'An interesting and very broad survey of much
reflection and intuition and their relation to pub
recognizing connections with social psychology, which is often neglected in
the literature and often unfamiliar to me.'

Jonathan Baron, *Professor Emeritus of Psychology, School of Arts*
and Sciences, University of Pennsylvania, USA

'The field of cognitive science is well served by this book, which expands
and extends the concept of cognitive reflection into broad-based areas that
are politically charged and full of real-world implications. This volume takes
reflection out of the laboratory and connects it to pressing cultural and
political debates.'

Keith E. Stanovich, *Emeritus Professor of Applied Psychology and*
Human Development, University of Toronto, Canada

REFLECTION AND INTUITION IN A CRISIS-RIDDEN WORLD

This book provides a definitive guide to the value of reflective thinking in the modern world, showing how today's most fundamental problems are, to an important degree, based on citizens' thinking styles.

The authors highlight the importance of reflection by systematically revealing the causes underlying differences in people's thinking styles and the consequences of thinking in different ways. These different ways of thinking contribute to sociopolitical views and can result in misunderstandings of complex issues such as beliefs in conspiracy theories and fake news, anti-vaccine attitudes, and even fundamentalism and extremism. By training and strengthening reflective thinking in society, via education and other means, we can encourage individuals to challenge misinformation, and their own belief systems around controversial topics. The book also explores the idea that reflection is not enough on its own and examines the shortcomings of reflection and the other skills that complement it positively, especially holistic and systems thinking. In doing so, the authors highlight how implementing a solid, science-based understanding of key issues in education and society at large can contribute to the solution of problems, from climate change to economic inequality.

By showing how we can put our reflective capacity to good use, alongside critically examining reflection in relation to modern problems experienced by humanity, this book is a fascinating reading for students, researchers, and academics in psychology, politics, and the broader social sciences.

S. Adil Saribay is Professor of Psychology at Kadir Has University, Istanbul, Turkey. His research focuses on cognitive style and face perception.

Onurcan Yilmaz is Associate Professor of Psychology at Kadir Has University, Istanbul, Turkey, and currently leads the Moral Intuitions Laboratory (MINT Lab). His research primarily focuses on the cognitive and contextual determinants of moral judgment and behavior.

Global Perspectives in Political Psychology
Series editors: Cengiz Erisen and Martijn van Zomeren

Global Perspectives in Political Psychology is a book series showcasing scholarly work over a wide range of areas within political psychology. The series welcomes theoretically and empirically informed scholarship, and the books in this series are designed to be authored or edited books on a circumscribed topic, including reviews and original research. Books may also take an applied approach, and offer practical guidance and interventions aimed at specific issues/contexts. Each volume in the series will make a conceptual contribution to the topic by reviewing and synthesizing the existing research literature, by advancing theory in the area, or by some combination of these missions. It is also expected that volumes will, to some extent, include an assessment of current knowledge and identification of possible future trends in research. The books should each consist of approximately 7–10 main chapters, well-structured and integrated to form a self-contained unit for the advanced reader.

Titles in this series:

Psychological Intergroup Interventions
Evidence-based Approaches to Resolve Intergroup Conflict
Eran Halperin, Boaz Hameiri and Rebecca Littman

Reflection and Intuition in a Crisis-Ridden World
Thinking Hard or Hardly Thinking?
S. Adil Saribay and Onurcan Yilmaz

For more information about this series, please visit: www.routledge.com/Global-Perspectives-in-Political-Psychology/book-series/GPPP

REFLECTION AND INTUITION IN A CRISIS-RIDDEN WORLD

Thinking Hard or Hardly Thinking?

S. Adil Saribay and Onurcan Yilmaz

Routledge
Taylor & Francis Group

LONDON AND NEW YORK

Designed cover image: Jorm Sangsorn via Getty Images

First published 2025
by Routledge
4 Park Square, Milton Park, Abingdon, Oxon OX14 4RN

and by Routledge
605 Third Avenue, New York, NY 10158

Routledge is an imprint of the Taylor & Francis Group, an informa business

© 2025 S. Adil Saribay and Onurcan Yilmaz

The right of S. Adil Saribay and Onurcan Yilmaz to be identified as authors of this work has been asserted in accordance with sections 77 and 78 of the Copyright, Designs and Patents Act 1988.

All rights reserved. No part of this book may be reprinted or reproduced or utilised in any form or by any electronic, mechanical, or other means, now known or hereafter invented, including photocopying and recording, or in any information storage or retrieval system, without permission in writing from the publishers.

Trademark notice: Product or corporate names may be trademarks or registered trademarks, and are used only for identification and explanation without intent to infringe.

British Library Cataloguing-in-Publication Data
A catalogue record for this book is available from the British Library

ISBN: 978-1-032-29176-5 (hbk)
ISBN: 978-1-032-28591-7 (pbk)
ISBN: 978-1-003-30036-6 (ebk)

DOI: 10.4324/9781003300366

Typeset in Sabon
by Newgen Publishing UK

*Dedicated to the legacy of Cavit Orhan Tütengil
and the countless others whose names may not
be recognized by the masses but whose good will,
hard work, and reflectiveness keep our crisis-ridden
world turning.*

CONTENTS

PREFACE

This book was written because we believe there is an ongoing need to emphasize the value of reflectiveness—i.e., thinking that is carefully carried out with cognitive effort, rests on proper information about the topic at hand, and uses tools such as logic and probability. We contrast reflectiveness with intuitiveness—i.e., thinking that is fast, rests on information that is irrelevant or peripheral to the topic at hand, and uses shortcuts. For some scholars, the scientific study of these ways of thinking is "one of the most fascinating and important challenges for psychological scientists" (De Neys, 2021, p. 1424). We could not agree more and this is the case even though emphasis on the importance of the former has been persistent throughout the known history of Western civilization. Despite this long history, the main message has not been integrated firmly into many cultures and it appears that it has still not been digested by a great number of human beings today. Some scholars view attempts to emphasize the value of reflective thought as "philosophically naïve, psychologically unsophisticated, and even politically suspect" or that it represents "a particularly Western white male viewpoint" (Bloom, 2016, p. 166). Being neither exactly White and Western, nor hopefully, after all these years in our careers, psychologically unsophisticated, philosophically naïve or politically ill-willed, we disagree. Maybe a point of agreement can be reached in the following sense: None of the issues we touch upon are simple and straightforward and it would absolutely not suffice if you stopped reading at this point and walked away thinking "more reflection is always better, in all domains, and solves all our human problems, individually and societally." The bottom line is that societies and science need to keep on reflecting on reflection (and intuition). However, it is clear that today's most pressing issues, like climate change and the unemployment problems brought on by artificial intelligence, cannot be solved through reflection alone. Just as people often turn to Eastern teachings like meditation in times of personal depression or social crisis, we should not intuitively dismiss Eastern cultural orientations—like holism—and their Western counterparts—like systemic thinking—in science today. Instead, we should seek to transition from overreliance on a form of reflection focused solely on detail and logical analysis to a type of reflection that considers the whole picture and evaluates alternative perspectives through a more integrative kind of thinking. We need to understand that this new form of reflection, supported also by virtues like open-mindedness and intellectual humility, can offer solutions to pressing contemporary problems like polarization, climate change, and poverty.

This is not a "how to think" type of book or a list of cognitive biases and illusions and ways to prevent them. This book's main concern is with the causes and consequences of thinking reflectively and intuitively and with the validity of this dichotomy. In Part I of the book, we first attempt to convince the reader that intuition has played a central role in the evolutionary journey of the human species (Chapter 1). We then cover the theoretical and empirical basis of the reflection-intuition distinction and how it is connected to issues such as rationality and bias (Chapter 2). Finally, we cover how reflective thought arises in development and how it can be further trained and strengthened (Chapter 3). In Part II of the book, we review the empirical literature examining how reflection is affected by situational forces, especially threat (Chapter 4). In the next few chapters, we delve into different domains to specifically examine the role of reflectiveness in the proliferation of and individual susceptibility to epistemically suspect beliefs such as supernatural and conspiracy beliefs (Chapter 5); sociopolitical views (Chapter 6), cooperation and morality (Chapter 7), and violent extremism (Chapter 8). In Part III, to balance it all out, we ask what the downsides of thinking reflectively might be and doing so naturally makes some of the underrated aspects of intuition clearer (Chapter 9). Finally, we try to demonstrate that the theoretical framework we rely on for all of the above is not infallible and that many intriguing issues concerning the nature of reflection and intuition await exploration (Chapter 10). We end the book with a brief section summarizing what we have learned from our experience as researchers actively working in this area. We argue that reflection runs the risk of simply confirming one's pre-existing views, unless one makes sure it involves high cognitive effort and takes advantage of cognitive mechanisms like decoupling and mental simulation that actually allow the thinker to entertain alternative viewpoints. Furthermore, unless synthesized with different, more integrative modes of thinking (e.g., holistic, systemic) and reinforced by virtues and motivations such as open-mindedness and intellectual humility, reflection will not facilitate finding solutions to major contemporary issues like political polarization, climate change, and economic inequality. Instead, without this synthesis, reflection may exacerbate these problems through motivated reasoning and a narrow, unproductive focus on a small number of dimensions underlying these highly complex issues.

The book is intended for both academics and the informed lay public. Each chapter necessitated a slightly different approach in terms of language and level of technical details. For instance, whereas Chapter 1 is a more broad and easy-to-read entry, Chapters 2 and 10 are more technically loaded. Our choice for inclusion of technical issues might not appeal to many readers. However, we were motivated by the realization that there is an important connection between scientific efforts directed at reaching an increasingly realistic and precise understanding of the human cognitive architecture and practical efforts directed at solving many individual and societal tasks and problems. In her response to a new model posing many challenges to the dual-process model of the mind, Osman (2023, p. 51) put it well when she stated that

> … there is a sense that we are at a point in our history where enlightenment is taking a bruising. Equivalences are drawn between facts and feelings. The study of reasoning is crucial to addressing this, and other worrying patterns that [are] emerging. The study of reasoning informs our understanding of how we develop sound arguments, how we identify sound arguments from bad, and how we reason from evidence. This is not only of scientific value, this is a given, the field is of value because the insights are essential in their applications to helping improve education, medicine, law, forensics, journalism, and public policy, to name but a few.

The inclusion of such technical material has probably made the book more difficult to read for those who lack prior exposure to psychology and science. We think the book is especially useful for informed individuals and scholars looking to increase the depth and breadth of their knowledge and to catch up with the cutting-edge empirical and theoretical developments. It could serve advanced undergraduate and graduate courses in psychology and related fields such as those mentioned above and beyond (e.g., communication). Practitioners who wish to create evidence-based programs to train individuals to think more reflectively may find material of value especially in Chapter 3 and Part II, but in the rest of the book as well if they are additionally seeking to motivate their efforts and/or to inspire others regarding the value of reflectiveness from a balanced and scientific point of view. That is, any individual seeking to be informed about why, how, and when reflectiveness is of benefit should find something (we hope, many things) of use in our effort.

Our unit of analysis is the mind, and our approach is based on psychology. The literature we present mostly resides in the subfields of social psychology, cognitive psychology, and political psychology. Where useful, we refer to work in related fields such as developmental psychology, cognitive science, behavioral economics, neuroscience, evolutionary psychology, political science, and philosophy. We are convinced that many societal phenomena are connected to individual-level reflectiveness, but we also understand that society is not reducible to the mind and analysis of cognitive processes cannot explain emergent higher-order phenomena. A bird's eye view of society from the perspective of fields like political science, economics, sociology, biology, and anthropology is needed for a more complete understanding. Even though we do not put those perspectives at the center of our effort, we include them where we can.

Nevertheless, the absence of an inclusive theoretical framework in the behavioral sciences, applicable across all disciplines, is a notable limitation (Muthukrishna & Henrich, 2019). This gap signifies the lack of a comprehensive social science theory to benchmark new inquiries and validate findings on a robust foundation, such as an overarching theoretical framework. One reason could be the problems concerning the application of the hypothetico-deductive method in the social sciences. Psychology, as many other fields of science, faces scrutiny in the wake of the open science movement, challenging the robustness of historical empirical knowledge and theoretical advancements (Open Science Collaboration, 2015). The "publish or perish" culture in academia and the methodological practices in psychology have significantly contributed to this issue. Beyond questionable research practices (e.g., John et al., 2012), a key issue is the inadequate focus on validity studies in psychology (Chester & Lasko, 2021; Flake et al., 2022; Schimmack, 2021; Vazire et al., 2022), particularly in multi-lab, cross-cultural replication studies that often leap from validity testing to direct hypothesis testing across different cultures.[1] Even foundational concepts like reflection and intuition and their respective experimental manipulations, despite their long empirical history, lacked systematic examination regarding their effects on performance until recently (Isler et al., 2020; Isler & Yilmaz, 2023). This deficiency hinders methodological unity and rapid knowledge accumulation, essential for discovering robust phenomena and theoretical development as in other well-established fields of science such as physics (Meehl, 1967). Psychology, yet to establish a paradigm akin to other well-established fields of science, is often fragmented with individual theories (Gigerenzer, 2010). Recent criticisms of the current use of hypothetico-deductive method in psychology have given rise to advocating for abductive reasoning as a pathway to theoretical progress, with practical implementations in psychological sciences (Borsboom et al., 2021; Haig, 2005, 2019; Muthukrishna & Henrich, 2019).

In essence, psychology's shortfall is a unifying theoretical framework. To construct such a framework, we must prioritize measurement validity, adapt tools to diverse cultures or locally develop culturally sensitive ones from scratch, and achieve methodological unity in manipulating and measuring psychological constructs to detect robust phenomena. After establishing robust phenomena with their boundary conditions, we must provide their verbal explanations (e.g., proto-theories) as underlying mechanisms. We must then attempt to model these explanations mathematically and compare them with alternative theories, drawing inspiration from more advanced fields, as Darwin did.[2]

Hence, the validity of tools and their cultural integration is paramount before we can expect accelerated theory development in psychology. The advent of artificial intelligence offers an opportunity to expedite the discovery of robust phenomena (e.g., Kliegr et al., 2020; Mac Aonghusa & Michie, 2020; Miller, 2019; Robila & Robila, 2020). Utilizing this advantage, psychology and other behavioral sciences can evolve into a *metadiscipline* capable of sound policy recommendations (IJzerman et al., 2020). Embracing abduction and diverse data from underrepresented non-WEIRD (Western, Educated, Industrialized, Democratic and Rich; Henrich et al., 2010) cultures is more crucial than ever. This book presents insights from researchers born and working in a non-WEIRD country, hoping their perspectives will help address psychology's pressing issues and contribute to the newfound excitement regarding the potential to become a much more scientifically sound discipline.

At the same time, a focus on "methodology per se doesn't resolve the issue" and can even exacerbate the risk of our field remaining "a vast menagerie of interesting facts with absolutely no big picture map of how these facts fit together into a coherent explanatory framework" (Henriques, 2013, p. 169; see also Ellemers, 2013). Researchers need better training in theory construction, selection, and integration (Gigerenzer, 2010; Kruglanski, 2001). Fortunately, we are in an era where both inspiring examples (see Van Lange, 2006) and practical guidance (e.g., Eronen & Bringmann, 2021; Gigerenzer, 2010; Henriques, 2013; Van Lange, 2013; van Zomeren, 2024) are readily available on this front. A perusal of such offerings makes it clear that both reflective thinking—e.g., being skeptical of data-analytic practices and thinking more carefully about one's implicit assumptions underlying research materials and procedures—and holistic thinking—e.g., appreciating the "broader story behind the theory one uses" and "putting different theories together within an overarching theory or meta-theory" (van Zomeren, 2024, p. 27)—are indispensable in science.

One may ask why our book is needed, especially given that a Nobel Prize winner already published a book on the same topic (i.e., Kahneman, 2011). As the above discussion signals, psychology is still a young and very dynamic discipline constantly reflecting on itself, innovating methods, and producing novel findings and theories. Concurrent with the publication of Kahneman's book, the field of social psychology[3] went head-on into a major crisis triggered by a couple of significant events—a colossal case of fraud and the publication of an article on Psi—a paranormal "phenomenon"—in our field's "top" journal (see Spellman, 2015). It has come to light that many published findings are not replicable (when new data is gathered to test the same hypothesis) or even reproducible (when the original data are re-analyzed with the hope of reaching the same statistical results) (for a review, see Nosek et al., 2022). These problems stem from widespread use of *questionable research practices*,[4] motivated by the incentive structure in academia which rewards publishing novel and statistically significant findings (Chambers, 2019). Luckily, rapid adoption of new tools offered by the *open science movement* such as preregistration (e.g., publicly committing to the whole research strategy before data collection) has been very helpful in beginning to separate the wheat from the chaff. Thus, it is necessary to periodically revisit the body of literature, to re-evaluate our interim conclusions, and self-correct when necessary. Obviously, this book is not the final word on the topic but a (hopefully important) step along the path to an increasingly accurate and deeper understanding.

Still, deciding what counts as solid research and trustworthy evidence has not yet become so straightforward. Seasoned researchers often warn readers that high-quality studies are lacking in their areas, especially those areas in which samples are difficult to recruit and/or to administer standardized measures to. One domain in which we encountered this situation more clearly during our effort is violent extremism (see Chapter 8). Furthermore, mixed findings and conflicting conclusions are more common than people sometimes assume. In some cases, there is an insufficient number of replications, making it difficult to resolve such cases. There is also limited knowledge about the cross-cultural generalizability of many findings we discuss. The good news is that large-scale cross-cultural replication and collaborations are becoming more and more common.[5] Such efforts typically use measures developed in one culture (typically the U.S.), in nearly identical forms, in other cultures. This suggests that there is further progress to be attained by paying closer attention to measurement validity in a cross-cultural context. Amidst these methodological complications, we have tried our best to prioritize solid research and to always communicate what we judged to be the conclusion favored by the weight of the evidence.

For us, it is strikingly ironic that these methodological complications have to do with the poor application of reflective thought during the creation of the very empirical evidence that we need to rely on to derive insights about reflectiveness. That is, the above-mentioned problems partly stem from scientists' failure to think slowly and more carefully about the research process and its central frameworks and tools such as *null hypothesis significance testing* and the *p-value* (Haller & Krauss, 2002).[6] That even scientists are having trouble applying reflective thought in their work is further proof that a continued emphasis on the value of reflectiveness is necessary in all domains of modern life.

Notwithstanding these human-centric problems concerning methods, psychology is a particularly difficult scientific field in terms of how complicated its subject matter is. Human behavior (including cognition) is overdetermined and context-sensitive. Consequently, the typical effect reported in psychology is relatively small in size (Götz et al., 2022; Richard et al., 2003).[7] Some effects tested in the published literature that are deemed to be present (real) and reliable are practically unimportant.[8] We place reflectiveness at the center of our focus and ask whether evidence supports the idea that it matters. Our aim is not to compare the effect of reflectiveness directly with other key determinants of behavior (e.g., emotion, motivation), though the importance of those determinants is undeniable and they come into our explicit focus via some concepts (e.g., motivated reasoning, threat) throughout the book. Those other determinants of course also matter in real life. Reflectiveness matters and it likely matters enough to care about it in most situations; but it is not easy to determine *how much* it matters in comparison to other relevant factors. In sum, given these facts—the overdetermined nature of human behavior and the smallness of the average effect size—the reader should be careful to not go to extremes while forming their own opinions based on our arguments.

The methodological complications about which we have tried to warn the reader above are not meant to encourage a pessimistic attitude. We think that, just as Vazire (2018) predicted, psychology and our careers have entered an era where it is becoming more difficult to attain feelings of progress, success, discovery, and conquest while true scientific progress is in fact becoming more common and rapid. Vazire characterizes the ongoing developments as "the credibility revolution' and we agree that the past decade has been nothing short of a revolution. We simply choose to not mask these complications and to do justice to the complexity of the matter. In case it is not clear from the rest of the book, we would like to take the chance here to affirm the reader of our excitement regarding the future of research on reflectiveness.

Amidst these complications, our exploration of many different lines of research often pointed us toward the idea that reflection is tremendously valuable but not sufficient by itself and needs to be complemented by other human capabilities. Sometimes what stands out in terms of this complementary role is intuition—the very concept that is seen as the major source of bias and pitted against reflection since Plato. At other times, it is a kind of broad, integrative, global thinking that we have most concretely been able to discuss via holistic and systemic thinking. This applies even to those human-centric problems we mentioned above and that have created complications in science: Researchers are probably sufficiently reflective; they conduct and report research carefully, paying a great deal of attention to each minute issue along the way, exerting intense cognitive effort to crack problems, and so on. Our problems in science may have more to do with losing the vision of the whole, forgetting that one's original goals were not to "publish papers" or "win awards," but to contribute to humankind, pursue the truth, make true discoveries, and establish important facts by evidence; failing to place our actions in broader context and to understand that they will affect our peers, students, and the public—that collectively we are shaping the future of science and of humanity. Hence, virtues such as open-mindedness, intellectual humility, and cooperativeness (the "disinterestedness" of Mertonian norms; Merton, 1973) must join reflectiveness. In any case, we think the field has shown tremendous progress since the 1960s and the time is now ripe to explore these interesting combinations of the different ways in which we humans represent, process, and relate to the world around us.

Many other developments have also happened since Kahneman's book. The topic has become extremely popular and so much more empirical work and new models now exist. The burgeoning of research on related topics such as morality and conspiracy beliefs, in addition to exciting developments in basic research on reflection and intuition, has increased the need for up-to-date reviews. This book is a part of a series on "Global Perspectives in Political Psychology." This series publishes books that synthesize a broad range of research areas related to political psychology. While our book addresses topics commonly explored in political psychology, such as ideological differences, moral beliefs, and extremism, it also delves into the general theme of the causes and consequences of reflection and intuition. In this respect, it offers insights beyond the traditional scope of political psychology. In other words, we have included a broader discussion of reflective and intuitive processes and not confined ourselves to sociopolitical phenomena narrowly defined. This is because (1) nearly everything seems to be political these days[9]; (2) more transfer of knowledge and ideas is needed across silos of the literature which we believe wider-scope reviews facilitate[10]; and (3) knowledge of the human cognitive architecture, which we include in our review, is necessary for understanding phenomena studied in fields like social and political psychology. That said, in different sections of the book, we have focused squarely on the role of reflection and intuition in politics—especially in Chapters 4 through 8—and emerged from our effort with an even stronger conviction that this is a vital focus for societies, as well as for social scientists of all types. Politics might bring out the worst in human beings and is a particularly good domain for observing the limitations of the human mind. Intuitions, strengthened by factors such as repetitive exposure to the same views in echo chambers and high-arousal emotions stemming from perceived threat, may heighten the risk of closed-mindedness, cognitive rigidity, and extremism. Reflection has an important role to play here but comes with its own limitations, sometimes adding fuel to the fire instead of extinguishing it. Exploration of the more positive functions of intuition that are more easily observed outside of politics suggests that as individuals, societies, and scientists, we need to work further on finding creative uses of human mental capacities. Accomplishing this in the domain of politics would be an extremely encouraging feat.

Notes

1 Our intention is not to criticize the well-meaning multi-lab studies that aim to swiftly identify robust phenomena for the scientific record. Much like questionable research practices such as p-hacking were the norm until the open science movement gained momentum in the 2010s, the primary issue in many multi-lab replication studies is their approach. Instead of directly conducting hypothesis testing with measurement tools translated through the translation-back-translation method, without prior validity studies, a better approach would be to divide the participating labs into two groups: one for validity studies and the other for hypothesis testing, especially when numerous labs from a single culture are involved. The crucial aspect is to recognize the necessity of validity studies before pursuing novel research and to establish a standard norm for not publishing studies where validity is uncertain, regardless of their novelty. Without confirming the validity of measurement tools, the non-replication of results could be attributed to the inappropriateness of the tools for the specific culture, rather than the absence of the effects.

2 Darwin employed abduction to develop his theory of natural selection. When he formulated the concept of natural selection based on existing evidence at that time, he drew analogies from artificial selection, asking why a natural counterpart would not exist (Haig, 2005). Similarly, in theory development, psychologists should consider established robust phenomena with their well-established boundary conditions and mathematical models from fields like population genetics, evolutionary biology, and behavioral economics, assessing their applicability to psychological research (Borsboom et al., 2021). While there are notable instances of successful analogical modeling in the areas covered in this book (e.g., Bear & Rand, 2016; Curry, 2016; Van Der Maas et al., 2006), this approach has not yet become mainstream across the behavioral and cognitive sciences (Guest & Martin, 2021; Perone & Simmering, 2017; Thelen & Smith, 1994). To establish this as a predominant methodology, it is crucial for interdisciplinary scientists to have in-depth knowledge of diverse fields and technical proficiency (Van Lange, 2006), particularly in applying mathematical models to social sciences. Another effective strategy involves collaboration in Big Team Science (e.g., Baumgartner et al., 2023; Coles et al., 2022; Forscher et al., 2023), bringing together experts from various disciplines. Our Moral Intuitions Laboratory (MINT Lab; www.moralintuitionslab.com) exemplifies such interdisciplinary collaborations.

3 The crisis, we hate to say, seems to be more general (Bausell, 2021; see for a pessimistic view, Ioannidis, 2005). The unique status of social psychology is that it was pushed into the crisis earlier than other fields. There are of course differences across fields (e.g., Fanelli, 2010) and even subfields (e.g., Youyou et al., 2023) in terms of how well they are generally doing.

4 To give an example, it is now completely clear to us that applying some flexibility in data collection (e.g., checking significance after the arrival of each new observation and continuing data collection until significance is attained) and analysis (e.g., using covariates as an afterthought) virtually guarantees that one will reach the desired (or at least a statistically significant) result (Simmons et al., 2011). These tactics are collectively termed *p-hacking* because they aim to get the p-value to fall below the threshold for statistical significance (see for a comprehensive list, Wicherts et al., 2016). However, there are other problems, as well, such as *hypothesizing after the results are known* which greatly reduces the interpretability, if not the veridicality, of conclusions reached under the null hypothesis significance testing framework (Kerr, 1998). There are also aggregate-level problems such as *publication bias*—i.e., the overrepresentation of statistically significant (vs. null) findings in the published versus unpublished research reports (e.g., Franco et al., 2014).

5 For a neat example, see the website of the Psychological Science Accelerator at https://psysciacc.org/

6 Others agree that this has to do with insufficient reflectiveness. In the words of Gigerenzer (2004, p. 587), "[s]tatistical rituals largely eliminate statistical thinking in the social sciences."

7 Effects may appear larger than they actually are due to questionable research practices (Schäfer & Schwarz, 2019).

8 The argument here is *not* that all small effects are unimportant, which is not true (e.g., Prentice & Miller, 1992). However, researchers sometimes exaggerate the importance of effects based on their statistical significance alone and fail to consider practical significance.

9 Our current favorite example is that supporting the Turkish women's volleyball team, which has been enjoying great success recently, is politicized (see www.nytimes.com/2023/09/03/world/middleeast/turkey-womens-volleyball.html).

10 One example covered in Chapter 9 of the book is the vastly different overall impressions of intuition harbored in cognitive psychology versus applied fields like management.

ACKNOWLEDGMENTS

Our collaboration started at Boğaziçi University when the second author became the first's master's student (2013–2015). The first author was himself trained at the same master's program a little over a decade earlier (2000–2002) and returned there as faculty (2010–2020). The Psychology Department at Boğaziçi had built a rigorous graduate program and during our time there, we were surrounded by brilliant colleagues and students and were supported by a 150-year-old institutional culture (going back to its roots in Robert College, the first American higher educational institution overseas) and an administration that made it possible to pursue our ideas freely. We are indebted to Boğaziçi University and its Psychology Department. Unfortunately, Boğaziçi became more and more isolated and under attack due to its free intellectual climate in an increasingly authoritarian Türkiye. Her meritocratic system and core principles are in the process of being torn down for political reasons. This is in essence an attack on reflectiveness and is deeply concerning. We hope that the Turkish public will soon come to realize that this and other similar attempts at sociopolitical engineering are really acts of self-destruction and change course.

We probably would not have had the chance to write this book if Cengiz Erişen, editor of the series which includes this book, had not approached the first author with the idea. We thank both him and Routledge for this precious opportunity. Cengiz Erişen also provided highly valuable and constructive feedback on drafts of this book, along with the other editor of this series, Martijn van Zomeren, and we are grateful to them both. We thank Gordon Pennycook for not only tremendously stimulating research in this area via his own rigorous and impactful empirical research and theoretical work, but also giving us a generous and enthusiastic review on our initial proposal to

Routledge. Most of our work toward this book took place in 2023 in which Türkiye experienced her worst natural (but in reality, largely human-made) disaster—a series of earthquakes that heavily impacted several major cities in the Southeast and ended the lives of more than 50,000 people. We also thank our editors and the staff at Routledge, especially Emilie Coin, Yashika Tanwar, and Tori Sharpe, for their patience and support as we struggled to finish the project in time amidst this catastrophe and other woes of society and academia.

We stand on the shoulders of many intellectual giants, such as the late Daniel Kahneman, who was probably the single most responsible person for popularizing this area of inquiry; and Keith Stanovich and Jonathan Evans who together sometimes seem to us to have discovered everything there is to be discovered about reflectiveness. We thank them and all the other researchers—too many to list here but whose names are scattered throughout the book in the form of citations—for generating the empirical and theoretical work we relied on to write this book.

We extend our deepest gratitude to Jonathan Baron for his invaluable contributions to the advancement of this field. His scholarly research and dedicated service as an editor have been instrumental. Jonathan Baron has not only rigorously investigated the potential implications of reflection and open-mindedness in socio-political contexts but, as the founding editor of *Judgment and Decision Making* (JDM), has also been pivotal in incorporating this work into the broader literature. His commitment to open science principles since the journal's establishment in 2006 sets a commendable example. If one were to illustrate ideal journal editorship, Jonathan Baron's approach would undoubtedly serve as a prime model. As authors of this book, our initial collaborative effort, the second author's master's thesis, was published in JDM. Years later, we were honored to join the journal's editorial board, an experience that showcased the epitome of editing and scientific review. We have greatly benefited from his editorial guidance, both professionally and personally, and take immense pride in being part of the editorial board of this trailblazing journal. We owe our thanks to Jonathan Baron and the entire JDM team for their exceptional work.

We also thank Kadir Has University, The Scientific and Technological Research Council of Türkiye, the Turkish Academy of Sciences, The Science Academy and its Young Scientists Award Program, and Templeton Religion Trust, for funding our research; all research participants for their time; and the many student assistants for their help.

The following individuals helped with the literature search: Halil Almaç, Nazlıcan Esatoğlu, Emre Kayatepe, Nagihan Özman, and the staff of Kadir Has University Information Center. The following individuals provided constructive feedback on parts of this book (listed in alphabetical order): Ayşe Altan Atalay, Emre Kayatepe, Merve Mutafoğlu, Gaye Soley,

Efe Tokdemir, Jaïs Adam-Troïan, and Berna Uzundağ. Ali Karaca, Selenay Keleş, Enes Kor, and İlayda Velioğlu checked the final draft for errors. We are especially grateful to Diane Sunar, who has mentored both of us and has contributed immensely to psychology in Türkiye, for reading the entire book carefully and providing constructive and detailed feedback at short notice. We thank all these individuals for their time and effort. Of course, all errors are solely ours.

Last but definitely not least, much love goes to our families for their patience, support, and understanding throughout the process. Adil would like to thank his wonderful parents Ali Yaşar and Tülin Sarıbay for teaching him the best uses of both reflection and intuition, his dear wife Merve Mutafoğlu and his precious feline daughter Baldo for being a constant source of the most enjoyable and meaningful reflective and intuitive responses, his extended family, especially Ayşe Akbaş, for their support, Karel Kleisner for being a great colleague and friend, and Jim Lemanowicz for the musings on music and life that provided much needed distraction during the writing process. Adil would also like to thank all his lab members for making work fun and his graduate mentors Susan M. Andersen, James S. Uleman, and Bilge Ataca for their support and positive influence.

Onurcan would like to thank his beloved Yılmaz family (B. Ceren, Güler, M. Ramazan, Sebile, Rafet, Seda, Birkan, and Gökre Yılmaz) and his close colleagues and friends Ozan İşler, Burak Doğruyol, Hasan G. Bahçekapılı, İlyas Göz, Mehmet Harma, Sinan Alper, and Fatih Bayrak for their unwavering support in all aspects of his life. He would also like to express his appreciation to the members of MINT Lab, especially Sevim Cesur, for her significant impact on his career. He is also deeply appreciative of his dedicated students at MINT Lab, listed alphabetically, Bengi Aktar, Berke Aydaş, Ensar Acem, Fırat Şeker, Gülce Günaydın, Halil Almaç, Melih Varol, Rozelin Vurgun, İlayda Velioğlu, and Yiğit Aşık, who have greatly contributed to his academic and intellectual journey. Finally, Onurcan would like to express his heartfelt gratitude to Nehir and Didem Doğruyol, as well as Piraye Harma and Hilal Şen, for significantly enriching and bringing joy to his life.

PART I

Reflection and Intuition

The Basics

1
THE INTUITIVE MIND

Have you ever found yourself engaged in philosophical or political discussions with friends, feeling as though you are conversing with someone from another world due to the difficulty in reaching a consensus? For instance, should everyone earn equal salaries, or should compensation be based on individual merit and contribution? Do you view climate change as the world's most critical problem or believe its significance to be exaggerated? Is the primary objective of a quality debate to uncover the truth or to emerge as the victor?

In each of these diverse scenarios, individuals often hold distinct intuitive beliefs, and sometimes these beliefs are so deeply entrenched that finding common ground in a conversation becomes nearly impossible. This rigidity often arises, because, in such debates, participants are more inclined to uphold perspectives that align with their personal worldviews than to consider the objective reality. Even when provided ample time or prompted to think slowly, carefully, and logically, these deeply held convictions persist. This is largely due to the human mind's inherent motivation to construct and maintain a worldview that resonates with its intrinsic intuitions, fortified further through reasoning. In this chapter, we will delve into some of the innate intuitive properties of the human mind and explore their profound implications for our social interactions and relationships.

A Working Definition of Reflection and Intuition

We start with a working definition of two key terms—reflection and intuition. At the heart of reflection lies subjectively effortful *cognitive engagement*[1] or, simply, thinking harder. Reflection is about taking time to think further instead of hastily drawing conclusions or acting in an impulsive

DOI: 10.4324/9781003300366-2

or careless manner. If we take time to think, we can ask questions, probe the contents of the mind—both in long-term memory (i.e., stored knowledge) and consciousness, check for errors in our thinking, and assess whether more information needs to be collected. The purpose of such activity is to reach better conclusions, formulate deeper and more coherent explanations, generate more solid ideas and arguments, and act in accordance with valued principles and chosen goals or, in other words, to be more rational. All these are uniquely human and amazing feats.

If one is not engaged effortfully, the alternative is not complete cognitive disengagement as this does not describe even comatose patients (Fischer et al., 2008). The mind is a constantly active evaluation and sense-making machine that does not seem to remain on standby even at rest, without a task (Raichle, 2015). The critical dimension of this ever-present activity concerns the degree to which cognitive effort is deliberately directed to the task at hand. Thus, the alternative to reflection is cognitive miserliness—a tendency to make do with the least effort possible to handle the situation. Most of the time when we are cognitively miserly, it is intuitive processes that fill in the role of reflective ones. *Impulsivity* is another term sometimes used to describe this way of responding.

But what is the output of mental processes when we are not making a deliberate cognitive effort but letting intuition do the work? First of all, a warning: The word "intuition" is often used rather loosely due to its popularity in pseudoscience (as in a "sixth sense," with which we have nothing to do) and is confounded with or used in place of many other terms, such as instinct, impulse, and insight (see Sadler-Smith, 2007, p. 30). Because of the more mysterious (i.e., less open to conscious analysis) nature of intuitive thoughts, this ambiguity is somewhat unavoidable and is also a problem in the scientific literature.[2] The word "intuitive" and the word "reflective" are, after all, linguistic abstractions that might obscure nuances. The *sources* of intuitive responses may indeed be varied and there may be meaningful subtypes (Pretz & Totz, 2007).

Take two different examples: In the first, you are hiking in the woods and abruptly shout and jump to the other side of the path, feeling a sudden rush of adrenaline. You recognize in mid-air that there is a snake in your path. Your *instinctive* response felt cognitively effortless. In fact, it is almost as if you consciously recognized the presence of the snake *after* you jumped. The source of your response can be attributed to an innate evolutionary adaptation that was present at birth.[3] This response will be quite difficult to modify, but you are glad it is an inherent part of your being.

Now, let us turn to the second example. Your office building where you have spent a decade has undergone complete renovation. On your first day back, you leave your room to grab a snack from the fridge. You notice mid-path that you took a left turn to where the kitchen used to be. You stop and walk back past your room to where the kitchen has moved. You repeat this mistake several times during the first week. Your *habitual* response (of turning left instead of right) felt cognitively effortless. The source of your response was a decade of behavioral repetition. This response is annoying, but you are glad that it seems to have been removed from your repertoire after that first week. It is obvious that the responses in these two examples are meaningfully different and stem from different sources. But for now, the important point is that it is the lack of deliberate cognitive effort that distinguishes intuitive processes from reflective ones.

When you think back to these events, you also recognize that those (intuitive) responses occurred not just cognitively effortlessly but also very fast, without conscious awareness, spontaneously (without intention), and seemed to have a life of their own independent of intentional control. In contrast, other mental events—like trying to hold a phone number in mind or imagining the consequences of a new policy you seek to implement at work as a manager—feel cognitively effortful and appear to be much slower. These relatively more reflective thought processes often necessitate conscious awareness, prove challenging to carry out under stress, fatigue, intoxication, and distraction, and seem to be under the control of your own will. These twin cognitive capacities—intuitive and reflective thinking—underpin many of our social attitudes and behaviors, influencing everything from our perceptions to our chosen actions. To delve deeper into these cognitive processes, let us begin by examining intuitive thinking.

Universality of the Intuitive Cognitive Mechanism

Many foundational pieces of theorizing in cognitive and behavioral sciences (e.g., Simon, 1955) posit that the mind endeavors to conserve energy by minimizing its cognitive exertion, enabling it to respond rapidly and automatically to various situations. Consider walking down a street, our mind is intrinsically primed for potential hazards or unforeseen scenarios that might emerge. Thus, our intuitive system is constantly active, processing pertinent stimuli from our surroundings, often unconsciously. This is why, amid a bustling crowd, we can distinctly recognize someone calling our name (Conway et al., 2001) or can swiftly spot an individual with an angry expression, especially if it is a male face (Fox et al., 2000), when everyone else bears a neutral demeanor. Such phenomena exemplify how our cognition often operates on "autopilot."

A significant benefit of this intuitive system is its tendency to foster large-scale cooperation within our social group. This intrinsic human proclivity for conformity and upholding societal norms primarily drives sustained cooperative behavior and shows the power of our intuitive cognitive system in fostering social cohesion.

When examining mammals in general, we observe that most of them live in groups and often differentiate their group members from others. While other animals form partnerships primarily based on kinship relations, the human species establishes relationships transcending genetic affinity (e.g., large-scale cooperation), allowing for long-term coalitions with out-groups to form through friendships. This psychological characteristic distinguishes humans from other animals significantly.

In addition to our intuitive cognitive mechanisms, shared with other animals, the human capacity for sustained engagement in activities over prolonged durations can be attributed to the evolution of self-control mechanisms. Such mechanisms have made unique practices possible, from honoring the dead to participating in marathons. In the realm of our current understanding, Homo sapiens stands as the only species endowed with the capacity to perform these extraordinary feats. To clarify, although cooperative alliances are a common occurrence among other primate species, among humans, the influence of these alliances on human lives spans a significantly broader spectrum and exerts a far more profound and lasting effect on our experience and behavior than those observed among other primate species. Examples of such coalitions include religions, nationalities, and various social groups and institutions, from sports teams to the United Nations. The underlying psychological mechanisms (e.g., emotional support, shared identity) acquired through evolution and subsequently shaped by the cultural process (Henrich, 2020), represent the fundamental factors underlying our capacity to form and maintain such coalitions. Even today, people on social media tend to follow individuals similar to themselves, creating echo chambers—an expression of a very primitive feature—homophily (Fu et al., 2012)—that remains present in modern humans. Throughout history, as a tribal species, humans have consistently favored their own groups and intuitively held biases against others, and this primitive mechanism lies at the root of conflicts between religions and nations (Clark et al., 2019; cf. Baron & Jost, 2019). These mechanisms were evolutionary adaptations that enhanced survival, as they played a crucial role in driving large-scale cooperation—the primary driving force behind the expansion of human communities. Ways to find partners, maintain cooperation, and enforce societal norms among group members could not have proliferated without our intuitive way of thinking. Subsequently, as social norms developed, it would not have been possible for people to automatically adapt to them without cognitive effort or for advertisers, for example, to influence people's purchasing preferences with specific persuasion techniques without human intuitive inclinations.

To understand this intuitive system better, a more detailed examination of the foundations of human evolution is necessary. Intuitive thinking can be simply defined as a mental process that enables individuals to make decisions quickly and seemingly automatically, directing their behavior. Throughout human evolutionary history, the need for solidarity and cooperation within groups was essential for survival and reproductive success. Consequently, individuals tend to form strong bonds with those sharing similar identities, leading to a sense of belonging and group cohesion among like-minded group members. Additionally, intuitive psychological mechanisms, such as emotional support or expected reciprocity, contribute to strengthening people's sense of identity and belonging. When individuals connect with groups sharing similar values, language, culture, or beliefs, they further experience a heightened sense of security and purpose, motivating them to deepen social bonds and collaborate within the community. Group boundaries and the associated emotional connection provided an evolutionary advantage during periods when groups competed and shared resources in the evolutionary past (Axelrod & Hamilton, 1981).

Hence, it is clear that intuitive psychological mechanisms facilitate social cohesion and cooperation. Groups with shared identities and values can collaborate more effectively and uphold societal norms, fostering solidarity and social order within the group. The tribal lifestyle evolved to promote this solidarity and trust within the community. For instance, consider the scenario of group movement during a perilous hunt in a hazardous environment. In such circumstances, the paramount concern is the establishment of trust among group members. The ability to foster instinctive emotional closeness and reciprocal trust within the group becomes imperative, as any absence of these crucial elements can significantly jeopardize the group's chances of survival.

An illustrative example of an innate mechanism that facilitates solidarity within a group is our tendency to comprehend and respect hierarchical relationships. In fact, human social structures, akin to those of most mammals, exhibit a hierarchical framework. Recognition and respect for hierarchy are established at an early age (e.g., Bas & Sebastian-Galles, 2021; Diesendruck & Shatz, 2001), similar to how a dominant alpha male gorilla claims all the females in its group. In various human societies, it has been observed that wealthy individuals often engage in polygamous relationships (Henrich, 2020). This behavior reflects an intuitive developmental tendency, where wealth serves as a key determinant of resource access and indicates one's social hierarchical status. Typically, such arrangements are acknowledged and accepted by other group members. Indeed, without this collective acceptance, it becomes unfeasible to sustain the hierarchical social structure (Haidt, 2012).

Given the recognition of these hierarchical systems, individuals in such contexts tend to adopt a dovish strategy, acknowledging authority and adhering to established hierarchies. However, in specific situations where power dynamics challenge the existing hierarchies, a hawkish strategy emerges, prompting confrontations and contests for leadership (Curry,

2016). This intuitive comprehension of hierarchical social relations by humans evolves into a fundamental guideline governing intricate social interactions.

Strong social bonds among group members also conferred a significant advantage in dealing with dangers and effectively sharing resources. When examining the hunting tendencies of humans in past environmental conditions, the advantages of this intuitive cooperation become evident. Humans partly evolved as a scavenger species, with the two most effective strategies being hunting in groups and following prey for extended periods (Pobiner, 2020). These features allowed humans to dominate nature to a greater extent than any other species. Comparing a tribe hunting individually with another tribe collectively pursuing a large prey, the evolutionary advantage becomes clear. Homo sapiens, collaborating as a group, could, for example, injure large prey from a distance with stones, then watch and wait for up to 2 days for the prey to become fatigued before attacking at the opportune moment. These evolved mechanisms enabled various forms of complex collaboration to be effortlessly realized.

Language

In the evolutionary history of humankind, tribal life held a significant place (Clark et al., 2019). During this period, characterized by hunter–gatherer groups, the emergence of language played a decisive role in the evolution of norms and social development, as language facilitated the rapid spread of intuitive structures within the culture.

Language stands as one of the most vital expressions of human cognitive capacity and serves as a distinguishing feature from other living organisms. Although other primates can acquire sign language, their language is characterized by a finite number of symbols and meaning worlds, lending clarity to the symbol's meaning through a code logic. However, the fundamental distinction of human language from other animal languages lies in its ability to generate an infinite number of meaning worlds from a finite number of symbols. We can liken this capacity to musical notes, where a finite set of notes can give rise to an endless array of compositions. Such infinite potential is a foundational characteristic of human language.

The evolution of the human brain plays a crucial role in language development. The human brain's larger neocortex and frontal lobes, compared to other primate species, are pivotal in the development of cognitive abilities such as complex thinking, planning, language processing, and social relations. The changes in brain structure during language evolution contributed to the emergence of the cognitive capacities essential for processing and producing language (Schoenemann, 2009). Language enables individuals to interact socially, conveying their feelings, thoughts, and information. This facilitation of cooperation and information sharing within groups also strengthens social ties and fosters solidarity within the community. Consequently, social interaction and communication played a crucial role in the evolution of language (Fitch, 2005).

Another mechanism through which language operates is gossip. Originally emerging in human societies as a low-cost form of punishment, gossip allows individuals to exert control over others without risking their own safety. For example, if a person attacks a weaker group member, intervening with that person intuitively (i.e., without forethought and calculation of potential costs) could jeopardize one's own survival. To deter such antisocial behaviors, gossip evolved as a fundamental form of punishment especially among small-scale societies where reputational concerns are more salient. Spreading stories (whether true or untrue) about individuals within the group by word of mouth was a common punitive practice in the past and still is to some extent in modern communities. This progress in language evolution through gossip facilitated large-scale cooperation by suppressing antisocial behaviors.

Cultural Evolution

Language is also closely linked to cultural evolution. It serves as a crucial tool for transferring cultural knowledge, allowing human communities to impart accumulated wisdom and experiences to future generations. Cultural transmission of language contributes to the formation of complex societies and enriches cultural diversity. Cultural evolution extends beyond the biological basis of human behavior and cognitive processes, encompassing the influence of social and cultural factors. It involves the transmission of elements like values, norms, and traditions shared within society from one generation to the next, ultimately shaping individual behavior and creating social order.

The interaction between culture and cognition leads to the shaping of human behavior and decision-making processes in line with the cultural norms and expectations of a given society. Culturally learned behavioral patterns are influential in shaping and guiding intuitive thinking. For instance, in societies where violence is considered acceptable and/or is the norm, individuals' intuitive thoughts may automatically lead to violent reactions. Conversely, in societies where violence is normatively condemned, intuitive thinking is more likely to trigger nonviolent responses (Pryor et al., 2018; Rand et al., 2014). Thus, while humans' intuitive tendencies themselves have an evolutionary history and tend to be universal, the specific behaviors they give rise to are shaped by cultural norms prevailing in a given locale and time. In line with that observation, modern evolutionary approaches adopt an interactionist paradigm, assuming that genes provide a blueprint while cultural factors shape this blueprint (Yilmaz, 2021b).

The emergence of behavior comprises a fusion of these two factors (genes and culture). For instance, theories advocating language as an adaptation (e.g., Pinker, 2003) posit that humans possess a biological predisposition to acquire language. This capacity is genetically inherent in human nature (similar to how horses can naturally gallop from birth). Nonetheless, when this biological predisposition is not met by exposure to certain critical environmental stimuli (such as human speech), the person may even fail to acquire advanced language skills, as exemplified by cases of feral children such as Dina Sanichar of India, who was discovered in a wolf den in 1872 at the approximate age of 6. Remarkably, he exhibited vocalizations akin to those of wolves and did not develop human language skills even after spending nearly three decades among humans (Malson, 1972). Building on such observations, the evolutionary perspective adopts an interactionist stance, emphasizing the interplay of both genetic factors and the environment.

In other words, while there exist evolutionarily acquired intuitive cognitive mechanisms, their application is contingent upon cultural practices. Pattern recognition, as an intuitive cognitive mechanism, for example, helps individuals make sense of complexity in their environment. This tendency is evident when we observe the seemingly endless and randomly scattered stars in the sky, likening them to culturally meaningful shapes and patterns, like an inverted coffee pot or the Big Bear constellation. Such perceptual categorization and simplification of complexity are made possible by the intuitive structure of our minds. However, if a community has never encountered a bear or used a coffee pot, the same intuitive mechanism would lead to results that superficially appear entirely different. Therefore, comprehending the intuitive mind and its implications necessitates an understanding of cultural evolutionary processes.

The formation of other culturally determined practices such as child-rearing practices significantly influences the development of people's intuitive thoughts and behaviors as well. Children are socialized by cultural norms and values, which shape the behavior patterns accepted by society. The evolutionary cultural approach posits that child-rearing practices, for example, reinforce adaptive behavior derived from the human evolutionary past. As children naturally exhibit intuitive tendencies, their development is guided by the adults around them, leading to adoption of the behavior patterns prescribed by society and fostering cultural evolutionary processes.

As a result, the evolutionary emergence and development of intuitive thinking confer substantial advantages to individuals and societies. Our human ancestors had to make swift and effective decisions to survive and reproduce in perilous environments. As the remainder of the book will make clear (see especially Chapters 2, 4, and 10), reflective processes are too slow and fragile to handle the challenges posed by such perilous environments. Consequently, intuitive thinking has emerged as a cognitive mechanism effectively employed in hunting, dealing with dangers, and engaging in social interactions. Throughout human evolutionary history, natural selection has enhanced the functionality of intuitive thinking, endowing the mind with faster and more frugal intuitive processes, resulting in a considerable advantage in terms of survival and reproductive success over generations. However, there is a critical cost to intuitive thinking: It can also lead to erroneous conclusions, particularly when confronted with complex decisions in modern, intricate societies that differ significantly from the natural environment. As such, human beings can be characterized as an ultra-social species living amid tremendous uncertainty, possessing evolutionarily shaped intuitive cognitive mechanisms to cope with this uncertainty. These intuitive mechanisms not only help us startle when hearing a strange noise while walking on the street but also provide insights into whom we should cooperate with and whom we should not trust; that is, intuitive processes support a large variety of responses, to good or bad effect. The tribal lifestyle, characterized by pronounced in-group favoritism, serves as a testament to the intuitive nature of human behavior. It is deemed a foundational trait that consistently manifests across individuals with diverse moral and sociopolitical convictions and is pervasive across various cultures (Clark et al., 2019).

Coda

Overall, the implications of intuition are not just limited to understanding biological tendencies; they also encompass the intricate interplay with existing cultural norms and practices. In this chapter, we introduced a working definition of the fundamental cognitive distinction between intuition and reflection and emphasized the pivotal role of the former in our social interactions. Moving forward, the subsequent chapter will delve deeper into the scientific foundations of this distinction. Subsequent sections of the book will then pivot toward an examination of intuition and reflection in the context of evolutionary and cultural influences, with a particular emphasis on their adaptability and the specific situations in which their influence is most pronounced.

Notes

1   The meaning of effort in this context has more to do with subjective experience than some other index of cognition, such as neural activity. For instance, some areas of the brain are even more active while dreaming than in waking consciousness (Nir & Tononi, 2010) but one does not have the subjective experience of exerting effort for dreaming. Thus, mere brain activity may not be a useful criterion here. On the other hand, there is a good reason for the relevance of a subjective sense of effort: The mental operations necessary for reflection are indeed computationally costly for the brain, as we will see later.

2 Topolinski (2017), for instance, argues that defining intuition based on its features, as dual-process models do (see Chapter 2), results in an overly inclusive definition of intuition.

3 This should not imply genetic determinism as environmental input is often just as critical as innate proclivities (genes) in determining behavioral outcomes (see the section on language).

2

DUAL-PROCESS MODELS OF THE MIND

Dual-process models of the mind are ubiquitous in psychology and cognitive science today. As the name implies, such models posit two sets of mental processes, having different characteristics and being described by different terms. This type of thinking is anything but new (Frankish & Evans, 2009). One can take it as far back as Plato (2002), who talked about passion (desire, emotion) versus reason (rational thought). Over the ages, it has lost none of its force: The cognitive psychologist Daniel Kahneman, well known for his book "Thinking, Fast and Slow," won the 2002 Nobel Prize in economics because of his work on this topic. For Plato, a good and happy life was possible if reason was in charge of one's actions. Throughout history, discussions have similarly tended to regard reason more favorably than passion, particularly in the Western context. As residents of a country, which has experienced a significant erosion of institutions and practices that are built on and operated by careful reasoning, we also carry a similar tendency. However, as scientists, our task in this book will be to critically evaluate the assumption that reason is superior to passion and that it will generally, if not always, lead to more valid beliefs and better decisions. In different domains and phenomena of social life taken up separately in the following chapters, we will guide the reader to interim conclusions based on whatever the most cutting-edge and solid scientific evidence shows in terms of the pros and cons of different ways of thinking and responding to life's challenges. We present such evidence selectively, with the most important criterion being scientific rigor. To make sense of the vast body of literature and seemingly unrelated findings we will present, we first need a theoretical framework of the human cognitive architecture.

DOI: 10.4324/9781003300366-3

We provided a working definition of reflection and intuition based on cognitive effort in Chapter 1. As our discussion there suggests, many features of intuitive and reflective processes exist. But which of these are central and which are peripheral? And when reflective processes are engaged, do intuitive processes cease entirely? From a subjective standpoint, it appears that sometimes one needs to suppress intuition, actively resist it from guiding behavior, and replace it with a more carefully calculated response. But is it possible that reflective and intuitive processes occasionally collaborate and interact? Furthermore, are there different kinds of reflective processes or distinct sources for such processes, like there are for intuitive ones? In short, even this attempt to introduce a simple dichotomy (i.e., reflection vs. intuition) and to identify a minimalistic definitional criterion (i.e., cognitive effort) ended up with several tough questions and a bit of confusion. Dual-process models of the mind are extremely useful for thinking systematically about these perennial complex issues. We provide an idealized dual-process model that will guide us through the variety of topics we cover in Part II of this book. In Part III, we revisit this idealized model to add more nuance.

Dual-Process Models in Cognitive and Social Psychology

Probably because dichotomies facilitate thinking about complex topics, psychology is replete with dual-process models. Most dual-process models focus on processes akin to reflection and intuition.[1] For instance, the distinction between automatic versus controlled mental processes—which partly corresponds to the reflection–intuition dichotomy—was central during the explosion of social cognition research in the 1990s (Chaiken & Trope, 1999). Smith and DeCoster (2000, Table 2) discuss several influential dual-process models, some of which stem from or explicitly focus on a single domain, such as stereotyping, attitudes, reasoning, memory, or decision-making. Others, such as Smith and DeCoster's own model, aim to be more integrative or general.

Most such models are in competition with other equally viable and influential models in the same domain. The proliferation of models is due partly to the desire of theorists to make different assumptions. For instance, the Elaboration-Likelihood Model (Petty & Cacioppo, 1986) was in competition with the Heuristic–Systematic Model (e.g., Chaiken, 1980) in the attitudes and persuasion domain. While the two focal processes (i.e., central route and systematic processing vs. peripheral route and heuristic processing) could be deemed equivalent, the models made some different assumptions about issues such as whether these processes were mutually exclusive or not (Chaiken & Ledgerwood, 2012).[2]

The use of different terms to refer to the two processes in these models may reflect slightly different conceptualizations of the same mental processes or even the fact that the theorists are focusing on different mental processes or subtypes of the same process. Can we assume, for instance, that automatic and terms used by other dual-process theorists—hot (Metcalfe & Mischel, 1999), heuristic (Chaiken, 1980; Evans, 1984), experiential (Epstein, 1994), impulsive (Strack & Deutsch, 2004), associative (Gawronski & Bodenhausen, 2006; Smith & DeCoster, 2000), reflexive (Lieberman et al., 2002), and so on—refer to the same thing or constitute a coherent constellation? Take just one of these terms—automaticity—and even then, one could be referring to different features of a mental process such as taking place outside of awareness, being unintentional, being efficient (requiring few cognitive resources), and being uncontrollable (Bargh, 1994). Even if we disentangle these features conceptually or in experiments, they might be correlated in life. Thus, a useful way out is to look for family resemblances and to remember that any overarching set of labels, such as reflection and intuition, represents *types* of processes.[3]

The development of domain-specific models subsequently allowed crosstalk and led to the realization of their commonalities, as well as their differences, and highlighted the subsequent theoretical challenges of integration (Chaiken & Trope, 1999; Sherman et al., 2014; Smith & DeCoster, 2000). Domain-specific models might be necessary to capture the nuances of those domains (and much empirical research is driven by such models) but for our purposes, we need a more general view of cognitive architecture that we can use to make sense of a wide variety of sociopolitical phenomena.

A General Dual-Process (and Tripartite) Model of the Mind

In our view, the work of cognitive psychologist Keith Stanovich offers the most comprehensive, well-organized, balanced, authoritative, and clear presentation of a general-purpose dual-process model of the mind. We rely on it extensively here and it is primarily what guides our thinking when we attempt to explain anything from the dual-process perspective.[4]

The Three Structures

The general dual-process model we rely on posits the reflective mind, the algorithmic mind, and the autonomous mind as three mental structures corresponding to reflection, intelligence, and intuition, respectively. To make sense of this tripartite view, one must note the distinction between *defining features* versus *typical correlates* of intuitive (Type 1) and reflective (Type 2) processes that Stanovich and colleagues (Evans & Stanovich, 2013a) raised in an attempt to reduce the confusion stemming from dual-process theorists' use of differing labels for the two processes. The defining feature of reflection is that it engages *working memory* and takes advantage of the human mind's ability to conduct *cognitive decoupling* and *simulation*. Intuition does not use working memory; it stems instead from an autonomous set of systems. All other features merely tend to be present when either type of process dominates a response. For instance, on tasks that require working memory (e.g., trying to memorize a phone number), thinking also tends to be slow, serial (processing one piece at a time), and conscious. On tasks that do not use working memory, thinking tends to be faster, parallel (processing multiple pieces at once), automatic, and nonconscious (see Evans & Stanovich, 2013a, Table 1).

Cognitive Ability: The Algorithmic Mind

The capacity that is exercised via working memory—the defining feature of Type 2 processes—is actively maintaining task-relevant information at the focus of attention (or in memory, ready to be brought to attention when required) while suppressing other, irrelevant or distracting, information (Kane et al., 2001);[5] such as when one is trying to commit a telephone number to memory while a bystander can be heard uttering irrelevant numbers. Or take the well-known Stroop task in which participants are required to report the color that words are printed in. This is particularly difficult when the word itself is the name of a color (e.g., "green") that is different than the color it appears in (e.g., red). Some individuals are faster and more accurate in such tasks than others, because they can inhibit the habitual response (developed through many years of education and leisurely reading) to read the word and replace it with the task demand (Kane & Engle, 2003); that is, individuals differ in *working memory capacity*. Those with higher working memory span are better able to keep task-relevant goals in mind and to resolve conflict between intuitive but task-irrelevant or counterproductive responses and what the current goals require. From this, it is clear that working memory is a capacity that is central to our ability to think reflectively, which also typically requires inhibition of intuitive responses.

Working memory is one of many computational capacities of the mind and is related to the broader construct of *cognitive ability* (i.e., intelligence). An especially relevant component of intelligence for reflectiveness is *fluid intelligence (Gf)*—which is about basic computations such as those that working memory is responsible for—as opposed to *crystallized intelligence (Gc)*—which is about stored knowledge such as one's vocabulary span. More specifically, Stanovich emphasizes an operation called *cognitive decoupling*, which he also argues is assessed by measures of fluid intelligence and is made possible by working memory (Evans & Stanovich, 2013a; Stanovich, 2011). Decoupling enables keeping mental representations of reality and hypothetical worlds separate. Sustaining the decoupled representation of the hypothetical world is necessary for running *mental simulations*—transforming the *primary representation* of the actual state of affairs into something else, a *secondary representation*—such as when you try to figure out whether implementing that new work policy would result in concrete improvements over the status quo. The ability to sustain decoupled representations is limited, because it is a computationally costly operation and because working memory is a limited resource.

Intuition: The Autonomous Mind

In stark contrast, intuitive responses are based on *accessibility* (Kahneman, 2003), which is about how easily a given mental representation can be brought to mind or more technically, the degree to which it is active in working memory (Higgins, 1996). Especially relevant is *temporary* (vs. *chronic) accessibility*, which occurs when an environmental stimulus or internal process temporarily activates mental content that otherwise would stay dormant in long-term memory. Accessible representations are ready to be applied to the task at hand and so are more likely to guide thought and behavior in that situation. One source of temporary accessibility is stimulus salience. For instance, *Prospect Theory* (Kahneman & Tversky, 1979)—a descriptive theory of human decision-making under risk—argues that psychologically, losses are more painful compared to how pleasurable gains of the same amount are, and therefore, that people are generally more risk-seeking in the domain of losses (vs. gains): A gamble with a worse outcome (i.e., lower expected utility) appears more attractive than a sure loss. Consequently, making losses versus gains more salient (hence, making one more accessible over the other) by framing choices differently leads to people responding in ways that violate the axioms of classical models (e.g., *expected utility theory*). Instead of staying consistent, people's choices shift between favoring risk-seeking versus risk aversion depending on loss- versus gain-framing, respectively.[6] Responding intuitively to a problem would mean that one is at the mercy of the particular way the problem is framed, while being unaware of this fact. Cognitive decoupling and mental simulation—i.e., reflective thought—would enable the decision-maker to imagine alternative frames and to become aware of their effects on the attractiveness of choices (Guo et al., 2017; cf. Igou & Bless, 2007; Wyszynski & Diederich, 2023).[7]

The source of Type 1 processes are called "the autonomous mind" and "the autonomous set of systems" (TASS) because this—autonomy—is their defining feature (Evans & Stanovich, 2013a; Stanovich, 2011). Autonomy here means that "the execution of Type 1 processes is mandatory when their triggering stimuli are encountered, and they do not depend on input from high-level control systems" (Stanovich, 2011, p. 19). One does not intend or consciously decide to initiate Type 1 processes; they are governed independently of the person's "will."

There is some mystery surrounding what the TASS includes, a topic we turn to in Part III of this book. This is parallel to the subjective feeling of surprise we experience at our own intuitive responses, whether it be a disappointing deviation from behavioral norms one is strongly committed to, a fast and accurate answer to a complex problem that only careful analysis seemed able to conquer, or an embarrassing Freudian slip. The sequence of mental events leading to an intuitive response is not transparent to the first-person perspective. The autonomous mind is not (easily) penetrable by conscious analysis.

Cognitive Style: The Reflective Mind

Once one accepts the reflection-versus-intuition distinction and that the former type of process requires cognitive ability, a conceptual gap presents itself: We called the source of Type 1 processes "autonomous," but we did not do the same for Type 2 processes. If those Type 2 processes are not autonomous, then what decides in each moment whether the resources available in the algorithmic mind are used for the purposes of reflection? Who or what demands working memory to simulate a world in which the new policy was implemented at work and compare its predicted outcomes to the representation of the current reality?

This gap is closed by positing a third structure—the reflective mind. Stanovich's model is dual process but tripartite (see Figure 1 in Evans & Stanovich, 2013a; see Figure 4.1 in Stanovich, 2011 for a more detailed version). Reflective (Type 2) processes (and rationality) are made possible by the joint workings of the reflective mind and the algorithmic mind. Intuitive (Type 1) processes stem from the autonomous mind. In this model, differences among individuals stem mostly from the properties of the reflective and algorithmic structures and to a much lesser extent from the properties of the autonomous mind. In this book, we are concerned mostly with individual differences in the properties of the reflective mind because as we will argue, this is probably the most important determinant of whether an individual is a reflective thinker.[8]

In other words, are there stable individual differences in the tendency to use (or to favor the output of) either set of processes? We can take it for granted that both reflection and intuition are used by everyone but do some people tend more toward reflection (or intuition) on average?[9] This is the idea of *thinking disposition* or *cognitive style*—that individuals have characteristic patterns of information processing as they attempt to solve problems, learn and reason about the world, make judgments and decisions, and so on. A large portion of the literature in psychology is directly or indirectly about cognitive style. The term appears to have originated in the writings of a prominent early social and personality psychologist, Gordon Allport (1937).

The cognitive revolution of the 1960s and 1970s in psychology resulted in an increased focus on the ways in which individuals construe, represent, and reason about the world, giving popularity to the cognitive style concept. For instance, in the 1970s, *learned helplessness*—the observation that dogs previously exposed to unavoidable shock failed to escape subsequent shock that was avoidable (Overmier & Seligman, 1967)—emerged as a significant discovery and eventually led to the insight that some individuals have an *attributional style* whereby they explain negative life events with reference to global, stable, and internal (as opposed to specific, unstable, and external) factors (Abramson et al., 1978). Such an attributional style—*hopelessness*—is depressogenic and is a stable trait of some individuals but can also be alleviated through treatment (Liu et al., 2015).

The work on hopelessness is just one example that illustrates that any pattern in perceptual and cognitive activity can fall under the umbrella term of cognitive style and that cognitive style can sometimes be a matter of life and death. We treat reflectiveness as a cognitive style and explore how and why it matters for the lives of individuals and societies. As with most psychological characteristics, cognitive styles develop as a function of both nature and nurture and as with hopelessness, there is always some hope of modifying them, as we explore in the coming chapters (see especially Chapter 3).

For us, what makes the reflection–intuition distinction so special is our belief that it is a more fundamental aspect of life than most of the other concepts discussed in the literature.[10] For instance, hopelessness develops by taking advantage of Type 1 processes to produce automatic negative thoughts (especially after a period of repeatedly making negative attributions). Due to how rapidly the mind carries out intuitive processes, their output is often mistaken for objectively given features of reality.[11] Subjective thoughts cannot be distinguished from objective reality and a self-perpetuating cycle emerges: If "reality" is so negative, I am right in feeling so depressed and the more depressed I feel, the worse my life becomes. Reflection in turn is the most readily available tool for cutting into this cycle (Zainal & Newman, 2022). Thoughts can be questioned, their validity checked against the world and the opinions of others, and alternative thoughts can be generated and entertained. Even reflecting on the negative affect most minimally—by just labeling it verbally—dampens it (Lieberman, 2011). Eventually, the cycle weakens and gives way to a more neutral, if not positive, way to experience existence. This is the gist of cognitive–behavioral psychotherapy.[12]

The above discussion is just a small demonstration that the scope of the topic at hand is much bigger than this book. Here, we focus on our specific interests as social psychologists and on the empirical evidence produced in (mostly) recent years. For now, the important point is that reflectiveness as a cognitive style is similar to a personality trait in being relatively stable, while also being somewhat malleable. The idea that some individuals are more reflective (or intuitive) across time and situations is at the heart of the present effort and we explore its implications focusing on several different domains, such as religion, morality, and politics, in subsequent chapters.

Coming back to Stanovich's dual-process model, one might think of cognitive ability and cognitive style as being similar to a car and a driver, respectively.[13] The driver steps on the pedals to propel and stop the car and turns the steering wheel for navigation. The car includes an engine that turns fuel into power for motion, a steering wheel connected to the tires, headlights, a dashboard with important device parameters, a climate control system, and other amenities to keep the driver functioning well, and so on. It is the driver that drives the car and it is the reflective mind that demands computations to be performed by the algorithmic mind.

The Temporal Interplay of Reflective and Intuitive Processes

Type 2 processes probably evolved in part to monitor and override Type 1 processes, as this ability affords our species much greater behavioral flexibility by inserting freedom in between stimuli and our immediate reactions to them. In other situations, Type 1 processes might provide useful ammunition for Type 2 processes. Whether they are competing or collaborating, there is constant interplay between the two sets of processes across time. Dual-process models differ in terms of assumptions about such temporal interplay. We subscribe to a *default-interventionist* (as opposed to a *parallel-competitive*) processing assumption (see Evans & Stanovich, 2013a) according to which individuals typically produce an intuitive response that is then, under some conditions, modified by reflective processes. This fits traditional notions of humans as cognitive misers (Simon, 1956; Taylor, 1981) and the fact that the operations governed by the reflective mind are computationally costly— we only think hard when we really have to and when we can afford to; or in other words, when we have the *motivation* and *capacity*. When we lack either, intuition dominates.

Some tasks used in empirical research—such as the extremely popular *Cognitive Reflection Test* (Frederick, 2005) discussed in the last section of this chapter—are designed specifically to trigger a wrong intuition and to test whether, without any explicit instructions,[14] the respondent will detect the need to override this intuitive response, inhibit it, and compute the correct response using an alternative, principled way of thinking (e.g., based on logic or mathematics). For such tasks, default-interventionism will of course seem true. However, not all situations are like this, so one must not assume that intuitive (and incorrect) responses will always occur first—in fact, some evidence suggests that they do not (Szaszi et al., 2018). Furthermore, intuitive responses, even when they do occur first, might be correct or valid in most mundane daily situations. After all, while there appears to be a growing number of "social media influencers" who are also potential candidates for the Darwin Awards,[15] the world's human inhabitants are not dying by the millions every day; most of us appear to get by fine, even if as a species we tend toward cognitive miserliness. Even theorists who emphasize reflectiveness and rationality, like Stanovich (2011, pp. 30–31), acknowledge that intuitive responses may generally serve us well; but they also argue—and we concur— that more reflectiveness would still help us achieve greater rationality. In Part III of this book, we examine whether intuition is obsolete in modern life.

Reflectiveness, Intelligence, Rationality, and Bias

In some of the chapters to follow, we explore the role of greater reflectiveness in various domains of social life. In most of this discussion, it is not easy to establish objectively what it means to be biased or which opinions and actions are (more) rational. For instance, is it irrational to subscribe to certain religious, moral, or political views (Chapter 6)? According to whom? Is it irrational to be selfish or to cooperate (Chapter 7)? Is it irrational to be a fundamentalist or extremist (Chapter 8)? In some other domains, there might be more hope for objectively establishing the rational position to take. Is it irrational to believe that the earth is flat (Chapter 5)? Yes! But even for conspiracy beliefs, things can get complicated: The idea that the CIA performed experiments with hallucinogens on innocent people in an attempt to control their minds may sound wacky until you learn about MK-ULTRA (Marks, 1991). The "conspiracy" label attached to the idea that coronavirus disease 2019 (COVID-19) leaked from a laboratory has recently become more tentative (Lenharo & Wolf, 2023).

Our task is not to provide a detailed treatment of rationality or cognitive biases in this book,[16] but it is important to entertain the fundamental question of whether thinking more reflectively aids rationality and bias prevention. Fortunately, for this purpose, cognitive psychologists have created tasks with objectively rational (i.e., normative) solutions and a significant risk of falling prey to a specific bias. This was the focus of the heuristics-and-biases research program (Tversky & Kahneman, 1974) that eventually won Kahneman the Nobel Prize in economics and the continued work along this direction is largely responsible for the dual-process view we present in this chapter. In this program, rationality takes a very concrete form: It is how close a response is to what is prescribed by the normative model (or the objective truth, if available) for the problem at hand; and it is the absence of bias (see Stanovich, 2011, p. 7).[17]

Some important insights emerged from such research. First, human beings appear quite prone to an ever-growing list of cognitive biases and illusions (Pohl, 2022). A classic case is when people make biased estimates because they judge the frequency of an event based on the ease with which they can recall instances of that event—the *availability* heuristic. For instance, one of the first demonstrations (Kahneman & Tversky, 1973, Study 3) found that the majority of participants estimated some consonant letters to be more frequent in the first compared to the third position in English words (even though the opposite is known to be true by an actual count), presumably because it is easier to think of words that start with a certain letter than words that have that letter in the third position. While such a bias may be trivial, Tversky and Kahneman's aim was to demonstrate how the application of a specific heuristic resulted in systematic and predictable bias. Further research focused on less trivial contexts, such as by showing that easier recall of one's own contributions to a group collaboration leads individuals to egocentrically attribute more responsibility to themselves for the ensuing group product (Ross & Sicoly, 1979).

Second, it appears that thinking more reflectively in fact aids bias prevention and consequently rationality. Some of this evidence is correlational, indicating that more reflective individuals are less susceptible to a variety of cognitive biases (e.g., West et al., 2008) whereas other evidence examines causal links either by focusing on situational factors that facilitate or inhibit reflection or on temporary activation or longer-term training of reflective thought. We cover this research in Chapter 3 of this book.

One might ask the question of whether it is really reflective thinking per se or cognitive ability that plays the most crucial role in rationality. They certainly both play a role: The driver and the car depend on each other for success at reaching the target location. More technically, when the reflective mind detects a need to override the autonomous mind, it initiates some key operations, such as hypothetical thinking to simulate an alternative version of reality, that require the computational power of the algorithmic mind, such as *cognitive decoupling*, which keeps the simulation encapsulated and separate from one's perception of reality and other irrelevant thoughts (see Stanovich, 2011, Chapter 3). The demand to create separate mental models is placed by the reflective mind and keeping these decoupled is the algorithmic mind's job. In other words, there must be close cooperation between the reflective and algorithmic minds and any failure in either structure would be fatal for rational thought and action.

In fact, cognitive ability and cognitive style are empirically related (e.g., Fleischhauer et al., 2010; Frederick, 2005). Some research has attempted to statistically control for the effect of one variable while examining the effect of the other. Controlling for cognitive ability, cognitive style is still uniquely associated with bias—with more reflective individuals showing less bias (e.g., West et al., 2008; see also Stanovich, 2011, footnote 4 in Chapter 2), but the relationship between cognitive style and cognitive ability is far from perfect. The same empirical findings showing their relationship also indicate a substantial degree of independence of cognitive style and ability from each other. Furthermore, the relationship between cognitive ability and susceptibility to cognitive biases is surprisingly weak (e.g., Stanovich & West, 2008; see Stanovich, 2011, p. 122).[18],[19]

Importantly, this body of research shows that individuals' cognitive style and cognitive ability have unique relations with their propensity to show bias, hence justifying a *tripartite* view of the mind.[20] The distinction between the reflective mind and the algorithmic mind also helps to make sense of *dysrationalia*—"the inability to think and behave rationally despite adequate intelligence ... demonstrated in thinking and behavior ... that is significantly below the level of the individual's intellectual capacity" (Stanovich, 1993, p. 503)—as exemplified by various well-known public figures (Lilienfeld et al., 2020; Stanovich, 2009b).

To come back to our car-and-driver analogy, we definitely prefer a driver at the wheel who is focused on figuring out how to navigate the car toward a target location. With such a driver, there is a much better chance that all that the car offers can be used in the service of the goal. We certainly do not prefer a driver who is absent, who is focused on their cell phone, who is sleeping in the back seat, who is trying to steer the wheel with the top of their head just for fun, and so forth. With a properly focused driver, a turn could be taken into the direction opposite of the target, but the error can be caught and a U-turn can put the car back on track. With a nonfunctional driver, good luck! The car itself is less important. Does it have the essentials? Then a functional driver can use it to get to the target location; maybe just a bit slower than if they had a fancy car. A fancy car and a dysfunctional driver are a much worse combination than a basic car and a functional driver.

Why Bias Occurs

In our reading of the literature, the evidence overwhelmingly supports the notions that (1) human beings are cognitive misers; (2) this makes them susceptible to a variety of biases (3) for which reflective thought is a protective factor. This is not just a matter of avoiding some innocent mistakes in trivial laboratory tasks: Reflective thinkers are also more competent decision-makers and better-behaved citizens in real life (Bruine De Bruin et al., 2007; Parker et al., 2018). Any idea that those with serious ambitions to be successful in modern society should just let their intuition run free simply crumbles under the weight of the evidence (e.g., see the references in Stanovich, 2011, footnote 2 in Chapter 2).

A dual-process perspective offers insight into both the ecological and the cognitive reasons why relying on intuition brings about bias. As Stanovich (2011) eloquently states:

> Increasingly in the modern world, we are presented with decisions and
> problems that require more accurate responses than those generated by

heuristic processing. Type 1 processes often provide a quick solution that is a first approximation to an optimal response. But modern life often requires more precise thought than this. Modern technological societies are in fact hostile environments for people reliant on only the most easily computed automatic response. Think of the multimillion-dollar advertising industry that has been designed to exploit just this tendency. Modern society keeps proliferating such situations where shallow processing is not sufficient for maximizing personal happiness—precisely because many structures of market-based societies have been designed explicitly to exploit such tendencies. Being cognitive misers will seriously impede people from achieving their goals.

(pp. 29–30)

This is the problem of *evolutionary mismatch* between the environment in which our psychological proclivities evolved and the modern environment (Li et al., 2018). Our tendency to prefer sweet foods was quite adaptive long ago when the sweetest foods available were actually healthy and food was scarce; but it is maladaptive currently because even the mildly sweet options now are very unhealthy and food is in abundance (Chang & Durante, 2022). As laypersons, we may be aware that market forces are taking advantage of our cognitive miserliness and that we may overcome this if we were to think harder to make better choices. Why then do we still resist thinking harder so often? Partly because cognitive effort feels aversive (David et al., 2022).[21] But why? For one, our cognitive effort is a *limited* resource that must be spent wisely on tasks that carry good reward potential and that connect to meaningful long-term goals. Whether there is a serious metabolic limitation—for instance, whether exerting cognitive effort depletes blood glucose—is unclear (Shenhav et al., 2017), but time is certainly limited for all of us mortals and we cannot focus our mental powers on multiple targets at once.[22] Thus, when we invest cognitive effort in one task or domain, we incur *opportunity costs*, because we are missing out on other tasks and goals in other domains we could be pursuing. The aversiveness of cognitive effort may simply be tracking the accumulation of such costs and might be a way to keep us from investing our limited cognitive resources in tasks that are unlikely to yield important benefits.[23]

From a more cognitive perspective, bias prevention requires at least three separate components: (1) *detection*—the realization that one's intuitive responses to the task at hand are inappropriate or suboptimal and that there is a better alternative; (2) *override*—cognitively inhibiting intuitive responses; and (3) *mindware*—the presence in memory of the "knowledge bases, rules, procedures and strategies" in such domains as "probabilistic reasoning, causal reasoning, scientific reasoning and numeracy" (Stanovich, 2018, p. 429) so that a superior response could be concretely generated.[24]

Thus, bias can result from a failure to detect a need to respond differently, a failure to sustain the necessary override of intuitive responses long enough, or the lack of proper mindware. In the first (detection failure), reflective processes are not engaged (intuition wins directly) and in the second (override failure), they are engaged but fail to overpower intuition. Stanovich (2018, see Figure 4) makes the interesting point that both these are interrelated with the third (mindware). For instance, with proper mindware in place, successful detection becomes more likely which in turn makes override a possibility. The importance of mindware makes it clear that merely thinking hard is not always sufficient for rationality (neither does thinking little guarantee irrationality; see Part III of the book for more on this) and that biased responses do not always indicate cognitive miserliness; they might just indicate lack of mindware (see Stanovich, 2018). For instance, one might not be able to use probability information to reach balanced conclusions without the mindware of probabilistic reasoning in place.[25] Importantly, reflective thinkers, tending generally toward greater information seeking (Cacioppo et al., 1996), should be more likely to recognize gaps in their mindware and fill in those gaps (Coutinho et al., 2005; Curşeu, 2011).

Operationalizations of Reflectiveness

We have defined reflectiveness as a tendency of individuals to spend cognitive effort on the task at hand as opposed to miserly information processing. We have argued that this is at the heart of rationality, playing an even greater role than intelligence, and is a relatively stable individual characteristic. Many measures attempt to assess this characteristic or a very similar one. We have already mentioned one extremely popular measure, the cognitive reflection test (Frederick, 2005). This is a performance-based (vs. self-report) measure designed to capture individuals' typical tendency to let an intuition guide their responses versus detecting the potentially misleading nature of the intuition, overriding it, and replacing it with a more effortfully calculated response. A sample item will make this clear:

A bat and a ball cost $1.10 in total. The bat costs $1.00 more than the ball. How much does the ball cost?

Most people have the intuition, created by the pattern of numbers in the question, that the ball costs 10 cents which is the cognitively miserly, but wrong, answer. With successful detection of the potential to fall into the trap laid by the question and successful override of the intuitive response, it is possible with knowledge of basic math (mindware) to calculate the reflective and correct answer, which is 5 cents. Performance on this bat-and-ball problem by itself has impressive predictive validity (see Pennycook,

2017, Table 2.1) and the reasons will become clearer as we move forward in the book.

Many other performance-based measures of reflectiveness exist (see the first "major dimension" in Stanovich, 2011, Table 10.1), differing significantly in surface features but tapping similar mental characteristics. Other measures directly ask respondents to make the assessment themselves, usually by indicating their level of agreement with statements on a rating scale. The *need for cognition* scale (Cacioppo et al., 1984) is a self-report measure that taps enjoyment of thinking with items such as "I find satisfaction in deliberating hard and for long hours" and "Thinking is not my idea of fun" (reverse-scored). The *need for cognitive closure*—the tendency to halt information processing as soon as possible—is a similar construct but in the opposite direction, with scale items such as "I usually make important decisions quickly and confidently" (Kruglanski et al., 1993). Some aspects of personality are also related to reflectiveness. For instance, in the most widely used model of personality—the Big Five (i.e., the five-factor model)— the dimensions of conscientiousness[26] and openness include facets obviously related to reflectiveness (see also Pacini & Epstein, 1999).

Many other tests and self-report measures are aimed at other aspects of rationality than reflectiveness, but they contain items that measure reflectiveness, or scores derived from them are correlated strongly with reflectiveness measures. In short, no single test or measure is perfect or process-pure (i.e., solely measuring reflectiveness)[27] and many criticisms and shortcomings of even the most commonly used tests have been discussed (sometimes along with rebuttals and counterevidence).[28] We aim to keep our focus squarely on reflectiveness as much as possible throughout the book but acknowledge that it is difficult to completely prevent sliding into related concepts because of the complexities of measurement (and sometimes also conceptualization). Fortunately, because each measure has unique limitations and strengths, the fact that the evidence is based on a wide variety of measures, rather than a limited number, allows us to detect converging evidence of generalizable mechanisms. We emphasize what the weight of the evidence supports instead of focusing on the unique features of individual studies.

Coda

This chapter aimed to introduce a general framework—the dual-process model based mostly on the work of Stanovich and colleagues—that will make it easier to appreciate the empirical research findings we present in the coming chapters. This framework is one of the most useful that we have encountered in our careers as psychologists and most certainly a superb entry point into the current topic. In our view, our field (and in fact, humanity in general) owes a great debt to this effort. Most of the research and the ensuing insight into human mind and behavior sampled in this book would not have existed without the work of the researchers chasing after these tough questions and importantly, no such work would have been possible without a great deal of reflective thinking.

The dual-process model of the mind and the research it has inspired and that it builds on make the value of reflection for human judgment and decision-making quite clear. It also highlights the interesting conflict and competition that sometimes occurs between reflective and intuitive processes. This is not the end of the story, however. Neither the dual-process model of the mind, nor the tasks designed to measure reflective cognitive style and other constructs (cognitive ability, rational thinking, etc.) are without criticism. We visit some limitations and novel theoretical proposals in Chapter 10 and introduce many other nuances in other chapters. Moreover, taking a more holistic view of human cognition and considering contexts in which it plays out other than the cognitive laboratory leaves one wondering whether reflection and intuition might enjoy a more collaborative relationship in other contexts. Does reflection never benefit from input from other types of human mental activity, such as intuition and emotion? Is it practical to assume that reflection, being a slower and more fragile process, should take the central role in all human affairs? Is reflection sufficient by itself for addressing today's fundamental issues like political polarization and climate change? After exploring the causes and consequences of reflection in depth in the subsequent chapters, we will argue at the book's conclusion how a new type of thinking—where reflection is still central but is complemented by other human capabilities—holds greater potential to address some of the most pressing problems of our time.

Notes

1 We focus on those kinds of models, as well, but there are also models in which the two central processes seem to be independent of the reflection–intuition dimension. There is, for instance, a domain-specific dual-process model of coping with bereavement that contrasts loss- and restoration-oriented activity (Schut, 1999); and a model in political psychology that focuses on the motivational bases of right-wing authoritarianism versus social dominance orientation (Duckitt & Sibley, 2010).

2 The relevance of these models to the topic at hand is demonstrated by how close their definitions of one type of process are to our definition of reflectiveness. For instance, in Chaiken's model, "systematic processing, involves attempts to thoroughly understand any and all available information through careful attention, deep thinking, and intensive reasoning (e.g., thinking carefully about the arguments presented, the person arguing, and the causes of the person's behavior)" (Chaiken & Ledgerwood, 2012, p. 247).

3 Initially, Stanovich (1999) had offered the terms "System 1" and "System 2" to refer to these two qualitatively different kinds of thinking and many others (e.g., Kahneman, 2011) adopted these terms. In recent years, there was a move to using "Type" to avoid the connotations of the term "System." For instance, many dual-process theorists do not wish to assume that there is correspondence to a single brain system for each type of process. In fact, Stanovich (2004) later started referring to "The Autonomous Set of Systems" (note the use of plural "systems") for the source of Type 1 processes.

4 There is a good deal of overlap across many works offered by Stanovich. We find his book *Rationality and the Reflective Mind* (Stanovich, 2011) to be a particularly good source for the technical details of our summary of his model here.

5 Many scientific terms are unnecessarily confusing as is the case here. As Stanovich (2011, see especially pp. 53–60) points out, working memory is relevant to sustaining decoupled representations, as we explain shortly. Thus, in layperson's terms, working memory is more about focus, concentration, and attention than about storage.

6 For example, the famous "Asian disease problem" presents participants with the scenario of an outbreak expected to lead to 600 deaths and, in the gain-framed version, the choice between two interventions that will either (A) save 200 of those lives or (B) save all 600 with a probability of one-third and not save any with a probability of two-thirds. In the loss-framed version, the alternatives will result in either (A) losing 400 lives or (B) losing no lives with a probability of one-third and losing all lives with a probability of two-thirds. The problem and the alternatives are identical in both versions. Tversky and Kahneman (1981) reported that the majority of participants exposed to the gain-framed version picked the more risk-averse alternative (A) whereas the majority exposed to the loss-framed version picked the more risk-favoring alternative (B).

7 It is wrong to assume that reflection will always reduce bias. For instance, Prospect Theory also argues that people tend to overweight small probabilities. One could use reflection to mentally simulate events of low probability, which could activate Type 1 processes and cause, for instance, a vivid sense of their affective consequences. As Evans (Evans, 2007, p. 115) has warned,

> our mental fantasy about winning the jackpot in the national lottery provides the event with a reality (and subjective weight) disproportionate to its minute objective probability. In the same way, the skilled insurance salesman increases the subjective weight of a potentially disastrous event, merely by persuading us to imagine its occurrence.

In short, reflection could trigger a cascade of Type 1 processes instead of focusing on aspects of a problem that facilitate better decisions, such as probabilities in the abstract. This is partly a matter of the amount of cognitive effort involved in the reflection, a topic that we turn to in Chapter 9.

8 What we mean by a person being reflective has a lot to do with, but is not exactly the same as, what Stanovich means by "the reflective mind" (or the "intentional level" in his earlier works) in his tripartite model. In his own words,

> the reflective mind is defined in reference to levels of control, not in terms of time. The term reflective mind is defined in terms of cognition involving high-level control change, not in terms of dictionary definitions of the term reflective (thoughtfulness, contemplation, etc.). As such, the term may be a bit

of a misnomer. High-level control change will often be extended in time, but not always.

(Stanovich, 2011, pp. 78–79)

Part III of this book will shed more light on this issue.

9 The assertion of stable differences across individuals in their overall tendency to be reflective does not preclude the assertion of substantial differences in the same person's tendency to be reflective across different situations. Person A behaving *less* reflectively in a specific situation X than person B is also not inconsistent with person A being much more reflective overall, across a wide range of situations and time, than person B (see Fleeson, 2004).

10 The fact that most dual-process models focus on reflection versus intuition (or something very similar) attests to this core importance, as well. The fundamental nature of this dimension of life is also demonstrated by the presence of inclinations toward either reflectiveness or impulsiveness in children (Kagan et al., 1964) and animals (Sih & Del Giudice, 2012). Note the parallels between Kagan and colleagues' description of the reflective child and our view of reflectiveness:

> Some children impulsively report the first hypothesis that occurs to them, and this response is often incorrect. The reflective child, on the other hand, delays a long time before reporting a solution and is usually correct. The reflective child considers the differential validity of alternative answers, makes fewer errors in reading prose or in recalling serially learned material, and persists longer with difficult tasks. The reflective child wants to avoid making an error and inhibits potentially incorrect hypotheses. The impulsive child seems minimally concerned about mistakes and makes his decisions quickly.
>
> *(Kagan et al., 1966, p. 583)*

11 This is similar to *naïve realism*, the belief "[t]hat I see entities and events as they are in objective reality, and that my social attitudes, beliefs, preferences, priorities, and the like follow from a relatively dispassionate, unbiased, and essentially 'unmediated' apprehension of the information or evidence at hand" (Ross & Ward, 1996, p. 110). Even our three-dimensional visual experience of the world is a mental reconstruction of the two-dimensional information falling into the retina but in domains such as vision, naïve realism may be good or even absolutely necessary as it would be detrimental to survival to not take for granted that the three-dimensional experience constructed by the mind and to constantly probe how it may differ from the objective world. In the social domain, where facts are much harder to establish and often just depend on arbitrary conventions and consensus, naïve realism can be a source of major difficulties (Ichheiser, 1970).

12 Ancient philosophers recognized the importance of cognitive style (and of reflectiveness), as also suggested by our reference to Plato earlier. Interestingly, the founders of cognitive–behavioral therapy explicitly acknowledge its roots in Stoicism (see Chapter 1 in Robertson, 2020), an Ancient Greek and Roman philosophical school that has become popular again recently.

13 We were unintentionally influenced by other similar analogies. We started the chapter with Plato, whose famous allegory presents a charioteer (the reflective mind) driving two horses (the algorithmic mind and the autonomous mind), with striking resemblance to the dual-process model we take as our basis here. Another similar analogy on a different topic likens the psychological sense of power to an accelerator and empathy to a steering wheel (Galinsky et al., 2014). Finally, we

were pleasantly surprised to find at least one sentence (perhaps there are others we missed) in Stanovich's own writings that suggests that our car-driver analogy is well-chosen: "When we measure [fluid intelligence], we measure a critical aspect of the engine of the brain but not the skill of the driver" (Stanovich, 2011, p. 183).

14 Letting respondents behave as they *typically* would do taps properties of their reflective mind whereas properties of the algorithmic mind are best assessed under *maximal* testing, e.g., by explicitly instructing respondents to do their absolute best (Stanovich, 2011).

15 The Darwin Awards are given to adults who, by acting idiotically despite having the capacity for good judgment, removed themselves from the gene pool by killing or sterilizing themselves (see https://darwinawards.com/).

16 Interested readers can consult many such treatments (Baron, 2023b; Hastie & Dawes, 2010; Kahneman, 2011; Pinker, 2021; Pohl, 2022; Stanovich, 2011; Stanovich et al., 2016).

17 We refrain from attempting to provide a more general definition of rationality. It is not only admittedly difficult but also somewhat out of our scope as it involves philosophy more than psychology. The different theoretical frameworks, definitions, and types of rationality discussed in a recent handbook (Knauff & Spohn, 2021) will make the complexity of the matter clear.

18 The judgment of the strength of correlation coefficients is difficult and dependent on context and expectation. For instance, Burgoyne et al. (2023) judged their observed correlations around $r = .5$ between rationality (good performance on several bias tasks) and cognitive ability as "strong." But such a correlation coefficient means that there is around 75% unshared variance between these two constructs. Consistent with such observations, a unique and important argument in much of Stanovich's work is that intelligence tests do not tap properties of the reflective mind and the latter has even more to do with rationality than the algorithmic mind (Stanovich, 2009b). All the fuss about intelligence in public discourse would make one think that rationality would be predicted strongly by intelligence, but the evidence does not support this.

19 The relationship between cognitive ability and cognitive bias susceptibility is actually a bit more nuanced. Stanovich (2011, Table 7.2) lists cognitive biases that do and do not correlate with cognitive ability and a detailed explanation of this pattern based on his tripartite model. The gist of his argument is that cognitive ability will be correlated with measures of bias to the extent that preventing bias on the task requires cognitive decoupling—a central and costly capacity of the algorithmic mind. Otherwise, performance will be related more to properties of the reflective mind.

20 Stanovich (2011, pp. 35–39) provides further justification.

21 To reflective thinkers, as captured by measures such as *the need for cognition* (Cacioppo & Petty, 1982), thinking hard is in fact enjoyable.

22 This was an insight that Wilhelm Wundt, the person considered by most to be the founder of scientific psychology, reached in his early days as a researcher (1860s) before the field officially existed (see Diamond, 1980).

23 Stanovich (2011) points out an interesting reason for why cognitive effort (specifically decoupling) is costly:

> Evolution has guaranteed the high cost of decoupling for a very good reason. As we were becoming the first creatures to rely strongly on cognitive simulation,

it was especially important that we not become 'unhooked' from the world too much of the time. Thus, dealing with primary representations of the world always has a special salience.

(p. 50)

In this light, there might be reason to be concerned about how realistic the fantasy worlds offered to us in modern society have become and consequently, how difficult it is to "become unhooked" from these worlds, sometimes fatally so (e.g., in distracted driving).

24 The reader might think that mindware is the same as crystallized intelligence but this is not really the case; see Stanovich (2011, p. 97). However, there are parallels so that Stanovich refers to proper mindware as "crystallized facilitators" of rationality (see Figure 10.1).

25 There is a different type of mindware problem—contaminated mindware—that we explain in Chapter 8 (see also Chapter 5).

26 While Stanovich does not focus on personality in his research or theorizing, he acknowledges that conscientiousness "taps the higher-level regulatory properties of the reflective mind" (Stanovich, 2011, p. 45).

27 Stanovich has attempted to organize these measures under the concept of *fluid rationality* of which avoidance of miserly processing (i.e., reflectiveness) is just one part (see Figure 10.1 and Table 10.1 in Stanovich, 2011). Consistent with our warning here, he also acknowledges that some measures of other aspects of rationality are confounded with reflectiveness. For instance, the careful reader will note that correct responses on the cognitive reflection test are both reflective and rational. In our reading, this is natural and perhaps unavoidable. There is little chance to succeed at any test of rationality without sufficient reflectiveness, even if that test itself is not designed to be a measure of reflectiveness. Evidence supports the centrality of reflection for rationality. For instance, reflectiveness (cognitive reflection test scores) predicts rationality (scores on a composite rational thinking battery composed of 15 measures) beyond and above cognitive ability, executive functioning, and other cognitive style measures combined (Toplak et al., 2011).

28 For instance, the cognitive reflection test has become so popular that we have encountered one of the items being asked on the Turkish version of the TV show "Who Wants to be a Millionaire?" Thus, one criticism is participant familiarity. Another is that it is confounded with mathematical ability (Sinayev & Peters, 2015). Some researchers have offered revisions and extensions of the original test to overcome these kinds of problems (Baron et al., 2015; Sirota, Dewberry, et al., 2021; Thomson & Oppenheimer, 2016; Toplak et al., 2014) and others have provided evidence that some such problems are practically insignificant (Bialek & Pennycook, 2018).

3
DEVELOPMENT AND TRAINING OF REFLECTIVE THINKING

Have you ever considered the possibility that your reflective thinking abilities could be influenced simply by the font in which you are reading this sentence compared to the normal font you see in the next sentence? A prominent psychology journal unveiled research suggesting that a phenomenon known as processing fluency had the potential to enhance reflective thinking (Alter et al., 2007; see also Song & Schwarz, 2008). Processing fluency refers to the ease with which individuals process information. High fluency denotes the simplicity, rapidity, and smoothness of information processing, whereas low fluency indicates the information's challenging nature (Unkelbach & Greifeneder, 2013). The underlying assumption is that presenting sentences in a difficult-to-read font will engage a cognitively challenging process in individuals, thereby activating reflective processes.

What if we were to ask you to gaze at Figure 3.1, depicting Rodin's "The Thinker," for a mere 30 seconds? Could we anticipate an improvement in your reflective thinking during subsequent tasks? In 2012, a study published in a leading scientific journal explored this very question (Gervais & Norenzayan, 2012). Participants who engaged in a 30-second contemplation of The Thinker image consistently outperformed their counterparts who engaged in a 30-second contemplation of the Discobolus of Myron in correctly answering cognitive reflection test (CRT) questions featured in Chapter 2. Intriguingly, these participants also demonstrated diminished scores related to belief in a divine entity, implying a potential link between reflective thinking and reduced religious inclination (Gervais & Norenzayan, 2012).

Now, imagine we prompt you to recollect a past situation where your reflective thinking led you down a beneficial path, and we request you to

DOI: 10.4324/9781003300366-4

articulate it within 6–8 sentences. Can this act trigger your reflective thought processes? Compose a paragraph of roughly 8–10 sentences describing an instance in which thoughtful reasoning guided you toward a positive outcome. By engaging in this exercise and subsequently taking a CRT or one of its variants, which can be found through a quick online search, you can check for any improvements in your performance relative to your typical results.

Although these techniques were initially offered with supportive evidence that they activate reflective thinking, subsequent investigations involving extensive participant pools have failed to consistently demonstrate their effectiveness (e.g., Deppe et al., 2015; Meyer et al., 2015). Therefore, while perusing a faintly presented text like the one in the beginning or pondering over an image like the one in Figure 3.1 for an extended time might induce

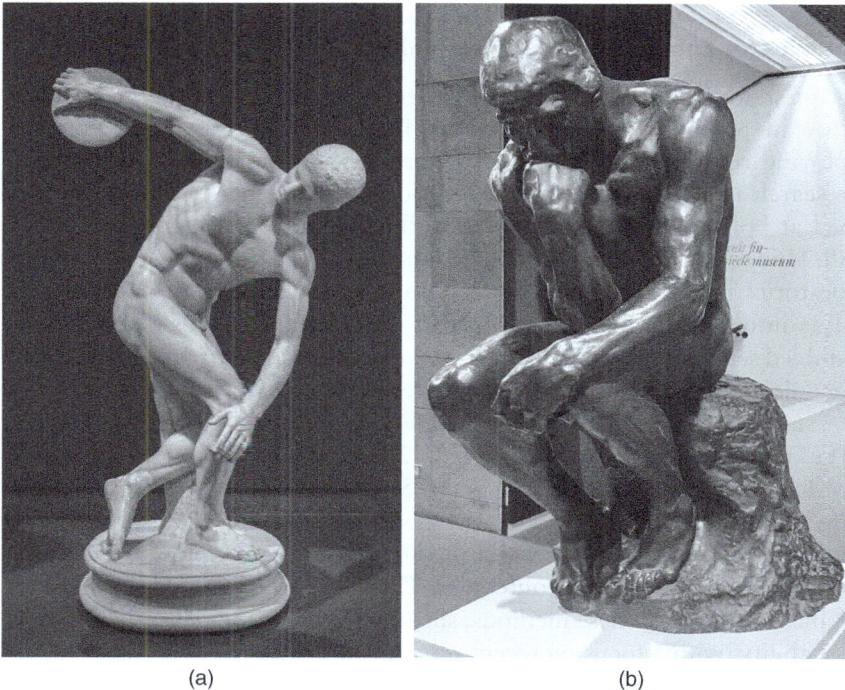

(a)   (b)

FIGURE 3.1   Discobolus (left) and the Thinker (right). Discobolus in National Roman Museum Palazzo Massimo alle Terme by Livioandronico 2013 is licensed under CC BY-SA 4.0. The Thinker by Auguste Rodin at Royal Museums of Fine Arts of Belgium by Yair Haklai is licensed under CC BY-SA 4.0.

a transient surge in reflective thought processes, it is essential to recognize that such effects are not universally applicable and do not endure (Isler & Yilmaz, 2023).

Nevertheless, these methods have persisted in the scientific literature as instruments for temporarily stimulating reflective thinking within experimental settings. Yet, the underlying question lingers: How can we foster reflection, given its fragility, when the intuitive facets of our cognition are profoundly entrenched in our developmental journey? In other words, despite the numerous cognitive biases acquired during our development that generally predispose us toward intuitive thinking, how is it possible to activate reflective thinking? In the sections that follow, we will embark on a multifaceted exploration. First, we will scrutinize the current scientific validity of techniques employed to augment reflective thinking in adults. Subsequently, we will broaden our perspective to encompass the development of reflection as well as the training of reflective thinking skills.

Strategies for Enhancing Reflective Thinking

The quest for methods to enhance reflective thinking has a longstanding history in psychology, exemplified by Dewey's (1933) seminal work on employing reflection for educational purposes. While a significant portion of research has concentrated on educational approaches and interventions aimed at bolstering critical thinking skills (Halpern, 2013; Hudgins et al., 1989; Hudgins & Edelman, 1988; Nilson et al., 2013), cognitive psychology laboratories have explored techniques to temporarily activate reflective (as well as intuitive) thinking in controlled experimental settings, such as the scrambled sentence task, cognitive disfluency, and visual priming, exemplified by iconic figures like The Thinker. Regrettably, many of these methods have suffered from a lack of replicability in subsequent studies (Bakhti, 2018; Deppe et al., 2015; Meyer et al., 2015; Sanchez et al., 2017; Sirota, Theodoropoulou, et al., 2021; Yilmaz & Saribay, 2016), rendering them ineffective, as shown by the previously mentioned examples. In the pursuit to enhance reflective thinking, several methods have been explored, each with its own set of challenges and outcomes. The first part of this chapter reviews and analyzes some of these methods, shedding light on their effectiveness and applicability, with a focus on recent research findings.

Ineffective Popular Techniques

One commonly employed method to experimentally stimulate both reflection and intuition is the time limit approach, as outlined by Rand (2016). This technique typically subjects participants to time constraints, such as a 10-second decision-making window, or introduces a time delay of 20 seconds (e.g., Teichert et al., 2014). It is theorized that decisions made under time pressure tend to be intuitive, while those deliberated upon for at least 20 seconds are considered relatively reflective. However, questions arise regarding the legitimacy of the time-delay manipulation, as it often lacks a control group such as a no time-limit condition. Furthermore, the arbitrary setting of time limits (e.g., 10 or 20 seconds) fails to account for potential variations in cognitive performance associated with different time frames and in different tasks. Recent research, conducted with high statistical power by our team, revealed that time pressure of 5 or 10 seconds indeed promotes intuitive thinking (Isler & Yilmaz, 2023). Contrary to expectations, the 10- or 20-second time-delay technique did not induce reflective thinking, with scores indistinguishable from those of the control group (no time-limit condition). Consequently, it appears erroneous to regard this frequently employed technique as a dependable means of inducing reflection. It is conceivable that prior attributions of effects to time delay as a reflection manipulation may actually be attributable to the influence of time pressure as an intuition manipulation (Everett et al., 2017; Isler, Gächter, Maule, et al., 2021; Isler, Yilmaz, & Maule, 2021). In essence, while time delay may serve as a control condition, the group subjected to time pressure emerges as the primary contributor to observed effects. Thus, time delay seems to lack effectiveness as a reliable reflection manipulation technique. One thing is more certain: strict time pressure leaves very little possibility for extensive reflection and thus, responses in this condition are intuitive.

In addition to the standard (e.g., between-subjects) time-limit manipulations, within-subjects versions of the time-limit approach have gained prominence in recent years (Yilmaz & Isler, 2019; see also Thompson et al., 2011). In this variation, participants initially make decisions under time pressure and subsequently contemplate their choices for 10 seconds, guided to engage in reflective thinking regarding their initial intuitive decisions (see also Chapter 10 for further discussion). Although this approach essentially translates the time pressure and time delay methods, typically implemented as between-subjects designs, into a single group (i.e., within-subjects design), there is insufficient evidence to assert that the second-stage time delay significantly enhances analytical performance. While some findings hint at substantial effects (e.g., Raoelison et al., 2020), it appears that, once again, the primary influence on performance arises from the manipulation of intuitive thinking induced by time pressure, with time delay failing to distinguish itself from the control group (Isler & Yilmaz, 2023).

Beyond the time-delay method, some researchers have tried to promote reflective thinking by instructing participants to rely solely on high-effort thinking or to employ reason (Eidelman et al., 2012; Kvarven et al., 2020). For instance, an experiment might contrast conditions in which individuals are instructed to make decisions using either reason (reflective) or emotion (intuitive). Although this approach has enjoyed popularity in cooperation-related studies (e.g., Kvarven et al., 2020), its impact on actual performance remained largely unexplored until recent years. A study by our group (Isler & Yilmaz, 2023) revealed that inducing emotion can enhance intuitive thinking, akin to the effects of time pressure, while reason induction failed to elevate reflection compared to the control condition.

The thought-priming method, as exemplified in the study by Isler et al. (2020), is one such approach that initially appeared promising. In this method, participants were assigned to either an intuitive-negative or analytic-positive condition. In the former, participants were instructed to recount an instance when their intuition or initial instinct led to an unfavorable outcome, while in the latter, they were asked to describe a situation where careful reasoning resulted in a positive outcome. Surprisingly, despite its initial potential, this method failed to yield significant effects on actual performance in recent high-powered studies conducted in both English and Turkish (Isler et al., 2020; Isler & Yilmaz, 2023; Saribay et al., 2020). Upon closer examination, it was discovered that a reduction in the required number of sentences to adapt the task to an online setting (Isler et al., 2020) and the application of the manipulation in a different language than the original study (Saribay et al., 2020) may have contributed to the lack of observed effects. Nevertheless, even when a direct replication with the original instructions was attempted, the method still failed to impact actual performance (Isler & Yilmaz, 2023). These limitations prompted a reconsideration of the thought-priming method's efficacy.

Effective Techniques

Recognizing the limitations of the thought-priming method, researchers have explored alternative approaches to activate reflective thinking. In a systematic study, Isler et al. (2020) experimented with three different methods, each demonstrating promising results.

The first approach involves an analytic training technique (Yilmaz & Saribay, 2017a, 2017b). Participants receive a 10-minute training session on reflective thinking and subsequently solve CRTs or base rate problems. In this training conducted within a laboratory setting, participants are initially asked to answer three different CRT questions. Subsequently, they receive feedback on the correct answer and the logic behind each question, presented in approximately one paragraph. The same questions are then posed again with altered numerical values to verify participants' understanding of the underlying logic. Following this, participants are presented with a base rate conflict question, wherein stereotypical knowledge is at odds with actual probability calculation. Feedback is provided on the correct answer along with its explanation, mirroring the earlier approach. This is followed by two additional base rate conflict questions to further assess participants' comprehension of the logic. The entire training session lasts about 10 minutes in the laboratory environment. This method has proven effective in various studies (e.g., Yilmaz & Saribay, 2017b) but posed challenges when integrated into the online environment due to its complexity.

Nonetheless, Isler et al. (2020) successfully adapted this analytic training for online use and generated a debiasing training technique with novel training questions, showing that training participants against cognitive biases led to improved cognitive performance, a result later replicated in a different sample (Isler & Yilmaz, 2023). In this online training, participants were presented with three questions and received feedback on the correct answers to these questions. One of these was a base-rate conflict question similar to the one exemplified in the task above. The other two questions involved semantic illusion and availability heuristics aimed at circumventing general cognitive biases (Kahneman, 2011). For instance, in the well-known Moses illusion question, "How many of each animal did Moses take on the ark?," most participants typically answer "two" or "a pair." However, more attentive readers might notice the error in the question, realizing that the correct answer should reference Noah, not Moses. As participants respond to each question, they are provided with feedback on both the answer and the logic behind the question. Subsequently, participants are asked to write an open-ended reflection on what they have learned during the training. Lastly, they are instructed to apply their reflective thinking to the subsequent task. In essence, providing individuals with brief training on cognitive biases and then testing their comprehension with similar novel questions activated reflective thinking.

This approach suggests the potential benefits of incorporating similar training modules into high school and undergraduate textbooks. In general, most critical thinking books and courses highlight that complex skills, be they cognitive or physical, are most effectively transferred through feedback and scaffolding techniques (Halpern, 2013). However, it remains unclear whether training individuals to avoid cognitive biases and consequently enhance their accuracy can be generalized to other contexts where bias plays a critical role, such as prejudice (Yilmaz, Karadöller, et al., 2016), and if so, which specific types of situations are most affected. Systematically examining this issue is crucial, particularly for educational applications. Nevertheless, the current empirical evidence does not provide a definitive answer to these questions.[1]

The decision justification technique in which participants are asked to justify their decisions on the cognitive performance task is widely recognized in the literature (e.g., Miller & Fagley, 1991), and has been known to enhance reflectiveness (e.g., increase accurate decisions in cognitive performance measures such as the CRT). Isler et al. (2020) conducted an online study with substantial statistical power, affirming the effectiveness of this method, a finding subsequently replicated (Isler & Yilmaz, 2023). Thus, simply requiring individuals to provide justifications before making decisions is likely to trigger reputational concerns, consequently activating reflective thinking processes through a monitoring mechanism. However, the fact that the decision context is both online and anonymous diminishes this alternative explanation. Typically, one would expect the context to shift away from anonymity for reputational concerns to become activated.

In conclusion, while some techniques, like thought priming, have proven ineffective in stimulating reflective thinking, others, such as debiasing training and decision justification, offer promising avenues for enhancing reflectiveness. These findings underscore the importance of continued exploration and refinement of techniques to cultivate reflective thinking, with potential applications in educational contexts and beyond.

Providing performance incentives is considered one of the key factors that can influence performance in cognitive tasks. Thus, another alternative technique previously established involves simply offering monetary incentives per accurate response in a set of trials. By enhancing motivation and attention, performance incentivization is anticipated to bolster task performance (see Hertwig & Ortmann, 2001; Vlaev, 2012). Despite its proven effectiveness, it is not a widely adopted approach in the literature due to its associated costs. Nonetheless, it serves as a valuable benchmark against which the efficacy of other techniques can be compared. It is worth noting, however, that even when an effect is observed in studies providing performance incentives, the effect size tends to be modest and contingent on the magnitude of the incentive provided (e.g., Isler & Yilmaz, 2023; Lawson et al., 2020; Yechiam & Zeif, 2023a, 2023b).

Overall, two reliable techniques for promoting reflective thinking have emerged: training and decision justification. Nonetheless, it is advisable to exercise caution when considering the latter, as it has the potential to inadvertently induce demand characteristics and response biases. This caution is particularly pertinent in domains like moral judgment such as prosociality, where social desirability carries substantial weight, making training the preferable option to investigate the consequences of reflectiveness (Isler & Yilmaz, 2023).

Consequently, analytic training (Yilmaz & Saribay, 2017a, 2017b), originally developed in laboratory settings, and its online adaptation, debiasing training, currently stand as the most prominent techniques in the literature for stimulating reflective thinking (Isler et al., 2020; Isler & Yilmaz, 2023). Notably, employing this technique to enhance reflective thinking has yielded promising results, including a marked reduction in belief in conspiracy theories. In contrast, the scrambled sentence task, a once-popular technique now considered ineffective, failed to produce similar outcomes (Sümer, 2023). This highlights the significance of replicating the effects associated with previously ineffective techniques using new and reliable methods.

These studies collectively highlight the challenge of fostering reflective thinking in individuals, primarily because of our inherent proclivity for intuitive thinking. Redirecting individuals toward intuitive thinking appears relatively straightforward, whereas elevating analytical thinking demands substantial effort because our cognitive architecture inherently resists expending effort without a clear purpose. Even modest incentives, such as a small bonus for each correct decision, prove insufficient to motivate reflective thinking (Isler & Yılmaz, 2023). To make reflective thinking possible, a more substantial time allocation for response generation, typically ranging from 1 to 2 minutes, akin to the time-delay technique, is required, but the crucial distinction lies in the need for guided training during this period. Unlike the unguided time delay, training provides essential conditions for eliciting reflective thinking, whether in a laboratory or online setting. Consequently, merely extending the time available without guidance is deemed ineffective, as only a small fraction of individuals naturally engages in analytical thinking in accordance with instructions (e.g., those with high levels of need for cognition). This underscores the challenging nature of even temporarily activating reflective thinking, which necessitates explicit and detailed instructions.

The challenge of activating reflective thinking within a short time frame in experimental settings can be attributed, in part, to the innate inclination of the human mind toward intuitive thinking. As we covered in the earlier chapters, our cognitive nature is deeply rooted in various intuitive tendencies developed since childhood, with reflective thinking gradually reshaping these intuitions over time. Throughout development, children primarily rely on intuitive thought processes for extended periods until the development of reflective thought processes. The next section will uncover the development of intuition and reflection during childhood.

Development of Reflection

Classical theories of development in psychology underscore the prominence of intuition in the early stages, with reflective abilities naturally evolving in tandem with cognitive development. Freud's (1905/2017) theory of development, for instance, posits that children initially exhibit intuitive behaviors stemming from evolutionary adaptations. The "id," described as an animalistic aspect of the self, impulsively interprets events through the lens of pleasure and pain. Furthermore, social norms acquired via society's influence contribute significantly to intuitive processes, driven by the development of the "superego." The emergence of the "ego" serves as the first inkling of reflective thought processes, acting as a balancing force between these two systems. Vygotsky (2012) posits that higher-order skills develop through interaction with the environment and social relations. Given that language and logical thinking are among these higher mental functions, his theory can be considered a classical approach to understanding the development of reflection. In Vygotsky's perspective, language is particularly viewed as a prerequisite for the development of higher-level skills, including reflectivity.

In addition, Piaget's (1965, 1967) theory of moral development links cognitive development with moral growth, highlighting the role of biological maturation and experience in social interaction in the development of reflective thought processes across various domains. As biological development unfolds, cognitive ability concurrently advances depending on the quality of social interaction. Contrary to traditional approaches in psychology, such as behaviorism,[2] Piaget's approach is highly influential in developmental psychology, and following his approach, these theories, while not explicitly detailing the developmental stages of reflection, implicitly emphasize its significance due to its active nature in development. Examining Piaget's (1952) classical theory, we observe, spanning ages 2–7, the maturation of symbolic thinking through the use of words and images, along with the development of egocentric thoughts. Children within this age range typically struggle with the conservation task. In this task, the same amount of liquid is transferred between two glasses: one tall and thin, the other short and wide. Despite observing the transfer, the child often perceives the taller glass as holding more liquid. Understanding the equality of the liquid amount in both glasses requires the development of reflective thinking, a skill that children at this stage generally have not yet acquired. The concrete stage, covering ages 7–11, showcases the initial emergence of reflection. Logical thinking becomes prominent here, with the child developing the understanding that situations can be viewed from multiple perspectives, leading to varied outcomes. Children in this stage are capable of recognizing that the amount of water is, in fact, equal in both glasses (e.g., conservation task). However, this stage primarily involves reflective thinking on concrete events, with hypothetical considerations about the future emerging in the subsequent formal operational stage. After about age 12, individuals begin to engage in metacognitive processes, involving systematic planning and hypothetical thinking. Piaget links these developmental stages to age and biological maturation and progressively more complex interactions with the environment, as characterized by the French phrase "penser est operer" (to think is to operate) that is often associated with Piaget's theory of cognitive development.

The Reflective Judgment Model (King & Kitchener, 2004) is another significant contribution in this field. It explains the development of reflective thinking from adolescence to adulthood, arguing that reflection's development is linked not to age, but to the understanding of epistemic beliefs and knowledge. This model delineates the evolution of individuals' conceptions of knowledge and its nature across seven stages, with each stage presenting a distinct perspective on how individuals comprehend and resolve complex problems. The centrality of the concept of evidence in the Reflective Judgment Model stems from the pivotal role evidence plays in individuals' processes of understanding and addressing complex and uncertain situations. The model was specifically developed to elucidate the development of individuals' thinking regarding knowledge and the evaluation of evidence.

While Piaget's theory offers predictions across all age groups, the Reflective Judgment Model focuses on the transition from late adolescence to adulthood. It outlines development through seven stages, grouped into three categories: pre-reflective stages (1–3 years of age), quasi-reflective stages (4–5 years), and reflective stages (6–7 years and beyond). Pre-reflective thinking involves making absolute judgments without considering evidence. Quasi-reflective thinking acknowledges evidence, but the link between this evidence and conclusions is not fully established. In the final stage in which full-fledged reflective thinking capacity becomes available, this connection is successfully made. The Reflective Judgment Model posits that knowledge and meaning are constructed entities. Although the model has a hierarchical structure, its stages are not rigidly defined or linear. Instead, they are complex, overlapping stages not directly tied to age. Furthermore, the model acknowledges that contextual cues can optimize reflective thinking. As such, an individual might exhibit stage 5 reasoning while in stage 4, given practical and contextual support (e.g., scaffolding and feedback). Thus, the model suggests that both age and education, which shape our understanding of knowledge, jointly influence the emergence of reflection. Accordingly, a developmental approach in education that aims to foster critical thinking should consider not only age but also the criteria regarding the nature of knowledge a person endorses.

Various developmental theories posit that different conflict situations often catalyze the emergence of reflective thought (e.g., Landy & Royzman, 2018; Pennycook, Fugelsang, et al., 2015). For instance, Freud's (1905/2017) theory of psychosexual development interprets the rise of the Ego as a reflective process balancing the id's biological impulses and the superego's moral aspirations. Similarly, Piaget's concept of equilibration (i.e., the balance between assimilation and accommodation) suggests that reflection arises from conflicts. Piaget emphasized that children actively gather information and form their own evaluations. During information acquisition, children engage in two processes: *assimilation* (integrating new information into existing schemas) and *accommodation* (modifying existing schemas to fit new information). In this process, the child actively assesses the compatibility of existing schemas with new data through cognitive effort, ultimately making decisions based on reflective thinking. Similarly, adult information processing, as Pennycook (2023) notes, involves two primary functions of reflection: motivated reasoning and cognitive decoupling. Motivated reasoning strengthens existing schemas, whereas cognitive decoupling adjusts schemas to new data or evidence. This process, sometimes labeled as *actively open-minded thinking*, may lead to attitudinal changes in adults (Baron, 2019; Baron et al., 2023). Pennycook's model also explicitly suggests that reflective thinking is triggered when there's a conflict between intuitions (see Chapter 10).

In the Reflective Judgment Model, reflection's role is fundamental, as individuals at each developmental stage (children, adolescents, adults) learn about and legitimize the nature of knowledge. This model underscores variations in epistemic norms among individuals (Metz et al., 2018). Reflection involves contemplating the limits, nature, and certainty of knowledge and evidence. While some individuals easily distinguish between evidence and belief, others struggle with this epistemic distinction, regardless of age. Education's role, then, is to bridge these epistemic norm differences and define "evidence" consistently. Baron (2020) highlights this in the concept of actively open-minded thinking, noting that epistemic norms differ between those educated in post-Enlightenment formal education and those rooted in pre-Enlightenment traditionalist thought. This divergence implies that scientific evidence may be interpreted differently across epistemic norms, suggesting that teaching reflection could have varied impacts.

A pivotal study on this subject by Metz et al. (2018) focused on the origins of opposition to evolution. It was found that this opposition stemmed primarily from the differing criteria used by opponents (vs. proponents) regarding their commitment to beliefs. For instance, while proponents of evolution cite scientific findings as evidence, opponents often refer to holy texts and religious authority. In a related study by our group, we explored the relationship between performance-based and self-reported reflective capacities and the cooperative behavior of religious individuals and atheists, with a 7-month interval between measurements (Acem, 2023). The findings revealed that reflective thinking significantly predicted anonymous cooperation among non-believers, but not among believers. A similar pattern emerged in another study by our team, where we investigated the impact of reflection on belief in God (Yilmaz & Isler, 2019). In this instance, reflection prompted atheists to reconsider their disbelief in God, yet it had minimal impact on the convictions of religious believers. These results imply that a universal standard for belief and evidence acts as a necessary condition for effectively influencing reflective thinking, given the variations in epistemic norms. Lacking this groundwork, reflective thinking risks being reduced to a tool that simply reinforces existing biases, a phenomenon often referred to as *motivated reasoning* (see Chapter 9).

Cognitive Reflection among Children

While it might be argued that reflection is involved in Piagetian tasks such as conservation, or in tasks used to measure theory of mind where a child is asked to consider their own or someone else's perspective, or in inhibitory control/executive function tasks (Gerstadt et al., 1994; Gómez et al., 2015; Wimmer & Perner, 1983), studies measuring reflection in children, akin to how it is assessed in adults, were quite rare until recent years. A pivotal factor contributing to this scarcity of research is the association of the CRT questions, developed in 2005 by Frederick, with arithmetic intelligence, rendering them challenging to administer to children. To address this constraint, Young and Shtulman (2020) introduced the 9-item CRT-D (where "D" stands for development). As Table 3.1 reveals, the questions do not necessitate mathematical knowledge. Although not without limitations, the CRT-D, much like its adult counterpart, exhibits acceptable internal validity values (Gong et al., 2021; Young & Shtulman, 2020).

This evolving landscape of research provides fresh insights into the development of reflective thinking during childhood and underscores the need for continued exploration into the intricate relationship between cognitive development and reflective abilities. Research on cognitive reflection has predominantly focused on replicating the relationship between CRT performance and rational thinking in adults. However, intriguing questions have arisen regarding whether elementary school-age children from diverse cultural backgrounds, such as the United States and China, exhibit differences due to these different cultures' tendencies to favor *analytical* versus *holistic* styles of thinking (see also Chapter 9). Surprisingly, the results have indicated that the CRT-D predicts rational thinking similarly in both cultures. Furthermore, the CRT-D has demonstrated its efficacy as a predictor of children's acquisition of scientific facts, especially those that run counter to intuition. Strikingly, it emerged as a significant predictor even after controlling for executive function (e.g., inhibitory control) (Tardif et al., 2020; Vosniadou et al., 2018).

In the context of adult cognition, CRT scores have been linked to performance on heuristics and biases tasks, even when controlling for executive function (see Chapter 2). Consequently, it appears that CRT-D, akin to its adult counterpart, represents a cognitive style, while executive function reflects cognitive ability, a distinction we made in Chapter 2. Remarkably, these two facets operate independently in elementary school-aged children,

TABLE 3.1 Cognitive Reflection Test for Children (CRT-D)

Question	Correct Answer	Common Misconception
If you are running a race and you pass the person in second place, what place are you in?	Second	First
Emily's father has three daughters. The first two are named Monday and Tuesday. What is the third daughter's name?	Emily	Wednesday
A farmer has five sheep, all but three run away. How many are left?	Three	Two
If there are three apples and you take away two, how many do you have?	Two	One
What do cows drink?	Water	Milk
What weighs more, a pound of rocks or a pound of feathers?	Same weight	Rocks
What hatches from a butterfly egg?	Caterpillar	Baby butterfly
Who makes Christmas presents at the North Pole?	Elves	Santa
Anna is playing four square with her three friends: Eeny, Meeny, and Miny. Who is the fourth player?	Anna	Mo

as they do in adults. While cross-sectional studies have demonstrated improved performance on traditional CRT questions during the transition from adolescence to adulthood, longitudinal evidence supporting this trend remains limited, with only one longitudinal study corroborating this observation (Toplak, 2022). Therefore, further longitudinal research is warranted in this area. Notably, as of the time of writing, no longitudinal study specifically focusing on CRT-D has been conducted.

To remove the demand for numeric ability present in the adult CRT, the CRT-D employs questions like "What do cows drink?" (Young & Shtulman, 2020). These questions are designed to elicit intuitive yet incorrect responses, particularly when posed to children between the ages of 5 and 12 years. It has been observed that CRT-D performance improves with age: Out of 9 questions, 5-year-olds typically answer 1–3 questions correctly, 9-year-olds manage 2–4, 12-year-olds achieve 3–5, and adults correctly answer 7–9 questions. Similar to adults, CRT-D scores are also linked with the performance of 8-year-old children on heuristics-and-biases tasks. A positive correlation was found between CRT-D performance and self-reported cognitive styles like Need for Cognition. While older children generally performed better on these tasks, a positive correlation between CRT-D and task performance persisted even when age was accounted for. These findings were also replicated in a study of Chinese children aged 5–12, with an average age of 9 years, suggesting the presence of a culture-independent cognitive reflection component. Therefore, while executive function is predictive of children's grasp of counter-intuitive concepts, cognitive reflection appears to be distinct from, yet related to, executive functions. However, longitudinal studies in this area are limited, and outcomes examined in the adult CRT literature, such as epistemically suspect beliefs, have not been extensively studied in children using CRT-D. Similar to debiasing training in adults (Isler & Yilmaz, 2023), we propose that such training based on CRT-D should be implemented with children to explore the extent of its impact on cognitive reflection.

Despite the extensive literature on the genetic transmission of capacities supporting reflective thought, such as intelligence (e.g., Deary et al., 2006), genetic studies employing CRT-D are noticeably lacking. In prior research, measures such as the rational-experiential inventory, need for cognition, or actively open-minded thinking scale were utilized, revealing genetic contributions to the variation in cognitive performance and reflective traits (Fletcher et al., 2014). To examine the longitudinal development of CRT-D in childhood while controlling for genetic factors, future investigations should employ actual performance metrics, instead of intentions. Similarly, while genetics has been associated with academic performance (Krapohl et al., 2014), no comparable study has explored the relationship between genetics and cognitive style. Intriguingly, genetic influences on intelligence appear to remain consistent across factors such as socioeconomic status (SES), while environmental influences are moderated by SES, highlighting the robustness of the genetics-intelligence relationship (Hanscombe et al., 2012). However, it remains uncertain whether these observations can be extended to cognitive styles.

Nevertheless, preliminary findings that suggest a parallel in heritability and its effects on educational achievement give rise to a novel hypothesis: reflectiveness (e.g., CRT-D scores) may exhibit similar patterns of genetic transmission. The consistent outcomes observed across different cultures hint at potential universal processes underlying the development of cognitive styles. While experimental interventions aimed at altering children's cognitive styles are yet to be explored, we anticipate the emergence of innovative methods in this direction. For instance, future research could examine the effects of providing feedback through CRT-D to various age groups, as a method of debiasing training and try to integrate it into the formal education system if successful implementations can be observed.

In addition to exploring the interplay between intelligence and education, a study conducted with adults focused on the consequences of cognitive style by directly measuring performance on the CRT. Robinson (2022) observed a correlation where the number of correct CRT answers increased with the level of education. Individuals who discontinued their education, particularly outside of the university setting, displayed lower CRT performance. Additionally, superficial attention, characterized by focusing only on faces in people, appearances in food, and headlines in newspapers, was linked to poor CRT performance. However, there is a lack of data on the development of these abilities in childhood. Consequently, to better understand the influence of education on reflective thought capacity, its association with age, and the limits of this effect, it would be reasonable to examine developmental trends through comparing CRT-D scores across various age groups. Despite these limitations, Robinson proposes the existence of a threshold in reflective thinking, below which individuals may be inherently resistant to reflective reasoning, irrespective of the nature of the reflection-requiring problems. Comprehensive longitudinal studies are needed to draw definitive conclusions on this matter.

Fuzzy-Trace Theory

Because of its focus on developmental issues and its unique predictions, *Fuzzy-Trace Theory* (Reyna et al., 2017) deserves mention at this point. Inspired by psycholinguistics and Gestalt theory, this dual-process model emphasizes the distinction between thinking based on *gists*—"fuzzy traces" and relatively vague impressions that capture the core meaning of information—and *verbatim* representations that are literal and more precise, such as in rote memory. Gist-based thinking is closer to concepts such as intuition, Type 1 process, and System 1 in the rest of the field while verbatim thinking appears to be what individuals typically need to focus on when they wish to think reflectively and analytically. Both types of representations are encoded under regular circumstances. For instance, right after a medical check-up where you were given evidence-based advice on your lifestyle, you may remember that regular exercise decreases the chances of a heart attack by about 38%. Simultaneously, you have extracted the gist of this information that it is a significant drop in risk and worthwhile. As this scenario should make clear, gist-based representations remain longer in memory (Brainerd & Reyna, 1990): The following week, you are likely to remember that exercise will significantly lower your cardiac risk but to have forgotten the precise percentage. According to Fuzzy-Trace Theory, even in cases where an individual's verbatim memory remains intact, they would still prefer to rely on the gist *to the extent that the task allows*[3] because of the advantages of fuzzy processing (e.g., longer memory retention). What is more interesting is that this *fuzzy-processing preference* becomes stronger with age (e.g., Reyna & Kiernan, 1994), as well as with increasing experience and expertise in a domain (Reyna et al., 2014).

To appreciate the significance of this for the development of reflection, consider the types of risky choice problems that Prospect Theory focuses on and in which the options may be framed in terms of either losses or gains. As we mentioned in Chapter 2 (see endnote 19), people (adults) typically prefer risk-aversion when gains are salient and risk-seeking when losses are salient and this is irrational because it involves inconsistency (i.e., the failure to choose equivalent options in different wordings of the same problem). Traditional theories of cognitive development emphasize the move away from intuitive and toward logical and quantitative thinking as the child grows older (Piaget, 1967), and thus, mainstream dual-process models would predict that, if anything, children would show more bias—i.e., stronger framing effects—than adults.[4] Fuzzy-Trace Theory predicts the opposite. As mentioned above, children start out with a stronger reliance on verbatim thinking and gradually grow a preference for gist-based thinking. However, it is gist-based, not verbatim, thinking that creates susceptibility to framing effects. For instance, the gist of the options in the gain-framed version of the "Asian disease problem" is the contrast between saving many lives for sure versus a gamble that could result in saving no one. In the loss-framed version, the gist of the options is the contrast between losing many lives for sure versus a gamble that could result in no one dying. These gists feel different, creating systematic differences in preferences. Working on the same problem with verbatim-based thinking dampens this difference and the reasoner can instead focus on the trade-off between risk and the magnitude of the outcome (see Figure 2 in Reyna, 2012). Consistent with this logic, Reyna and Ellis (1994) found in a study with children that the group least susceptible to framing effects were the youngest—preschoolers, compared to second and fifth graders. Because they employed verbatim-based thinking and focused on quantities, they were unaffected by loss or gain framing. Subsequent experiments supported this explanation by demonstrating that inducing gist- (vs. verbatim-) based thinking increases framing effects (e.g., Reyna et al., 2014). It is not that children's capacity for reflection decreases as they grow older—there is no doubt that it increases. However, as they grow more able to focus on the core meaning of information and develop world knowledge, the information activates more associations, leading to an "increased need to deal with tempting heuristics" (De Neys & Vanderputte, 2011, p. 439). Based on a similar rationale, Fuzzy-Trace theorists have also predicted and shown that false memories are *more* common in adults and adolescents compared to younger children (Brainerd et al., 2002). Compared to younger children, older groups of people simply have more (and richer) representations they have to mentally inhibit! Thus, ironically, the same mechanism (gist extraction) that allows mature individuals to excel at real-world tasks makes them prone to bias under some circumstances.

Another interesting application of these ideas concerns adolescent risk-taking. Adolescents are characterized by increased reward sensitivity and sensation-seeking (Steinberg, 2008). Thus, their risky behavioral tendencies are often analyzed in terms of weak impulse control and inhibition. Fuzzy-Trace Theory provides an interesting twist by predicting that adolescents should make more rational choices—in the sense of respecting expected utility—than adults. Because they are comparatively weaker in gist-based processing, adolescents tend to employ more deliberative processing of details (e.g., probabilities and the magnitude of outcomes) in risky choice situations (Kwak et al., 2015). This may facilitate decisions based on risk–reward trade-offs. For instance, an adolescent may understand that the probability of getting HIV from a single unsafe sexual encounter is very small while judging the benefits to be of large magnitude. This reflection on the risk in relation to the reward justifies the trade-off (i.e., taking the risk is worth the benefit of a sexual encounter). In comparison, older age groups apply gist-based thinking to such scenarios leading them to more easily make a categorical rejection (of the "possibility" of getting HIV), and hence, to make a safer choice. In this scenario, the adolescent is more rational—in fact, "hyper-rational"—in the economic sense of choosing on the basis of properly computed expected utility. However, less effortful thought focused on the gist of the choices (i.e., the "possibility"—vs. numerical probability—of catching HIV) is superior in that it results in the successful aversion of a debilitating disease. As this implies, Fuzzy-Trace Theory differs from many other models in terms of its definition of rationality, as well (Reyna & Farley, 2006). We must also note that Fuzzy-Trace Theory acknowledges the adaptive nature of some forms of risky behavior in adolescence because, especially for adolescents with strong reflective capacity, such behaviors enable exploration and create meaningful life experiences that can feed into wisdom later on (Romer et al., 2017).[5]

Coda

In this chapter, we have explored the activation of reflective thinking in adults and traced the developmental trajectory of reflective processes in children. Although a limited number of studies are currently available, the alignment of findings across different age groups suggests that the conclusions drawn throughout this book may apply to children as well. However, comprehensive longitudinal investigations are required to draw definitive conclusions on this matter. In our homeland, the Turkish Early Enrichment Project, which started in the 1980s, left an important legacy by demonstrating the positive effects of early intervention. To summarize briefly, over a few years, mothers of preschoolers from socioeconomically disadvantaged families were intensively trained to conduct educational activities with their children and received support and guidance through group meetings. The activities were designed to specifically target cognitive development. Immediate and 7-year follow-up assessments (Kagitcibasi et al., 2001) showed clear benefits for preschoolers' cognitive ability (as well as many socioemotional benefits). At 19 years post intervention (Kagitcibasi et al., 2009), the preschoolers had become young adults in their mid-20s, and the effects of mother training were still evident on educational attainment and occupational status, except for the group of preschoolers who were particularly cognitively impaired at baseline. Such intervention programs and their longitudinal assessments make it clear that efforts to improve cognitive functioning, and by consequence the capacity for reflective thought, are worthwhile even if challenging.

The unique perspective put forth by Fuzzy-Trace Theory raises some interesting questions. The superior performance of adults over children in many tasks does not seem to be a simple matter of stronger reflective capacity in the former group. Experience (more general and domain-specific knowledge) certainly contributes, as well, but that is not it either. Adults seem to benefit from a more developed *intuitive* capacity—i.e., better ability to extract and use gists. They arrive at the "bottom line" of information more easily and use it more effectively to guide cognition and behavior. Thus, the foundation of adult levels of competence might be *the combination of stronger reflective and intuitive* capacity compared to children. A narrow, antagonistic approach to reflection as being uniformly superior to and universally in competition with intuition becomes questionable. The use of the phrase "hyper-rational" by Fuzzy-Trace theorists highlights the possibility that too much reflection may even do more damage than good. A more holistic or systemic view of the mind as consisting of different capacities that each have a positive role to play in real-world competence—as well as weaknesses—might be more productive. We explore these issues further in Chapter 9.

Notes

1 Recent research by Boissin et al. (2023) has unearthed intriguing evidence suggesting that encouraging individuals to deliberate less while concurrently providing debiasing training can lead to an increase in accurate decision-making. These findings hint at a potentially more effective approach—promoting intuitive thinking over short-term reflective thinking—to facilitate lasting attitude changes. As a result, it becomes pertinent to contemplate potential implications for the education system and consider a restructuring that aligns with these insights. Although empirical research on this matter remains limited, it is imperative for future studies to delve deep into the nuances of how the effects of such training interventions may vary under conditions of intuitive and reflective thinking. It is important to note, however, that many studies have purported to enhance reflection through the utilization of a time-delay approach, employing the two-response paradigm as outlined earlier. As summarized previously, the observed distinctions in these studies are primarily attributable to the time pressure effect inherent in the initial stage. Consequently, characterizing the intervention in the second part as boosting reflective thinking may be somewhat tenuous, as it does not exhibit a discernible departure from the control group in terms of participants' performance (Isler & Yilmaz, 2023).

2 Behaviorism, the dominant school of thought from the 1920s to the 1950s, posited that the mind does not play an active role in behavior. This approach

asserted that the development of psychological faculties and behaviors can only be understood through the examination of stimulus-response associations (Kukla & Walmsley, 2006).

3 Throughout the book, we draw attention to the role of the context of the research and the particular materials used in the conclusions drawn. Fuzzy-Trace theorists similarly note that "[w]hen researchers contrive tasks that require exact numbers or precise wording to perform, the ability to use gist is constrained or eliminated, and such tasks do not necessarily reflect how people make judgments or decisions in the real world" (Reyna et al., 2017, p. 84; see Figure 1 in Reyna, 2012). That is, overreliance on tasks that require the use of precise information for correct ("rational") solutions may make intuitive processing appear less capable or more susceptible to failure than it might generally be.

4 Fuzzy-Trace theorists criticize this "illusion of replacement"—the idea "that development moves away from reasoning operations that are intuitive, qualitative, or heuristic toward reasoning operations that are analytical, computational, or logical" (Brainerd & Reyna, 2002, p. 42).

5 There are other interesting implications and applications of this theory. For instance, the lack of gist-based thinking characteristic of individuals with autism spectrum disorder could explain both their reduced susceptibility to framing effects and the difficulties they experience in social interactions (see Miller et al., 2014). We revisit other implications in Chapter 9.

PART II

Reflection and Intuition in a Crisis-Ridden World

4

SITUATIONAL INFLUENCES ON REFLECTIVENESS

Threat and Politics

Have you ever found it hard to think reflectively when deciding how to budget for the end of the month or when assessing the risk of catching a virus while using public transportation during a pandemic? Such threats tend to trigger intuitive cognitive mechanisms, overshadowing reflective thinking capabilities. A predominant reason is that perceived threats inhibit the capacity and motivation to pursue reflection in the decision-making process. But what exactly do we mean by "threat"?

Threats appear in various forms, from an epidemic disease to the shaking of an earthquake, but regardless of the form, they all signal an impending danger of some sort and exert a distinct positive or negative influence on behavior, compelling us to seek remedies to avoid or combat the danger. For example, the perception of an imminent invasion or the looming potential of a fire ravaging one's surroundings incites an immediate quest for escape routes. The need for quick assessments and decisions reduces our ability to think reflectively and pushes us toward reliance on more intuitive processes. The effects of this reliance can be far-reaching: not only may it determine our immediate responses to the threat, but it may also have implications for our social and political attitudes, judgments, and choices. The effects of threats span a broad spectrum, from human physiology to health, finance, and moral decision-making. For instance, it is known that stress induced by environmental and societal threats influences cortisol levels via the hypothalamic–pituitary–adrenal (HPA) axis (e.g., Kassam et al., 2009). This chronic state of stress often leads to suboptimal decision-making in health by overlooking long-term benefits, inhibits the delay of gratification in financial decisions by favoring short-term goals, and prompts selfish choices in moral decisions by prioritizing personal survival (e.g., Clark et al., 2012; Graham

DOI: 10.4324/9781003300366-6

et al., 2010; Pedroni et al., 2014; Porcelli & Delgado, 2009; Potts et al., 2019). Additionally, these threats also directly impact political attitudes and indirectly contribute to social polarization. In line with the scope of the book, in this chapter, we will explore how threats shape people's ideologies and ideological attitudes.

In other words, in this section, we will delve into the influence of threats on human psychology and decision-making processes, including social and ideological choices, and consider how we might preserve our analytic faculties amidst threats, especially when our cognitive resources are limited. However, before doing so, we must first acquaint ourselves with a broader understanding of the role of affect in cognition and politics and the diverse theories proposed in the realm of threat and the underlying assumptions they entail.

Affect and (Political) Cognition

Much work in psychology and related fields has explored the role of *affect*[1] in cognition and the interplay of these.[2] Starting especially from the 1960s, cognition was assumed to be a determinant of affect: It is how one subjectively interprets an event and its physiological repercussions (e.g., arousal) that provokes a particular affective response to it (e.g., Schachter & Singer, 1962). Some form of higher-order thought—a cognitive appraisal or attribution—was seen as necessary for a specific affective response to arise (Lazarus & Smith, 1988). Zajonc's (1980) seminal *primacy of affect* thesis—that affect often precedes and can occur without cognition (e.g., upon simply perceiving a stimulus)—forced researchers to consider the reverse causal order. For instance, people develop a stronger liking of stimuli that they are repeatedly exposed to compared to novel ones—the *mere exposure effect*—even when the exposure is arranged in a way that prevents recognition of these stimuli (e.g., Kunst-Wilson & Zajonc, 1980). This was interpreted as a demonstration that affect was independent of cognition (Zajonc, 2001; but see Storbeck & Clore, 2007).

Affect appears to share much with what we call intuition in this book. For instance, unlike explicit thoughts but similar to intuitive ones, affective states often subjectively pop up as the end result of a non-traceable and involuntary mental process. Accordingly, affect is typically viewed as stemming from Type 1 processes and as a ubiquitous source of intuitive responses (Evans & Stanovich, 2013a; Isler & Yilmaz, 2023). In turn, and in line with Zajonc's argument and influential neuroscientific models (e.g., LeDoux, 1996), dual-process models generally predict that affect temporally precedes cognition more of the time than vice versa. This should give affect an edge in terms of stealthily influencing downstream cognition and behavior (as well as a critical role to cognition in downregulating affect). This role of affect in cognition is exemplified nicely by the *feelings-as-information* theory (Schwarz, 2012) Accordingly, feelings provide feedback about the current environment and the status of the organism's goal pursuit—such as when negative affect arises because the expected sequence of events (and consequently, one's goal pursuit) is disrupted. Such "problematic" situations motivate detail-oriented, effortful thinking, whereas "benign" situations signal, via positive affect, that it is fine to rely on relatively effortless thought, dominant responses, and familiar knowledge structures (e.g., cognitive scripts, schemata, heuristics, and stereotypes). Moreover, memory representations are tagged with affect (reflecting one's learning history) and these tags can be quickly summed into an overall impression (e.g., "highly positive") providing a quick way to make judgments and decisions—*the affect heuristic* (Slovic et al., 2002). In sum, affective states arise in particular situations either *incidentally*—unrelated to the focal objects and goals, such as affect caused by the music that happens to be playing in a public space—or *integrally*—about the psychological situation itself, such as affect caused by a personal conflict one is tackling with (see Västfjäll et al., 2016)—and exert influence on the quality and content of cognitions.

These emerging realizations of the role of affect in cognition, combined with impressive demonstrations of the impact of nonconscious processes (e.g., Bargh et al., 2001; cf. Harris et al., 2013), the distinction between implicit and explicit attitudes (e.g., Wilson et al., 2000), and the wide impact of the heuristics-and-biases research program across the social sciences, provided new impetus for analyzing political cognition and behavior, as well. One of the best-known examples of this perspective in the political domain is Lodge and Taber's (2013) challenge to the idea of a deliberative citizenry pursuing rationality, "a vestige of Enlightenment mythology" (p. 21) misleading the field of political science. According to their model, it is not that citizens cannot think rationally but that this is very difficult and thus a rare occurrence in politics because of the ubiquitous and insidious role of affect (and nonconscious cognition). Based on vast literature and their own experimental research, these researchers argued that, for instance, the affect associated with political stimuli (e.g., leaders, groups, issues, policies) in memory can be activated with minimal input and without cognitive involvement, and automatically shapes subsequent thoughts and behaviors. Moreover, even incidental affect may influence downstream processing significantly. These are biasing influences and present a challenge to rationality in politics. For instance, arguments that are affectively congruent with one's extant affective associations are prioritized (faster responses, better memory) in information processing. By the time conscious deliberation about a political issue kicks in, a great deal of nonconscious affect and cognition (e.g., by way of spreading activation along the associative network in memory) have already taken place such that this conscious deliberation can no longer begin from a neutral, objective starting point but rather assumes the role of providing rationalizations for the direction this background activity has sent the individual towards. Due to the limitations of working memory, the individual might consciously be focused on a few salient considerations only and remain unable to detect this insidious influence of background Type 1 processes. Because of how rapidly and efficiently it can sort incoming information and judge its alignment with prior knowledge; and how persistent it is in long-term memory, affect assumes and maintains a central role in political cognition and behavior. The current levels of affective polarization in many countries in turn probably have the effect of individuals being repeatedly exposed to pairings of strong affective responses with political stimuli, cementing this central role of affect. Dishearteningly, Lodge and Taber also find that individuals with greater knowledge of and interest in politics are far from being immune from this biasing influence of affect. If anything, this group is the least open to belief revision. Political sophisticates simply have more nodes in their associative networks and so they are able to bring an even greater number of attitude-congruent thoughts to mind, making them even more biased than politically unsophisticated individuals. In sum, most of what individuals' "reasoning" actually plays more of a rationalizing role, and thus, Lodge and Taber conclude that confirmation bias and motivated reasoning are rampant in politics. The concluding sentence of their book—*The Rationalizing Voter*—states that this might be "as rational as we *homo sapiens* can be" (p. 234).[3] We come back to the broader topic of motivated reasoning in Chapter 9.

Threat had a special place in Zajonc's formulation of the *primacy of affect* thesis. A neurological or mental system that constantly monitors the environment, rapidly detects the presence of potential threats, alerts the organism via negative affect, and motivates vigilant processing and attention to detail has clear adaptive advantages for survival, especially if such a system works independently of other systems (e.g., those governing conscious thought). Because negative affect provokes vigilant processing, a perceived threat may facilitate careful thinking, as some research in the feelings-as-information tradition suggests (Schwarz & Bless, 1991). Likewise, research in political psychology has found negative affective states to be associated with a stronger tendency to seek information about the world, which implies a desire to engage in further deliberation. For instance, Erişen (2013) reported that experimentally inducing fear regarding the Syrian crisis increased participants' likelihood of requesting new information by 40–60%, compared to a control group and a hope-induced group. On the other hand, it seems possible that negative affect itself, especially if strong and prolonged and for individuals with impaired emotion regulation, can be a mental distraction, eating up the finite cognitive resources that reflective processes so critically rely on (Anticevic et al., 2010; Garrison & Schmeichel,

2022; Moran, 2016). From a different—Prospect Theoretical—perspective, the threat of loss is more psychologically impactful than the prospect of gain, which Kahneman (2011, pp. 281–282) views as a "System 1" characteristic stemming from our evolutionary history. Thus, threat may push people into a risk-seeking style with the goal of averting the loss (Tversky & Kahneman, 1981; see Chapter 2 of this book) and this could lead to rash and impulsive responses. Classical and emerging lines of research in the modern psychology literature have attempted to uncover the nature of the relationship between threat and reflectiveness, especially in the political domain, as we explain in the next section.

Dominant Theories of Threat

Research into the psychological ramifications of threats on human behavior has been going on for many years, with emerging consensus indicating that certain types of threats—such as terrorism—increase tendencies toward in-group favoritism and political conservatism (Jost et al., 2017). However, recent studies have revealed that the magnitude of this effect may be contingent upon the specific nature of the threat (Eadeh & Chang, 2020). The literature reveals a stable correlation between terrorist or mortality salience threats and shifts in political ideology (Jost et al., 2017; Sibley et al., 2012). Nonetheless, there are many diverse theoretical frameworks making contradictory predictions about the influence of threats on human behavior. Foremost among these is the Terror Management Theory (TMT).

According to TMT, subsequent to the evolution of consciousness, humans harnessed reflective thinking to exert dominion over nature and cultivate culture. However, this heightened consciousness inadvertently spawned a non-adaptive side effect: the awareness of impending mortality (Greenberg et al., 1986). As the sole species known to have such awareness, individuals contend with heightened death anxiety, expending cognitive resources to mitigate and suppress this apprehension (Trémolière et al., 2012, 2014). Specifically, the clash between the inevitability of death and the innate drive to survive engenders existential dread (Greenberg et al., 1986). Through the cognitive effects of this clash, individuals become more predisposed to particular social and cultural worldviews, strengthening their preexisting convictions (Pyszczynski et al., 2004). Embracing these worldviews confers a sense of purpose and manufactures a semblance of immortality—albeit symbolic—by constructing a stable and secure reality (Pyszczynski et al., 1999). In studies of this nature, participants assigned to the experimental condition are typically instructed to write about their thoughts and feelings concerning their own mortality. Conversely, those in the control condition are often presented with neutral tasks, such as watching television, or are exposed to a pain condition that carries an emotional negativity similar to that associated with mortality. While difficulties in replicating these findings in studies with high statistical power pose challenges for TMT (for discussion, see Klein et al., 2022; Schindler et al., 2021), past classical findings suggest that a reminder of one's mortality induces a heightened attachment to existing worldviews, as defending these worldviews furnishes symbolic immortality, thereby assisting individuals in coping with death anxiety (Rosenblatt et al., 1989). Subsequent studies applying the principles of TMT reveal that reminding individuals of their mortality leads to more positive perceptions of in-groups and more negative perceptions of out-groups (Greenberg et al., 1990, 1992, 1994, 2001).

TMT sheds light on the phenomenon of increased polarization by positing that individuals, when confronted with threats, bolster their defense of existing worldviews to manage these threats. This is evidenced by the tendency for left-leaning individuals to lean further left and right-leaning individuals to veer further right under mortality salience (Pyszczynski et al., 2015). While a general consensus exists within the literature regarding the influence of threats on human social behavior, an ongoing debate concerns the mechanisms underlying this effect (e.g., Crawford, 2017; Hibbing et al., 2014). Additionally, the TMT framework has encountered substantial critique due to its ambiguous evidential basis and problems with theoretical falsifiability (Martin & Van Den Bos, 2014), and the potential influence of researchers on results (Yen & Cheng, 2013). Furthermore, certain high-powered large-scale replication studies have revealed conflicting results (Chatard et al., 2020; Klein et al., 2022; Sætrevik & Sjåstad, 2022; Schindler et al., 2021).

Beyond these points, counter to TMT, alternative findings have emerged with respect to the direction in which threats impact human psychology and behavior. For instance, investigations conducted following the September 11 terrorist attacks indicate that the threat did not necessarily intensify individuals' commitment to their existing worldviews; instead, it contributed to a conservative shift among both liberals and conservatives (Bonanno & Jost, 2006; Cohen et al., 2005; Landau et al., 2004). In a seminal study, participants reminded of their own mortality or the 9/11 attacks displayed heightened support for then-conservative leader George W. Bush. Remarkably, this effect was consistent across both liberals and conservatives (Landau et al., 2004).

Another theoretical framework that accounts for these findings is motivated social cognition, which asserts that conservatism serves as a defense mechanism to manage uncertainties and insecurities (Jost et al., 2003, 2017). In line with this alternative perspective to TMT—i.e., that the threat of death and/or terrorism leads to a conservative shift in opinions—the central focus of this framework is to understand the origins of political divergences (Jost et al., 2003). Extensive research in political psychology over the past 50 years, primarily involving American participants, has demonstrated that liberals exhibit greater cognitive openness and a stronger inclination for deliberative thought compared to conservatives (Jost et al., 2003). In line with this difference in cognitive style, conservatives harbor a stronger desire to uphold the status quo and favor the preservation of societal hierarchies than liberals (Jost et al., 2003). A meta-analysis examining over 22,000 respondents across 88 studies conducted in 12 countries found that these tendencies broadly align with the motives of preference for stability versus change (also known as *resistance to change*) and preference for hierarchy versus equality (also known as *opposition to equality*).[4] In essence, conservatives are more inclined than liberals to safeguard the existing order and maintain the hierarchically structured network of relationships to fulfill fundamental motivational needs. This *conservatism as a motivated social cognition* perspective asserts that political conservatism functions as a protective mechanism against threats and anxieties in daily life, simplifying complexities, reducing uncertainty, and stabilizing the relatively intricate external system. This standpoint resonates with classical theories linking fear and right-wing ideologies from the early days of political psychology (Adorno et al., 1950).

In accordance with this outlook, conservatism functions as a psychological motivation to counteract threats. When threats become palpable, individuals enhance their endorsement of certain moral foundations such as in-group loyalty (Alper et al., 2020; Van De Vyver et al., 2016), system justification motives[5] (e.g., Ullrich & Cohrs, 2007; Van Der Toorn et al., 2014), religiosity and patriotism (Bonanno & Jost, 2006), authoritarianism (Echebarria-Echabe & Fernández-Guede, 2006), support for military expenditure (Janoff-Bulman & Usoof-Thowfeek, 2009; Landau et al., 2004; Nail & McGregor, 2009), racially conservative policies, and the likelihood of adopting conservative political ideology (Craig & Richeson, 2014). A time series analysis scrutinizing the impact of global terrorist threats between 1994 and 2013 found evidence that terrorist threats (e.g., global terror intensity) tend to increase the intention to vote for conservative parties (Akay et al., 2020). In harmony with this perspective, a meta-analysis encompassing over 369,000 participants across 134 studies conducted in 16 countries revealed a positive association between fear of death and conservatism, further demonstrating that reminders of death-related stimuli also influence conservatism (Jost et al., 2017). These findings suggest that threats provoke a conservative shift in worldview rather than merely defense of one's extant worldview, thereby supporting the motivated social cognition framework over TMT. Several prior meta-analyses with smaller sample sizes corroborate the core findings reported here (Burke et al., 2013; Onraet et al., 2013).

Notably, in one of these meta-analyses (Burke et al., 2013), both the "conservative shift" and the "worldview defense" hypotheses garnered support, with equivalent effect sizes. However, certain studies point to findings inconsistent with the motivated social cognition framework. For instance, Lambert et al. (2010) conducted a study investigating the impact of threats on attitude change. They found that reminders of the 9/11 attacks increased support for Bush's assertive military policies in Iraq. However, these reminders did not have a significant effect on overall political attitudes. Similarly, other studies have indicated that attitudes toward immigration policy remained unaffected by events such as the Charlie Hebdo and Hyper Cacher attacks (Solheim, 2021), the Mumbai terrorist attacks (Finseraas & Listhaug, 2013), and the Paris terrorist attacks (Brouard et al., 2018; Castanho Silva, 2018). In fact, comparisons made before and after the 2011 terrorist attacks in Norway revealed a heightened positivity toward out-groups post attack (Jakobsson & Blom, 2014).

An alternative idea—the *reactive liberal hypothesis*—attempts to reconcile these contrasting perspectives and findings by proposing that the "worldview defense" notion holds true for conservatives, while the "conservative shift" applies to liberals (Nail et al., 2009). Accordingly, under threat, conservatives experience a leaning toward heightened conservatism. However, an intriguing dynamic emerges as liberals display a conservative shift in their moral judgments. This perspective asserts that liberals exert cognitive effort to counteract the conservative shift effect induced by threats, temporarily aligning them with conservatives when their cognitive resources become depleted. This viewpoint is consistent with observations that liberals who are subjected to cognitive load, hindering reflective thought, tend to attribute the cause of an event using personal attributions, mirroring the tendencies of conservatives (Skitka et al., 2002). In a study conducted by van de Vyver et al. (2016), the shift in moral judgments and prejudiced attitudes in response to the terrorist threat was examined using two distinct representative samples, collected six weeks prior and 1 month after the 2005 London suicide bombings. Comparative analysis of these samples revealed a surge in the moral foundations related to in-group loyalty and nationalism, coupled with a general decline in the significance attributed to the moral judgment of "fairness." This effect was particularly pronounced among participants identifying as liberals, whose stronger negative attitudes towards Muslims and immigrants accounted for these shifts in moral foundations. Thus, there exists supportive evidence in the literature for the reactive liberal hypothesis.

Nonetheless, this seminal study bears certain limitations, with the foremost among them being the comparison of disparate samples in pre- and post-tests and the absence of a standardized and valid measure to gauge moral foundations. To address these constraints, our research group undertook a study in Türkiye, a non-WEIRD country (Muthukrishna et al., 2020), that sought to surmount these limitations (Velioglu, 2023). Specifically, we reengaged the same participant cohort that had previously been analyzed 1 month prior to the terrorist incident on Istiklal Street, Istanbul in 2022. We divided the participants into two groups: one group was reminded of the terrorist threat, while the other was not. Subsequently, we employed incentivized economic games to gauge actual cooperative behavior and utilized a validated metric for assessing moral foundations that we had also administered in the pre-test. The findings may underscore the influence of culture and cultural norms on the nexus between threats and ideologies: The threat of terrorism induced Turkish conservatives to display a heightened reactive tendency to de-emphasize care and fairness. Left-leaning individuals (similar to liberals in the U.S. American context) did not manifest a similar reactive response to threats. Consequently, the applicability of the reactive liberal hypothesis cannot be universally extended as an exclusive expectation for secular Western nations in most scenarios. A more comprehensive model is needed to reconcile the mixed findings that diverge across diverse cultural settings.

While a definitive consensus regarding the precise impact of threats on human behavior remains elusive, a small number of longitudinal and physiological studies lend credence to the argument that the disparities discussed here are indicative of relatively stable dispositional differences. For instance, a longitudinal study of preschool children found that individuals who exhibited relatively liberal tendencies in adulthood were characterized 20 years earlier as "relatable, confident, energetic, stoic" children, whereas those adults who leaned conservative were described as "touchy, indecisive, fearful, fixed, timid" during childhood (Block & Block, 2006). There is a growing belief that certain genetic inclinations contribute to the variance in political opinions (Bouchard & McGue, 2003; Hatemi et al., 2010, 2014). The central argument posits that specific genetic traits predispose individuals to certain personality attributes, which in turn render them more inclined toward adopting particular ideologies. While still nascent, empirical evidence from twin studies suggests that identical twins exhibit greater similarity in political attitudes compared to fraternal twins[6] (Alford et al., 2005; Bouchard et al., 2003). Although not without challenges in replication (Johnston & Madson, 2022), some data indicate the existence of neurophysiological characteristics distinguishing liberals from conservatives. For instance, Schreiber et al. (2013) demonstrated greater activation in the insula and amygdala regions among conservatives, whereas Kanai et al. (2011) highlighted that conservatives possess more gray matter in the right amygdala than liberals.[7] Hibbing et al. (2014) contend that these physiological and neuropsychological disparities collectively point to a fundamental divergence between liberals and conservatives in terms of *negativity bias*—the notion that negative situations hold more prominence, dominance, and strength than positive ones (Rozin & Royzman, 2001).

Hibbing et al. (2014) posited that the foundation of the outlined physiological disparities rests in conservatives' heightened sensitivity to negative stimuli. Accordingly, when confronted with disturbing images (e.g., a bloodied face), conservatives exhibit more pronounced activation in their sympathetic nervous system compared to liberals (Oxley et al., 2008). Dodd and colleagues (2012) demonstrated that conservatives dedicate more time to observing negative imagery than their liberal counterparts. Furthermore, conservatives display delayed responses to negative stimuli in the emotional Stroop test[8] (Carraro et al., 2011). Similarly, Vigil (2010) revealed that conservatives attribute more negative and threatening emotions to ambiguous facial expressions than liberals. The findings of this study are consistent with the broader body of literature indicating that liberals exhibit conservative traits when exposed to threats (e.g., Nail et al., 2009).

The evolutionary rationale behind the negativity bias is that negative events like injury, infection, and death bear higher costs than the benefits of positive occurrences. Prioritizing negative events and shaping decisions accordingly enhances the prospects of survival. Pioneering evidence of the negativity bias originates from Kahneman and Tversky's work (Kahneman & Tversky, 1979; Tversky & Kahneman, 1991), which demonstrated that the framing of choices in terms of losses or gains significantly influences decision-making. For example, people generally exhibit risk-averse behavior when presented with a positive frame, whereas they are more inclined to take risks when a negative frame is employed. For instance, in the scenario of an epidemic expected to kill 600 lives, individuals are more likely to favor the option framed as "saving 200 lives," despite there being no substantive difference between this option and the alternative frame of "failing to save 400 lives." In other words, the value attributed to an equal magnitude of loss is not the same as that of an equal magnitude of gain.

To date, the negativity bias has undergone extensive investigation across various tasks as explained above. While the findings generally support the notion that conservatives are more prone than liberals to associate ambiguous facial expressions with threatening emotions (Hibbing et al., 2014), the assertion that the negativity bias varies between political groups has faced some criticism within the literature. Brandt et al. (2014) argue that both liberal and conservative individuals utilize similar strategies and tactics when faced with threatening or adverse situations. Aligned with this logic, research proposes that both liberals and conservatives show bias against out-groups that contravene their values, with value congruence acting as the driving force of this effect (Voelkel & Brandt, 2019). Crawford (2017) expanded on this perspective, suggesting that political divergences in negativity bias might not become apparent in contexts associated with the "realm of meaning," such as discrimination against value-violating out-groups. However, these biases could become evident in scenarios related to physical stimuli that elicit fear, like the presence of predators.

To ascertain which political faction exhibits greater responsiveness to negative stimuli and to juxtapose the aforementioned theoretical perspectives, our research group (Salter et al., 2023) conducted three experiments with Turkish samples. One of them was a lab (vs. online) experiment and it found that rightists displayed greater negativity bias than leftists, in line with the literature discussed above although online experiments did not replicate this effect during the pandemic. However, under conditions of cognitive load manipulation in a lab setting, both leftist and rightist participants demonstrated comparable (and stronger) negativity bias. This suggests that leftists mitigate negativity bias by expending cognitive resources, and when deprived of those resources, they exhibit a level of negativity bias on par with conservatives. These results align with both the negativity bias and the reactive liberal hypotheses.

However, as mentioned earlier, the proposition that negativity bias diverges based on political affiliation has faced criticism within the literature. For instance, Brandt et al. (2014) contend that both liberal and conservative individuals adopt similar strategies and employ comparable tactics to navigate threatening and adverse scenarios. In essence, they posit that negativity bias is not exclusive to conservatives; rather, liberals, like conservatives, manifest heightened sensitivity and bias toward groups that challenge their values (see also ; Ditto, Clark, et al., 2019; Ditto, Liu, et al., 2019). As an illustration, conservatives have been observed to harbor unfavorable attitudes toward atheists, while liberals have exhibited unfavorable attitudes toward religious fundamentalists (Crawford et al., 2017). These criticisms collectively underscore the imperative for an entirely novel theoretical framework that can integrate these mixed findings.

In recent years, a model known as *issue ownership* has been incorporated into the realm of social psychology to reconcile the aforementioned findings (Eadeh & Chang, 2020). This model posits that threats will not directly trigger a conservative shift or worldview defense but that their impact on ideology will fluctuate based on the nature of the threat. Eadeh and Chang propose that the reason the threat of terrorism increases conservatism is that individuals associate conservative leaders and policies with societal order and view them as the resolution to events like terrorism. Thus, experimental activation of a threat such as terrorism augments the propensity to favor conservative policies, as people perceive a robust conservative party or leader with stringent policies as the solution. This relationship has also garnered support through a meta-analysis (Jost et al., 2017).

However, in alternative threat scenarios where liberal (vs. conservative) leaders and policies might be perceived as the solution, the threat could engender liberalization rather than a shift toward conservatism, potentially diminishing group partisanship rather than amplifying it. To test this hypothesis, three experiments demonstrated that activating situations wherein liberals are stereotypically viewed as the solution—such as environmental threats and limited healthcare access—incites a shift towards liberalism instead of conservatism (Eadeh & Chang, 2020). This suggests that ideological transformation hinges on the specific nature of the threat. Moreover, prior studies indicate that the perception of issue ownership—i.e., ideas regarding the domains that different ideologies are seen as relatively more competent—persists as an enduring attitude (Seeberg, 2017).

Although the issue ownership model has been employed within political science for a considerable time (Lefevere et al., 2015; Petrocik, 1996), its recent adaptation into experimental social psychology introduces a nuanced perspective. In contrast to the relatively straightforward picture observed in the earlier literature (Jost et al., 2003), this model posits that threats are not homogenous and that diverse threats, such as terrorism, scarcity, or pandemics, may induce varying impacts on human behavior. Correspondingly, a large-scale study employing World Values Survey data from 56 countries (N = 60,378) uncovered associations between different threat types and ideological orientations (Brandt et al., 2021). While economically oriented threats aligned with left-wing ideologies, violent threats correlated with right-wing ideologies, consistent with the prior literature. Hence, when applying this model, discerning which group individuals perceive as the focal point for solutions becomes pivotal for predicting the impact each threat will exert on political beliefs.

Apart from the beliefs related to issue ownership, it is also important to consider who is more affected by threats. For instance, while events like 9/11 or subway bombings pose a common threat to everyone living in that city, the impact of terrorist attacks on specific places of worship such as churches, synagogues, mosques, etc. is often more intensely felt by those who identify with the targeted group. This is because empathy in such threatening situations is typically limited to one's in-group, thus biased, selective, and parochial (Bloom, 2016). Therefore, in understanding the effects of threats, it is crucial to consider not only issue ownership but also perceptions of victimization.

Another form of threat that directly impacts human life is the inherent risk of viral infection and potential loss of life. Humans possess a psychological mechanism known as the *behavioral immune system*, believed to have evolved as a defense against diseases and infections. This system motivates individuals to avoid harm by altering information processing and behavior to mitigate the risk of infection and pathogen transmission (Ackerman et al., 2018). Initially, the system identifies potential sources of environmental threats and then prioritizes cognitive and emotional responses aimed at minimizing contact with these sources of threats. For instance, when one encounters spoiled food while hungry, the system detects the potential threat of pathogens in the food, eliciting a feeling of disgust that subsequently motivates avoidance behavior (Terrizzi et al., 2013). This mechanism effectively operates as a behavioral defense mechanism, significantly enhancing survival chances, especially in pathogen-prone regions. However, the behavioral immune system is also known to influence various social behaviors (e.g., Faulkner et al., 2004; Navarrete & Fessler, 2005; Schnall, 2017; Stewart et al., 2020; but see Van Leeuwen & Petersen, 2018).

When pathogens are widespread within a community and ecological conditions heighten the risk of contamination (as in the case of the recent pandemic), prior social psychology research suggests that behavioral adaptations linked to high infectious disease prevalence, such as conformity to established traditions and avoidance of potentially infectious stimuli (e.g., unfamiliar individuals and out-groups), become more pronounced (Faulkner et al., 2004; Fincher & Thornhill, 2012; Navarrete & Fessler, 2006). More precisely, the activation of the behavioral immune system through threat-related stimuli prompts individuals to avoid unfamiliar social groups and stick more closely to familiar ones. Experimentally inducing such threats motivates individuals to steer clear of harmful pathogens, leading to increased hostility towards out-groups and a greater inclination to embrace existing traditions and the status quo (Helzer & Pizarro, 2011; Inbar et al., 2009; Jones & Fitness, 2008; Murray & Schaller, 2012; Wu & Chang, 2012). Notably, individuals with a heightened perception of infection risk tend to adopt conservative attitudes more readily (Terrizzi et al., 2013). Consequently, the *parasite stress model* predicts a correlation between conservatism and the prevalence of pathogens in the environment, suggesting that a pathogen like coronavirus may drive a global trend toward conservatism. Past research demonstrates that regional variations in pathogen distribution align with more ethnocentric, collectivist, and conservative social attitudes. Specifically, the increase in parasite stress within a region corresponds to a rise in socially conservative attitudes over time (Murray et al., 2013; Terrizzi et al., 2013; Thornhill et al., 2009; but see Horita & Takezawa, 2018). Consequently, the parasite stress model anticipates that the COVID-19 threat will prompt a resurgence of conservatism across diverse cultures. There is some evidence supporting this conjecture (Karwowski et al., 2020; Kempthorne & Terrizzi, 2021).

In addition to pathogens and parasites, scarcity and mortality are the two main threats that directly influence survival. Scarcity is a phenomenon that may be experienced in different domains and at different levels throughout life, such as in economic crises and natural disasters. Resource scarcity has been studied in a variety of fields ranging from psychology (e.g., Griskevicius et al., 2013; Sherif, 1988) to economics (e.g., Banerjee & Duflo, 2012), political science (e.g., Grossman & Mendoza, 2003), business (e.g., Sharma

& Alter, 2012) and sociology (e.g., Booth, 1984). The concept of scarcity is also central to modern economic theory which defines rational choice as the efficient use of scarce resources and assumes that the relative scarcity of goods and services determines supply, demand, and prices through market relations (Mankiw, 2014).

Threats as Mental Burdens

Recent studies, mostly in psychological sciences, suggest that resource scarcity is a psychological variable (Mullainathan & Shafir, 2013; Shah et al., 2012; Spiller, 2011). For example, when people think that resources are scarce, they lose cognitive resources (Mani et al., 2013), become more selfish (Roux et al., 2015), and, more importantly, engage in specific behaviors by adopting a general scarcity psychology. For example, the rarer an object is in the environment (such as gold or bitcoin), the more valuable it is perceived to be, regardless of its use value (Mittone & Savadori, 2009).

At the same time, a person who has a scarcity mindset due to factors such as low socio-economic status may prioritize subsistence. Research suggests that people living under a sense of scarcity are able to direct their cognitive resources to issues related to overcoming scarcity (e.g., finding ways to make money) but their cognitive performance decreases on other issues (Mani et al., 2013). This was replicated in a field context, among Cambodian smallholder farmers (Bruns et al., 2022). Therefore, it may be unrealistic to expect individuals burdened with scarcity to engage in reflective thought, especially if the issue at hand is unrelated to their subsistence concerns.

Likewise, previous studies show that reminding people of their own mortality undermines their reflective thinking tendencies (Trémolière et al., 2012, 2014), which in turn influences their moral judgments (Yilmaz & Bahçekapili, 2018). Although TMT's mortality salience studies had mixed results on worldview defense, the effect of mortality salience on cognitive styles has been replicated more successfully (Goldenberg & Arndt, 2008; Hayes et al., 2010; Pyszczynski et al., 1999; Trémolière et al., 2012, 2014).

According to this prediction of TMT, when people are confronted with the awareness of mortality, they spend cognitive effort to suppress it; consequently, reminding people of their own mortality should lead to a decline in their cognitive performance. Likewise, as mentioned above, scarcity is known to have a similar effect (Mani et al., 2013). When people think that their resources are scarce, they lose cognitive resources (e.g., executive functioning) and experience a loss of cognitive performance in activities other than those directed at finding resources. Therefore, since both threats increase people's tendency to think intuitively and automatically, it can be predicted that people become more receptive to external political propaganda or messages (e.g., nudges) under the concerns of mortality and scarcity. This is because such threats put people in a general heuristic thinking mode, which increases compliance and obedience. This suggests that environmental conditions can easily render people's thinking intuitive, reverting them back to primitive tribal tendencies, which can sometimes be maladaptive for our modern world.

So, in a world where we find ourselves surrounded by threats, should we simply accept this inherent intuitiveness, or should we strive to develop strategies to better handle it? To answer this question, let us present a radical example to highlight the dangers of relying solely on our intuitive instincts.

As we discuss in Chapter 9, it is evident that intuitive thinking can lead to beneficial outcomes in specific scenarios, such as when someone possesses expertise or demonstrates unconditional cooperation during crises like the COVID-19 pandemic. Certainly, for example, an experienced firefighter can often make more accurate decisions in emergency situations by relying on their well-honed intuition, which has been developed through countless repetitions. Similarly, citizens can intuitively follow recommended preventive measures by scientific authorities during a pandemic. It is akin to a skilled pianist using intuitive processes to hit the right notes in rapid succession. So, if you are an expert in a particular field, trusting your intuition can be justified (Isler & Yilmaz, 2019). However, for individuals lacking expertise in a relevant domain, intuition can have detrimental effects, particularly in terms of implicit discrimination.

Consider the case of Amadou Diallo in 1999, where four police officers, initially searching for a suspect linked to a year-old rape case, encountered Diallo on the street. Seeing the policemen, Diallo panicked and escaped into a building. Followed by the officers, he reached for his wallet to show his ID. Shockingly, the officers fired a total of 41 shots at him without hesitation, leading to his tragic death. Diallo was, in fact, an innocent man with no criminal record, simply going about his business. This incident piqued the interest of social psychologists, prompting them to investigate the underlying mechanisms behind this tragic outcome. They explored whether people's stereotypes of African Americans, including those held by police officers, influenced their perception of someone holding an object resembling a gun. New paradigms were developed wherein researchers manipulated, for instance, the race of target individuals (African American or White) shown on a computer screen to participants and whether the target was armed or unarmed (e.g., shown holding a gun or a regular object such as a cell phone). Participants were tasked with (symbolically) shooting when they perceived a gun in the target's hand but were to refrain from shooting when they recognized an object other than a gun. Researchers focused on the error rates made by participants, the speed with which they reacted to the trials, and whether these varied based on the manipulations. The results of several studies using this paradigm revealed that participants made more errors in the form of shooting an unarmed Black target compared to an unarmed White target or failing to shoot an armed White (vs. Black) target more often. Even correct decisions involved a bias measured in terms of time whereby the decisions to shoot an armed Black (vs. White) target and to not shoot an unarmed White (vs. Black) target were faster on average. This suggests that processing a constellation involving a gun and a Black face demands less cognitive effort than that involving a gun with a White face (see Correll et al., 2002; Essien et al., 2017; Payne, 2001).

Research on these types of biases demonstrates that intuitive cognitive mechanisms do not always lead individuals in the right direction; in many cases, they lead them astray. The multitude of disasters encountered on a daily basis, especially those faced more intensely and consistently by individuals living in certain regions (e.g., the Middle East), such as death, pathogens, economic crises, earthquakes, floods, and forest fires, can easily push individuals into an intuitive mode of responding. This may serve as a reminder that in such perilous situations, it is in general a good idea to exert more cognitive effort before arriving at a final decision if the situation permits. This is easier said than done but still valuable to promote as an idea because what makes situations chaotic and unconducive to reflection is not only their material and physical reality (e.g., imagine the lack of resources critical for survival such as food and water in the immediate aftermath of an earthquake) but also the human factor—that is, people's reactions being too fast to be thoughtful enough to contribute to collective well-being and the restoration of peace and order. As more individuals behave thoughtlessly, chaos can grow and force more and more individuals into thoughtless behavior in a kind of positive feedback loop.

Coda

In this chapter, we introduced affect as a situational factor influencing and interacting with cognition and subsequently explored alternative theoretical models aimed at predicting how different types of threats can influence human behavior, especially in the sociopolitical domain. We also identified that these threats could exert specific causal effects on human social interactions and cognitive processes. Notably, the culture-specific nature of these effects warrants further investigation because the perilousness of individuals' living environments often places a heavy cognitive burden on them.

When we grapple with financial troubles or face threats like terrorism, our focus naturally shifts toward the imperative of survival amid intense environmental challenges. Consider individuals facing financial hardships; their primary behavioral and cognitive motivation may revolve around addressing these financial difficulties. Compare the experiences of an average person living in a Scandinavian welfare state to one living in a corrupt dictatorship in the

Middle East in terms of financial troubles and access to material resources. It becomes evident that people living in regions where the diverse forms of threats discussed in this chapter (e.g., terrorism, pathogen prevalence, resource scarcity) are significantly less prevalent and where the social system operates under secular rule of law and impartiality are better positioned to maintain their capacity for reflective thinking. In such environments, it is easier to channel that reflective thinking capacity toward intellectual pursuits beyond mere survival, such as science, philosophy, art, and philanthropy.

In the years leading up to the Second World War, particularly during 1931–32, discussions about the rise of fascism in Europe raised fundamental questions about human aggression and its role in instigating wars, as Sigmund Freud argued in his letters to Albert Einstein (Freud, 1946). Is our inherently aggressive nature, as Freud posited, responsible for conflicts that future generations are doomed to repeat endlessly? Or is there a possibility that we can harness our reflective thinking to prevent the negative consequences of our intuitive biases?

Answering this philosophical question is undoubtedly challenging, but it appears that in a world governed by our intuitive biases, especially in a globalized society where we interact extensively with people who possess different and often incompatible intuitions, establishing and maintaining peace may necessitate transcending the divisive nature of our intuitive cognitive architecture (Sauer, 2015). This might involve reevaluating or revising, through a deliberate process of reflection, some of the moral convictions that our intuitions generate. At the same time, it is increasingly becoming important to realize that reflection alone falls short in its protective role against the effects of threat. Guided by one's social identities and affective investments, it is easy for reflection to proceed in a selective manner and to end up strengthening one's pre-existing beliefs. Thus, the virtues and motivations of open-mindedness and intellectual humility are needed to prevent us from engaging in such motivated reasoning when confronted with ideas that challenge our intuitions or leave us feeling threatened. Without such efforts, achieving and sustaining peace in a world where intuitions are at odds with one another becomes a daunting task.

Importantly, reflection may serve more laudable goals than simply boosting one's pre-existing views if one adopts a holistic view. More and more, individuals feel threatened simply by the thought of encountering political adversaries. Discussions with these others frequently leave both sides even more threatened and polarized. In such encounters, reflection may work better by asking oneself what political debates are for. If the answer is to win arguments and dominate others, then why even waste time discussing matters with opponents? When a society becomes obsessed with winning, motivated reasoning is the most that reflection will produce (Mercier & Sperber, 2017). Of course, the actual purpose behind engaging in a political discussion is to test one's views against alternatives, to find the weaknesses and strengths in each, and to arrive at an even better position via this mutual influence. Thus, reflection may begin to function in a way that makes belief revision possible if we adopt a holistic view that allows us to see that what matters, in the long run, is to get closer to the truth. Rosenberg (2002) made a similar point when he argued that individuals who take a more holistic view of society while also being highly reflective (*systematic thinkers* in his words) understand that political debates "provide a means whereby individuals may enter each others' reflections on their interpretations and evaluations and thereby contribute to the construction of a better understanding of truth and right" (p. 78). Interestingly, this is also not that different from the situation we mentioned in this book's Preface of the scientists who fail to think holistically and to connect their day-to-day activities to the actual goal of science, which is also truth-seeking.

One of the most significant challenges of our century lies in the fact that social media users often tend to sensationalize every event, reinforcing their moral convictions in echo chambers by selectively consuming and promoting information that aligns with their preconceived beliefs. In this regard, the contemporary world presents one of the most pressing social dilemmas we face, as moral convictions continue to harden under existential threats, and even the content we encounter within the social media ecosystem has the power to exacerbate polarization. Therefore, it is crucial to comprehend how threats, cultural norms, cognitive style, and decision-making processes interact with each other in affecting polarization. This understanding can guide us in formulating clearer strategies for preserving and nurturing reflective thought in our environment, ultimately contributing to a more harmonious world. In summary, maintaining reflective thought processes, especially in the face of existential threats, is challenging yet clearly beneficial. Contemporary scientific insights can help foster reflective thinking in these contexts.

Notes

1 We use the word *affect* broadly to refer to a variety of neurophysiological arousal states and subjective experiences, such as *emotion* and *mood*. The varieties show differences amongst each other (and a good deal of variation within each) when analyzed at a finer level: The arousal may be diffuse, such as a pleasant feeling or positive mood, as well as discrete, such as fear or joy. The latter are *basic* emotions but there are emotions that are *self-conscious*, such as pride and shame, as well. Moods last longer, whereas affect and emotion are typically shorter-lived. Russell's (2003) framework may be helpful to readers seeking further clarity. Collectively, these varieties and their relation to cognition make up an enormous body of literature that is not possible to cover in detail here. Dual-process theorists also acknowledge that they often "ignore emotion altogether" (Evans, 2008, p. 256), probably because of the same reason—that it is too challenging to do justice to the complexities of affect while keeping dual-process models and research manageable.

2   On the one hand, it is possible to argue that affect and cognition are independent human functions realized by distinct neuroanatomical structures—the "low" limbic and the "high" cortical roads, respectively (LeDoux, 1996). On the other hand, this could be simply a practically useful distinction that does not necessarily correspond so well to reality (Duncan & Barrett, 2007). This might be a matter of interpretation. As Cacioppo and Berntson (2007, p. 1353) noted "what appears to one investigator to be a minor difference in neural circuits may represent qualitatively different functional mechanisms to another." We discuss a similar issue regarding the distinction between reflection and intuition in Chapter 10.

3   Lodge and Taber's model focuses on affect in the sense of a positive versus negative reaction that is deeply embedded in the fabric of our moment-to-moment experience. One could also consider discrete negative emotions, such as anger, which can also have similar biasing effects on political cognition. For instance, Suhay and Erisen (2018) found that anger is associated with the tendency to favor attitudinally congruent (vs. incongruent) arguments on political issues. See Gadarian and Brader (2023) for a comprehensive review of the role of emotion in politics.

4   In the past, there have been criticisms that suggest conservatives have received more attention in research compared to liberals, possibly due to a liberal bias in the social psychology literature. Additionally, some studies have depicted certain conservative traits using biased language (e.g., Duarte et al., 2015). Consequently, while the original terminology of "resistance to change" and "opposition to equality" is still employed in the literature, in this book, we opt for more neutral terminology: "preference for equality" versus "preference for hierarchy."

5   System justification theory posits that people possess an inherent motivation to uphold the status quo, a drive that spans epistemic, existential, and relational domains. Epistemic needs concern the management of uncertainty, whereas existential needs pertain to the mitigation of existential threats and anxieties. Upholding the status quo serves a palliative function, as it envisions a certain and predictable world. The final category encompasses relational needs, which are fulfilled when individuals foster positive relationships with others who operate within the same system, often by advocating for the perpetuation of the existing social order.

6   Identical twins possess genetic material that is virtually identical, while fraternal twins share a level of genetic similarity akin to that of regular siblings.

7   The amygdala and insula, as components of the limbic system in the brain, play crucial roles in emotion regulation. The amygdala is particularly sensitive to fear and threatening stimuli, whereas the insula has been linked to behaviors involving avoidance and disgust sensitivity.

8   In the classical Stroop test, researchers examine variations in participants' response times when the written words and their corresponding ink colors are either congruent or incongruent. The emotional Stroop test, on the other hand, employs words with emotional significance in place of color words. The underlying premise is that participants encounter interference when processing emotionally charged words, thereby resulting in increased response times.

5

EPISTEMICALLY SUSPECT BELIEFS

Homo sapiens are skilled storytellers, often weaving narratives that involve supernatural occurrences. While some individuals literally believe in the reality of these supernatural events, others view them as literary devices. This dichotomy in worldviews is mirrored by variations in cognitive styles (Yilmaz, 2021a). In recent years, empirical studies linking cognitive style disparities to endorsement of epistemically questionable belief systems, such as belief in the supernatural or conspiracy theories, have surged. The consensus in the current literature indicates that as reflective thinking decreases, there tends to be an uptick in the endorsement of beliefs that are epistemically dubious, such as those pertaining to the supernatural, conspiracy theories, and the paranormal (Baron, 2020; Binnendyk & Pennycook, 2022; Yelbuz et al., 2022).

Epistemically suspect beliefs can be defined as a broad and umbrella category encompassing paranormal, conspiracy, or supernatural beliefs that often stand in opposition to established scientific facts (Lobato et al., 2014).[1] While research on these belief systems predominantly focused on individual variables and the examination of personality traits associated with individuals who hold such beliefs (e.g., Pennycook, Cheyne, et al., 2012), it is crucial to recognize that these systems, which contravene established scientific knowledge, can readily propagate through the intuitive inclinations of our minds. This poses a significant challenge in situations where quick decisions, such as during pandemics, are required, potentially leading to public health concerns, particularly in terms of vaccine hesitancy. Moreover, these belief systems can also jeopardize individual health by promoting the adoption of pseudoscientific practices like alternative medicine (Lindeman, 2011). Therefore, it is imperative to gain a comprehensive understanding of

DOI: 10.4324/9781003300366-7

the cognitive origins underpinning these belief systems. In this section of the book, we will elucidate how humans' intuitive thought processes predispose them toward embracing epistemically questionable belief systems.

However, it should be noted that all types of beliefs correspond to mental states which, by their nature, are challenging to validate and thus are epistemically uncertain. These beliefs may span a spectrum from ideologies (see Chapter 6) to conspiracy-like explanations and even to dogmatic adherence to science (Sheldrake, 2012). While this chapter will explore the role of cognitive style in shaping these beliefs, it is the more distal mechanisms, such as cultural upbringing, that predominantly determine belief formation (Gervais et al., 2021). Nonetheless, cognitive style as an individual difference may also play a role in strengthening or initiating these belief systems (Baron, 2020; Birnendyk & Pennycook, 2022). Our primary focus here is to understand the relationship between cognitive styles, belief in conspiracy theories, and, particularly, religious beliefs.

Origins of Epistemically Suspect Beliefs

Although sociologists define religion as a set of cultural practices binding people through sacred moral norms (Durkheim, 1912/2008), recent research argues that religious belief may have evolutionary roots, transcending a purely cultural analysis (Atran, 2002; Barrett, 2004; Boyer, 2001; Henrich, 2020; Johnson, 2016; Norenzayan, 2013). Recent studies posit that religious belief is not solely a product of cultural learning; rather, several universal cognitive abilities also incline humans toward acquiring religious and supernatural beliefs. Although a debate lingers over whether these cognitive traits are specialized for religious belief, it is clear that humans have a disposition to acquire them due to the evolution of either specialized or more generalized cognitive capacities, such as agency detection or theory of mind abilities (Bahçekapili et al., 2019; Bellah, 2011). These inherent capacities, which serve adaptive functions within the human species, could have provided the cognitive foundations for the emergence of religious beliefs (Norenzayan, 2013). Additionally, religious belief, along with the accompanying belief of fear of supernatural punishment, may have an adaptive function of its own, serving to enhance cooperation among individuals who are not closely related genetically (Johnson, 2016). Regardless of whether they are evolutionary adaptations or the byproducts of broader cognitive capabilities, the cognitive biases that facilitate religious belief, such as mind–body dualism (Bering, 2006), pattern recognition (Douglas et al., 2019), teleological thinking (Kelemen, 2004), agency detection mechanism (Barrett, 2004), and anthropomorphism (Epley et al., 2007) have been evident since early stages of human development (White et al., 2021). This approach elucidates why religious faith and belief in supernatural agents are ubiquitous across all known human cultures.

The human brain's proclivity for recognizing patterns constitutes a cornerstone of belief formation. Early humans, living in a world fraught with unpredictability, gained a vital survival edge through the ability to discern patterns—whether in the short (e.g., prey movement) or long run (e.g., recurring seasons). This cognitive trait engendered various cognitive biases, including attributing intentions to natural occurrences, thereby paving the path to the development of supernatural belief. In the earliest religions, the rustling of leaves indicating a lurking predator or interpreting water movement or tree shadows as the actions of concealed spirits marked the origins of initial animistic beliefs (Norenzayan, 2013). Analogously, just as we liken stars in the sky to patterns like coffee pots (e.g., Ursa Major), ancient humans sought to mitigate existential uncertainty by discerning stimuli in their environment and thinking of them as forming patterns. This cognitive mechanism paved the way for the emergence of cognitive biases, leading to the attribution of unexplained natural phenomena to supernatural agents that resemble humans, with tendencies to reward and punish others' behaviors (i.e., anthropomorphism) with the help of the emergence of theory of mind skills (Norenzayan & Gervais, 2013). This pattern recognition mechanism was also pivotal for early humans to differentiate between intentional actions, such as a hunter's pursuit, and natural events such as wind, a distinction which has a high survival value. These evolved cognitive traits formed part of the cognitive substrate for the evolution of religious belief.

A different cognitive ability, known as theory of mind, is another aspect of this cognitive substrate. It enables us to comprehend that minds beyond our own are agents capable of thought and mentalization (Baron-Cohen, 1991). While more rudimentary forms of the theory of mind are believed to exist in animals, such as great apes (Krupenye & Call, 2019), it is considered a complex construct unique to humans and a crucial driver of intentionality (Tomasello, 2001). In other words, although it is possible to observe these skills in other animals, this capability is less developed in them, if at all, causing them (e.g., cats) to perceive a moving ball, for example, as a living agent and to chase it. In contrast, human infants can distinguish between human-like objects (with eyes and ears) and non-human-like objects from an early age (Hamlin et al., 2007). Some argue that religious beliefs emerge as a byproduct of this ability (Bahçekapili et al., 2019; Boyer, 2001). Much as we recognize others as thinking agents, we can also ascribe intentionality to unseen supernatural agents when unexplained natural events occur. In this light, anthropomorphized gods, or rituals aimed at appeasing unseen spirits or gods, likely resulted from this cognitive capacity, as individuals sought to uncover the intentions of supernatural entities and to influence their actions through interactions such as prayers or sacrificial rites.

Mind–body dualism, the concept that the mind and body are distinct entities, likely emerged as an offshoot of the theory of mind. Early humans, observing their own actions and intentions, may have projected analogous mental experiences onto natural phenomena and readily embraced the notion of spiritual beings with agency separate from physical bodies (e.g., ghosts, angels). Hence, mind–body dualism is an intrinsic feature of adult intuition and its development can also be observed from an early age (Forstmann & Burgmer, 2017). In this sense, these cognitive biases are inherent in humans from birth, rendering the human species receptive to religious beliefs.

Teleological thinking, denoting the inclination to perceive purpose in natural occurrences (Dubray, 1912), has also significantly contributed to epistemically suspect belief formation. The unpredictability of the environment spurred the quest for explanations, propelling early teleological interpretations. For example, the movement of the Sun in the sky was attributed to a divine force guiding its path. These intuitive cognitive features collectively establish religious belief as a fundamental human trait, rather than a cognitive error.

This same perspective can be applied to other epistemically suspect beliefs, such as paranormal beliefs[2] or conspiracy theories. Paranormal beliefs are often considered byproducts of religious beliefs (Lindeman & Svedholm, 2012), frequently encompassing dubious systems concerning magic, unidentified flying objects (UFOs), and other phenomena that are not addressed by traditional religions. The mechanisms underlying the formation of traditional religious beliefs are also applicable to paranormal beliefs (Yilmaz, 2021a).

Conspiracy theories may be viewed as products of this heuristic system as well, closely intertwined with the mechanisms of pattern recognition (Douglas et al., 2017), causal attribution, and theory of mind. Conspiracy theories are unfounded beliefs attempting to elucidate the origins of emerging events. Often relying on frail arguments devoid of scientific rationale or factual accuracy, these theories occasionally align with reality but primarily serve as palliative explanations, aiming to alleviate uncertainty (Wood & Douglas, 2018). While a few conspiracy theories might be valid, the majority are fashioned for the purpose of uncertainty reduction. Typically, conspiracy theories invoke notions of concealed power and gain traction within society due to their resonance with intuitive cognitive processes. These theories fulfill a shared objective: mitigating uncertainty by presenting explanations for intricate events, by employing simplistic and feeble arguments. Making connections between seemingly unrelated events is a common trait across all conspiracy theories (Douglas et al., 2019). In essence, conspiratorial minds can establish a link between two apparently unrelated events, such as the implantation of a chip in the body and the development of a scientific vaccine against coronavirus disease (COVID-19). The basis for these connections lies in our overactive pattern recognition mechanism (Narmashiri et al., 2023), which in turn activates our cognitive alarm system.

In addition to the pattern recognition system, the tendency to believe in epistemically questionable beliefs lies in the desire for control, mechanisms pertaining to cognitive dissonance, and the allure of concealed knowledge. For instance, conspiracy theories thrive in circumstances marked by high uncertainty and greater difficulty in cooperation (Liekefett et al., 2023). In such contexts, identifying suitable partners for cooperation and accessing accurate-seeming information become crucial for survival. Consequently, anyone claiming that information is being concealed (e.g., by the government or corporations) and that reality contradicts conventional understanding rings alarm bells in our mental framework, capturing our attention. As this proposed explanation seemingly resolves a particular uncertainty for a believer of that conspiracy (such as the cause of a pandemic), people often cling to such conspiracy-like interpretations even in the absence of compelling evidence (Van Mulukom et al., 2022). Failing to make sense of an uncertain situation can lead to anxiety and stress, reducing our sense of control and rendering us more susceptible to embracing conspiracy theories (Van Prooijen & Acker, 2015).

The cognitive dissonance mechanism elucidates why individuals persist in their belief in conspiracy theories, even when confronted with substantial evidence against them. Cognitive dissonance refers to a psychological state arising when our actions contradict our beliefs (Festinger, 1962). For instance, you may possess an affinity for alcohol, while being aware of its potential harm to internal organs through regular and heavy consumption. Such a situation engenders a conflict between your behavior and your cognitions. To address this dissonance, individuals can opt to cease alcohol consumption or modify their beliefs about it, introducing additional cognitions. For instance, novel cognitions may serve to justify the behavior, such as "I consume alcohol for stress relief," "I exercise to counter alcohol's negative effects," or "alcohol doesn't really pose serious health risks." Similarly, when exposed to opposing evidence, individuals might gravitate toward narratives that align with their existing beliefs concerning conspiracy theories, which in turn can lead to an increase in the motivation to pursue positive self-esteem (Cichocka et al., 2016) and the need for uniqueness (Lantian et al., 2017). These tendencies facilitate the perpetuation of conspiracy beliefs within our intuitive mindset.

In line with the motivated reasoning account (e.g., confirmation bias), people do not pursue the truth in the way a scientist does but rather play the role of a lawyer, seeking to legitimize and validate their current beliefs and perspectives. Consequently, the structure of our minds can sustain beliefs with questionable epistemic foundations, allowing them to persist in the face of diverse contrary evidence. For this reason, reflection can sometimes function to support, rather than suppress, intuitive inclinations (Kahan, 2013).

The alliance detection mechanism also plays a pivotal role in the development of both supernatural and conspiracy beliefs. Humans and most other mammals inhabit groups and establish coalitions by cooperating with those who share similarities. Consequently, when forming trust-based relationships like partnerships, friendships, or business ties, we instinctively place more trust in individuals who share our worldview (Tomasello, 2016). The knowledge that another person has similar moral convictions as oneself is taken as an indicator of trustworthiness (Čehajić-Clancy et al., 2023). Throughout history, this mechanism has engendered homophily in social networks (McPherson et al., 2001) and segregation of societies along group membership by, for instance, leading Christians to trust fellow Christians and Muslims to trust fellow Muslims. This automatic mechanism guides us in discerning who belongs to our in-group and who merits our trust. Sharing religious views or conspiracy beliefs serves as a fundamental cue that triggers this system.

Although the predisposition toward both conspiracy theories and supernatural beliefs stems from evolutionary traits, social factors shape these predispositions, as well. For instance, in countries characterized by high levels of corruption and perceived injustice, conspiracy beliefs tend to be more prevalent—partly due to the increased likelihood of real conspiracies in such environments (Alper, 2023). Consider Putin's request for a COVID test from Macron.[3] If this had occurred between two Scandinavian heads of state, the possibility of one's DNA being stolen would not have crossed the mind. However, the closed nature of a country like Russia elevates the plausibility of such concerns. In cultures with low corruption, educational attainment tends to negatively predict conspiracy beliefs. However, in countries with high corruption, educational attainment either loses its predictive ability or predicts these beliefs less strongly (Alper et al., 2024), as the likelihood of conspiracies being true increases their perceived plausibility (Alper & Yilmaz, 2023). The same applies to religious belief: In countries where the rule of law is not well-functioning, religious beliefs tend to increase, whereas in countries where the secular rule of laws and institutions work well, religious beliefs tend to decrease (Norenzayan, 2013).

Nonetheless, individual variations still exist among people residing within the same culture and under the same social conditions. For example, anxiety, stress, and the inclination for intuitive thinking are significant factors (Douglas & Sutton, 2023). Notably, while experimental findings remain inconclusive regarding the causal effect of cognitive style on conspiracy beliefs (Bago et al., 2022; Stall & Petrocelli, 2023; Sümer, 2023; Swami et al., 2014; Većkalov et al., 2024), meta-analytic evidence indicates that individuals who are more reflective are less inclined to believe in conspiracy theories (Yelbuz et al., 2022). The same pattern also applies to supernatural and paranormal beliefs (Yilmaz, 2021a).

Indeed, there are three primary human motivations (Jost et al., 2008) that drive people toward epistemically suspect beliefs (Douglas et al., 2017).

The first is epistemic motivation. People generally desire clear information and are motivated to gain its psychological benefits, even if the information is incomplete or inaccurate. Acting intuitively and believing something, even if it is incorrect or unplausible, fulfills this epistemic need by reducing uncertainty. The second fundamental motivation is existential needs. People generally seek a stable and secure environment, and existential threats are psychologically challenging to accept. To reduce feelings of a lack of control and alleviate anxiety, such beliefs help satisfy existential needs. The third basic motivation is social or relational needs. People live as members of specific groups and desire a positive perception of themselves and their groups. Therefore, they often aim to fulfill this relational need by engaging in shared rituals or pursuing common goals. When a conspiracy theory involving one's own group emerges, individuals are more likely to defend it, even if false, as long as it reinforces their group's self-perception.

Understanding the evolutionary functions of these epistemically suspect beliefs is crucial, but it is equally important to comprehend their proximate mechanisms through the psychological motivations they fulfill. These beliefs easily permeate society because they appeal to our intuitive system and satisfy three fundamental human needs. However, if religious and related beliefs are natural outcomes of intuitive cognitive biases that predispose us to these convictions, along with their underlying motivations, how does religious disbelief emerge?

Origins of Disbelief

Norenzayan and Gervais (2013) proposed four distinct pathways that lead to religious disbelief. The first is *mind-blind atheism*, which refers to deficits in mentalizing ability, which may facilitate religious doubt, as individuals with theory of mind deficiencies are less prone to mentalize supernatural agents (Norenzayan et al., 2012; but see Maij et al., 2017). The second has been called *InCREDulous atheism*, which refers to lower exposure to religious symbols in a country, leading to religious disbelief. The third is *apatheism*, which denotes an absence of existential insecurity, such as physical and social instability, diminishing the need for religion. Finally, there is *analytic atheism*, or skepticism toward prevailing cultural beliefs resulting from higher levels of reflective thinking. A dedicated body of literature has emerged for each of these paths. While the magnitude of effects varies, and cognitive style variables generally perform like the secondary factors in understanding the formation of religious beliefs beyond the main factors like cultural learning mechanisms (White et al., 2021), each pathway has been linked to religious belief (e.g., Gervais et al., 2021).

However, an increasing number of recent empirical findings have established a connection between reflectiveness-intuitiveness and religious belief. Particularly, since religious belief hinges on automatic assumptions formed during the socialization process, the corrective Type 2 model of dual-process cognition anticipates that individuals prone to reflective thinking are more likely to scrutinize and rectify initial intuitive conclusions (Baron, 2020; Yilmaz, 2021a). This leads them to question and challenge religious teachings and beliefs—a notion often referred to as the *intuitive religious belief hypothesis.* Substantial evidence now supports this hypothesis (Gervais & Norenzayan, 2012; Pennycook, Cheyne, et al., 2012; Shenhav et al., 2012; but see Gervais & Norenzayan, 2018), and this association persists independently of cognitive ability, demographics, and personality variables (Pennycook, Cheyne, et al., 2012; Saribay & Yilmaz, 2017). A meta-analysis of 31 studies conducted in Western countries concluded that a weak but significant negative relationship exists between reliance on reflection and religious belief (Pennycook et al., 2016). Self-identified atheists also exhibit a stronger inclination towards reflective thinking than self-reported believers. This negative correlation extends to non-Western cultures, including Türkiye (Bahçekapili & Yilmaz, 2017; Yilmaz & Saribay, 2016), India (Stagnaro et al., 2019), and Singapore—but not China (Gervais et al., 2018). Gervais et al. (2018) tested this hypothesis across 13 different cultures, identifying a weak but generally significant negative relationship, albeit not universal.

Our research group recently discovered an interesting qualification for this negative association between reflectiveness and religious belief. In a series of studies (Bahçekapili & Yilmaz, 2017), we explored whether this relationship varies based on types of religious motivations, revealing that the negative association holds true for both intrinsic (belief for personal righteousness or spirituality) and extrinsic (like avoiding social exclusion) religious motivations. Intriguingly, a third kind of motivation exhibited the reverse pattern. The tendency of individuals to resist dogmatic answers to religion and to question religious tenets (i.e., *quest religiosity*, Batson & Schoenrade, 1991) was *positively* associated with reflectiveness. This discovery underscores the fundamental role of religious motivations in understanding the intricate relationship between religion and cognitive style. Therefore, it seems that aside from whether one is religious or not, an important factor here is the religious motivation one has in the belief maintenance.

Despite various moderating variables, the intuitive religious belief hypothesis finds consistent support in correlational findings. However, experimental results are less straightforward. The notion that religious belief is grounded in intuitive thinking was initially tested experimentally by Gervais and Norenzayan (2012) and Shenhav et al. (2012), revealing that activating intuitive thinking heightens religious belief, while activating reflective thinking diminishes it. Furthermore, Yilmaz, Karadöller, and Sofuoglu (2016) examined this relationship in a Turkish sample, demonstrating that reflective thinking reduces religious belief when controlling for participants' baseline religiosity assessed four weeks before the experiment.

However, the clarity in the initial experiments has been muddied by subsequent replication failures. Gervais and Norenzayan's (2012) experiment (Study 2) could not be replicated in a later study with high statistical power (Sanchez et al., 2017). Similarly, the experiment conducted by Shenhav et al. (2012) failed to replicate in another high-powered study (Saribay et al., 2020). Another study noted that activating reflective thinking did not lead to a decrease in religious belief (Yonker et al., 2016). Farias et al. (2017) also reported that various methods of activating intuitive thinking did not affect religious belief. However, it remains uncertain whether these studies successfully activated relevant cognitive styles (e.g., Sanchez et al., 2017; Saribay et al., 2020; Yonker et al., 2016), and had sufficient statistical power (e.g., Farias et al., 2017). For instance, the first of the three manipulation techniques used by Gervais and Norenzayan (2012) did not yield consistent results in the studies of Sanchez et al. (2017) and Deppe et al. (2015). The manipulation technique employed by Yonker et al. (2016)—which assumes that attempting a cognitive reflection test or a Stroop test, initially designed for measuring reflective thinking, promotes reflection—probably has very small effects, difficult to capture in standard sample sizes. Similarly, the technique originally used by Shenhav et al. (2012) did not work well in influencing actual cognitive performance (Isler & Yilmaz, 2023; Saribay et al., 2020). In a similar vein, in a small-sample study (n = 37), Farias et al. (2017) imposed cognitive load on participants, investigating potential differences in supernatural attributions compared to a control group. Thus, two general issues—effectively activating reflective thinking and ensuring sufficient statistical power—plague this literature.

To address these limitations, our research group (Yilmaz & Isler, 2019) further examined whether activating reflection influences religious belief in two high-powered experiments using the time pressure/delay method reinforced with intuitive or reflective thinking prompts commonly employed in the literature (e.g., Isler & Yilmaz, 2023). Half of the participants responded to the question regarding belief in God within a time constraint of 10 seconds (which forces them to rely on intuition), whereas the other group of participants deliberated on this question for a minimum of 20 seconds (which enables reliance on reflection). Contrary to the intuitive religious belief hypothesis, the results of the first between-subjects experiment revealed that reflective thinking increased religious belief, particularly among atheists and agnostics. Subsequently, a preregistered experiment employing a within-subjects design was conducted.[4] Participants were asked to make decisions under time pressure initially, followed by the opportunity given to revise decisions under time delay. Although the results were seemingly aligned with the notion that reflection increased religious belief, particularly among non-believers, additional analyses indicated that the overall change in mean religious belief tended towards the middle of the scale (i.e., uncertain) for both believers and non-believers, supporting the reflective religious doubt hypothesis (reflection intensifying self-questioning about intuitively held beliefs). Although this work provided a novel hypothesis regarding the influence of reflection on religious belief, it seems clear based on the current state of the art that we need well-designed cross-cultural experiments using stronger manipulation techniques (e.g., Isler & Yilmaz, 2023) to reach a consensus on the causal effect of intuition and reflection on religious beliefs.

Possible Explanations

The corrective Type 2 thinking style (which we covered in Chapter 2) or conflict detection mechanism (which suggests that reflective thinkers are more attuned to conflicts between immaterial supernatural beliefs and the realities of the material world) might explain the negative association observed between religious belief and reflective thinking in correlational findings (Pennycook et al., 2016). However, certain boundary conditions exist: (1) the association is applicable only to specific types of religious motivations (intrinsic and extrinsic, but not quest religiosity; Bahçekapili & Yilmaz, 2017) and (2) specific cultures (Gervais et al., 2018). A majority of previous findings are based on data collected from North American or online WEIRD (Western, Educated, Industrialized, Rich, Democratic) samples (Henrich et al., 2010), with rare exceptions such as Türkiye (e.g., Bahçekapili & Yilmaz, 2017). Gervais et al. (2018), referring to the sole cross-cultural dataset on this association, asserted that reflective thinking could not be a global predictor of religious belief. However, the lack of standardized methods and testing procedures across different cultures has made reliable cross-cultural comparisons impossible to date.

Considering the current evidence challenging the cross-cultural universality of the association between reflective thinking and religious belief (Gervais et al., 2018), three distinct competing hypotheses can be proposed to account for the moderating role of culture. The *social foundations hypothesis* (Morgan et al., 2013) posits that there is no inherent causal link between reflective thinking and religious belief. Instead, culture shapes both. In collectivist cultures, networks of relationships may promote intuition and religiosity at the same time, making the endorsement of both easier.

The second possibility is that a causal relationship exists, but its strength is higher in tight (vs. loose) cultures (Gelfand, 2018).[5] Rigorous social norms in tight cultures necessitate robust reflective thinking for dissent (i.e., religious disbelief).[5] Since reflection may lead to overall non-conformity, and non-conformity can manifest as religious disbelief in more traditional societies (e.g., tight cultures), a stronger association might be expected in more traditional countries. In contrast, in cultures with looser norms (e.g., Western Europe), religious disbelief might be facilitated through mechanisms other than reflective thinking (e.g., lack of existential insecurity). Tentative evidence can be observed in the cross-cultural fluctuations in the direction of association between reflection and belief in God (Gervais et al., 2018). According to this observation, a negative, albeit small, relationship exists between reflection and religiosity in the overall sample, and this association tended to be stronger in more religious countries, in line with the dual-process model. In these nations, questioning prevailing norms may result in reduced religious belief because the norms and beliefs are aligned. However, if this logic holds true, highly secular countries should display a positive relationship. This is because questioning the prevailing norm of secularism would result in an increase in religiosity more often than not. While direct empirical support for this evolutionary cultural model is lacking (e.g., Baimel et al., 2021; Stagnaro et al., 2019), Yilmaz and Isler's (2019) experimental findings summarized above, which indicated an increase in religious belief upon reflection in a highly secular context, particularly among atheists and agnostics, suggest that reflecting on the existence of God caused a small but statistically significant rise in belief in God. This increase is characterized by a general uncertainty toward religious belief, as reflected by scores clustering around the midpoint of the response scale (e.g., "not sure"). That is, these non-believers are not suddenly reporting belief in God in an absolute sense after being made to think more reflectively, but their responses are still shifting from a position of no belief to uncertainty. Future studies should assess these alternative hypotheses using demographically representative samples, such as those collected in the World Values Survey.

The third possibility postulates that in tight cultures, strict norms leave individuals with less freedom to defy those norms compared to individuals in loose cultures. Straying from these norms could result in stigmatization. More specifically, the *constraining environment hypothesis* (Caldwell-Harris et al., 2020) emerged, suggesting that the negative association between reflection and religious belief relationship might be weaker or absent in tight cultures, where people lack the opportunity to make choices compared to the loose cultures.

Another explanation can be proposed to reconcile varied experimental findings in the literature: the psychometric tools employed to measure religious belief might probe stable opinions that are resistant to change through experimental manipulation. These opinions, ingrained as defining characteristics of one's identity throughout life, reside in memory (i.e., they are not necessarily constructed on the spot when participants are asked to report them). For instance, participants scoring either 0 or 100 on a question about belief in God may remain unswayed by experimental manipulations, as their belief status has already solidified throughout the years as a stable facet of their identity. Experimental manipulations might show stronger effects on individuals less certain about the existence of God because attitudes that are less certain tend to be more situationally malleable (Petty & Krosnick, 1995). Another prospect is that reflection neither heightens nor diminishes religious belief as a general effect but fosters self-questioning among both believers and non-believers. Yilmaz and Isler (2019) observed that a majority of subjects initially reporting under time pressure that God definitely or probably exists or doesn't exist subsequently revised their responses to hover around the middle of the scale (i.e., the "not sure") when provided a chance to revise their initial answers under time delay. Therefore, it appears that reflection may foster a general tendency toward self-questioning about one's intuitively held beliefs which in turn either diminishes or promotes religious belief depending on what those intuitively held beliefs are in the first place.

Coda

Evaluating the current state of the art in studying the relationship between reflectivity and religious belief, it seems that there is a negative relationship between holding religious and related beliefs and relying on reflective thinking (Baron, 2020; Yilmaz, 2021a). Yet, experimental evidence remains inconclusive. There is support for the negative impact of reflection (Gervais & Norenzayan, 2012; Shenhav et al., 2012), no impact of reflection (Farias et al., 2017; Sanchez et al., 2017; Saribay et al., 2020), and a positive or self-questioning impact of reflection (Yilmaz & Isler, 2019) in the current literature. Consequently, further high-powered studies are necessary on this matter, particularly ones that examine the aforementioned boundary conditions using robust reflectiveness manipulations (e.g., Isler & Yilmaz, 2023) to achieve greater clarity on the issue.

Furthermore, as mentioned earlier, cognitive style variables should be regarded as secondary factors for understanding the establishment of religious belief. The primary influences stem from cultural exposure and filial upbringing. In this regard, an evolutionary approach alone falls short of fully grasping the emergence and development of these belief systems. Hence, contemporary models frequently turn to cultural evolutionary frameworks to gain insight into these belief systems (Henrich, 2020; Norenzayan, 2013; White et al., 2021).

According to the cultural-evolutionary framework (e.g., White et al., 2021), while the likely origins of religious belief correlate with specific cognitive biases, this alone does not account for the cultural transmission of religion. Certain religious belief systems gained a direct advantage in fundamental survival contexts such as intragroup cooperation, intergroup competition, and reproductive success. As a result, they are swiftly and efficiently disseminated through cultural evolutionary processes. In this light, it is argued that religions featuring significant moralizing deities arose as solutions to conflicts in harsh environments—that is, geographical regions characterized by resource scarcity and intense conflict (Norenzayan, 2013). These religions found greater ease of dissemination and achieved reproductive success among their adherents (Moon, 2021), conferring advantages in intergroup competition and further propagating globally.

Hence, while the predispositions of the human mind play a pivotal role in the emergence of religious belief, the transmission of religions in society underscores the imperative for a cultural evolutionary explanation. For instance, the development of nuclear families after the Catholic Church prohibited kin marriages led to the development of individualism prevalent in the Western world today (Fukuyama, 2011). This shift, in turn, led to the emergence of impartial secular institutions, contributing to relatively reduced corruption, and more egalitarianism, compared to kin-based institutions (Henrich, 2020). Such a perspective exemplifies the necessity of incorporating cultural evolutionary mechanisms alongside cognitive factors when endeavoring to comprehend the evolution of religious beliefs.

In summary, while reflection plays a crucial role as an individual factor in shaping epistemically suspect beliefs, it remains unclear from experimental evidence under what conditions engaging in reflection leads to change in beliefs and attitudes toward a more epistemically sound direction, such as via cognitive decoupling, versus reinforcing preexisting attitudes, as seen in motivated reasoning, regarding epistemically suspect beliefs. To advance our understanding in this area, future studies should aim to identify the characteristics of beliefs and the specific conditions that prompt individuals to engage in cognitive decoupling versus motivated reasoning. Additionally, as we also mentioned at the conclusion of Chapter 4, an open question remains regarding the changes that could be brought to people's belief systems by incorporating virtues and motivations like holism, systemic thinking, open-mindedness, and intellectual humility into reflection, enabling them to consider different perspectives.

Notes

1   While established scientific facts are undoubtedly based on findings determined by the current paradigm or scientific consensus, it is important to recognize that new findings may lead to changes in these established facts. However, when a belief system contradicts fundamental scientific facts such as natural selection, cell theory, germ theory, etc., defending such belief systems becomes more challenging. This is because extraordinary claims require extraordinary evidence. Similar to Bayesian probability calculus, strong evidence is needed to substantiate low-probability events. Therefore, although scientific knowledge does not represent absolute truth, it serves as an epistemic norm, making certain beliefs more defensible than others.

2   Paranormal beliefs encompass phenomena that elude explanation through ordinary experiences or current scientific understanding. These beliefs are not inherently divine or spiritual in nature; for instance, the purported existence of UFOs falls under the category of paranormal beliefs. The foundational premise of paranormal beliefs does not necessarily challenge scientific principles; rather, it acknowledges the possibility of phenomena, like the power of thought, that science has yet to elucidate (Irwin & Watt, 2007). Supernatural beliefs, in contrast, pertain to events beyond our direct experience and observation—phenomena that lie outside the realm of scientific explanation (Slone, 2004).

3   In 2022, during a visit to Russia amid the pandemic, French President Macron was mandated by the Russian authorities to undergo a COVID-19 test to be permitted in the same room with President Putin. Macron declined, citing concerns that his DNA could be collected. Consequently, they were seated at a considerable distance from each other around an expansive round table (see: www.reuters.com/world/europe/putin-kept-macron-distance-snubbing-covid-demands-sources-2022-02-10/).

4   In a standard between-subjects design, different participants are recruited for the experimental and control groups. This approach, when combined with a large sample size and random assignment (e.g., randomly assigning participants to the groups), ensures that potential confounding variables, which were not explicitly measured in the study, are evenly distributed between the two groups. Consequently, it enables more robust causal inferences to be drawn. On the other hand, within-subjects designs involve using the same participants in both the experimental and control conditions. While within-subjects designs offer higher statistical power by minimizing individual differences, they can be susceptible to response biases like fatigue or order effects. The application of both these methods in the study conducted by Yilmaz and Isler (2019) represents a notable strength of the research, as it allows for a more comprehensive examination of the phenomenon under investigation.

5   In accordance with the tight versus loose culture dichotomy, a key framework utilized in cultural psychology for categorizing diverse cultures, tight cultures are those characterized by stringent social norms, where departing from these norms is generally met with disapproval. In contrast, loose cultures exhibit more relaxed social norms, where deviations from these norms are often deemed acceptable.

6   See also Chapter 8 for further discussion.

6

IDEOLOGY

In 2018, the Turkish version of "Who Wants to Be a Millionaire?" presented a question that went viral on social media due to an incorrect answer. In this instance, a university student contestant faced the following challenge: "In a supermarket where the combined cost of a chocolate bar and chewing gum amounts to 11 Turkish liras, the chocolate is 10 liras more expensive than the chewing gum. How much does each cost?" She had 45 seconds to provide an answer.

Attentive readers will recall that this question is a modified version of those found in the Cognitive Reflection Test (CRT), which we initially introduced in Chapter 2. As we have discussed in that context, research has shown that people's initial response to such questions is often intuitive but incorrect, especially under time pressure and stress (Kahneman, 2011). The common instinctive answer is 1 lira. However, if the chewing gum costs 1 lira, the chocolate would then cost 11 liras, resulting in a combined cost of 12 liras, not 11. The correct pricing should be 50 kurus for the chewing gum and 10.5 liras for the chocolate to meet the combined total of 11 liras. This seemingly straightforward question's incorrect answer led to criticism of the Turkish education system and mockery of the contestant on social media.

What is often overlooked in such situations is how questions like this spotlight the difference in human thought processes, specifically between intuitive and reflective thinking—a subject we have touched upon throughout this book. Readers might remember our discussion on the dual-process model of the mind, which proposes that our minds function using two primary systems of thought (Kahneman, 2011). Type 1 (or System 1) thinking is intuitive, effortless, and autonomous. In contrast, Type 2 (or System 2) engages during tasks that require cognitive effort.

DOI: 10.4324/9781003300366-8

For example, once individuals learn how to ride bicycles or drive cars, operating these vehicles becomes second nature. These acquired skills become automatic, requiring no conscious thought. Similarly, an experienced waiter can adeptly carry a tray laden with glasses, minimizing attention and errors due to their familiarity with the task. This dual-system thinking likely evolved in ancient times, playing an adaptive role in human evolution. In essence, our predisposition toward automatic thinking is energy-conserving: Imagine the mental toll if every time we sat in a car, we had to relearn its operations or reconsider the nuances of using the clutch. Such constant deliberation would be draining.

As we discussed in the first chapter of the book, while intuitive thinking is beneficial in many life scenarios, conserving our mental resources, it also leads to inherited cognitive pitfalls. As demonstrated by Daniel Kahneman, a Nobel Prize-winning economist, and his colleague Amos Tversky, numerous cognitive biases stem from intuitive thinking. For instance, previous chapters highlighted that individuals with a stronger analytical inclination are less prone to logical mistakes when posed with probabilistic questions. They suppress stereotypical information, focusing on base rate information. An illustrative example is the renowned "Linda problem":

Linda is 31 years old, single, sincere, and jovial. She holds a philosophy degree. During her student years, she was passionate about discrimination and social justice, and participated in anti-nuclear protests. Which of the following descriptions is more probable?
a) Linda is a banker. b) Linda is a banker and an active feminist.

Individuals with a strong analytical thinking inclination can discern more readily that option A is statistically more probable than option B. This is because it is more likely for something to be exclusively "A" than for it to be both "A and B." To put it differently, being a "banker" encompasses the category of being both a "banker and a feminist" (meaning, all B's are necessarily A's). Given the larger population of the "banker" category, Linda is inherently more likely to be an A. Conversely, those who lean heavily on intuitive thinking often overlook this base-rate information, making them more susceptible to choosing the erroneous option B. This propensity arises because the description presented immediately invokes a feminist profile in one's mind. Hence, intuitive thinkers often gravitate towards this option without extensive contemplation.

Mathematical challenges frequently demand tasks that engage the Type 2 cognitive mechanism for most individuals. For instance, if you encountered the initial question for the first time, you would likely need to employ Type 2 thinking to deduce the right answer. Frederick (2005), the pioneer behind this task, introduced three distinct questions to gauge the extent of reliance on reflective thought. The logic underlying the first question closely mirrored our introductory challenge, while the other two prominently featured a misguided answer derived from intuitive thought. One might wonder, then, what bearing political ideologies hold on the responses to these queries.

As we have observed, these cognitive processes profoundly influence numerous daily attitudes and actions, particularly in the realm of epistemically suspect belief systems (Pennycook, Cheyne, et al., 2015). Individuals with heightened intuitive thinking tendencies display a greater proclivity toward embracing religious, paranormal, and conspiracy beliefs as we discussed in Chapter 5, including susceptibility to fake news (Pennycook & Rand, 2019). Furthermore, such individuals tend to prioritize traditional moral values (Pennycook et al., 2014), demonstrate altruistic behaviors, and display increased cooperative tendencies in economic games embedded with social dilemmas (Isler & Yilmaz, 2019; Rand, 2016). Simultaneously, those with strong intuitive thinking leanings exhibit a higher affinity for right-wing ideologies and conventional convictions (Alper et al., 2021).

While the concept of ideology typically refers to moral attitudes encompassing cognitive, motivational, and emotional elements (Jost, 2006), in accordance with the overall theme of the book, this chapter aims to examine the influence of intuitive and reflective thought processes on the formation and maintenance of political identities (left-wing vs. right-wing). In the following section, we will clarify our interpretation of ideology and then discuss the role of intuitive and reflective thought processes in the development and persistence of political identities, including their cross-cultural relevance.

What Is Ideology?

Tracing back to the etymology of "ideology," we encounter "idée" (idea) and "-ologie" (science). Although introduced in the late 18th century, the term garnered prominence through the writings of Marx and Engels (1970). They employ "ideology" in two distinct contexts. The first pertains to abstract and symbolic meaning systems prevalent even today. The latter, more condescending, alludes to a distorted reality or a "false consciousness." Modern social scientists rarely adopt the latter definition. Nowadays, ideology often encompasses a psychological perspective and is described as a collection of ideas shaping the moral, political, philosophical, and cultural ethos of a particular political or class orientation. Social scientists often define ideology as static, deep-seated beliefs, while social psychologists associate ideology with dynamic psychological constructs such as attitudes, values, and motivations (Jost, 2006). Broadly, political ideology embodies moral and political views informed by cognitive, emotional, and motivational facets, serving as a pivotal gauge explaining human actions.

The left-right dichotomy, originating from a session of the French National Assembly, might appear reductionist, but currently holds weight as a significant predictor of people's political and moral conduct. Ideology, traditionally operationalized in a one-dimensional format, aligns with the liberal-conservative divide in the U.S. and the left-right distinction in Europe (Feldman & Johnston, 2014; Gerber et al., 2010). Earlier approaches often categorized ideology dualistically as in dual-process models of the mind: Eysenck (1954) positioned the left as radical and the right as conservative, Lipset (1960) distinguished ideologies based on success versus equality metrics, Scott (1960) equated ideology with global peace versus nationalism, while Alford et al. (2005) discerned two political phenotypes. Seeking commonalities among these perspectives, Jost et al. (2003) conducted a meta-analysis and demarcated left and right-leaning ideologies based on their proclivity for change and equality (Jost, 2017).

But, do these categorizations genuinely capture political behaviors? Evaluating U.S. participants' self-identified positions on the liberal-conservative spectrum reveals significant predictive power concerning political actions (Jost et al., 2009). Empirical evidence indicates consistent self-placement along this spectrum, notwithstanding minor discrepancies (Feldman, 2003; Knight, 1999). Remarkably, 90% of American college students select a position on this axis, even when provided alternatives like "I don't know" or "I've never thought about it" (Jost, 2006). Data from the American National Election Studies (ANES) further substantiates this, linking liberal-conservative self-placement to voting patterns from 1972 to 2004. These insights underscore ideologies' pivotal role in influencing political stances, even amongst the less politically inclined, suggesting that ideologies are cognitive frameworks that structure values and beliefs, orienting individuals towards political actions, including voting. Thus, defying arguments by proponents of the "end-of-ideologies" school of thought like Fukuyama (1992) and Bell (1962), it is evident that, when afforded an opportunity, people tend to align with specific ideologies, even if imperfectly, and these alignments significantly influence their cognitive processes.

Cognitive Style and Ideology

Many researchers have sought to understand the relationship between cognitive styles—particularly those operationalized on the basis of intuition and reflection—and ideology. The CRT, developed by Frederick (2005), has been widely utilized to contrast the responses of right-wing and left-wing individuals. Initial research identified a notable negative correlation between conservatism (right-wing) and reflective thinking (Deppe et al., 2015; Iyer et al., 2012; Pennycook, Cheyne, et al., 2012; Talhelm et al., 2015; Yilmaz

& Saribay, 2016). However, further studies failed to reproduce these findings (Baron, 2017; Kahan, 2013; Landy, 2016; Piazza & Sousa, 2014).

The primary reason why some studies find an effect on ideology and others do not may be attributed to the initial research in this area, which often used a single-item political identity measure to operationalize ideology (liberal vs. conservative). Most of these studies were conducted with participants from the United States and WEIRD (Western, Educated, Industrialized, Rich, and Democratic) societies (Jost et al., 2017). However, a significant issue arises with the single-item political orientation measure (liberal vs. conservative), especially in the U.S. context, as it fails to capture some important nuances. Ideologies are commonly analyzed along two main axes: social (cultural) and economic (fiscal) attitudes. Within this framework, the single-item liberal-conservative measure may not accurately represent some respondents. For example, in the U.S., respondents who identify as libertarians have social attitudes similar to liberals, but their economic attitudes align more closely with conservatives (Boaz & Kirby, 2006; Iyer et al., 2012; Janoff-Bulman & Carnes, 2016; Swedlow & Wyckoff, 2009; Yilmaz, Saribay, et al., 2020). When presented with a single-item question, these respondents typically identify as conservative (Feldman & Johnston, 2014). This poses a significant challenge, particularly in examining the relationship between ideology and cognitive style. Although conservatives and libertarians may share similar economic attitudes, both groups often align themselves more with conservative options on the single-item question. Interestingly, the reflective abilities of libertarians surpass those of both liberals and conservatives (Iyer et al., 2012; Yilmaz, Saribay, et al., 2020). The tendency of studies using the single-item question to not adequately identify self-identified libertarians, or to not control for them in the analysis, has led to mixed findings (Yilmaz, Saribay, et al., 2020). As a result, subsequent studies have sought to analyze the relationship between social and economic attitudes and reflectiveness separately to achieve a more nuanced understanding.

In a meta-analysis, Jost, Sterling, and Stern (2017) found a negative correlation between social conservatism and reflective thinking. Intriguingly, they observed only a weak correlation with economic conservatism. This suggests that there are nuances within the association between cognitive style and ideology. This pattern suggests that opposition to concepts like euthanasia or capital punishment—social issues—have more intuitive roots than economic opinions, such as support for neoliberal policies. Even when factors like intelligence or religiosity are controlled for, these observations remain consistent (Saribay & Yilmaz, 2017).

Furthermore, the results are similar when alternative measures of reflective thinking replace Frederick's original CRT questions (Yilmaz & Saribay, 2017d). In a study testing the robustness of those associations, we hypothesized that the instrument employed to gauge reflective thinking disposition might act as a moderating variable. Notably, the CRT, which we initially introduced in Chapter 2, is composed of three mathematical questions (e.g., "If it takes 5 minutes for 5 machines to make 5 widgets, how long will it take 100 machines to make 100 widgets?"), is the predominant tool in this field. While reflective thinkers tend to suppress the intuitive (yet incorrect) answer with cognitive effort, we posited that the relationship between reflective thinking and conservatism might be influenced by the specific tool used to measure analytical propensity (Yilmaz & Saribay, 2017d). Consequently, the CRT did not correlate with any ideology metrics. However, other reflective thinking assessments consistently showed a negative correlation with social conservatism. This sheds light on why earlier studies using the CRT might have reported no significant link between reflective thinking and conservatism. More importantly, social conservatism was found to be significantly negatively associated with the overall reflectiveness score, which was derived from combining three different reflection measures (standard CRT, verbal version of CRT, also known as CRT-2, and base-rate conflict problems that we illustrated in the beginning of the chapter with the Linda problem), whereas the relationship with economic attitudes was not significant.

Expanding on our own work, we probed another potential moderator: motivations underlying political ideologies (Yilmaz & Saribay, 2018a). Jost et al. (2003), in a comprehensive meta-analysis combining findings from the existing literature, discovered that ideologies roughly correspond to two basic motivations. This approach, known as "Conservatism as Motivated Social Cognition," suggests that ideological orientations are primarily determined by motivational differences, consisting of epistemic and existential needs. The term "epistemic" pertains to the need to manage uncertainty, while "existential" refers to the need to manage threat perception (Jost et al., 2003, 2007; Jost & Amodio, 2012). Epistemic needs align with cognitive-motivational variables such as tolerance for uncertainty, openness to experience, and the need for cognitive closure. Conversely, existential needs relate to variables like fear of death, terrorism, and system instability.

Jost et al. (2007) demonstrated that epistemic needs influence political orientations through resistance to change, and existential needs through opposition to equality. Essentially, the primary motivations driving people toward conservative ideologies are their need for order to cope with uncertainty and their preference for stability. The latter need aligns with a preference for maintaining hierarchical systems as opposed to equality. In our study, we focused on determining which of these two types of motivations—epistemic or existential—is more closely related to reflectiveness.

We hypothesized that only one facet of conservatism, as outlined by Jost et al. (2003)—resistance to change (preference for stability)—correlates with diminished reflective cognitive styles, whereas another facet—opposition to equality (preference for hierarchy)— does not (Yilmaz & Saribay, 2018a). Our findings, based on three Turkish samples, supported our premise. When we incorporated an alternative reflective thinking metric alongside the CRT, the outcomes persisted. This indicates that the resistance to change aspect of conservatism consistently correlates with reflective thinking across various measures.

The nature of ideologies, which varies from culture to culture (Malka et al., 2014), and the context-specific content of sociopolitical attitudes (e.g., capital punishment, stem cell therapy) suggest that studying the cross-cultural stability of the relationship between ideology and reflectivity using the motivations defined by Jost et al. (2003) would be more effective as Jost et al. argue that the motivations behind ideologies have a culture-free nature. For instance, while there are many scales developed to measure social and economic attitudes (e.g., Everett, 2013), the items on these scales are both culturally influenced and shaped by the current debates within that culture. However, these scales, mostly based on debates in the U.S. and reflecting the more stable political identities there, may not be suitable for other cultures.

In contexts like Türkiye, where political climates can rapidly change, we observed that the items we developed in our political ideology measures exhibited low stability over the years. This instability makes it challenging to use standardized measures of political attitudes, especially in non-WEIRD contexts where political identities are fluid. The relevance of economic political attitudes outside the U.S. also remains uncertain (Malka et al., 2014). In our studies in Türkiye, for example, we found that a scale measuring economic attitudes, inspired by U.S. examples, showed very low inter-item consistency and thus was not included in the analysis (Yilmaz & Saribay, 2017b).

The motivations defined by Jost et al.'s (2003) conservatism as motivated social cognition account correlate with the underlying drives behind social and economic attitudes. A preference for stability aligns with the motivational elements underpinning social attitudes, whereas a preference for hierarchy aligns with those leading to economic attitudes. Developing a tool to measure these motivations cross-culturally is essential for testing their stability, but currently, no such universally applicable tool exists in the literature.

While there is currently no tool to measure these motivations cross-culturally, recent debates have suggested that the different moral intuitions defined in Moral Foundations Theory (Haidt, 2007) may actually be a product of the motivated cognition account (Hatemi et al., 2019). This theory posits that the content of morality is based on at least five different evolved moral intuitions. The first two of these, fairness and care (avoiding harm), correspond to individualizing foundations, while the other three—loyalty, authority, and sanctity—constitute binding foundations (see Chapter 7 for further discussion).[1] However, recent findings have faced criticism that these moral foundations simply repackage differences defined in political ideology (Federico et al., 2013; Jost, 2012; Kugler et al., 2014; Milojev et al., 2014; Sinn & Hayes, 2017). While subsequent studies indicate that moral intuitions cannot be directly reduced to political differences (Yilmaz & Saribay, 2018b), other studies have argued that binding foundations, defined in Moral Foundations Theory, correspond to epistemic and existential needs due to their uncertainty-reducing functions, with some empirical evidence supporting this view (Strupp-Levitsky et al., 2020). Additionally, the Moral Foundations Questionnaire (Graham et al., 2011a), designed to measure moral foundations, is a standardized instrument that has been translated into various languages for both WEIRD (e.g., Davies et al., 2014) and non-WEIRD cultures (e.g., Yilmaz, Harma, et al., 2016). This allows for the use of its binding subscale to examine the cross-cultural stability of the relationship between reflection and conservatism. This approach is particularly useful as it aligns with the motivations outlined by Jost et al. (2003), thereby providing a more comprehensive understanding of this relationship across different cultural contexts (Strupp-Levitsky et al., 2020).

Adopting this perspective, our group explored the cross-cultural relationship between reflection and binding foundations, aiming to harmonize divergent results in academic discourse (Yilmaz & Alper, 2019). A meta-analysis of data from over 7,000 individuals spanning 30 distinct cultures revealed a nuanced relationship. While a general negative association was observed between binding foundations—characterized by "nationalism," "support for hierarchies," and a "reverence for religious lifestyles"—and reflective thinking tendencies in line with the past literature (Jost et al., 2017), this relationship manifested more robustly in WEIRD contexts, such as the U.S., and less so in non-WEIRD contexts, exemplified by Türkiye. This underscores an essential observation: the majority of these studies draw predominantly from WEIRD populations, and the association between ideology and cognitive style appears more pronounced within these cohorts!

Another noteworthy aspect that we introduced at the beginning of this chapter is that many of these studies overlook the libertarians, a group that differentiates itself from both liberals and conservatives through certain characteristics. Iyer et al. (2012) highlighted that libertarians as a unique political group in the U.S. lean toward socially liberal values while simultaneously endorsing economically conservative stances. Intriguingly, libertarians consistently demonstrate higher scores in reflective thinking disposition compared to both liberals and conservatives. Yet, when resorting to the frequently used single-item political ideology scale, ranging from 1 (liberal) to 7 (conservative), libertarians often identify more conservatively (Feldman & Johnston, 2014). This presents potential challenges for studies exploring the relationship between economic conservatism and reflection in the U.S. context. The difficulty arises because some individuals who score higher in economic conservatism may not actually adhere to conservative ideologies; instead, they are libertarians (Boaz & Kirby, 2006; Iyer et al., 2012; Janoff-Bulman & Carnes, 2016; Swedlow & Wyckoff, 2009; Yilmaz, Saribay, et al., 2020). This distinction is important as it influences the interpretation of findings related to cognitive style and political beliefs.

More importantly, while libertarians are typically recognized as a U.S.-specific political group, similar groups with analogous characteristics may exist in different countries, albeit under different names. For example, while liberal means left-wing in the U.S. context, in Türkiye, the distinction between left and right is more pronounced, and even a single-item left-right scale demonstrates significant explanatory power (Saribay & Yilmaz, 2018; Sarıbay et al., 2017; Yılmaz et al., 2016). However, in Türkiye, self-identified liberals align more closely with the characteristics attributed to libertarians in the U.S. On a 1–7 left-right scale, Turkish liberals, akin to social democrats (left of center), score lower than social democrats on a single-item religiosity measure related to binding foundations (Yılmaz et al., 2016). This suggests that the issue observed in the U.S. context, where different groups with distinct names may create confounding effects similar to those caused by libertarians, could also be relevant in other cultural contexts. Therefore, when examining the relationship between ideology and cognitive style, it is important to consider this potential confounding factor, not only in the U.S. but also in a cross-cultural context.

Recapping the foregoing discussions, the relationship between economic conservatism and cognitive style has produced mixed results: some findings indicate a significant negative correlation between reflection and economic conservatism (e.g., Jost et al., 2017), others suggest no significant correlation (e.g., Yilmaz & Saribay, 2017d), while a few even hint toward a slightly positive correlation (Deppe et al., 2015). A plausible explanation for such variation across studies might stem from the proportion of libertarians within the samples. Given that libertarians tend to score higher in reflective thinking, a higher libertarian representation might nudge the correlation to appear more positive. In an extensive study by our group (Yilmaz, Saribay, et al., 2020) involving 8,648 participants, findings indicated a positive correlation between reflective thinking and economic conservatism when libertarians were part of the sample. However, once libertarians were omitted, the correlation's strength dwindled, close to zero. This supports the initial conjecture, highlighting the complexity libertarians introduce, especially when a single-item political orientation scale is employed, causing them to skew conservative. The possibility that political groups similar to libertarians exist in non-WEIRD cultures, potentially leading to variations in reflection scores that could distort the relationship between political orientation and cognitive style, is an important consideration. This factor should be carefully accounted for in future cross-cultural studies to ensure a more accurate understanding of the interplay between ideology and reflectivity across different cultural contexts.

Yet, despite these intricacies and boundary conditions, it is apparent that some facets of conservatism, like a preference for stability, correlate with a more intuitive thinking style. It is crucial to understand that these conclusions are based on correlation, not causation. In correlational research, whether one variable directly influences the other remains ambiguous. Alternatively, an unmeasured third variable might be driving the observed relationships between the two primary variables, as for libertarians discussed above. That is why it is necessary to look at the experimental findings to infer causality.

Causality

Eidelman et al.'s (2012) study was pivotal in probing the direct causal link between cognitive style and ideology. Their research hinted that low-effort thinking may propel political conservatism. More specifically, when individuals were primed toward intuitive thinking, they displayed a more pronounced inclination toward right-wing ideologies. Despite its groundbreaking nature, the study had glaring limitations:

- The sample sizes were very small (total N for each study ranged from 34 to 38), making it challenging to infer significant results from such small groups.
- Political orientations of participants were not controlled. Even though the priming was randomly applied, with such limited sample sizes, randomization may not eliminate important differences between the groups.
- The research did not distinguish between social and economic political attitudes in their outcome measures.
- Conservatism and liberalism were treated as distinct scores, rather than opposite ends of a continuum, which may affect the results.

Challenging Eidelman et al.'s (2012) findings, we could not replicate the study, despite having a sample size more than twice as large (Yilmaz & Saribay, 2016).[2] However, small sample-size studies by Zitek and Tiedens (2012) and Van Berke et al. (2015) supported Eidelman et al.'s claims. Their findings underscored that right-wingers' hierarchical sensitivities are more intuitive, while left-wingers' equalitarian tendencies require more cognitive effort. While studies demonstrating an effect primarily utilized WEIRD samples, and those with failed replications often employed non-WEIRD samples, the identification of significant effects of cognitive style manipulations in similar non-WEIRD samples, as shown by Yilmaz and Saribay (2017a, 2017b), indicates that cultural differences alone may not be sufficient to explain the observed disparities. That is, factors beyond mere cultural differences might influence the impact of cognitive style manipulations on research outcomes. Hence, to achieve a thorough understanding of the causal influence of cognitive styles on political attitudes, it is essential to consider a range of elements, including methodological approaches and contextual factors.

Addressing these inconsistencies, Talhelm et al. (2015) proposed that mindset manipulations might only affect opinions under active processing (e.g., contextualized opinions) but not entrenched (e.g., stable) beliefs. Among cultural orientations, increasing analytical thinking led to greater liberalism on social issues (compared to economic issues). In contrast, increasing holism was linked to greater conservatism, but only in contextualized opinions expressed through newspaper reports, not in stable opinions measured by standard scale items (Talhelm, 2018; Talhelm et al., 2015). We proposed a similar link between cognitive style and political inclinations (Yilmaz & Saribay, 2016). Two experiments (Yilmaz & Saribay, 2017b) reinforced the idea that brief analytic thinking exercises induced more liberal views in contextualized opinions but not in stable ones. In this methodology, participants do not receive standard measures of political ideology as outcome measures, unlike in the study by Eidelman et al. (2012). The rationale is that the attitudes measured by items on such scales are based on relatively stable views formed over time, and these measures are likely to be resistant to experimental manipulations. However, in the case of contextualized opinions, participants are presented with semi-fabricated news articles addressing a policy issue (e.g., gay marriage) in a format commonly encountered in daily life, such as a newspaper article. Within this article, participants read contrasting opinions on the issue, and then form their own stance. The findings indicate that participants who received analytical training did not alter their long-standing political opinions. However, they were more inclined to adopt liberal positions when it came to contextualized opinions. This approach highlights the potential influence of analytical thinking on more flexible, context-based opinions, as opposed to deeply entrenched political beliefs.

Regardless of this clarification, the use of experimental manipulations to stimulate reflective thinking remains unsettled due to the ineffectiveness of existing techniques for experimentally activating reflection. Various techniques have been tried, but their purported effects have all been met with partial or complete failure to replicate. Deppe et al. (2015) attempted to test changes in stable political opinions using methods such as the scrambled sentence task and visual prime to activate reflection, but these methods were not successful in effectively activating reflection. As outlined in Chapter 3, the visual prime technique involved showing participants Rodin's "The Thinker" or a neutral photograph (Discobolus of Myron) with the assumption that observing "The Thinker" would activate reflective thinking. However, this method was ineffective in Deppe et al.'s study. The findings of Gervais and Norenzayan (2012), who originally used this method, were also not replicated in later high-powered experiments (Sanchez et al., 2017).

In the scrambled sentence task, participants construct meaningful sentences from a set of words, some of which are intended to trigger reflective thinking (e.g., ponder, analyze, reason). Despite initial assumptions, recent studies have indicated that this task is generally ineffective in activating reflection (Deppe et al., 2015; Većkalov et al., 2024). Other methods from the literature, aside from reflection training, have also been found ineffective in recent high-powered replication studies (Isler & Yilmaz, 2023). Therefore, the results of studies using these now-determined ineffective methods should be approached with skepticism. It is suggested that future replications should utilize reflection training methods like debiasing training (Isler et al., 2020), which can be easily adapted for online environments.

In summary, while the relationship between cognitive style and political ideology is a topic of interest, there are significant challenges encountered in experimentally manipulating cognitive style and achieving consistent findings. The literature reveals that eliciting reflective thinking experimentally remains a predominant issue (Isler & Yilmaz, 2023).

Coda

The prevailing issues make it challenging to definitively ascertain whether reflective thinking causally impacts the outcome measure, namely political ideology, as also discussed in Chapter 5 in the domain of epistemically suspect beliefs. However, a synthesis of the existing evidence hints at the possibility that traits associated with conservatism, such as a preference for stability, might be influenced in part by intuitive thinking. These conclusions are tentative, and further empirical studies, particularly those involving cross-cultural comparisons, are essential to determine the causal links between reflective cognitive style and conservatism. But the intricate connection between cognitive styles and political views, as summarized above, raises an intriguing question: Why might right-wingers lean toward relatively more intuitive thinking, while left-wingers seem relatively more reflective?

The underlying motivations of right-wingers and left-wingers differ. If we assume that everyone's primary objective is to satisfy their motivations as fast and efficiently as possible, the difference in the degree of reflectivity may lie in its usefulness in achieving this objective. For individuals who view conventions as inviolable rules that are to be internalized and adhered to without contemplation, there's no impetus to ponder alternatives; their course is set by the societal norms they have embraced. In contrast, for those intent on societal transformation—even if it necessitates revolutionary measures— the challenge lies in critically assessing and determining alternatives to the current system. Corroborating this, we carried out a series of studies (Yilmaz & Saribay, 2018a) showing that, between the two core tenets of right-wing ideology—defending traditions and endorsing hierarchies—it was primarily the defense of traditions that correlated with intuitive thinking. This facet alone accounted for a significant proportion of the statistical variance between right-leaning ideologies and intuitive thought processes.

The findings outlined in this section indicate a relationship between social (as opposed to economic) conservative attitudes and reflective thinking. Notably, this relationship appears more pronounced in WEIRD cultures than in non-WEIRD ones. The need for additional research on this topic is clear. First and foremost, the universality of the link between social conservatism and reflective thinking should be explored through cross-cultural studies using probabilistically representative samples. Additionally, the cross-cultural reliability of the aforementioned experimental results warrants further testing. Multi-lab experiments employing rigorous manipulation techniques should be carried out to ascertain the robustness of these findings. The advent of multi-lab replication studies in recent times promises to offer more definitive insights on this matter in the near future.

In synthesizing the prevailing evidence, it appears that there might be a foundational distinction in the cognitive styles of right-wingers and left-wingers, influencing their worldview. The observation that these divergent worldviews can even affect their performance on a mathematical problem suggests that the distinctions in cognitive styles could reflect deeper differences inherent to human nature. As we continue to uncover new insights in this rapidly evolving and fruitful domain, we inch closer to elucidating one of the age-old perennial questions of human cognition.

In this chapter, we have explored the role of cognitive style in forming and maintaining political identity. However, it is important to recognize that these cognitive style traits also shape political ideologies in conjunction with other personality traits and cultural orientations. For instance, reflective thinking can lead to cognitive decoupling, which corresponds to attitude change, as demonstrated in our examples. However, reflection can also manifest as motivated reasoning, serving to justify existing attitudes rather than changing them (see Chapters 4 and 9). Moreover, findings suggest that actively open-minded thinking (AOT), which is defined as the willingness to revise existing beliefs when presented with new evidence, is a component of reflection that supports cognitive decoupling (Baron, 2019; Baron et al., 2023). People with high AOT tend to evaluate opposing views more objectively and are more open to changing their attitudes. Consequently, AOT might be more effective in explaining political differences than standard measures of reflectiveness (Baron, 2019). There is also evidence of a stronger correlation between AOT and ideological measures compared to standard reflection measures (Yilmaz & Saribay, 2017d), further supporting the potential of AOT in better explaining political differences than standard reflection measures. However, the literature to date has not comprehensively established when and by whom these different motivations of reflection are utilized and their frequency (Pennycook, 2023).

Moreover, although holistic (vs. analytic) cultural orientation increases conservatism on social issues (Talhelm, 2018; Talhelm et al., 2015) and reflective (vs. intuitive) thinking decreases it, we lack data on what a combination of these two would look like and how it would affect political attitudes. In other words, we do not have clear information on how political attitudes would change if we considered the tendency to think in an effortful and detailed way alongside the tendency to think holistically and systemically. To us, it seems possible that adopting a more holistic thinking style along with strong reflectiveness, may enable individuals to place their momentary goals and actions in a broader context and clarify how they are connected to overarching motivations and life goals. It could also help them see their political existence as an element that is part of a bigger system (e.g., neighborhood, some institution, city, or even the entire society and humanity). Especially combined with a healthy sense of morality and a cooperative orientation, this could maximize the potential of reflection and free human thought from the trap of motivated reasoning.

Notes

1 According to the moral foundations theory, care and fairness are categorized as individualizing foundations due to their focus on individual rights, while loyalty, authority, and sanctity are termed binding foundations, reflecting their role in fostering group cooperation (but see Janoff-Bulman & Carnes, 2013; Sinn & Hayes, 2017, for alternative perspectives).

2 We later made a conceptual replication attempt with over 1000 participants but still could not confirm Eidelman et al.'s conclusions (Yilmaz & Saribay, 2017c).

7

MORALITY AND COOPERATION

Have you ever wondered about the basis upon which individuals who choose to oppose or support stem cell therapy or euthanasia formulate their positions? Do conflicts about these issues primarily stem from politically driven preferences forged through a process of rational deliberation, or are they rooted in clashes of intuitively acquired fundamental moral principles? Are people intuitively selfish or cooperative? Do they instinctively cooperate exclusively within their in-group? Can the realization of a universal moral framework be achieved solely through the application of reflective thought processes? This chapter attempts to demonstrate how individuals' intuitive cognitive mechanisms lead them to embrace specific moral principles and behaviors in distinct circumstances, while also exploring the potential of diverse cognitive processes in mitigating the polarization and in-group bias that often characterizes political disagreements.

The first theoretical framework to address these questions is Moral Foundations Theory (MFT) (Haidt, 2007; Haidt et al., 2009), which we initially introduced in the previous chapter. By framing morality in terms of intuitions, MFT challenges earlier monistic moral paradigms articulated in terms of reasoning and notions of care and fairness (e.g., Kohlberg, 1969). MFT posits that the human species has evolutionarily acquired not just these two foundations, but at least three other distinct moral foundations. These five foundations encompass, first, the *care* dimension, reflecting the instinct to protect and nurture offspring or those in vulnerable positions; second, *fairness*, which pertains to the moral dimension that emerges as individuals coexist within groups, striving to identify and deter those who engage in deceit and disrupt group cohesion, including a sensitivity to justice; third, *loyalty*, emphasizing the significance of exhibiting loyalty to one's

DOI: 10.4324/9781003300366-9

own group and refraining from acts of betrayal; fourth, *authority,* which centers on preserving social order by upholding respect for authority figures within a hierarchical structure; and finally, *purity*, which pertains to a moral dimension associated with both physical and spiritual purity, emphasizing the veneration of sanctity while restraining worldly desires (see also Atari et al., 2023, for a refinement in the theory).

While liberal (e.g., politically left-leaning) individuals have been found to predominantly emphasize the care and fairness dimensions as moral imperatives, conservative (e.g., right-leaning) individuals accord relatively equal importance to all five dimensions (Graham et al., 2011). Graham, Haidt, and Nosek (2009) contend that care and fairness represent *individualizing* foundations that pertain to the needs and rights of individuals, while the remaining three moral principles constitute *binding* foundations that serve to strengthen group cohesion and suppress tendencies toward selfishness within the group. In essence, conservatives' perception of cooperation aligns more closely with the theme of binding foundations, whereas that of left-leaning individuals gravitates toward the domain of individualizing foundations, shaping the contours of cooperative social relations through aspects such as equality and care.

Core Moral Convictions

Moral psychology has evolved significantly from the era of Kohlberg's (1971, 1981) dominant paradigm, which emphasized care and equality as primary moral intuitions, suggesting a hierarchical moral understanding. Later research, particularly from non-WEIRD (Western, Educated, Industrialized, Rich, and Democratic) cultures, challenged this view, highlighting cultural differences in moral priorities due to varied environmental pressures. Shweder et al.'s (1997) cultural approach, utilizing discourse analysis, proposed that non-Western cultures might prioritize moral foundations beyond care and fairness. Binding foundations, such as loyalty, authority, and sanctity, gained prominence in areas with increased threats, fostering in-group cooperation (Di Santo et al., 2022; Gelfand et al., 2017). In contrast, the Western emphasis on enlightenment and secular institutions led to a focus on universalistic values of care and fairness. Amidst these debates, MFT emerged, critiquing Kohlberg's hierarchical model and proposing five normatively equal foundations. This theory provides a more inclusive framework, accommodating the diversity of moral reasoning across cultures.

The theory not only addresses cultural differences but also offers insights into variation across individuals and subgroups within the same culture. It suggests that these individual differences are the fundamental moral divisions that drive culture wars and political polarization. According to this framework, the specific moral foundations that individuals emphasize significantly influence their political viewpoints, contributing to the profound ideological polarization seen in many societies, particularly in highly polarized nations like the U.S. (Haidt, 2012). The question of which moral foundations hold greater primacy stands as one of the most contentious debates within this theory.

Haidt and Kesebir (2010) contend that all individuals, by virtue of evolution, possess all five distinct moral dimensions outlined, and the disparity between liberals and conservatives can be attributed to the influence of the Enlightenment era. This historical period is posited to have defined morality in a manner that aligns with the liberal perspective, consequently downplaying the significance of binding foundations. Substantiating this viewpoint is the reactive liberal hypothesis (Nail et al., 2009) that we discussed in Chapter 4. According to this hypothesis, the primacy of care and fairness foundations for liberals depends on reflective processes, and when they are faced with threats or cognitive burdens that reduce their ability to reflect, they exhibit behavioral patterns akin to those of conservatives. For example, under a cognitive load, liberals tend to ascribe personal responsibility to victims similar to the attributions of conservatives (Skitka et al., 2002). Essentially, under conditions of limited capacity for intensive cognitive processing, liberals' attributions appear to converge with those typically made by conservatives.

Moreover, a study conducted by Van de Vyver et al. (2016) investigated moral foundations and prejudice using two distinct representative samples, one conducted six weeks before and another 1 month after the 2005 London suicide bombing incident. Their findings indicated a general increase in the importance accorded to loyalty foundations and a concurrent decrease in the emphasis on fairness. Notably, this shift was more pronounced among liberals than conservatives. It is this alteration in moral foundations that elucidates the growing prejudice among liberals towards Muslims and immigrants in recent times. Given that terrorist attacks, such as 9/11, are known to elicit effects akin to mortality salience (e.g., Landau et al., 2004), and mortality salience shares similarities with the impact of cognitive load (Trémolière et al., 2012, 2014; Yilmaz & Bahçekapili, 2018), it may be inferred that terrorist attacks induce a shift in moral foundations by inducing individuals into an intuitive mindset.

Conversely, Graham (2010), utilizing implicit measurement methods, demonstrated that liberals exhibit a more pronounced disparity between their explicit moral foundations and their implicit moral foundations as compared to conservatives. This observation lends support to the argument that liberals may also indeed possess binding foundations as everyone but consciously suppress them by expending cognitive effort when articulating them at the explicit level. Indeed, the theory posits that everyone possesses these five moral foundations due to evolutionary adaptations, but individuals may prioritize them differently depending on the situation. For instance, if loyalty is more valued than fairness, one might choose to help a close friend by sharing answers during a test. However, this act can compromise the fairness norm for other students who do not cheat, potentially leading to an unfair academic advantage for the friend. Such dilemmas highlight the varying priorities people place on individualizing versus binding foundations. Similarly, moral priorities can shift with changing environmental conditions and social norms. While harming another human is generally considered morally wrong, in the context of war, such actions become normalized. This illustrates how moral intuitions adapt to different circumstances

The opposing viewpoint to this perspective is presented by Jost et al. (2003), in the framework of conservatism as motivated social cognition. According to this model, while every individual possesses the fundamental moral dimensions of care and fairness as a baseline, conservatives amplify the importance of binding foundations by investing additional cognitive resources. This heightened focus on binding foundations is believed to arise from conservatives' "resistance to change" and "opposition to equality" motivations, as well as their inclination to utilize binding foundations as a coping mechanism in response to uncertainty and existential threats (see also Jost, 2012). Consequently, following this viewpoint, it is anticipated that when their cognitive processing capacity is compromised, conservatives will reduce their emphasis on binding foundations, making them more similar to liberals. This position contrasts with the predictions of the reactive liberal hypothesis, which suggests that threats or reliance on intuition in decision-making will make liberals more like conservatives.

In a thorough investigation designed to directly compare these two theoretical approaches, Wright and Baril (2011) explored whether subjecting liberals and conservatives to cognitive load or depleting their cognitive resources (in comparison to a control group) would induce changes in their moral foundations. Surprisingly, the study did not yield any significant main effects. However, when the data from both experimental groups were combined, a noteworthy finding emerged: conservative participants in the cognitively distracted group (comprising the load and ego depletion conditions) displayed a decrease in the significance they attributed to binding foundations. This result lends support to Jost's (2012) argument that conservatives emphasize the role of binding foundations, suggesting that the core moral principles valued by individuals at baseline are care and fairness. It is important to note that while Wright and Baril's findings are insightful, they are based on a single experiment and may lack robust statistical power. Additionally, in contrast to these results, another study reported a significant increase (i.e., a main effect) in the importance assigned to the care and authority dimensions by participants under cognitive load (Van Berkel et al., 2015). Furthermore, in another study that we employed using Turkish participants, reflective thinking activation instead of cognitive load demonstrated a significant increase in the importance attributed to the dimensions of care and fairness, which contradicts Wright and Baril's findings, and displayed no interaction with political orientation (Yilmaz & Saribay, 2017a). This adds complexity to the debate and underscores the presence of mixed findings. One limitation of Wright and Baril's study lies in the amalgamation of two distinct experimental conditions (load and ego depletion), making it unclear whether differences exist between the individual experimental conditions and the control group. Consequently, a more comprehensive understanding of the matter is warranted.

Furthermore, there is an ongoing debate in the literature regarding the susceptibility of scale items, which are used to measure moral foundations, to experimental manipulations (Deppe et al., 2015; Talhelm, 2018; Yilmaz & Saribay, 2017b). Deppe et al. reported that some moral attitude items displayed no alterations even after undergoing an analytic thinking manipulation, despite the absence of a direct measurement of moral foundations. Our group (Yilmaz & Saribay, 2017b) adopted a similar experimental design but distinguished the dependent variable into two categories: contextual and stable attitudes. Through two separate experiments, it was revealed that liberal attitudes shifted in certain contextual scenarios following analytic thinking training (e.g., care and fairness); however, no discernible change was observed in the scale items. In essence, the reflective thinking manipulation did not impact scale items representing individuals' relatively stable opinions but did induce changes in contextualized and novel narratives presented as newspaper articles (similar effects can be found in Talhelm, 2018; and Talhelm et al., 2015). Given the extensive use of the moral foundations questionnaire in research, especially in online platforms like Amazon Mechanical Turk and Western university samples, it is possible that these scale items have become entrenched attitudes for participants, rendering them resistant to experimental manipulations. In other words, participants from WEIRD college or online samples, who might repeatedly encounter these statements, could develop standard responses, potentially obscuring the effects of experimental manipulations. In light of these considerations, Clifford et al. (2015) introduced moral foundations vignettes that offered a more contextual and novel approach, in addition to the standard moral foundations questionnaire.

To address these limitations comprehensively, our research group conducted a conceptual replication of Wright and Baril's (2011) study as a registered report,[1] employing a high-powered and pre-registered experimental design (Isler, Yilmaz, & Doğruyol, 2021). To enhance individuals' inclination towards intuitive thinking, we employed a time-pressure manipulation, a technique widely recognized in the literature for its effectiveness. However, it is noteworthy that this intuitive thinking manipulation yielded no discernible effects on the endorsement of different moral foundations. Furthermore, the use of moral foundations vignettes instead of the standard moral foundations questionnaire, as developed by Clifford et al. (2015), failed to yield significant effects. These outcomes further accentuate the complexity surrounding the ongoing debate concerning the malleability of moral foundations. In light of these challenges and the diverse findings in the literature, it is evident that future research endeavors are warranted to achieve a conclusive resolution to this pressing issue.

Intention-Behavior Gap

A major challenge in this domain, particularly within social psychology, is the prevalent use of hypothetical scenarios or intention/attitude scale items when investigating the precursors and consequences of moral judgments. Yet, behavioral economics literature frequently demonstrates significant disparities between individuals' actual moral conduct and their professed moral intentions (Bostyn et al., 2019; Sheeran & Webb, 2016). In empirical research, it is often challenging to directly assess all the distinct moral foundations or those proposed in alternative theories like morality as cooperation theory (Curry, 2016) through behavioral measures. Nevertheless, these theoretical models share a common theme, emphasizing that valuing these moral principles promotes cooperation (Curry, 2016; Graham & Haidt, 2010). Consequently, the field of behavioral economics has amassed a substantial body of empirical work exploring the cognitive underpinnings of cooperative behavior. This is achieved through the utilization of specific tasks designed to gauge cooperation via real-life actions.

Cooperation is crucial for societal success (Rand & Nowak, 2013) with humans naturally equipped with cognitive mechanisms that predispose them toward cooperative behavior (Rand, 2016). In extensive societies, cooperation with anonymous individuals yields public benefits and enhances social well-being, particularly during pandemics or societal crises. Fundamentally, policies fostering cooperation hold profound significance for societal functioning. Despite humans being characterized as a cooperative and ultrasocial species (Bowles & Gintis, 2011; Tomasello, 2016), the sustainability of this large-scale cooperative success remains uncertain. This uncertainty largely stems from the fact that most individuals cooperate based on the expectation that others will reciprocate their cooperation (Fehr et al., 2002; Fischbacher et al., 2001; Hermes et al., 2020; Isler, Gächter, et al., 2021; Isler, Yilmaz, & Maule, 2021). Furthermore, this cooperative capacity undergoes daily testing from new environmental and social challenges, including pandemics, climate change, and mass migration. While our intuitive system readily responds to evolutionarily familiar threats such as food scarcity, a condition reflective of the environments in which humans evolved as described in the concept of the

Environment of Evolutionary Adaptedness (Bowlby, 1969; Foley, 1995), it often struggles with evolutionarily novel, global-scale challenges like mass migration. In these situations, an increased reliance on reflective thought processes becomes crucial for effectively responding to such threats.

In addition, the decision to cooperate or not presents a social dilemma for individuals. This dilemma arises because cooperation, while enhancing overall gains, often incurs personal costs for the cooperating individual. Consider, for instance, the widespread adoption of mask-wearing in society to combat the coronavirus disease 2019 (COVID-19) pandemic, which effectively reduces virus transmission rates (Mitze et al., 2020). While such behaviors are conducive to cooperation and collective welfare, they can entail a net personal cost in terms of time, money, and effort, especially for individuals not at high risk for COVID-19. Another example is the rush of individuals to markets just before curfews, where they purchase more goods than necessary, negatively impacting cooperation by making essential products less affordable for those in need. Similarly, imagine a scenario on a water-scarce summer day, where some individuals squander water needlessly instead of collectively conserving it. These examples highlight the inherent social dilemmas that cooperative behavior presents in everyday life, also known as the *tragedy of the commons* (Hardin, 1968).

The aforementioned instances of cooperation challenges in daily life are systematically studied in behavioral economics through economic games. For instance, consider a scenario in which you can transfer any portion of the $100 in your possession to a stranger you will never meet again, with the amount you transfer being doubled before reaching the other party. If you opt to transfer $50, you retain $50, while the recipient receives $100, thereby increasing the total welfare from an initial $100 to $150 due to your action. In such experimental settings, the more money you choose to transfer to the other party, the greater the enhancement of total social welfare, indicating a higher degree of cooperative behavior. In essence, participants in these games, labeled as "cooperators," opt to elevate overall welfare despite the potential personal cost. This delicate balance between social benefit and personal sacrifice presents a challenge in explaining the psychological underpinnings of cooperative behavior using conventional mechanisms.

Evolution of Cooperation

Cooperation stands as a crucial element of adaptive significance across various species, augmenting the odds of successful hunting and resource acquisition through the formation of coalitions. Although different species rely on varied evolutionary mechanisms, in humans, engaging in cooperative behaviors is critically important for survival. This is because the resources obtained through cooperation are often exclusive to contributors, making cooperation an evolutionarily stable strategy. Moreover, the emergence of intuitive cognitive mechanisms, such as language and moral cognition, is believed to be linked to their role in bolstering cooperation (Curry, 2016; Salahshour, 2020).

In the realm of social beings, humans exhibit a remarkable capacity for cooperation, extending their sociability to genetically similar as well as dissimilar individuals. This spectrum of sociability encompasses interactions with relatives, friends, and even transient encounters with anonymous individuals. The vast scale of human sociality sets it apart as a distinctive feature, distinguishing it from the social behaviors observed in other mammalian species (Tomasello, 2016).

Examining the development of cooperation over the history of the human species, the initial forms of altruistic intuitions manifest within mother–child interactions. In essence, mutual altruism arises facilitated by hormones such as oxytocin, serving the purpose of nurturing offspring and fostering both physical and emotional attachments. Subsequently, this altruistic behavior extends to close relatives (Hamilton, 1964). The fundamental logic underpinning this extension is the understanding that aiding relatives constitutes an indirect investment in one's own genetic legacy, given the shared genetic material with kin, determined by the degree of relatedness.

Human sociality also transcends the bounds of kinship relations. Humans engage in cooperative interactions with genetically dissimilar individuals, even extending assistance at the risk of their own lives. The underlying evolutionary mechanism accounting for this phenomenon is the principle of reciprocity (Trivers, 1971). Reciprocity can manifest through direct or indirect means. In direct reciprocity, bonds of friendship are established, and individuals provide assistance with the expectation of receiving similar help in the future. Essentially, this expectation of mutual aid underpins the formation of friendships. In contrast, indirect reciprocity involves one person assisting another out of concern for their reputation. By helping another individual, the helper indirectly enhances their likelihood of receiving aid from others who witness their benevolent actions. For instance, assisting a beggar encountered on the street serves as an example of indirect reciprocity. This act of kindness is not directly tied to an expectation of reciprocation from the beggar; rather, it signals to others the possibility that, if needed, the helper can also receive help from other members of the group in the future. Consequently, this behavior elevates their reputation and increases the likelihood of receiving assistance when they encounter challenges in the future.

Cognitive Origins of Cooperation

While the nature of cooperative behavior in human societies has been extensively studied (Boyd & Richerson, 1989; Gintis, 2003; Gouldner, 1960;

Hamilton, 1964; Tomasello, 2016; Trivers, 1971), standard mechanisms fail to account for cooperative behaviors like those mentioned earlier—one-shot, anonymous, and devoid of reputational concerns.

To address this, the Social Heuristics Hypothesis (SHH) has been proposed as an alternative explanatory framework (Rand, 2016; Rand et al., 2012, 2014). According to this hypothesis, individuals develop intuitions aligned with cooperation through their social experiences, rendering them habitually predisposed to cooperate. This approach is grounded in the dual-process model of the mind (Evans & Stanovich, 2013a), which posits that the mind operates via two fundamental systems—intuitive and reflective. As elaborated in the preceding chapters, the dual-process model contends that intuitive cognitive processes strive to conserve energy, often resulting in swift, automatic responses. Social processes are similarly characterized by predominantly intuitive and automatized cognitive mechanisms.

The SHH specifically explores the relationship between intuitive thinking and social dilemmas, particularly cooperation, within the framework of the dual-process model. The SHH predicts that individuals tend to be more cooperative when thinking intuitively and more self-centered when engaging in reflective thinking in social dilemma situations (Rand, 2016; Rand et al., 2014). This is because reflective thinking highlights that cooperating in one-shot economic games may carry more personal costs than benefits. However, given the advantages of cooperation in daily life's repeated interactions, intuitions favoring cooperation tend to form, resulting in increased spontaneous cooperation. The initial experimental study supporting this intuitive cooperation account was conducted by Rand et al. (2012), who demonstrated that activating intuitive thinking (e.g., through time pressure) leads to heightened cooperative behavior. However, subsequently, large-scale studies raised doubts about the SHH due to methodological limitations, such as the exclusion of participants who did not comply with manipulation instructions (Bouwmeester et al., 2017; Tinghög et al., 2013; Verkoeijen & Bouwmeester, 2014). Conversely, some independent high-powered replication attempts supported the SHH (e.g., Isler et al., 2018). A meta-analysis of these findings showed a significant overall effect of intuitive cooperation (Rand, 2016). A recent meta-analysis highlighted the significance of the effect in certain specific scenarios, such as when an emotional prime was employed as the method for intuition manipulation. However, it also indicated a diminished effect size (Kvarven et al., 2020). Notably, the analysis revealed that when six individual experiments that utilized an emotional prime were omitted from the meta-analysis involving 88 experiments, there was a failure to demonstrate a significant effect of intuition.

Some studies suggest that the inherent human inclination toward cooperation may primarily be activated toward in-groups rather than out-groups. These studies, employing varying methodologies, have yielded mixed results regarding the interplay between "manipulation of intuition" and "group identity" (Dreu et al., 2015; Ma et al., 2015; Ten Velden et al., 2017). While some studies report a significant interaction, others do not (Artavia-Mora et al., 2018; Everett et al., 2017; Rand et al., 2015). Consequently, achieving a definitive consensus on this matter remains a challenge within the current literature.

Upon closer examination of these studies, methodological distinctions become apparent. Notably, studies reporting a significant interaction used manipulations other than time pressure, such as oxytocin induction or various other priming techniques. Conversely, studies that did not find a significant interaction consistently employed time pressure manipulation. However, these latter studies vary in crucial aspects. For example, Everett et al. (2017) defined group identity using artificial groups (Eagles or Rattlers), while Rand et al. (2015) employed the contrast between Barack Obama and Mitt Romney supporters in the 2012 American presidential elections. Artavia-Mora et al. (2018) aimed to create an out-group identity using a Muslim figure wearing a headscarf in a field study conducted in the Netherlands whereas Isler et al. (2021) used other natural groups (e.g., atheists and Christians) as the group identity. Nevertheless, it is important to acknowledge that these studies have methodological constraints when it comes to making generalized claims about intuitive cooperation such as not having enough statistical power to detect an interaction effect.

One other key issue is the duration of time pressure manipulation. Studies conducted in laboratory settings by Everett et al. (2017) and Rand et al. (2015) utilized a notably lengthy time pressure manipulation, which raises questions about its ability to activate intuition effectively. Myrseth and Wollbrant (2017) argue that time pressure manipulations in the range of 10–15 seconds may not genuinely activate intuition. Their argument centers on the belief that 10 seconds of time pressure affords participants minimal deliberation time, best described as "low deliberation," while intuitive decisions necessitate a maximum of 4 or 5 seconds of pressure. Consequently, prior studies employing 10-second manipulations may suffer from significant internal validity issues (i.e., they may activate low deliberation rather than intuition). The ongoing debates in the literature notwithstanding, a recent study conducted by our group with high statistical power demonstrated that both 10-second and 5-second time pressure manipulations significantly enhanced cognitive performance compared to a control condition (Isler & Yilmaz, 2023). Nevertheless, no unequivocal conclusions can be drawn based on the existing evidence.

Although the Self-Control Hypothesis (SCH) has been largely overlooked in the context of intuitive cooperation, it suggests that, under specific conditions such as when intense time pressure is used, reflective thinking can enhance cooperation (Capraro & Cococcioni, 2016; Martinsson et al., 2014). SCH posits that individuals' intuitive and emotional responses tend to be selfish, but with sufficient cognitive resources (i.e., reflective thinking), automatic selfish reactions can be overridden, leading to increased cooperation (Isler, Gächter, et al., 2021). Supporting this hypothesis, recent findings indicate that reliance on intuitive thinking, either induced by intense time pressure or in scenarios like the maintenance dilemma evoking scarcity (Gächter et al., 2022), tends to reduce cooperation (Capraro & Cococcioni, 2016; Isler, Gächter et al., 2021; Isler, Yilmaz, & Maule, 2021; see also Capraro, 2024).

In a recent pre-registered, high-powered experiment, our group directly tested the SHH and the SCH, with the results strongly supporting SCH (Isler, Yilmaz, & Maule, 2021). This study involved more than 2500 practicing Christians and atheists in the U.S., who participated in an online experiment centered around the one-shot continuous Prisoner's Dilemma game, a standard tool to measure cooperation. Participants engaged with their in-groups, out-groups, or anonymous participants. In this game, participants allocated actual money to the other party, with the transferred sum being doubled and equally divided, making higher transfers indicative of greater cooperation. Half of the participants were required to make decisions within a 10-second time constraint, accompanied by instructions that explicitly encouraged the use of intuition, thereby promoting intuitive thinking. The other half of the participants were allotted a minimum of 20 seconds for deliberation, along with instructions that specifically advocated for reflective thinking. The results yielded some evidence in favor of SCH, challenging the prevailing paradigm in the literature. Notably, our participants, particularly Christians, exhibited the capacity to resist selfish impulses and cooperate, regardless of their group membership, when afforded time for reflection. Importantly, this effect remained robust when considering participants who correctly understood the economic games' internal logic or those playing the game for the first time.

In summary, our findings provide substantial support for the model of intuitive selfishness and deliberated cooperation proposed by SCH. This main result was also replicated in another experiment using a similar cooperation game with a punishment option (e.g., Mieth et al., 2021).[2] These results suggest that reflection can mitigate cooperation challenges among members of different religious groups. This perspective offers a fresh lens through which to view the existing literature, implying that intuitive tendencies in fostering cooperation may not be as straightforward as previously assumed. Consequently, the literature on the impact of intuitive and reflective thinking on cooperation presents a complex and nuanced picture.

Recent efforts have culminated in the development of a more comprehensive model—the Contextualized Reciprocity Model (CRM)—aimed at reconciling discrepancies between SHH (e.g., intuitive cooperation) and SCH (reflective cooperation) (Isler, Gächter, et al., 2021; Isler, Yilmaz, & Maule, 2021;

Yilmaz & Isler, 2024). CRM posits that the influence of intuition and reflection on cooperative behavior hinges on a combination of contextual (e.g., dilemma types and situations) and individual factors (e.g., intuitions, preferences, and personality traits). According to CRM, SHH may hold true under certain conditions, just as the SCA may be applicable in others. For instance, in environments where scarcity prevails, people's intuitive responses, shaped by their social interactions, may lean towards selfishness. Conversely, in situations of resource abundance, intuition might foster cooperative behavior, reflecting the prosocial nature of everyday interpersonal interactions. It is also important to note that scarcity does not always lead to selfishness; individual beliefs, preferences, and motivations can influence how reflection is utilized in decision-making. The CRM framework seeks to comprehensively explain one-shot cooperation behavior, incorporating contextual and dispositional factors such as expected cooperation levels and individual preferences. Although there remains insufficient data in the literature to definitively resolve one of the oldest philosophical questions— whether humans are inherently inclined toward cooperation or selfishness— for now, the current state of the art allows some predictions. In specific situations, such as interactions with in-group members who share prosocial heuristics with expected cooperation, particularly during times of diverse threats (e.g., pandemic, war), intuitive thinking may heighten cooperative inclinations toward in-groups. Conversely, cooperation in certain situations, such as with out-group members in ambiguous environments, may necessitate the engagement of reflective thinking to suppress instinctual selfish reactions. In the context of a pandemic, when the local economy is severely impacted, it gives rise to an environment that is both uncertain and threatening. In such circumstances, our intuitive cognitive architecture may tend to exhibit in-group bias, emphasizing binding foundations, while downplaying the sensitivities related to care and fairness, which are traditionally associated with the endorsement of universal morality (Kohlberg, 1971; Pennycook, 2017). Consequently, our intuitions may discourage us from cooperating with unfamiliar individuals in such challenging environments, which in turn leads to the argument that engaging in reflective thought processes becomes a prerequisite for fostering cooperation in such harsh conditions (Isler, Yilmaz, & Maule, 2021). Therefore, it is essential for future research to systematically investigate these insights within the evolving landscape of this field of study.

This chapter provided a concise overview of scientific findings on core moral convictions and the cognitive processes influencing individuals' propensity to cooperate in one-shot, anonymous interactions. Although existing scientific evidence does not offer a definitive answer, it provides valuable directions for future research. Especially in anticipation of impending crises expected to impact our lives dramatically in the near future, such as pandemics or climate change, understanding the circumstances under which intuitive and reflective decisions steer us toward large-scale cooperation is a pressing scientific inquiry. Future studies, especially those with cross-cultural experimental designs, should further explore this fertile area of research.

Coda

As previously discussed in this chapter, the literature engages in a normative debate based on empirical findings by Wright and Baril (2011). Haidt and Kesebir (2010) propose that as moral disparities between different ideologies originate from intuitions, resolving these differences necessitates one side (e.g., liberals), recognizing the moral foundations (e.g., binding foundations) considered vital by the other group (e.g., conservatives), but previously excluded from the moral framework. In this perspective, if liberals were to expand their moral framework from two to five, matching conservatives' existing five foundations, it could potentially reduce political disagreements (Haidt, 2012). Conversely, Sauer (2015) argues that this approach is asymmetrical and suggests that reducing conservatives' moral framework to two (instead of broadening liberals' framework to five), particularly if there is already a consensus on the moral relevance of these two dimensions, could more readily diminish disagreement. Furthermore, as political agreement can often be reached at the reflective rather than intuitive level during political negotiations, the increased emphasis on individualizing foundations when individuals engage in reflective thinking (e.g., Capraro, 2024; Isler, Gächter, et al., 2021; Isler, Yilmaz, & Maule, 2021; Van Berkel et al., 2015; Yilmaz & Saribay, 2017a) may lend support to Sauer's (2015) normative standpoint. If both liberals and conservatives attach greater importance to individualizing foundations under the influence of reflection, it might signify a movement toward a consensus on universal morality when both sides have ample time to consider the issue, thus, when thinking reflectively (Kohlberg, 1971). In this scenario, conservatives might accentuate individualizing values, rather than requiring liberals to expand their foundations to encompass binding ones.

While empirical findings cannot be directly employed to substantiate normative claims (Black, 1964), the observation that individuals place a greater emphasis on universal values such as care and fairness during moments of reflective thought (Van Berkel et al., 2015; Yilmaz & Saribay, 2017a, 2017b) aligns with the principles elucidated in traditional theories of moral reasoning (e.g., Kohlberg, 1971). Moreover, individuals often exhibit enhanced cooperative behaviors upon reflection on their interactions with in-groups, out-groups, and even anonymous individuals (Isler, Yilmaz, & Maule, 2021), particularly in specific dilemma situations (e.g., Isler, Gächter, et al., 2021), and when grappling with intense intuitive pressures (Capraro & Cococcioni, 2016). While these findings indicate that reflective thought processes may indeed be a prerequisite for nurturing universal cooperation and effectively curbing tribalistic inclinations, especially in times of crises, which encompass the endorsement of what has been termed "binding foundations" in the literature (Haidt, 2012), they alone may not suffice to mitigate political polarization and promote extensive cooperation among individuals with differing perspectives. Undoubtedly, the motivations (e.g., striving for virtue, humility, open-mindedness) and objectives (e.g., pursuing financial gain, maintaining a consistent life) that accompany reflective thought processes should be regarded as pivotal determinants in whether those processes polarize or nurture cooperation. As we have emphasized throughout the book, adopting a holistic and systemic perspective that goes beyond justifying one's own intuitions via reflection and considers alternative viewpoints is essential for addressing political polarization, one of today's most pressing problems. Without this approach, each group tends to use reflection to reinforce their political intuitions, which only exacerbates polarization.

Indeed, some researchers contend that group-based foundations including loyalty, authority, and sanctity, commonly labeled as "binding," might be inaccurately named (Sinn, 2019; Sinn & Hayes, 2017). This is because the endorsement of these binding foundations often acts as both a binding force and a divisive factor, exacerbating polarization and prejudice. Consequently, these foundations could pose a hindrance to the establishment of universal cooperation. Therefore, the role of reflective thinking in critically filtering these aspects of our intuitive cognitive architecture becomes crucial for fostering large-scale cooperation, particularly in what we term the "crisis-ridden world," where our tribalistic tendencies undergo transformations and exert a profound impact on our lives within a broader global context. In particular, rather than attempting to reject our tribalistic moral intuitions embedded in human nature, considering how we can process them through the filter of reflection with a holistic perspective in a changing and globalizing world can greatly benefit us in addressing problems like polarization.

Notes

1 The registered report is a publication format in which authors submit a study proposal and receive peer reviews at Stage 1. Following the acceptance of their proposal in Stage 1, the authors proceed to collect data and present their findings in Stage 2. This format is specifically designed to reduce publication bias.

2 In the punishment version of the game, players are given the opportunity to impose punishment on each other after deciding to cooperate or defect. If a

player disagrees with the other player's decision, they can opt for a punishment. In this game, the punishment options are structured as follows: selecting a 0 cent punishment results in no punishment while opting for a 1 cent punishment leads to a deduction of 10 cents from the punished person. This design allows researchers to investigate under what circumstances enforcing cooperative norms through punishment, especially when cooperation is violated, becomes an evolutionarily stable strategy.

8

VIOLENT EXTREMISM

The first author of this book was born in 1978 to a student of Prof. Cavit Orhan Tütengil, a renowned sociologist at Istanbul University. Prof. Tütengil sent a congratulatory note upon the birth of his student's child. The note, addressed to the newborn, read "Welcome to our crisis-ridden world." A little more than a year later, on the morning of December 7, 1979, Prof. Tütengil was killed in a crossfire while walking from his house to the bus stop to go to work. The clear suspects, ultra-nationalists, were never brought to trial. The act was premeditated, so much so that about two weeks prior to his death, Prof. Tütengil allegedly said "I guess it's my turn" (referring to several other Turkish academics assassinated in the late 1970s). Tütengil's "fault" was to care deeply about his nation's problems, especially those of rural Türkiye, and to analyze them on scientific grounds.

A year before the assassination of Tütengil, the country experienced one of its worst massacres in the Southeastern city of Kahramanmaraş, where more than a hundred religious minority citizens (Alawites) were killed. A witness to the events reported that when they caught one of the perpetrators and demanded his reasons for participation in the massacre, his response was: " 'We are killing the infidels,' they said, so I went and killed" (Açıkgöz & Alp, 2014, p. 200).

The two incidents paint very different pictures of the minds of individuals engaged in ideological violence, even though both sets of perpetrators are from the right wing.[1] The latter was apparently driven by "heat of the moment," Type 1 processes with no sign of premeditation or calculation of its consequences.[2] The former involved quite a bit of Type 2 processing, from choosing the victim to seeking information about his residence and hours of commute, to deciding on the placement of the assassins to leave no

DOI: 10.4324/9781003300366-10

chance of survival, and to planning their safe escape. Members of terrorist organizations and other perpetrators of violence can be quite rational, at least in the instrumental sense—they have no trouble taking actions that facilitate goal pursuit (Wintrobe, 2006).[3] While there is no agreed-upon definition of terrorism, a significant portion of available definitions includes the "purposive, planned, systematic tactic" component (Schmid, 2011). Acts of terrorism are patterned, suggesting that terrorists conduct cost–benefit analyses of their options (Duru et al., 2021). It is even possible to argue that certain violent actions (e.g., suicide bombing) are rational for the perpetrator to commit because, for instance, they may produce greater effect (e.g., change in society in the desired direction) than the individual would ever be able to otherwise in their remaining time in life (Greenland et al., 2020). To consider violent extremists as reflective and rational can be disturbing, but to characterize all of one's ideological opponents, whether violent or not, as unreflective and irrational in one stroke would be naïve at best and a form of myside bias, and can hinder balanced analysis of their actions (Abulof, 2015), which is necessary if societies are to successfully tackle the problem of violent extremism.[4] It is hard to argue on the basis of evidence that violent extremists are psychologically *completely and categorically* different than the rest of us. For instance, there is no consistent evidence that violent extremists—with the possible exception of *lone actors*[5]—are more likely to suffer from mental health issues than the general population (for a meta-analysis, see Sarma et al., 2022).[6] However, a focus on psychopathology is unlikely to be completely baseless and we come back to this topic later in the chapter. We concur with Adam-Troian et al. (2021, p. 23) that "violent extremism stems from adaptive feelings and concerns of individuals" while asserting that responses to those feelings and concerns (i.e., violence, not for self-defense but to terrorize for gain) are categorically unacceptable and dysfunctional. In this chapter, we review the arguments and evidence for a potential role of (weak) reflectiveness in radicalization into and engagement with violent extremism.

Some (Other) Cautionary Notes on Violent Extremism

Before we delve into the literature, several other cautionary notes are due. First, many findings presented in Chapter 6 included data from respondents that placed themselves at the edges of the ideological spectrum, such as by choosing "1" (e.g., "extremely liberal") or "7" (e.g., "extremely conservative") on a 7-point Likert-type scale, and were hence labeled "political extremists" (e.g., Brandt et al., 2015; Costello & Bowes, 2023). This is in parallel with a long tradition of attitude research in which extremity is defined based on self-placement at the end points of measurement scales (Abelson, 1995). It would be wrong to assume that extremists defined in this narrow manner would have a great deal in common with violent extremists. A major difference is that the latter are *willing to fight and die* for their chosen cause or in-group (whether it be political, religious, or other).

That said, the study of nonviolent extremism does inform our understanding of violent extremism because they are not unrelated. First, becoming cognitively (vs. behaviorally) radicalized may simply be a phase prior to becoming a violent extremist. Moghaddam's (2005) well-known staircase model of terrorism metaphorically places all individuals on a ground floor of a building, where perceptions of injustice and relative deprivation are widespread. An increasingly smaller proportion of individuals gradually climbs the stairs if they believe that viable normative options for addressing those negative perceptions are lacking (first floor); blame out-groups for their problems (second floor); replace a mainstream understanding of morality with that defined by a violent organization (third floor); accept the organization's means as legitimate (fourth floor); and are able to overcome mechanisms that normally inhibit violence against noncombatant civilians (fifth floor). Thus, there is continuity between being a regular citizen on the ground floor and a perpetrator of violence on the top floor and much of this gradual climb involves well-understood social–psychological mechanisms that also occur in the nonviolent sphere with lesser intensity. In fact, the influence of cults on the individual (i.e., "brainwashing") is also best understood not as a mysterious process involving exotic techniques (e.g., hypnosis, hallucinogens, electroshock) but as an intense and concentrated version of mundane social influence tactics practiced by legitimate agents in daily life (Andersen & Saribay, 2012). Second, in the era of populist politics, violence may be moving closer to being a norm versus an exception, as recently evidenced by former U.S. President Donald Trump's inflammatory rhetoric (Kinsman & Frimer, 2021) and the January 6 attack on the U.S. Capitol. In fact, as the boundary between violent and nonviolent spheres in society became more blurred (Kallis, 2013), psychological theories that originated as attempts to explain violent extremism have become applicable to nonviolent politics (Van Prooijen, 2021).

Adding to the complexity of the matter, not all types of extremism are violent, repulsive, or detrimental to human progress; some may even be laudable (Fleeson et al., 2022). Cassam (2022) goes into great detail about the many distinctions that can be made within the category of extremism and also between extremism and related terms such as fundamentalism, fanaticism, radicalism, or even being principled. While most of these terms have a strongly negative connotation, they do not all point to the same problematic phenomenon. For instance, not all fundamentalists support violent extremism. In fact, some scholars point out that terms such as fundamentalism have received an unwarranted degree of derogation in the social sciences, along with myths and stereotypes that obscure our understanding of their true meaning and actual manifestations in society (Hood et al., 2005). Even if a certain act is labeled as an episode of extremism and punished by law or derogated in a certain context or time, that same act might be regarded as heroic in the future or in a different context. This is unlikely for episodes of violent extremism[7] but is a serious possibility for other types of acts, such as extreme acts of protest intended to draw attention to environmental issues. To find our way through these complications and confusions, we leave aside these more ambiguous cases and focus on violent extremism that violates noncombatant civilians' right to live and prosper. The latter presents clear dangers to human societies, especially when organized by groups (vs. performed by lone actors[8]) and continues to be a pressing global issue,[9] with no ideology or culture being immune from the risk of producing violent extremist movements.[10] We also draw from research on cults because of their similarities to violent extremist groups (Galanter & Forest, 2006; Gaub, 2016) and on measures of support for/willingness toward extremist violence even though some such data are collected from nonradicals.

Sociostructural and Demographic Factors

An analysis of violent extremism confined to cognitive factors could run the risk of explaining little. Many researchers have noted the necessity to approach violent extremism from a multidisciplinary perspective (Decety et al., 2018) and many factors outside of individual cognition (and outside of other microlevel factors whose effect could be captured by studying the individual, such as the family environment), from the macro (global, nation-level) to meso (group-level) levels, appear to play a role in the emergence and growth of extremist movements and terrorist organizations. We briefly touch upon these here to place the role of reflectiveness in a broader context.

At the group and community level, some scholars (Iannaccone & Berman, 2006) have argued that what makes violent extremist organizations effective is their ability to provide public goods and services (e.g., healthcare, education, supernatural/religious services, financial support).[11] These become especially valuable to locals when the actual government fails to provide them. Thus, sympathizers and supporters of violent extremist organizations—whether they themselves eventually take part in violence or not—are more than backward-thinking fanatics[12] and ideology or theology plays a limited role in this analysis. Data from the Middle East suggest that religious organizations that are reliable providers of public goods and services are more effective in conducting suicide attacks than organizations that do not serve this role (Berman & Laitin, 2008). Thus, echoing our earlier cautionary note, Iannacone and Berman state that "it is a serious mistake to view violent religious extremists as pathological drones enslaved by theologies of hate.

One gets much more analytical mileage from an approach that treats militant religious extremists as social and political entrepreneurs" (p. 123). That is, these religious organizations may sometimes appeal to the public because they provide them with support for their essential daily struggles, rather than merely because they bombard the public with irrational extremist discourse.

Turning to the macrolevel, "The Fundamentals," a series of essays published in the early 20th century advocating the preservation of the basic tenets of Christianity, was a reaction to changes in American society. Similarly, today's extremists may be reacting to significant worldwide changes such as modernity and globalization, sometimes with violent means. Globalization is responsible for rapid and significant changes in the demographic composition of societies and the distribution of wealth across and within nation-states (Stiglitz, 2003). Much research and theorizing has focused on material conditions in relation to violent extremism with mixed findings. While Krueger (2008) concludes that "terrorism should be viewed more as a violent political act than as a response to economic conditions" (p. 90), some other research suggests that economic development is negatively associated with the number of terrorist incidents (e.g., Li & Schaub, 2004), and yet others find nonlinear effects (Boehmer & Daube, 2013).[13]

Two interrelated insights may help elucidate the role of sociostructural factors in violent extremism. First, as many scholars argue, there is no single trajectory to violence (Gill et al., 2021) and microlevel (individual, psychological) factors have the potential to resolve mixed findings by moderating the links between sociostructural factors and violent extremism. Second, the effect of many sociostructural factors is truly understood only by tracing their impact on the psychology of the individual. In other words, what appears as a sociostructural factor (e.g., globalization, economic development) or a mere demographic pattern (e.g., young males being especially likely to enact violent extremism; Silke, 2008) may have its effects primarily via psychological mechanisms at the individual level. As Moghaddam (2005, p. 161) put it succinctly, "terrorism can best be understood through a focus on the psychological interpretation of material conditions." In fact, one prominent (de)radicalization scholar warned of the "need for concepts of radicalization that focus more on the psychological mechanisms behind the process as such, rather than individual factors and root causes" (Koehler, 2020, p. 16) while another one noted that "the field urgently requires more psychologists" (Horgan, 2017, p. 200). Consistent with these views, psychological factors were more closely associated with radicalization compared to some other classes of factors (e.g., sociodemographics) in a recent systematic review (Wolfowicz et al., 2021). In the puzzling case of economic factors, Piazza (2011) discovered that it was not so much poor economic development of a country but whether its minorities were subject to economic discrimination that predicted (domestic) terrorism. This makes sense from a psychological perspective emphasizing the effects of such material factors on personal feelings of significance, as we discuss below.

Psychological Theories and the Role of Reflectiveness

Notwithstanding the importance of sociostructural factors that are more aptly studied with the conceptual and methodological tools of fields like political science, anthropology, and sociology, social psychology still features prominently in analyses of the processes by which individuals become violent extremists. However, this is not because of a focus on the role of cognitive style,[14] but rather because social psychology has a long history of studying relevant topics such as social identity, intergroup relations, within-group dynamics, and social influence (Borum, 2011). Post (2010, p. 15) informs us that one of the conclusions reached at the 2005 Madrid international summit on terrorism was that "it is not individual psychology, but group, organizational, and social psychology, with a particular emphasis on 'collective identity,' that provides the most powerful lens to understand terrorist psychology and behavior." A close look at the literature within psychology reveals that reflectiveness (or more broadly, cognitive style) is in fact not the first factor that jumps out in terms of the attention it has received in the context of violent extremism, as is also the case for the other topics (e.g., epistemically suspect beliefs, politics, cooperation) covered in this book. Given that humans are cognitive misers on the whole, if miserliness was a direct cause of violent extremism, human societies all over the globe would be in complete chaos. Furthermore, even in the most developed societies—those that cherish education, democracy, science, rationality, and reflectiveness the most—such as Western Europe and the United States—violent extremism unfortunately continues to be a significant threat (Mattsson & Johansson, 2022). Moreover, contrary to popular opinion, terrorists tend to be highly educated on the whole and educational attainment is positively associated with involvement in terrorism (e.g., Berrebi, 2007).[15] At first glance, these findings suggest that, even among psychological (let alone sociostructural) factors, individuals' (lack of) reflectiveness plays a limited role in violent extremism. A more nuanced picture emerges when prominent psychology theories and findings are examined closely, as we do below.

The Militant Extremist Mindset

Cassam (2022) points to the importance of *mindset* for characterizing extremism and draws attention to the work of Saucier et al. (2009) on the *militant extremist mindset*. Defining extremism with mindset at the center moves it closer to cognitive style. To reveal the militant extremist mindset concretely, Saucier et al. (2009, see p. 260, Table 1) identified 16 themes from linguistic materials pertaining to militant extremist groups. In further work applying factor analysis to responses of regular participants (i.e., those who are not members of militant extremist groups) across many cultures, Stankov et al. (2010) found that the militant extremist mindset is characterized by (1) pro-violence; (2) belief in a vile world; and (3) divine power (which they later called *nastiness*, *grudge*, and *excuse*, respectively; Stankov et al., 2018).

A narrow examination of the content of these themes suggests connections to cognitive style, on the basis of other research. One example is "dehumanization of the enemy"—commonly encouraged by violent extremists as a strategy to overcome the inhibitions that normally keep individuals from harming innocents (Bandura, 1990). Dehumanizing others indicates reduced reflectiveness in the sense of lower activity in the social–cognitive neural network (Harris & Fiske, 2011).[16] More broadly, thinking about others can require significant cognitive effort, which is why people have been characterized as "cognitive misers" not just by dual-process theorists in cognitive psychology but also by social cognition theorists (Taylor, 1981). For instance, social categorization and stereotyping save cognitive resources and indicate a cognitively simplistic approach to the social world (Macrae et al., 1994). To the contrary, individuating people (i.e., acknowledging their unique characteristics instead of stereotyping them; see Brewer, 1988; Fiske & Neuberg, 1990) and treating them as fully human is facilitated by effortful thinking, which is required to go beyond simplistic frames (e.g., stereotypes) and egocentric biases. Individuals with lower cognitive capacity (e.g., working memory) or whose cognitive resources are currently taxed (e.g., with a distracting secondary task) are worse at reading the minds of others (Lin et al., 2010) and experimentally activating reflectiveness improves empathic accuracy (Ma-Kellams & Lerner, 2016). Individuals even appear to avoid empathy and compassion because they are cognitively costly (Cameron et al., 2019; Scheffer et al., 2022).

Examination of other specific themes identified by Saucier et al. (2009) gives the impression that militant extremism is not simply reducible to cognitive style generally or to weak reflectiveness particularly. For instance, it is not easy to argue that themes such as the "perception that modernity is disastrous" or the "perception that one's group is obstructed" would be weakened by reflective thought, even though thinking further and collecting more information on those issues with a high accuracy motivation (i.e., not simply to support one's extant beliefs; overcoming confirmation bias) should lead to more balanced and moderate views. However, there is a different, broader sense in which reflectiveness is relevant here that we discuss later.[17]

Significance Quest Theory

Another prominent contemporary theory of violent extremism is called *Significance Quest Theory* (Kruglanski, Molinario, Jasko, et al., 2022) because it views individuals' *need* to attain personal significance and the quest they undertake to satisfy it as the main driver of extremism. The theory is also referred to as the *3N Framework* because it asserts that how this need is concretely satisfied is determined by two other factors, *narrative* and *network*. We give a central position to this framework here because it is a comprehensive analysis of social–psychological mechanisms that is also empirically well supported (see for a meta-analysis, Da Silva et al., 2023). We examine each of these components with an eye toward uncovering a potential role of reflectiveness.

Need

The theory views significance (i.e., social worth and recognition) as a basic human need, while acknowledging that differences exist across cultures and individuals in the strength of the need (Kruglanski, Molinario, Jasko, et al., 2022). Many individuals strive for significance, as we do in writing this book or an athlete in training for a tournament. Problems occur when this need is chronically unsatisfied and/or there are strong incentives and opportunities to satisfy it deeply (e.g., by being recognized as a hero in one's community due to an extreme act of altruism). If any need is personally strong and yet is chronically frustrated, it may dominate the person's thoughts, feelings, and behavior at the expense of other needs, motives, and goals. In the recent literature, this *motivational imbalance*—the disproportionate allocation of one's resources to the satisfaction of a single need (Kruglanski, Kopetz, et al., 2022; see also Bélanger, 2021)[18]—is recognized as a common factor underlying many different types of extremism (e.g., involvement in extreme sports). Under normal circumstances, various needs and goals of an individual constrain each other. For instance, our desire to have fun and get rest, to maintain our significant relationships, to fulfill our administrative and academic duties at the university and be good mentors to our students, and to be physically active and healthy has kept us from working on this book 24/7 regardless of how rewarding and important it felt. The dedication to a single need or goal, which is rooted in a chronic motivational deficiency causing that need or goal to overshadow others, lifts such constraints, making extreme behavior possible.

Loss (or felt absence) of significance can stem from a variety of factors (e.g., being economically disadvantaged, politically marginalized, or socially excluded) and may trigger a quest for significance. Significance provides an important psychological bridge between various sociostructural factors and violent extremism, helping to resolve some of the mixed findings mentioned earlier. For instance, it is likely that poor economic conditions contribute to radicalization primarily if they trigger feelings of personal, or especially, group-based relative deprivation, which in turn has been associated in research findings with intentions toward violent extremism (Obaidi et al., 2019). If one does not feel relatively deprived, which may be the case regardless of objective conditions if one is focused on downward (vs. upward) social comparison, personal significance may not be hurt, and the quest for significance is not triggered. This may explain why Western-born (vs. native) Muslims are more at risk for terrorist engagement[19]—they are more likely to compare themselves to the well-off majority surrounding them and to feel deprived.[20]

Our assessment reveals that there are several ways in which reflectiveness is relevant to the need component of Significance Quest Theory. First, chronic frustration of basic needs, especially when other means of satisfying them are blocked, fosters obsessive, as opposed to harmonious,[21] passion (Lalande et al., 2017). When the need in question is about *significance*, the obsession can turn ideological and set off a cascade of processes that radicalize the person into violent extremism (Bélanger, 2021). Obsessive passion is a precursor of violent extremism, with a larger effect size than nearly all other predictors of the latter (Wolfowicz et al., 2021). Obsessive passion shares a basis with obsessive–compulsive disorder (OCD) in which unwanted thoughts repetitively intrude into conscious awareness (Adam-Troian & Bélanger, 2024). The ability to inhibit thoughts and responses is a key deficiency of OCD patients (Chamberlain et al., 2005; Mar et al., 2022) and OCD is comorbid with impulse control problems and addiction (Ruscio et al., 2010). Higher levels of OCD symptoms in healthy populations are associated with cognitive rigidity (Ramakrishnan et al., 2022). Thus, OCD and obsessive passion (and by extension, violent extremism) are incompatible with reflectiveness, which requires self-regulation of impulses and shielding of conscious awareness from persistent intrusive thoughts.

Second, the processes which link ideological obsession to violent extremism (see Bélanger, 2021, Figure 1) are also problematic for reflectiveness in their own right. For instance, over time, obsessive passion might lead to an exclusive reliance on a violent extremist ideology/group for satisfying significance. Self-worth being so highly contingent on one entity (i.e., the ideological group or belief system) renders it particularly fragile and in need of constant defense, leading the individual to show extreme, often aggressive, reactions to any attack on that entity (Golec De Zavala et al., 2013; Kernis et al., 1989). This creates a cycle of high sensitivity to ego threats, insecurity about self-worth, the experience of heated (and cognitively consuming) emotions such as anger, and a constant struggle to ward off the perceived threats. Such heightened arousal works to the advantage of malevolent organizations because it decreases the capacity for critical thinking and renders the individual more pliable (Baron, 2000). Group-based anger commonly accompanies shared grievance and is associated with violent intentions (Obaidi et al., 2018). Critically, the experience of anger has been shown to decrease reflectiveness in several different ways (Tiedens & Linton, 2001). Any thinking that occurs while angry is likely to be directed at confirming existing views (Suhay & Erisen, 2018).[22] In sum, unless the individual is especially competent in emotion regulation and self-control (which are inconsistent with experiencing extreme anger and harboring violent intentions in the first place), any serious level of reflectiveness becomes unlikely under this combination of factors.

Third, heightened significance needs and associated emotions (e.g., humiliation, shame) may trigger self-uncertainty and motivate cognitive closure—the desire for certain and complete resolution of ambiguity that extremist ideas and groups are good at providing (Hogg, 2021). Across both religious and ethnic extremism, radical (e.g., terrorists in prison) and nonradical participants, and field (correlational) and experimental studies, Webber et al. (2018) found that significance loss is associated with a greater need for cognitive closure, which in turn is associated with attraction to (violent) extremist ideas. Because cognitive closure stands directly in opposition to reflectiveness, these findings highlight another way in which the latter is relevant to violent extremism. Moreover, Zedelius et al. (2022) found that, compared to *interest curiosity* (i.e., seeking information for intrinsic purposes like enjoyment), *deprivation curiosity* (i.e., need-induced epistemic curiosity) is associated with lower intellectual humility and susceptibility to epistemically suspect information (e.g., fake news, *pseudo-profound bullshit*).[23] Tolerating (self-)uncertainty, as opposed to seeking to get rid of it via immediate and complete closure, requires greater reflectiveness,[24] as well.

Fourth, the quest for significance can motivate sensation-seeking—the pursuit of exciting and thrilling experiences—which in turn is associated with support for violent extremism, at least in the absence of exciting but peaceful options (Schumpe et al., 2020; see also Cottee & Hayward, 2011). Sensation-seeking shares cortical circuitry with aspects of impulsivity (Holmes et al., 2016) and supports rash and risky, rather than prudent and reflectively supported action. Using a data-driven approach on responses collected via 37 perceptual and cognitive tasks, Zmigrod et al. (2021) discovered that both sensation-seeking and impulsivity (and lower working memory capacity) were associated with support for extreme pro-group attitudes including support for violence.

Narrative

Most people are hesitant to engage in violent acts, bringing us to the importance of narrative. Significance Quest Theory asserts that the individual comes to view particular actions as having the potential to fulfill the quest for significance through narratives. Research on conspiracy theories, the militant extremist mindset, and much other work across the social sciences have independently revealed the central themes and the beliefs and perceptions promoted by the narratives propagated by violent extremist organizations (see the "composite narrative" on p. 265 of Saucier et al., 2009). In short, these narratives (see Levine & Kruglanski, 2021) take advantage of and provoke significance threats and shared grievances (e.g., by emphasizing relative deprivation, political injustices) and portray violence as legitimate and even desirable and moral (e.g., because it is in defense of sacred group values that are being attacked by evil, dehumanized out-groups). Violent extremist narratives are simplistic, binary (e.g., evil–good, them–us), absolutist, and consequently have particular appeal for those on a significance quest with heightened closure needs (Kruglanski & Orehek, 2011). Violence (compared to other means) has an upper hand, because it may be particularly effective in restoring feelings of self-certainty, agency, control, power, and hence, significance (Hogg, 2021; Molinario et al., 2021), while also fulfilling the sensation-seeking motive.

A clear relevance of reflectiveness in this component is uncovered in the literature on *integrative complexity*. Supported by reflective processes,[25] integratively complex thought (typically measured by analysis of written and verbal communication) differentiates the multiple dimensions and opposing ideas regarding an issue and recognizes the interactions and connections among them (Suedfeld, 2009). Narratives of violent extremist groups are lower especially on integrative complexity, even compared to ideologically similar nonviolent groups (L. G. Conway et al., 2011).[26] Low integrative complexity predicts support for and engagement in ideological violence (Suedfeld et al., 2013).

Research on conspiracy beliefs independently highlights the relevance of reflectiveness, as we discussed in Chapter 5. Conspiracy theories often provide the foundation for these narratives (Kruglanski, Molinario, Ellenberg, et al., 2022) and are relevant here for three reasons. First, analysis of propaganda by violent extremist organizations from Neo-Nazis to ISIS reveals that conspiracy theories are actively circulated and not only do they promote violence but sometimes also attempt to create the perception of significance loss itself (Baele, 2019; Kruglanski, Molinario, Ellenberg, et al., 2022; Schut, 1999). Second, conspiracy theories in fact have this intended effect: Belief in conspiracy theories is directly linked with greater support for and willingness to engage in violence. Anecdotally, conspiracist thinking appears to have played a central role in some of the worst acts of terrorism in recent years, such as those committed by Breivik in Norway and Tarrant in Christchurch (e.g., Fekete, 2012). Moreover, experimentally heightening participants' belief in a conspiracy-governed world (vs. low levels of such belief) increased their intentions for illegal, nonnormative political acts including physically attacking people (Imhoff et al., 2021). A correlational study on a nationally-representative German sample supports the association between conspiracist thinking and violent extremist intentions while also suggesting some qualifications (Rottweiler & Gill, 2022a). For instance, and most interestingly, the association does not hold for individuals high in self-control—a characteristic that enables stronger reflectiveness. Third, Chapter 5 presented evidence that conspiracist thinking goes along with weak reflectiveness. Consequently, reflectiveness is a preventive factor, because it gives the individual greater ability to see through the epistemically suspect nature of extremist narratives[27] as well as the ulterior motives (e.g., getting the individual to believe that violence is justified and even morally desirable) underlying the use of those narratives in violent extremist organizations. For the already radicalized members, the role of reflectiveness in the decision to disengage from violent organizations is implied by the common finding that *disillusionment* (which involves *critical evaluation* of group goals and means and identifying inconsistencies and hypocrisies) is a central push factor in disengagement (Koehler, 2017; Schut, 1999).[28]

Network

Narratives are compiled and circulated by a network of group members with shared goals. Critically, via its social functions, the network imbues narratives with psychological weight, transforming them from lifeless messages into *shared reality*—a common understanding of the world that promotes subjective feelings to the status of objective reality (Higgins et al., 2021). Thus, epistemic (narrative) and relational (network) factors are intertwined. The sense of shared reality and joint activities (e.g., rituals) taking place within the network also facilitate *identity fusion,* a "unique form of alignment with a group, one that entails a visceral feeling of oneness with the group ... [and] increased permeability of the boundary between the personal and social self" (Swann et al., 2012, p. 441). Identity fusion in turn facilitates extreme pro group self-sacrifice, such as fighting and dying.

The network component of the 3N Framework highlights the role of reflectiveness in at least four distinct (but related) ways. First, a key driver of attraction to a violent extremist network is social exclusion[29] (Ezekiel, 2002), because it activates the quest for significance. Importantly, being socially excluded appears to reduce reflectiveness. Experimentally manipulating social exclusion (vs. inclusion) reduces both the motivation and the ability to exert proactive (vs. reactive) control, that is, preparing for events and responses in advance by giving forethought (Xu et al., 2020); reduces performance in complex tasks requiring cognitive effort (Baumeister et al., 2002); and reduces the motivation to inhibit impulses (Baumeister et al., 2005).[30] Weakened reflectiveness means a low capacity to resist social influence and persuasion, such as being unable to think critically about misleading conspiracist narratives. Furthermore, social inclusion is contingent on unquestioning acceptance of the narratives, which should further decrease the new recruit's motivation to subject the narratives to serious scrutiny and to calculate the long-term consequences of accepting the short-term social rewards that the violent extremist organization offers. Such organizations often target socially excluded and marginalized individuals precisely for the ease with which they can take advantage of the deficiencies in their social needs and their weakened reflectiveness.

Second, though individuals may respond to acute social exclusion by increasing their congeniality to obtain acceptance (e.g., Cheung et al., 2015), repeated social exclusion may set in action a vicious cycle of increasing resentment and distrust toward others in society and decreasing prosociality, met by further exclusion from others in return (Stavrova et al., 2020).[31] This may result in the individual becoming *informationally isolated* from the broader society and relying increasingly on only the narrative and network provided by a violent extremist organization as it steps in with the promise to fulfill the social (belonging) and epistemic (certainty) needs of the individual. Such organizations often require the new recruit to sever all their external social ties (Everton, 2018). Individuals' attitudes tend to be stronger, more certain, and consequently more resistant to change if their network consists of attitudinally similar individuals (Visser & Mirabile, 2004). As many classic social psychology studies attempted to demonstrate (e.g., Asch, 1956), social (normative) and informational processes within homogeneous groups (e.g., unanimity in opinions) facilitate artificially high levels of conformity and motivated reasoning (Janis, 1982; Levitan & Verhulst, 2016). Limited exposure to alternative opinions and information[32] might thus foster rigidity in beliefs and attitudes, a cognitive characteristic conducive to violent extremism (Zmigrod et al., 2019). On the contrary, attitudes tend to be more ambivalent when individuals are embedded in heterogeneous networks. Moreover, such individuals seek novel, particularly counter-attitudinal, information more (Levitan & Wronski, 2014), process persuasive messages more reflectively (Levitan & Visser, 2008), and show greater tolerance for alternative worldviews (Mutz & Mondak, 2006). Ambivalence[33] may support the capacity and willingness to doubt a violent extremist group's narratives and doubt—a reflective process (Gilbert, 1991)—is known to be an important factor in deradicalization (see Koehler, 2017, p. 16).

Third, paranoia toward the outside world and increasingly exclusive reliance on the group for information facilitate the establishment of a charismatic leader (or text) as having epistemic authority (Lifton, 1961). The network's capacity to address the social needs of the individual (i.e., belonging, inclusion, admiration), strong group cohesiveness and the appearance of uniformity within the group, and the charisma of the leader combine to produce an exceptional level of trust of and submission to the group. The group's narratives transform to shared reality and "rather than being subjected to critical examination, (…) are likely to be 'swallowed hook, line, and sinker'" (Levine & Kruglanski, 2021, p. 107). Deference to a charismatic leader—often posing as the sole arbiter of truth by way of special (e.g., supernatural) powers—means one is "bypassing moral deliberation" (i.e., failing to reflect on the right course of action on one's own behalf) in followers (Flanigan, 2013). Reflection becomes unnecessary as the judgment of what to do is left to others.

Last but not least, it is known that cults and violent extremist organizations do not reveal the full extent of their aims to new recruits. Their influence strategies are deceptive and coercive (Andersen & Saribay, 2012). The clearest reason for this is that having full access to the end goals of such organizations would give individuals an easy chance to refuse entry, based on reflective thought. Malevolent organizations also create heightened levels of arousal and stress to break down the individual's capacity for reflection (Baron, 2000). Thus, these organizations attempt first to trap the individual via the operation of narrative (e.g., establishing conspiracist beliefs and a militant mindset) and network (i.e., establishing identity fusion, a charismatic leader, and strong pressures toward conformity) factors such that reflective critique of organizational goals and means becomes unlikely. A similar dynamic occurs for members who wish to exit the group. Unsurprisingly, these individuals are subjected to significant maltreatment (e.g., Koehler, 2017, see pp. 22–23) instead of civilized persuasive attempts based on reflective processes (e.g., offering reasons for staying or improvements to group life).

Contaminated Mindware: The Memetics Perspective

Another interesting approach, which is not exactly a psychological theory but very much relevant to reflectiveness, may contribute to the discussion. The literature gives the impression that both violent extremist organizations and deradicalization interventions are focused much more on *what* their members should believe (i.e., ideological indoctrination) than *how* they should think (i.e., cognitive style). However, our review so far indicates that reflectiveness (i.e., the *how* of thinking) is involved in various ways. The what and how of thinking are not independent of each other. The following discussion of the concept of *memes* should make this, as well as the role of reflectiveness in violent extremism, clearer.

Borrowing heavily from Dawkins (1976), Stanovich (2004) distinguishes between replicators (genes) and vehicles (the organism that houses the genes and interacts with the environment), whose interests overlap only partly. Unlike other animals, humans have evolved to a degree of complexity that no longer permits their genes to directly control the vehicle via "short-leash goals" (i.e., specific, rigid, preprogrammed stimulus–response couplings, such as a fear of snakes). Instead, in promoting their primary interest of self-replication, genes have to suffice with "long-leash goals"—general, nonspecific directions for action. This gives the vehicle some wiggle room to bypass control by replicators, as in having sex only for pleasure by using birth control. Human cultures are also quite complex and contain a wide variety of ideas and information that can be adopted by organisms. These informational packages are called memes (and when they combine, *memeplexes*) and are viewed as roughly corresponding to genes in that their main interest is self-replication. Just as with genes, memes do not necessarily serve their vehicles (the minds they inhabit) but instead "[t]hey exist because, through memetic evolution, they have displayed the best fecundity, longevity, and copying fidelity—the defining characteristics of successful replicators" (Stanovich, 2004, p. 176). Thus, this view puts the emphasis on the characteristics of ideas and beliefs (i e., memes) that make them more successful in terms of the number of minds they come to inhabit, as opposed to the characteristics of individuals that determine the beliefs they adopt.

Memes can be adopted intuitively, with little or no critical evaluation, or after long deliberation and intense scrutiny. Importantly,

> [m]emes having passed many selective tests that we reflectively apply are more likely to be memes that are resident because they serve our ends [as vehicles]. Memes that we have acquired unreflectively—without subjecting them to logical and/or empirical scrutiny—are statistically more likely to be parasites, resident because of their own structural properties rather than because they serve our ends.
>
> *(Stanovich, 2004, pp. 183–184)*

While genes are forced to cooperate with other genes in the same body and to keep that body alive until at least reproduction, memes are free of these constraints and can therefore be much more dangerous.[34] Thus, it is critical for vehicles to be able to evaluate memes before they are allowed to inhabit the mind. Stanovich (2004, pp. 184–192) provides four rules for meme evaluation, two of which appear particularly relevant to extremism. The rule Stanovich claims might be the most important of all is "avoid memes that resist evaluation." For example, Christianity enjoys the greatest number of adherents among the religions in the world today, and for much of its history, it sanctioned violence against those who attempted to revise or abandon its official dogma (Clarke, 2014).[35,36] Many other belief systems threaten punishment or the loss of rewards if their basic tenets are questioned. Reflection should allow one to see through the function of such evaluation-disabling beliefs by questioning the grounds on which the belief is deemed unquestionable.

The other rule of meme evaluation relevant here is to not allow any memes that prevent other memes from being hosted in the mind. A certain memeplex dominating one's mind could lead to a dangerous situation if this memeplex is incompatible with other memeplexes and personal goals. This is in fact what many extremist organizations and cults attempt to do—to get the person to commit completely to their cause at the expense of all other life goals, as discussed earlier. For the suicide bomber, the only worthy goal may be martyrdom. Reflection should lead one to question the reasons why any particular need or goal should have such a disproportionately high status in one's life given the high level of complexity and diversity characteristic of the human motivational system (Higgins & Pittman, 2008).[37] This second rule from Stanovich is important because once radicalized, deradicalization is not easy. Counternarratives—messages designed to discredit violent extremist propaganda (e.g., by pointing out logical inconsistencies)—have limited, if any, deradicalizing effect (Bélanger et al., 2023; see for a systematic review, Carthy et al., 2020).[38] This is consistent with the idea that violent extremists reside in attitudinally homogenous networks and already harbor evaluation-disabling beliefs and obsessive passion, factors that make them susceptible to an extreme degree of confirmation bias and resistant to persuasion. Moreover, Bélanger et al. (2021) demonstrated that when their beliefs are contested, ideologically obsessed individuals show psychological reactance by increasing, rather than decreasing, their willingness toward violent political actions. This suggests that more of our societal resources should be directed to prevention than intervention.

Co-Radicalization

As the previous sections make clear, reflective thought itself has allowed science to identify pathways into violent extremism and the deceptive strategies of malevolent organizations. Reflection is also the capacity that identifies a more complicated process visible only at a macrolevel and over a longer time span—*co-radicalization* (i.e., the mutually radicalizing effect that two groups have on each other, such as when a terrorist attack by an immigrant drives greater support for anti-immigration attitudes in the host culture). An immediate goal of many radical organizations is to garner more public support and/or new recruits. Their violent actions are designed in part to radicalize competing entities, for instance, by provoking the government to adopt increasingly forceful oppressive measures (Kydd & Walter, 2006).[39] When this occurs, they use rivals' extreme and aggressive responses to justify their narratives and draw the sympathies of a wider audience (see Molinario et al., 2021, p. 261). Thus, different agents are radicalizing each other, a dynamic that is best visible in today's Western Europe involving the Muslim minority on the one hand and far-right anti-immigrant groups on the other (see Verkuyten, 2018, pp. 26–27). Co-radicalization is probably heavily involved in the blurring of the boundaries between violent and nonviolent spheres we mentioned earlier—violent extremism moves closer to being the norm as different factions of society mutually reinforce the positive feedback loop of radicalization. Reflection makes it possible for individuals to become aware of this trap, giving them a chance to break free from this cycle of polarization and violence. Failure to collect information on the broader society and "the other side" because of informational isolation (see the "Network" section) or to give serious and open-minded thought to such information because of weak reflectiveness means that the individual is unlikely to comprehend the self-fulfilling (and hence, questionable) nature of the in-group's narrative (e.g., claiming victimhood that is in part self-generated by radicalizing competing entities). Under such conditions, it becomes easy to develop false *metaperceptions* about out-groups. For instance, U.S. Democrats and Republicans tremendously overestimate the degree of the rival groups' support for and willingness to conduct political violence (Mernyk et al., 2022). This metaperceptual bias radicalizes individuals and correcting the bias has been found to reduce one's support for and willingness toward political violence at practically significant levels, with some long-term stability. By facilitating the critical examination of one's metaperceptions, reflectiveness should help to prevent radicalization. A holistic view of society and one's place in it should thus aid reflectiveness to play this positive role.

Reflectiveness as a Preventive Factor

Earlier, we covered how reflectiveness can be strengthened (Chapter 3; see also Caroti et al., 2023; Halpern, 2013) and how it facilitates guarding against epistemically suspect beliefs (Chapter 5) and cognitive biases (Chapter 2). The conclusion emerging from our review is that reflectiveness has the potential to weaken many mechanisms feeding into violent extremism, especially in preventive fashion. In fact, this potential appears to be gaining greater recognition in more recent times (Stephens et al., 2021). A good example is the finding from a nationally representative U.K. sample that the association between relative group deprivation and violent extremist attitudes and intentions is significantly lower (though still positive) for individuals higher in self-control and critical thinking (Rottweiler & Gill, 2022b). A similar protective effect of self-control (mentioned earlier) was found in the association between conspiracy beliefs and violent extremist intentions (Rottweiler & Gill, 2022a).

Earlier, we covered how low integrative complexity goes along with violent extremism. One of the most promising efforts in countering violent extremism has recently emerged in this area. Close to 100 studies in a wide range of cultures and samples (including detained violent extremists) find a highly consistent, large, and persistent effect of interventions designed to increase integrative complexity, accompanied by other positive effects such as value pluralism, empathy, and a shift toward more prosocial conflict resolution styles (e.g., Liht & Savage, 2013; for a review, see Nemr & Savage,

2019). Using integrative complexity training with at-risk youth could be especially fruitful, because such programs focus on cognitive style without attacking particular beliefs that individuals may hold, thereby bypassing the problem of psychological reactance. We suspect that the future will bring many similar attempts in educational settings (see the comment by Vezjak in Sardoč et al., 2022).

Surely, other factors at the macro-, meso-, and microlevels are not unimportant. A test of the relative importance of reflectiveness vis-à-vis these is lacking. For instance, based on Significance Quest Theory, one might argue that more priority be given to addressing significance needs. Our review suggests otherwise. Practically, it may be more difficult to intervene on significance (e.g., via restoring social inclusion and belonging), because even if one were to successfully undertake the difficult task of arranging for a socially excluded individual to be reconnected to others, there is no guarantee that the individual will retain the benefits.[40] On the other hand, once attained, thinking skills and mindware are the individual's to take wherever they go. Theoretically, as we have attempted to show, reflectiveness can guide the person to more prudent action when faced with need deficiency and negative emotional arousal. To add further evidence, mindfulness—a mental state that supports greater reflectiveness by short-circuiting intuitive responses and improving metacognition (Kang et al., 2013)—dampens the effect of social rejection on aggressive behavior (Heppner et al., 2008). Thus, reflectiveness is the overarching factor—it improves optimal responding to most, if not all, radicalizing factors (e.g., need, narrative, network)—and strengthening it early in life should have wider-ranging and longer-lasting effects.

Coda

Among the characteristics Cassam (2022, p. 112) considered, such as attitudes, preoccupations, and emotions, he argued cognitive style to be the weakest candidate for being a core (vs. peripheral) element of extremism. However, many scholars who have tackled extremism more broadly draw attention to the role of reflectiveness, such as when mentioning the "need to cultivate the skills of self-questioning, recognizing our own limitations, and attentive listening to those who differ" (Morson & Schapiro, 2021, p. 15).

Setting aside the methodological and sociopolitical challenges surrounding the topic, we faced the additional challenge that reflectiveness (and related variables, such as intelligence) is not featured explicitly and centrally in the literature examining radicalization into violent extremism (Wolfowicz et al., 2021) and the deradicalization and disengagement literature (Koehler, 2017), even though related variables (e.g., cognitive rigidity vs. flexibility) are examined in research involving broader sample of participants who are nonviolent but show variability in terms of endorsement of violent means (e.g., Brandt et al., 2015; Zmigrod et al., 2019). This necessitated an in-depth analysis of the (de)radicalization process, the factors that make individuals vulnerable, and the workings of violent organizations across a highly scattered literature. We emerge with the conclusion that violent extremist organizations actively work to reduce individuals' capacity for emotion regulation, impulse control, and cognitively effortful thinking, especially of the open-minded and critical sort. Combining the case studies, anecdotal reports, and quantitative work in the violent extremism literature with research on basic mechanisms in psychology, it becomes clear that strong reflectiveness undercuts pathways into violent extremism via its effects on various phenomena involving the need (e.g., obsession, anger, sensation-seeking), narrative (e.g., conspiracy beliefs), and network (e.g., social exclusion, informational isolation) components. Reflectiveness is an overarching factor that plays into the other, more widely discussed ones (e.g., motivation, emotion, attitudes). Like fog in a forest, reflectiveness permeates the landscape of radicalization into violent extremism, difficult to grasp or point to, but omnipresent. Why violent organizations ranging from the Neo-Nazi to the Salafi Jihadist commonly follow certain strategies in recruitment and social control and promote certain narratives becomes clear when they are examined through the lens of reflectiveness. These organizations discourage and suppress all truly open-minded reflective thought because otherwise they would fail.

Just as Krueger (2008) opined from a macrolevel perspective that lack of education and poverty are not root causes of terrorism but can be part of the solution, our review makes clear that the same holds true for reflectiveness at the microlevel. Reflectiveness works best as a preventive factor (for a converging opinion, see Moghaddam, 2005). A mind already taken over by violent extremism is unlikely to easily revert to moderatism. Outside intervention to replace extremist beliefs with more socially acceptable ones often backfires. The best hope may be that the previously gained rational mindware and reflective skills of the individual trigger reflective processes like doubt (Dalgaard-Nielsen, 2013). Once again, this suggests that reflectiveness should be nurtured earlier in life, without waiting for individuals to get tangled up in messy situations.

This view has the practical advantage that cognitive style is relatively easy to modify (see Chapter 3 of this book), and it bypasses the problem of psychological reactance by focusing on *how* to—not *what* to—think. If we can train and motivate people early on in life to regulate their emotions and impulses better; to be more cognitively flexible, intellectually humble, and integratively complex; and to separate motivated reasoning from true reflection involving cognitive decoupling—all of which require high levels of cognitive effort—we can make it significantly harder for them to fall prey to violent extremism. But as individuals, we must make sure that our powers of reflection, supported by appropriate mindware, are directed at our own minds without the motivation to confirm our preexisting beliefs. Those who are able to avoid extremism are "profoundly skeptical of the mind" and remain "attentive to its many cognitive biases and our tendency to self-deception" (Morson & Schapiro, 2021, p. 44). Metacognition, as a particular flavor of reflective thought, is especially critical.

This should not be taken to imply that reflection will or should always lead to moderate views. And moderatism and radicalism are not themselves vices or virtues (Cassam, 2022). The goal of strengthening reflectiveness is not to create moderate, docile, compliant citizens with a mainstream worldview but to support cognitive flexibility and complexity (Davies, 2009). A reflective thinker stands a better chance of adopting any orientation—whether it be moderate or radical—that the situation demands, to do so based on defensible grounds and, we hope, with respect for human life.

Notes

1 Türkiye has had its share of left-wing terrorism, as well. In fact, the most casualties by any terrorist organization (upward of 30,000 Turkish citizens) have been caused by the PKK, an ethnic (Kurdish) organization with Marxist–Leninist ideology. We do not assume correspondence between the ideology (e.g., right-wing vs. left-wing) behind violent extremist acts and the cognitive style of the masterminds and perpetrators (e.g., reflective vs. intuitive; see also endnote 10).

2 This analysis takes the perspective of the individual perpetrators mentioned in the text. We do not wish to argue that the massacre in Kahramanmaraş did not involve a masterplan.

3 See Caplan (2006) and van Um (2011) for more nuanced discussions of terrorist rationality.

4 The same cautious approach is necessary in deradicalization interventions as these might get tangled up with the political and economic interests of mainstream society and "could easily become an excuse to prevent political activism for promoting democracy, political dialogue or the promotion of minority rights ... [and] could serve as a justification for avoiding deeper societal changes" (Hansen & Lid, 2020, p. 3).

5 The issue is complicated even for lone actors, individuals who engage in terrorist acts on their own, without apparent ties to an organization (Holzer et al., 2022). For instance, Baele (2017) shows that the writings of lone-actor terrorists are just as cognitively complex (i.e., indicating high reflectiveness) compared to writings of pacifist exemplars (e.g., Mahatma Gandhi) and *more* complex than a control sample of nonemotional text.

6 Gill et al. (2021, p. 18) wisely note that

> even for those who become violently radicalised and who also suffer mental health problems, the role the latter plays differs from case to case. Where present, it might be a driving force, it might inflame other stressors and have a snowball effect, it might be a by-product of violent extremism behaviours, or it might be playing no role whatsoever.

Post (2010) draws attention to the fact that, logically, terrorist organizations select out psychologically unstable individuals due to the risks they would pose for the organizations' security, which is an argument against portraying such organizations as consisting of "crazed fanatics." More broadly, it also does not seem possible to uphold the idea of a "terrorist personality" (Corner et al., 2021; Horgan, 2014). On the other hand, our review will demonstrate that certain psychological factors make individuals susceptible to radicalization into violent extremism, including some that represent mental health issues.

7 Operation Valkyrie, the failed assassination of Adolf Hitler, is an example of an exception because had it been successful, millions of lives could have been saved. Another example could be the violence exhibited as the only choice to die a certain death with dignity or to realize one's slim chances of escape and survival, at the hands of cruel and unjust oppressors (e.g., Jews in Nazi camps; see Haslam & Reicher, 2012). See also attempts to distinguish benevolent from malevolent forms of radicalization (Reidy, 2019).

8 Many arguments we advance in this chapter probably apply to lone actors, as also suggested by the blurry distinction between lone actors versus groups (Schuurman et al., 2019).

9 See www.visionofhumanity.org/maps/global-terrorism-index/

10 Many religious and political ideologies have been co-opted in this manner (Almond et al., 2003; Clarke, 2014; Gaub, 2016; Gentile, 2006; Holbrook & Horgan, 2019; Webber et al., 2020), and supernatural beliefs (divine power) emerge as an important overarching component of violent extremism (Saucier et al., 2009). At the same time, much work indicates that religion *per se* is not the driver of violence (Ginges et al., 2009; Wolfowicz et al., 2021). For instance, among British Muslims, religiosity, frequency of religious practice (e.g., mosque attendance), and even belief in Sharia law are *not* associated with support for terrorism (Ahearn et al., 2021; for a review, see Desmarais et al., 2017). If anything, deeper knowledge of religion may provide more ammunition for reflective thought processes to defend against terrorist propaganda. Consistent with this reasoning, a nationally representative survey of Pakistanis found that greater knowledge of Islam is associated with *less* support for terrorism (Fair et al., 2017). Other belief systems that enable violence are probably confounded with religion, as well. For instance, endorsement of honor culture, which is common in our native Türkiye, is associated with both stronger religiosity and support for and propensity to engage in violence (see Molinario et al., 2021).

11 See also the literature on *rebel governance*, which suggests that it is common for armed rebels to create quasi-state institutions (Albert, 2022).

12 One example of this is the finding that endorsement of liberal democratic values (e.g., free speech) and support for militant organizations (e.g., Taliban) were *positively* associated among Pakistanis, especially if they believed that such organizations are acting in defense of Muslims' right to self-determination (e.g., in Indian Kashmir; Fair et al., 2014).

13 Researchers rely on different datasets varying in quality as well as content (e.g., time period, region of focus, terrorist groups included) which makes mixed findings less surprising. These nuances are out of our scope and do not detract from the main points that emerge from our analysis of the literature.

14 The situation seems different for the literature on crime in general (e.g., drunk driving) where constructs with a reflective core (e.g., self-control, impulsivity, thoughtfully reflective decision making) seem to feature more prominently (Mamayek et al., 2015).

15 The *content* of education probably matters (Berrebi, 2007; Davies, 2009) but this is unlikely to explain away the puzzle here. For instance, Sageman (2004) reports that the majority of a sample of religiously motivated (Salafi mujahedin) terrorists he compiled received *secular* education. From an economics perspective, Krueger (2008) argued that "although lack of education and income are not important root causes of terrorism, they can be part of the solution" (p. 51). Interestingly, Krueger seems to have suspected that the key role of education would be to strengthen reflectiveness, as he also added that

> [i]f education is to be part of the solution, I believe it is important that we concentrate on the content of education. I do not think that merely increasing years of schooling with the same curriculum that exists now will improve the situation. Research is necessary to learn what subject areas and educational materials lead to greater tolerance and respect for nonviolent forms of protest rather than self-righteousness and extremism.
>
> *(p. 51)*

In addition, it is important to analyze the effects of education at a macro level, longitudinally tracking how it changes societal norms for open dialogue and contributes to economic prosperity.

16 More specifically, dehumanization is accompanied by decreased medial prefrontal cortex activity, suggesting that this is a socio-emotional type of reflectiveness, not simply "cold" cognition. The latter is accompanied by activity in regions such as the dorsolateral prefrontal cortex. In social tasks involving empathy and compassion, these two regions are sometimes found to be in an antagonistic relationship (Fehse et al., 2015). Thus, reflectiveness in the sense of "cold" cognition alone may do more harm than good; it could facilitate violence by dampening affective responses (e.g., to a victim's pain).

17 Also relevant is work by Knežević et al. (2022) who found in a multi-ethnic sample from Serbia that closed-mindedness was associated with all three components of the militant extremist mindset. However, closed-mindedness here was a latent factor derived from many sociopolitical variables (e.g., conservatism, religiosity, ethnic narcissism, quest for personal meaning) among which we would only consider the need for cognitive closure to capture (low) reflectiveness directly.

18 The same insight appears to have been attained independently by others in the violent extremism literature. For instance, Koehler (2020, p. 16) notes that

> [a]t the end of the process [of radicalization within a violent extremist group], the recruit only recognizes one problem subsuming every other or simply being much more important than all other issues, only one viable solution and one perfect vision for the future.

19 See www.newamerica.org/future-security/reports/terrorism-in-america/who-are-the-terrorists

20 This assumes that these individuals are viewing the situation through the lens of a social identity (i.e., self as a Muslim) and attributing relative deprivation to group membership rather than to individual factors (e.g., one's laziness). In general, identity is multifaceted and sensitive to context and it is possible that the same individual adopting a different perspective (e.g., individual vs. collective self) would respond differently to the same situation (Sedikides & Brewer, 2015).

21 Obsessive (vs. harmonious) passion toward an activity feels more aversive, less under one's control, and is more likely to create conflict with other activities.

22 For a warning against equating anger with irrationality wholesale, especially in oppressed groups, see Carman (2022).

23 In one of the studies by Zedelius et al., performance on the cognitive reflection test was associated negatively with receptivity toward epistemically suspect information but surprisingly, not deprivation curiosity.

24 As Kahneman (2011, p. 80) succinctly put it, "[u]ncertainty and doubt are the domain of System 2." Moreover, "tolerance for ambiguity combined with a willingness to postpone closure" (Stanovich & West, 1997) is an explicit part of the "actively open-minded thinking" scale, a metacognitive measure of reflectiveness.

25 Higher integrative complexity requires more cognitive effort and is definitionally similar to a low need for cognitive closure, cognitive flexibility, high need for cognition, and actively open-minded thinking (Conway et al., 2008).

26 For more nuance, see the difference between dialectical and elaborative complexity, which can move in opposite directions (Conway et al., 2008).

27 Going further in the same direction, Cassam (2022) argues that extremism as a label is only applicable if the beliefs that result from the narratives (e.g., the preoccupations identified in the work on the militant extremist mindset) are not properly aligned with reality. However, in many situations, reality might be difficult, if not impossible, to define objectively and is instead defined by the narratives in the first place.

28 While we do not know of a direct and prospective test of how reflectiveness may facilitate disengagement and/or deradicalization (which is very difficult to conduct as it would require testing cognitive characteristics of individuals while they are active members of violent organizations and before they show explicit signs of disengagement or deradicalization), anecdotal accounts are supportive of our interpretation. For instance, Kruglanski et al. (2019) report how German Neo-Nazi interviewees, in the process of disengagement, "began to see things that previously might have escaped their attention" (p. 194) and "recognized weighty contradictions and discrepancies between what they expected from the movement and what they found to be the case" (p. 195).

29 For the sake of brevity, we use social exclusion to refer to a variety of similar experiences including ostracism, rejection, physical isolation, humiliation, embarrassment, derogation, and discrimination.

30 Loneliness has similar damaging effects on cognitive fitness (Cacioppo & Hawkley, 2009).

31 Williams (2009) proposes that a *reflexive* stage of emotional (e.g., pain) responses to social exclusion is followed by a *reflective* stage of appraisals and coping attempts. Though he does not seem to mean that this stage is characterized by conscious and effortful cognitive processes, it is clear that reflective processes may dampen the negative consequences of and the vulnerabilities that stem from social exclusion, for instance, by helping to regulate negative emotions, to control the impulse to immediately restore needs, to modify appraisals and construals toward a more constructive direction (e.g., attributing exclusion to temporary, situational factors rather than stable and personal ones), looking for social support elsewhere, and to question the need to find a scapegoat (on the latter, see Pellegrini et al., 2021). Paradoxically, the very experience of exclusion harms one's motivation, if not capacity, for reflectiveness, as discussed.

32 A similar effect has been discovered in the domain of morality. The perception of convergence on moral views in one's social network is causally linked to the willingness to fight and die for the in-group (Atari et al., 2022).

33 The reader is warned that attitudinal ambivalence or moderatism is not always desirable. For instance, similar to Popper's (1971) well-known *paradox of tolerance*, having an ambivalent attitude toward violence (i.e., whether harming innocent civilians for political purposes is justified) is not something we would recommend to anyone if they are faced with the task of resisting persuasive attempts by a violent organization. In this case, a strong, certain, and negative attitude toward violence would serve one better as it would be more resistant to persuasion (Bassili, 1996). The same goes for the effects of exposure to alternative views, whose attitudinal effects are not uniformly softening, because such exposure also motivates defense of one's views and production of counterarguments (Wojcieszak, 2011) and may thereby harden preexisting attitudes. Here, we base our arguments on the weight of the evidence that is most relevant to the social structure and dynamics of violent extremist groups and the process of radicalization.

34 For instance, compare the rate of transmission of a meme via linguistic communication to the rate of gene transmission via biological reproduction. As Atran (2001, p. 354) states,

> [m]emes could even afford to kill off their hosts if given the time and the medium to broadcast themselves to new victims before the hosts' demise, as with well-publicized cases of religious or political martyrdom. With Internet and globalization of information transmission, the evolutionary rate of memetic change appears to be once again on the verge of exponential takeoff, with unforeseeable evolutionary consequences. Now there is even less pressure on memes to guarantee the physical survival of brains, as more and more memetic activity shifts from biospace to cyberspace.

35 The reader must be warned that memetics has had its share of criticism, including being called "scientifically empty" (Pigliucci, 2007), and that viewing religious belief systems as memeplexes is unlikely to provide the most complete scientific understanding of religion currently (see Norenzayan, 2013; but see also Boudry & Hofhuis, 2018). In fact, one of the most prominent proponents of memetics has revised her opinions on this matter (Blackmore, 2010). Our reason for including this discussion of memetics is that, as Stanovich (2004, pp. 197–198, see also endnote 20 in Chapter 7) also argues, the very concept facilitates reflective scrutiny of one's own beliefs, as well as helping us make the argument that reflectiveness plays an important role in (the prevention of) violent extremism.

36 Once again, our emphasis here is not on Christianity per se but on the fact that what is perhaps the most successful belief system in the history of the world has had explicit and strong evaluation-disabling components. To be sure, many other belief systems, including secular ones, protect themselves similarly (e.g., *thought-terminating clichés* in Communist China, Lifton, 1961).

37 In fact, activity in other life domains (e.g., desire to start a family, employment, education) is commonly viewed as facilitating terrorist disengagement and/or deradicalization (Altier et al., 2014). The role of reflectiveness in the decision to restore motivational balance by pursuing such alternative domains is not known but a significant amount of cognitive effort probably precedes the decision in favor of such major life changes as starting a family or getting a new job at the expense of responsibilities in a violent extremist organization.

38 From a different vantage point (i.e., genetics), McDermott (2022, p. 41) made a parallel, though disheartening, observation in the nonviolent sphere:

> Importantly, many of the most well-documented differences [between U.S. liberals and conservatives] are in emotional domains, showing that, once again, information alone may be insufficient to change the minds of the most politically committed. Thus, models stressing the value of deliberation, however valuable for the less entrenched, may be ineffective for the vast majority of the ideologically committed.

See also the discussion of motivated reasoning in Chapter 9.

39 Koehler (2017, p. 294) made the converging observation that "deradicalization, reintegration, or rehabilitation programs for extremist and terrorist offenders are logical consequences of static and repressive counter-terrorism policies." However, we must also note that competition (e.g., between an insurgent group and the state or among insurgent groups) does not uniformly drive radicalization among competing factions. While the earlier literature argued that terrorist organizations are motivated to demonstrate their expertise in and capacity for armed violence and that, consequently, competition among such organizations would result in each becoming more violent (Kydd & Walter, 2006), subsequent evidence failed to support this (Findley & Young, 2012). Tokdemir et al. (2021) showed that some organizations may even become more moderate in an effort to differentiate their ideological products offered to the public.

40 This is partly due to the assimilative nature of cognitive schemata. For instance, once a person develops sensitivity to social rejection, they are more likely to readily interpret ambiguous social cues as evidence that they are being rejected (Downey & Feldman, 1996). Moreover, feelings caused by exclusion such as loneliness are more closely tied to the perceived quality of one's relationships than objective social isolation (i.e., quantity of relationships and frequency of social interaction; Cacioppo & Hawkley, 2009).

PART III
The Future of Reflectionism

9

REVISITING REFLECTIONISM

A central argument of this book is that reflective thinking is a necessary, even indispensable skill for modern human beings—a *reflectionist* position (Pennycook, 2018). In contrast to reflection, we have so far painted a somewhat negative picture of intuition, as necessitated in part by the weight of evidence. Intuition appears to be mostly associated with processes (e.g., production of impulses and emotions that could lead goal pursuit astray) and outcomes (e.g., bias, irrationality) we deem undesirable in the context of modern life. There are some good reasons for such prejudice toward intuition: Compared to reflective responses, intuitive ones are much less reproducible, if at all, because the steps involved are not accessible to introspection and cannot be formally specified; they also lack generalizability and may be context-specific in unknown ways. In social situations that require accountability—the need to explain and justify our decisions and actions and persuade others— reflection is clearly much more advantageous. In fact, some scholars argue this fact was a key driver in the evolution of our reflective capacities (Mercier & Sperber, 2017). For instance, reflection is the modus operandi in science. Theoretical and empirical advances critically depend on reflective thought employing explicit linguistic, logical, and mathematical assertions. Others can then use their own powers of reflection to scrutinize these assertions and convergence enables the establishment of useful concepts, methods, and theories. In contrast, by definition, individuals have at most superficial access to intuitive thought even though it also may play a key role in reflective endeavors such as science (Byrd, 2021; Chandrasekharan, 2014; Monsay, 1997). It is typically impossible to penetrate intuitive output and to lay it out in sequential steps as we do for reflective output. Consequently, we have much less first-hand knowledge of intuition and it has remained a much more

DOI: 10.4324/9781003300366-12

mysterious mental capacity. This must be part of the reason for the prejudice against it.

Does all this imply that reflection is by itself sufficient for individuals to successfully navigate modern society or to solve all our global problems or that intuitive processes ought to be inhibited, even removed from the cognitive arsenal if it were possible? Going to such an extreme is not warranted. At the least, as dual-process theorists explicitly acknowledge, an abundance of processes carried out by the autonomous mind feed into and support the operations of the algorithmic mind (see Pathway G in Figure 4.1 in Stanovich, 2011). As Evans (2008, p. 271) put it directly, "Type 2 processing requires supporting Type 1 processes to supply a continuous stream of relevant content into working memory." Without the background work of intuitive processes, reflection has very little to play off.[1] Intuitive processes comprise perhaps the majority of our mental activity and are much older evolutionarily, as explained in Chapter 1. Moreover, Type 1 processes not only provide background support for Type 2 processes but they may also by themselves be responsible for effective action. One example of a beneficial intuitive process is *habit* (Galla & Duckworth, 2015)—i.e., a behavioral sequence triggered automatically by environmental cues, without intent or reflection. As we will explore, the human mind's capacity to delegate complex action sequences to Type 1 processes seems to greatly facilitate effective action under pressure. Taken to an extreme and combined with the idea that reflection harms such intuitive operations, this line of thought can lead to *intuitionism*, the opposite of reflectionism.

In any case, despite its serious shortcomings, intuition continues to enjoy wide popularity (e.g., Liebowitz, 2021).[2] Some appeals to intuition may be based on *bullshit*[3] more than anything else and therefore are still dangerous (e.g., the harm done to individuals via "alternative medicine"). However, it is interesting that the word intuition derives from the Latin word "intŭēri" which means, among other things, "to consider, contemplate, pay attention to" (Simpson, 1968). Perhaps, in older times (or currently, outside of scientific circles), intuition was or is regarded as a more integral part of contemplation and a more valid way to make sense of the world and to make judgments and decisions (Davis, 2009). Even Enlightenment philosophers, from Bergson (1903/1999) to Kierkegaard (1846/2009), wrote highly of the human capacity for intuition (for other examples, see Descartes, 1641/2013; Moore, 1903/2004). In modern times, intuition enjoys a relatively good reputation in some applied fields such as organizational research and management. Writing from the perspective of those fields, Sadler-Smith (2007, p. 31) warns readers that

> [l]ife and business opportunities may be squandered or missed if intuitions are overlooked, ignored or practised covertly in an uneducated fashion.

Moreover, when—not if—a decision-maker encounters a situation where rational analysis is inappropriate, ineffective or impossible, informed intuitive judgement presents a viable alternative to paralysis-by-analysis, "groping in the dark", or passive inaction.

The bottom line is that many individuals continue to value intuition and rely on it for their judgments, decisions, and actions, raising the suspicion that there might be more to intuition than we are willing to admit at first. Part of the reason for diverging opinions on intuition is that it involves a wide set of distinct processes, as Stanovich's (2011) term "the autonomous set of systems" implies. With the term intuition, we have mostly emphasized rapid, initial responses that do not involve conscious deliberation, but others appear to have a different sense of intuition in mind. In this chapter, we explore some of these nuances, as we ponder the potential downsides of reflection and how, sometimes, intuition may compensate for those. This, we hope, will place the reader in a better position to judge the merits of reflectionism, as well as intuitionism.

Sluggishness and Fragility

In Herbert Simon's (1997) view, the limits of rationality arise because our modern world is too complex, messy, and unstable for our minds to handle. Individuals are often forced to act under time pressure, stress, fatigue, incomplete information, and many other constraints, even when they may wish to engage in extended periods of cognitive reflection. Typical correlates of reflective processes include being slow and being capacity-limited in the sense of relying on working memory—a finite resource (Evans & Stanovich, 2013b). Thus, they are particularly ill-suited to producing optimal performance under heavy constraints. Sometimes, such a constrained environment is an integral part of one's job, and intuitive processes—being faster and high capacity—may rise to the task. This was the case in a very impressive feat performed by driver Juan Fangio in the 1950 Monaco Grand Prix (described in Sadler-Smith, 2007). Apparently, Fangio—without any reason known to him—chose to brake while exiting a tunnel and this move eventually earned him first place. It turns out that his decision was based on his detection of an unexpected cue in the periphery of his vision: The faces of the audience, normally turned toward the car exiting the tunnel, were turned toward the opposite direction because of an accident and the pile-up of cars that Fangio would have crashed into if he had not processed the change in color (due to the direction of faces) in this peripheral area of vision. While many post-hoc reports of impressive feats are suspect in terms of whether they can safely be attributed to intuitive responding, the short time window in which all this occurred combined with the fact that the cue was in the periphery of his vision makes Fangio's responses non-reflective by definition. This was most likely the work of intuitive processes; reflection is too slow to come to aid in such circumstances. Even though one can probably find just as many cases in which apparently intuitive decisions are wrong or lead to disaster (or cases in which reflection leads to correct or better decisions when reflection is possible), we still take the value of rapid intuitive decisions seriously, as sometimes, as in Fangio's case, deciding intuitively is our only option anyway.

Skillful Action Under Pressure

The popular idea that reliance on intuitive processes is the better choice for performing under pressure or more generally for skillful behavior is consistent with the idea that reflective processes are too slow and fragile. It is well-established that through practice and repetition, behaviors requiring conscious control can be automatized and delegated to intuitive processes (Fitts, 1964; LaBerge & Samuels, 1974; Shiffrin & Schneider, 1977). This is a welcome part of growing up, enabling a wide range of behaviors from brushing one's teeth to reading to driving a car to become faster and less effortful, thereby freeing up cognitive capacity for other tasks. Taking this to an extreme level by deliberately practicing a skill for a prolonged period (e.g., a decade) may turn one into an elite performer (Ericsson et al., 1993).[4] Elite performers are those who have succeeded in turning the subcomponents of skillful action into automatized procedures that no longer demand conscious attention and working memory involvement. They can therefore engage in external tasks while displaying their skills, without a reduction in performance levels (Beilock et al., 2002).

This highlights the immense benefit of not just intuition (i.e., behavior practiced to automaticity and now under the control of Type 1 processes) but also reflectiveness: Effective practice requires, in the short run, being highly attentive and thoughtful as well as delaying gratification and regulating emotions. Moreover, managing such a regimen of practice and other aspects of one's career in the long run also requires a great deal of planning and therefore, sustained reflection. This exemplifies the true meaning of stepping (and staying) out of one's comfort zone. But there may be a cost of reflectiveness for performance, as well. *Choking under pressure* is a widely discussed phenomenon whereby performance in critical situations (e.g., a penalty shoot-out in a high-profile football match) is decreased to a level that greatly mismatches the performer's skill level. One classic view of choking is that the pressure (and anxiety) heightens the performer's conscious attention—a reflective process—to their own motor behavior which in turn deranges the automatic processes that normally execute such behavior (Baumeister, 1984). The heightened self-focus stems from a need to ensure optimal performance (due to the high stakes involved) but conscious thought is ill-suited because it lacks the know-how (i.e., to execute the necessary skills) that intuitive processes possess and the speed that is required for real-time control of fine-grained motor behavior.

At first glance, evidence supports the idea that self-focused attention to monitor and control the execution of overlearned motor behavior impairs the performance of experts (Beilock et al., 2002, 2004). Three points bring further nuance. First, the type of pressure (e.g., when the outcome is critical vs. the performer is being watched by an audience) and the type of task (e.g., how much it relies on reflective processes) matter (DeCaro et al., 2011). For instance, outcome- (vs. audience-) related pressure is more likely to distract attention to task-irrelevant items (e.g., "What will my coach think of me if I lose?") and eat up working memory capacity. Thus, it should hurt performance, especially on reflection-dependent tasks (i.e., those that rely on working memory and conscious attention) but much less on intuitive tasks. Second, this line of work has been criticized for showing only a correlational, not causal, link between self-focused attention and performance impairment, as well as for other issues such as lack of ecological validity and the presence of serious methodological inconsistencies (Christensen et al., 2015). Third, Papineau (2015) makes a crucial distinction between reflecting on *basic actions* versus their *components*. For skilled performers, components of actions are heavily automatized chunks of behavior and reflecting on these would disrupt performance. An expert football player does not need to reflect on how to dribble the ball. However, focusing on basic actions is necessary for performance. The player still needs to decide to dribble the ball against other options (e.g., a pass or cross), as well as the speed and direction of the dribble. Because each performance situation is dynamic and uncertain, such higher-order skills are unlikely to be fully automatized.

Overall, then, reflective processes support performers to sustain the mental activation of task-relevant intentions and direct attention properly (e.g., prevent distraction), coordinate components of basic action into a coherent performance, and flexibly respond to novel challenges and make ongoing adjustments to their behavior (Bermúdez, 2017).[5] It also clearly helps a performer to automatize and chunk as much of the action sequences involved as possible. Without delegating complicated action sequences to the fast-acting intuitive mind through heavy (and deliberate) practice, it is impossible to perform skillfully, let alone at an elite level, especially under pressure. Such delegation frees up cognitive resources so that reflective processes can work on higher-level aspects of task execution and goal pursuit. In sum, undoubtedly, both intuition and reflection are indispensable in many skillful performance situations. This cooperation between intuitive and reflective processes is exemplified by the fact that elite performers can rely on rapid, intuitive judgments and decisions *because* they have already acquired the skills and knowledge necessary to do so via reflective processes. The potential for reflection to harm performance exists but is much more limited than many people believe and pales in comparison to the benefits of reflective processes.[6]

The Alarm Signal Function of Intuition

Many of the above-mentioned positive capacities of intuitive processes make possible the rapid detection of threats in the environment without having to rely heavily on cognitive resources like controlled attention. What Juan Fangio's mind registered as he exited the tunnel was the potential presence of an unknown threat—a pattern that signaled that something was wrong and his life or his goal of winning was at risk. Humans are known to efficiently process valence (i.e., the overall positivity/negativity) of environmental stimuli (Bargh et al., 1996). The *dual implicit process model* (March et al., 2018) goes one step further and proposes that automatic *threat* detection is a unique mental capacity, not only compared to reflective thought but compared even to automatic valence processing. It is sensible that throughout evolution, humans evolved a distinct mechanism to detect, process, and respond to survival threats and that this mechanism gained not only a high degree of efficiency but also priority over any other task or mechanism. There is evidence supporting this view: Stimuli that pose an immediate survival threat (e.g., gunmen) elicit faster and stronger physiological and perceptual responses (e.g., startle-eyeblinks) than other categories of stimuli, including negative but not immediately threatening ones (e.g., feces) (March et al., 2017).[7] These responses occur within a few hundred milliseconds and are not likely to be reflective. More definitive evidence that this is an intuitive capacity is in fact available: Presenting the same categories of stimuli subliminally (i.e., outside of conscious awareness) produced converging findings (March et al., 2022). This function of intuitive processes—detecting and rapidly responding to threats—is also evident in very different, real-world research settings where it often works through detecting the deviation of complex constellations of stimuli from expected patterns. We discuss this in a subsequent section.

Fast and Frugal Heuristics

While Kahneman and Tversky's highly influential heuristics-and-biases line of work led to an explosion of research, other researchers, inspired by ideas of humans as boundedly rational and as satisficers (vs. maximizers), attempted to demonstrate the value of thinking less. Heuristics are mental shortcuts for solving problems with much less information than full-fledged deliberation might entail but with the benefits of speed, reduced effort, and equal or even better accuracy. The general idea is that the human mind is an "adaptive toolbox" that possesses a variety of useful heuristics, whether they are generated by the individual, culturally transmitted, or take advantage of evolved capacities (Gigerenzer, 2008a). When information is lacking or costly to obtain or process, heuristics can provide an easy way out. A good example is the *recognition heuristic* or estimating some aspect of an entity as being of a higher value if one recognizes the entity. Consumers frequently rely on brand name recognition to infer the quality of a product. More surprisingly, stock portfolios built on the basis of whether various groups of people (e.g., German and U.S. American laypersons) recognized the company name was found to prospectively (i.e., six months following data collection) outperform traditional benchmarks such as market indices (e.g., Dow 30) and mutual funds (Ortmann et al., 2008; for other examples and other heuristics, see Goldstein & Gigerenzer, 2009; Gigerenzer & Gaissmaier, 2011). Of course, the validity of such heuristics critically depends on the structure of the environment[8] and one's mental representations (Goldstein & Gigerenzer, 2002). Consider the question of whether Detroit or Milwaukee has a larger population. U.S. Americans do worse at this than Germans because they recognize both cities equally well whereas Germans are more likely to recognize the bigger city, Detroit, which indeed has the larger population. For the same reason, experts (given they recognize entities in their domain uniformly) cannot use the recognition heuristic. However, the importance of heuristics in expertise, particularly in natural environments, has been widely demonstrated in the literature (Gigerenzer, 2008b; Gigerenzer et al., 2011; Gigerenzer & Todd, 1999). For instance, in social contexts, ordinary people use heuristics to determine if someone is trustworthy or caring. As social animals, humans excel at recognizing these cues due to their evolutionary and cultural history. Similarly, intuition can be valuable in financial decisions. Those who succeed in the stock market often are not Economy PhDs but investors who have spent years in the industry, honing their intuitions to an art form. Intuition also plays a significant role in medical decision-making. In emergencies, where quick decisions are required, experienced doctors can make more accurate diagnoses by developing smart intuitions based on prior experience. More experienced firefighters also tend to perform better in emergencies, like fires, because their intuition has been sharpened by experience. This demonstrates that qualified professionals in specialized fields can make effective decisions by developing and relying on smart intuitions (Isler & Yilmaz, 2019). Lau and Redlawsk (2001) reported parallel findings showing how experts (but not novices) could benefit from the use of heuristics in politics.

Overall, it seems safe to conclude that heuristics can help individuals overcome the limitations concerning cognitive resources and the time required by reflective processes, as well as information overload, under some conditions (Kahneman & Klein, 2009). However, it does not seem possible to claim that all heuristics are intuitive. The *gaze heuristic* is used by baseball players to catch a flying ball (McBeath et al., 1995; see the discussion in Gigerenzer, 2008a). Players appear to be unaware of it and it seems to be closer to an intuitive response that has been honed over experience and practice, like those discussed in the section on skillful action above. Contrast this with fast-and-frugal decision trees used in medical diagnosis, which are also called heuristics (Marewski & Gigerenzer, 2012). These involve explicitly identified steps, each of which requires a decision. For instance, the difficult problem of whether a patient with chest pain should be sent to the coronary care unit may be simplified into a sequence of three questions. The first asks whether there is an anomalous electrocardiogram reading with the patient being sent to coronary care if affirmative. If not, the next question is considered, and so on. Nothing is unconscious, the steps are explicit, and the decisions need reflection. Thus, the literature on heuristics should not be taken as uniformly demonstrating the limitations of reflection and the advantages of intuition. Heuristics can be reflectively derived, committed to memory, and used more automatically with practice, and re-evaluated and edited via reflection as needed.

Reyna and Lloyd (2006) similarly found that more experienced physicians relied on a *smaller* number of information dimensions in assessing risk and making decisions in scenarios involving cardiac patients, and were still able to discriminate better between low- and high-risk patients. However, these researchers approached the issue from a distinct perspective, that of Fuzzy-Trace Theory, whose interesting developmental predictions are discussed in Chapter 3. The theory is relevant in this context due to its distinction between thinking based on gist (global, imprecise impression focused on essential meaning) versus verbatim (surface form, precise, detailed) representations. Similar to how heuristics take on a more positive meaning in Gigerenzer's work, Fuzzy-Trace Theory views intuitive (gist-based) thinking in a much more positive light than mainstream dual-process models. In fact, it goes further by placing "intuition—defined as meaningful gist-based thinking—at the apex of advanced cognition" (Reyna et al., 2017, p. 82). Compared to verbatim thinking, gist-based thinking is more advanced and advantageous in various senses, such as that (1) development and expertise both entail increasing reliance on gists; (2) gists are more memorable and accessible; (3) gists entail conceptual and context-sensitive understanding of meaning (and not just associative processing); and (4) gist-based intuitions often lead to better decisions in the real world, as discussed in Chapter 3 (see also Blalock & Reyna, 2016; Reyna & Mills, 2014).

Fuzzy-Trace Theory views gist and verbatim representations as independent and makes the interesting case that gists can be grasped even when one is unable to reflect on or verbalize them (Reyna & Mills, 2007). In parallel, an early realization by Fuzzy-Trace theorists concerned dissociations between memory and reasoning: Under some circumstances, reasoning performance is uncorrelated with memory for problem features and less verbatim memory can go along with even better reasoning (see Reyna & Brainerd, 1995).

Sometimes people may have more wisdom than they are able to verbally report!

Low-Effort and Misdirected Reflection

It is often the case that people accept the value of reflectiveness and think they are acting in accordance but actually fail to engage in true reflection in terms of the amount of cognitive effort they exert and its direction. What we wish to point to here is not a downside of truly reflective thought but of other forms of cognitive activity carried out by the same set of (Type 2) processes. The two need to be clearly separated.

Serial Associative Cognition with a Focal Bias

We have presented an idealized version of Type 2 processes at the outset of the book. However, dual-process model theorists point out that Type 2 processes do not always involve the costly mechanisms of hypothetical thinking and cognitive decoupling that excel at fine-grained analysis. The *typical* Type 2 activity might actually not involve much cognitive decoupling or effort. Kahneman (2011, p. 24) argued that "System 2 is normally in a comfortable low-effort mode, in which only a fraction of its capacity is engaged." There are two ways of being cognitive miserly (see Stanovich, 2011, p. 66). We have mostly discussed the primary one, which involves relying on Type 1 processes by default and in which Type 2 processes are never initiated or if initiated, were unsuccessful. However, remember that the intuitive mind learns slowly and needs experience or the help of evolutionary modules to generate responses. Many situations in modern society are too novel and complex for any intuitive response to be even produced, let alone to be helpful. Type 2 processes come to aid but with a catch: In the absence of sufficient motivation (e.g., high personal relevance and importance), a less resource-heavy version of Type 2 processes will be employed; the low-effort mode that Kahneman's quote above mentions. Stanovich (2009a, p. 68) called this *serial associative cognition with a focal bias* and defined it as "cognition that is not rapid and parallel such as [intuitive] processes, but is nonetheless rather inflexibly locked into an associative mode that takes as its starting point a model of the world that is given to the subject." This is the consequence of the reflective mind's tendency "to deal only with the most easily constructed cognitive model" (Stanovich, 2009a, p. 69)—the focal model. This also converges with the idea that cognitive ability translates to performance in reasoning and problem-solving especially or exclusively when a need to think effortfully is detected by the reasoner (Stanovich, 2011; see also Chapter 2) or is made explicit by task features (e.g., Evans et al., 2010).[9] This mode of operation has been confused with intuitive processes by researchers[10] and we suspect that it is easily confused with reflection from the perspective of the layperson doing the thinking. It is thus sneaky and dangerous; it creates the illusion of true reflection but does not possess some of its critical characteristics.

Consider a concrete example: When faced with a sales pitch or even shopping on your own, the communication and physical environment are arranged to give you various attractive options. This activates many thoughts relevant to a possible purchase (e.g., the pros and cons of this brand and model vs. that other one). You might be engaged in cognitive effort and have many conscious thoughts. But such cognitive activity flows from the immediate situation (i.e., it is serial associative cognition); you are rarely given the option to not take any of the alternatives and just walk away without buying anything. You have to think of this yourself, with higher-effort cognition, as it is not easily constructed based on salient cues. Switching from a serial associative cognition with a focal bias to true reflection is probably what people are trying to get others to do when they ask them "to think outside the box" (i.e., in technical language, to simulate alternative models other than the focal model). This also suggests that reflection can play a key role in creativity. In fact, there is evidence that individuals with a stronger reflective cognitive style and those who enjoy thinking more are also more creative in some senses (Barr et al., 2015).[11]

The Anchoring-and-Adjustment Heuristic

Knowledge of serial associative cognition with a focal bias helps to make sense of other phenomena. For instance, the well-known *anchoring-and-adjustment heuristic* occurs when a reference point—the anchor—influences a judgment (for a review, see Furnham & Boo, 2011). The anchor may be integral to the judgment task (e.g., one's first guess) or it may even be a random value.[12] In an early demonstration (Tversky & Kahneman, 1974), participants were first shown the experimenter spinning a rigged wheel of fortune that stopped at either 10 or 65. They were then asked to provide a numeric estimate such as the percentage of African nations within the U.N., by first stating whether their estimate would be above or below the number revealed by the wheel of fortune—thereby bringing this arbitrary value into focus—and then to work toward their final estimate from that anchor. There was a sizeable difference between estimates in the group of participants exposed to different anchors—median values of 25% versus 45% for the 10 and 65 groups, respectively—and this effect still held when participants were incentivized to provide accurate estimates or were briefly educated about the effect and asked to prevent it (Wilson et al., 1996; cf. Epley & Gilovich, 2005; Simmons et al., 2010). A prominent explanation of this effect is that participants fail to sufficiently adjust their estimates and end up staying in the vicinity of the anchor (Epley & Gilovich, 2006). However, recent research suggests that people adjust their degree of adjustment in response to features of the problem space. For instance, when errors are more costly, more adjustments are made, reducing the anchor's biasing influence whereas when time is costly, people resort to faster responses with smaller adjustments, leading to greater anchoring bias (Lieder et al., 2018).

The anchoring-and-adjustment heuristic has wide application. For instance, it is a good reason why first offers are good predictors of the final deal in negotiations (Galinsky & Mussweiler, 2001). Salespersons attempt to take advantage of this by carefully choosing the price of goods. Getting a deal at a somewhat lower price than the initial offer leaves the customer satisfied while starting with a high anchor ensures the desired amount of profit for the salesperson. In the legal system, a question from a journalist may bias, by serving as an anchor, the sentencing decisions of even experienced trial judges (Englich et al., 2006). From a methodological perspective, anchoring effects need to be considered in the design of research materials because respondents may be influenced by the anchors provided in item stems or response options, even when reporting their own recent behavior (Cheek et al., 2015). Finally, anchoring may underlie various egocentric biases in the social realm because when attempting to infer the thoughts of others or take their perspective, individuals often start by using knowledge of themselves as an anchor. For instance, participants who were made to feel thirsty (vs. not) via exercise were subsequently more likely to predict that others in a different situation—lost mountain hikers without supplies—would also experience thirst (vs. hunger) as their main concern (Van Boven & Loewenstein, 2003). Likewise, people tend to overestimate the extent to which others in the social environment notice them—*the spotlight effect*—and the extent to which their internal states (e.g., thoughts, knowledge) are seen by others—*the illusion of transparency* (Gilovich & Savitsky, 1999). Both these might be specific cases of anchoring-and-adjustment whereby one's phenomenological experience serves as the anchor. Such egocentric biases are amplified under conditions that make reflection difficult, such as time pressure (Epley et al., 2004). Note that in the kinds of situations studied in this literature, people are making judgments using explicit information. Thus, it is not the case that they are not thinking; in fact, they may be viewing themselves as doing a great deal of thinking. However, their thinking appears to suffer from a focal bias. A greater degree of cognitive effort is needed to realize or break free from the influence of the anchor on their final judgments or to make a greater degree of adjustments away from it.

Motivated Reasoning and Actively Open-Minded Thinking

Throughout this book, we have occasionally touched upon one of the biggest dangers of reflective thought—that it may sometimes serve to uphold our pre-existing beliefs in light of our preferences, desires, and motivations rather than to calibrate our beliefs to reality. That is, sometimes individuals already know what they want to believe, the conclusions they want to reach in the debates they engage in with others, and the actions they want to take next. In Chapter 4, for instance, we mentioned Lodge and Taber's (2013) view that thinking harder may result in even more bias in one's political beliefs. These kinds of findings appear to challenge the idea that reflection is necessary for rationality. Others have challenged accounts like Lodge and Taber's by arguing that they focus on a subpar, "learning and memory-driven" version of reflection instead of a stronger form that "actively reshapes, redefines and reframes" what has been learned, memorized or is contextually cued (Rosenberg, 2017, p. 378). Such challenges have serious merit!

The beliefs, desired conclusions, and actions that constrain our reasoning often stem from intuitive thought more than careful deliberation; they may represent basic human motivations to see the self and in-group in a positive light. Guided by such motivational states, individuals use reflective thought (or what superficially appears to be reflection, as discussed above) to arrive at those pre-determined end states. This phenomenon has been discussed under the term *motivated cognition* or *motivated reasoning* (Kunda, 1990). The tendency to search for, selectively attend to, remember, and interpret information in ways that confirm a focal hypothesis or one's pre-existing beliefs can be seen as specific instantiations, studied under terms such as *confirmation bias* (Nickerson, 1998) and *myside bias* (Stanovich, 2021). Converging with the above discussion, pre-existing beliefs (or one's current motivations) have a special psychological import in the sense of being highly accessible anchors to work from in responding to the world. They can be used with minimal cognitive effort while maintaining the appearance, to oneself and others, of careful reasoning.

While much work on dual-process theory leaves one with an idealized impression of reflection, the *primary* assumed function of Type 2 processes in the earliest dual-process frameworks in the 1970s was in fact *rationalization*—i.e., "to construct a justification for [one's] own behavior consistent with [one's] knowledge of the situation" (Wason & Evans, 1974, p. 149), even when the behavior is at fault or when the justifications have little or nothing to do with the actual causes of one's behavior (Evans, 2019).[13] There is abundant evidence for rationalization. In an earlier demonstration, Evans and Wason (1976) contrived three wrong (but plausible) solutions and offered one of these as the correct solution to a reasoning problem for each of the three groups of participants. A fourth group received the actually correct solution. Participants were required to explain why the solution was correct and report their confidence in their explanations. All were able to do so and generally with high confidence! This implies that not only do people happily fabricate explanations for why something is valid without realizing that it is invalid, but they also may *not* be experiencing genuine insight when they appear able to explain the reasons for why a valid response is so.

This initial emphasis on rationalization converges with social psychological research of the same era which focused on how actions may cause beliefs by mechanisms such as *cognitive dissonance* (e.g., Festinger & Carlsmith, 1959). Post-hoc rationalization of behavior is indeed widely discussed in the literature at least since Freud (1900/1953) identified it as a defense mechanism, with humans characterized as "masterful spin doctors" (Wilson, 2002) and "rationalization machines" (Mercier & Sperber, 2017). The extent to which rationalization is employed in daily life and is adaptive versus a source of problems is a topic of contemporary debate (see the target article by Cushman, 2020 and responses). Importantly, some recent dual-process models imply that the rationalizing function of reflection has greater affinity with low-effort thought than with true reflection involving cognitive decoupling: Rationalization may not exactly be miserly but it may favor a focal intuition at the expense of alternative ideas, similar to serial associative cognition with a focal bias. For instance, Evans' (2019) model assumes that reasoners proceed by default as if their initial intuitive response is right and use reflective thought to justify it. Unless otherwise motivated (e.g., by a general inclination to think reflectively or by the personal importance of the problem at hand), this is where they stop. Thus, in many situations, we can imagine intuitive processes as simply doing their best to provide any useful initial response. Reflective processes might be more to blame for our limitations as reasoners because they do a poor job of filtering intuitive responses and instead, often provide justifications for them, which creates the illusion of well-reasoned beliefs and actions.[14]

This function of reflection—to confirm our pre-existing beliefs and rationalize our intuitions or actions after the fact—stands in opposition to its function to support good (e.g., logical or optimal) reasoning. These two functions are not mutually exclusive in the sense that Type 2 capacities can be used to perform either function (Evans, 2019), but it greatly matters which function is implemented at any given time. The distinction between these functions is most clear in research on *actively open-minded thinking*[15] (Baron, 2019; Baron et al., 2023; Stanovich & Toplak, 2023b). While various conceptualizations and operationalizations of this construct exist, they commonly emphasize factors that would reverse or weaken the tendency for motivated reasoning, such as belief flexibility (i.e., the willingness to change one's beliefs in light of evidence) and consideration of information that contradicts one's beliefs (e.g., see Table 1 in Stanovich & Toplak, 2023b). Baron (2019) points out that while reflectiveness and actively open-minded thinking are necessarily related[16] (e.g., because considering information that counters one's pre-existing beliefs will simply increase the amount of time one spends thinking per se), the direction of thought is typically more important in real life than its amount. Stanovich and colleagues consider actively open-minded thinking "the most important thinking disposition" (Stanovich & Toplak, 2023b, p. 2) among the many measures they have compiled to assess rational thinking (Stanovich et al., 2016). In fact, scores on their measure of actively open-minded thinking are correlated with scores on nearly all those rational thinking measures even while controlling for cognitive ability (Stanovich et al., 2016). Moreover, actively open-minded thinking is negatively correlated with a variety of epistemically suspect beliefs (e.g., Pennycook et al., 2020).[17] Thus, actively open-minded thinking represents a set of norms for good thinking that maximize the value one can derive from cognitive effort (Baron et al., 2023). If we wish to be fair and objective and calibrate our beliefs and actions to evidence rather than to our desires, motivations, and impulses, mere cognitive effort or superficial forms of reflection will not suffice. To fulfill its true potential, reflection needs to break out of the riverbed carved by intuitive and low-effort forms of thought.

Rumination

Rumination[18] is one type of cognitive activity that at first appears to be reflective—in fact, overly reflective (i.e., overthinking, overanalyzing)—because it has been defined as "thinking perseveratively about one's feelings and problems" (Nolen-Hoeksema et al., 2008, p. 400) that occurs "in the absence of immediate environmental demands requiring the thoughts" (Martin & Tesser, 1996, p. 1). It also appears similar to reflectiveness because it is assumed to be driven by a "[c]onscious motive … to understand the deep meanings of events, gain insight, and solve problem" (Nolen-Hoeksema et al., 2008, p. 407).

However, upon careful examination, rumination has greater affinity with intuitive than reflective thought. First, rumination is experienced as an intrusive, aversive, and persistent cognitive activity (Papageorgiou & Wells, 2001) accompanied by difficulty in disengaging attention from certain themes (e.g., negative self-relevant thoughts; Koster et al., 2011), suggesting that it does not stem from the person's consciously controlled (i.e., reflective) thoughts. Ruminative thoughts are repetitive and become automatized over time, making them intuitive, spontaneous, passive, and habit-like (Watkins & Nolen-Hoeksema, 2014). Second, as the above implies, rumination stands in direct opposition to reflectiveness empirically. For instance, weaker Type 2 capacity (e.g., executive functions, working memory) is associated with a ruminative tendency (see Watkins & Roberts, 2020) and the role of such capacity is likely to be causal (Siegle et al., 2014). The failure to inhibit negative self-relevant thoughts, even when the task at hand requires it, may underlie the negative consequences of rumination such as increased depression (Johnson et al., 2009), anxiety (Ruscio et al., 2011), and obsession (Grisham

& Williams, 2009; see also Chapter 9). Thus, rumination is not only intuitive but also irrational because it is a maladaptive coping strategy that amplifies the stress response and stretches it out across time, leading to a wide range of negative effects on both mental and physical health (Nolen-Hoeksema et al., 2008; Watkins & Roberts, 2020).

Ruminators hold positive beliefs about rumination, such as that it helps them to cope with adversity (Papageorgiou & Wells, 2001). This does not hold up in light of evidence on the harmful effects of rumination just mentioned, but it leaves open questions: Why does rumination exist, why is it so common, and why do individuals believe it has positive aspects? The literature in fact distinguishes between maladaptive and adaptive forms and consequences of rumination (Trapnell & Campbell, 1999; Watkins, 2008). Research suggests that for rumination to be beneficial, the individual should take a self-distanced[19] (vs. self-immersed) perspective, as in viewing events from a third- (vs. first-) person perspective (for meta-analyses, see Moran & Eyal, 2022; Murdoch et al., 2023). For instance, experimentally manipulating individuals to adopt self-distancing (vs. self-immersion) reduces depressed affect and rumination after recall of a depressive episode (Kross & Ayduk, 2008), especially when they were encouraged to ask more abstract "why" (vs. more concrete 'what") questions (Kross et al., 2005).[20]

When one ruminates from a self-distanced perspective, the cognitive activity that ensues is no longer rumination as an intuitive, automatic process but more like proper reflection. Rumination pretends to be reflection but is not. Overall, the former is harmful and the latter beneficial.[21] In sum, the weight of the evidence suggests that the motivation behind rumination—to understand and process one's feelings in response to a stressful event—can be addressed by the flexible use of reflective processes in a much more adaptive way, especially via downregulating negative affect and boosting attentional control, compared to letting intuitive processes run rampant.

Directionlessness

Motivated reasoning, discussed above, is a problem where reflection has a pre-determined direction and fails to be fair, balanced, neutral, and objective. The opposite, directionless reflection, is also a problem. Individuals sometimes appear to reflect for prolonged periods on a certain task or topic without much practical benefit. The thought involved can be low in effort and highly repetitive, as in rumination, or it can be highly effortful and focus on various unique aspects of the topic. Putting these aside, the important question that arises in these cases is whether "too much reflection" is a thing. In other words, should one strive to maximize the amount of reflection across the board or is that a bad idea after all? If one's aim is to be rational, one should strive to maintain high levels of reflectiveness (and other useful dispositions such as "belief flexibility") but should *not* strive to maximize it because at maximal levels, the "person might get lost in interminable pondering and never make a decision" or "end up with a pathologically unstable personality" (Stanovich, 2011, pp. 39–40). In our modern world where many of us are faced with an overload of information and choices, there is a serious risk of suffering from paralysis-by-analysis or indecision. Research suggests that even individuals high in cognitive ability and incentivized to perform well on an experimental task have difficulty prioritizing information in their decisions (Aßmann et al., 2022). Moreover, cases of individuals with localized brain lesions exemplify the above-mentioned risk. For instance, an individual with damage to the ventromedial prefrontal cortex may have intact intellectual capacity but may be unable to make decisions that move them forward in any given task (Damasio, 1994). According to Damasio's *somatic marker hypothesis*, this may be due to an inability to generate and integrate bodily and emotional responses to ongoing considerations. That is, normally, the subtle cues from our intuitive responses constrain the problem space, prune options to a manageable set, and facilitate making choices and decisions. We desperately need these intuitive "go, stop, and turn signals … for much decision making and planning on even the most abstract of topics" (Damasio, 1996, p. 1417).[22] Without them, reflection leads into a dead-end street. In sum, successfully overcoming information overload and preventing indecisiveness or paralysis-by-analysis may require the recruitment of intuitive, even emotional and bodily, processes to narrow down options and to reserve the finite resources fueling reflective processes for the things that really merit further reflection. This view also converges with the perspective of Fuzzy-Trace Theory, discussed earlier in this chapter and in Chapter 3, that what counts in the real world is not necessarily "processing more" but "processing more meaningfully" by focusing the essence of information rather than its surface details (Reyna et al., 2017).

This idea can be applied in the domain of morality where it may matter more. Without a moral compass, reflective thought can do more harm than good by serving evil better than intuitive thought can. A carefully planned sneak attack can be much more effective on the target than an impulsive burst of aggression. Having a strong reflective tendency by itself is no guarantee that an individual will distinguish what is good from evil and choose to follow the former. In Chapter 8, we discussed how some forms of reflective activity, such as doubt, may facilitate disengagement from violent extremism. Moral emotions, which we would consider to originate more from intuitive than reflective processes, can also serve a similar function, such as when one is disgusted by the brutality of fellow members (Speckhard & Yayla, 2015).

As Bloom (2016, p. 180) stated, "[r]eason and rationality … are not sufficient for being a good and capable person … but … they are necessary, and on average, the more the better." Of course, the last part of this quote needs to be supplemented with the warning above regarding maximal levels of reflective dispositions. Consistent with the discussion above, Herbert Simon (1997) and many others recognized the importance of intuitive processes for providing motivation and direction to reflective thought. This idea applies at a very broad level. At the outset of the book, we mentioned two meanings of rationality—instrumental and epistemic. The former is about one's ability to reach desired goal states using available resources. Note that at the top of the structure, there lies a *desired goal*, which is about motivation and valence, not symbolic cognition devoid of these. There is an important role of valence and evaluation even in the other sense of rationality. Instrumental rationality is about whether one's beliefs accurately represent the world. But what is the agent forming beliefs about? One cannot mentally represent the entire world, so what are they attending in the world? Surely, people do not just expose themselves to information about random objects or events they come across. Especially in the modern world, this is a recipe for becoming dysfunctional quickly. We filter out what we *want* to learn and develop beliefs about what we find *pleasurable* to attend to. In sum, to serve the individual and society well, reflection needs direction from both intuition and guiding principles other than just mindware concerning logic and probability.

Atomism and Piecemeal Processing

Dual-process theories commonly mention serial processing as a correlate of Type 2 processes (Evans & Stanovich, 2013b). Because of the limits of working memory, there is a small number of elements that can be reflected on at any given moment. This forces thinkers using reflective thought to consider elements in a problem space in a piecemeal fashion, handling them one at a time or in small chunks. In contrast, a correlate of Type 1 processes is parallel operation, which makes them better overall at handling a greater number of elements simultaneously. This could place reflection at a comparative disadvantage. For instance, complex patterns, which characterize much of our modern environments, cannot be detected by focusing on elements one at a time.

Implicit Learning and Pattern Recognition

Juan Fangio's example was worth repeating because it demonstrates not only the speed advantage of intuitive over reflective processes but also the superior pattern recognition capacity of the former. After all, Fangio responded to an unexpected *pattern* of color in the stands where the audiences were seated. The pattern Fangio responded to was visually simple and did not involve extensive prior learning in a narrow sense. More complex patterns can be learned slowly if they are regularly encountered and then recognized rapidly by Type 1 processes—a widely discussed example being patterns on a chess board (Chase & Simon, 1973). One reason why expertise takes so much time and first-hand experience is the slow speed with which Type 1 processes learn.[23] If the goal is to develop expertise, the study of patterns is probably best done consciously and with cognitive effort (i.e., with Type 2 processes; Ericsson et al., 1993) but their storage and organization in long-term memory and their recognition when encountered (i.e., matching the stimuli with memory representations) is up to Type 1 processes.[24] Upon recognition of a pattern with the help of Type 1 processes, Type 2 processes can engage in further computation (e.g., of alternative responses) so that the optimal action can be taken. Evans (2020, p. 186) emphasizes how crucial this interplay between Type 1 and Type 2 processes is when he writes that

> [t]he recognition of which moves deserve attention, cued by patterns learnt by long study, is what gives humans playing strength. These rapid recognition processes (Type 1, autonomous) greatly reduce the load of explicit calculation (Type 2, engaging working memory). If we think of rationality as depending simply on explicit calculation and reasoning, then we do our species a great disservice. Our working memories are small and slow but our capacity for implicit learning of patterns is vast.

On the basis of this insight, Evans also notes how Type 1 processes appear necessarily less intelligent in novel laboratory tasks—which form the majority of evidence that dual-process models are based on—because participants have no prior experience with them and are therefore unable to use any of their natural pattern learning and recognition skills.

This serves as a good warning against any prejudice toward Type 1 processes (e.g., intuition = error-prone), which is supported by evidence in other domains of expertise. For instance, in medical diagnosis, experienced clinicians are able to rely more on Type 1 processes—e.g., for recognizing patterns of illness based on similarity to previously encountered cases—but Type 2 processes are more important for clinicians with less experience and for difficult (e.g., atypical) cases (LoGiudice et al., 2021). As in chess, intuitive pattern recognition helps expert clinicians generate a feasible number of diagnostic alternatives, greatly reducing the further work that Type 2 needs to undertake, such as in verifying a particular diagnosis (Brush et al., 2017). If expertise is both supported by Type 1 processes and associated with better performance (e.g., more accurate diagnosis), then it is illogical to place the blame for diagnostic error only on intuition. There is evidence that faster diagnostic decisions—more likely to stem from intuitive pattern recognition than reflection—are *more* accurate (Sherbino et al., 2012). Detailed analyses of diagnostic errors yield the conclusion that both Type 1 and Type 2 processes are responsible for them (Norman et al., 2017). Consistent with our occasional emphasis on metacognitive flexibility throughout the book, evidence suggests that instructing medical students to use *both* Type 1 and Type 2 processes (e.g., compared to no particular instruction) improves diagnostic accuracy (Eva et al., 2007).[25]

Another line of research highlighting the importance of intuitive pattern recognition, as well as how intuitive processes function to detect threat, was carried out by Klein et al. (2010) who interviewed firefighters—more specifically, highly experienced fire ground commanders—to identify decision points in critical incidents. The majority of decisions were made under extreme time pressure, within a minute and usually even less. Leaving aside the difficulty of carrying out serious reflection under stress, deliberating over options was not feasible and almost none of the 156 decision points analyzed involved deliberation and option comparison. Instead, the overwhelming majority of decisions were based on pattern recognition. That is, firefighters matched the current incident to their prototypical one, which immediately revealed the actions needed; they did not even feel like they were making any decisions. The mismatch between the current incident and the prototype can serve as an intuitive alarm signal[26] as demonstrated by one of the cases Klein et al. reported:

> ... a firefighter led his men into a burning house, rounded back to the apparent seat of the fire in the rear of the house, and directed a stream of water on it. The water did not have the expected effect, so he backed off and then hit it again. At the same time, he began to notice that it was getting intensely hot and very quiet. He stated that he had no idea what was going on, but he suddenly ordered his crew to evacuate the house. Within a minute after they evacuated, the floor collapsed. It turned out that the fire had been in the basement. He had never expected this. This was why his stream of water was ineffective, and it was why the house could become hot and quiet at the same time. He attributed his decision to a "sixth sense."
>
> *(pp. 194–195)*

The attribution to the sixth sense—the inability to explicitly justify the action—suggests that the decision was largely intuitive. The case also exemplifies the value of rapid, intuitive decisions under pressure. If this decision had been left up to reflection, this crew could have perished! Based on such insights, Klein (1998) developed a model of *naturalistic decision-making* that emphasizes intuitive decisions that flow directly from pattern recognition, much in line with the pioneering work of Herbert Simon. In sum, it seems clear that intuition, in the form of learning patterns over long periods of experience and recognizing them rapidly, comprises an indispensable component of expertise.

Seeing the Forest: Holistic and Systems Thinking

Many modern problems, such as climate chaos, are wide in scale and involve a very large number of distinct but interconnected elements. Our mental representations of the world do not seem to match the complexity of some of the critical problems we are faced with (Wallis & Valentinov, 2017). The serial nature of Type 2 processes—bringing informational units into working memory one at a time—may give rise to the by-product of a piecemeal approach that prioritizes isolating objects at the expense of their interconnectedness and at the expense of attaining a view of the forest rather than just single trees. This may be a serious deficiency for attacking problems that require a more global view with an understanding of interconnections between the parts and of part–whole relations (Mungan, 2023b).

Holistic Thinking

In the cross-cultural literature, *analytic thinking* is placed in opposition to *holistic thinking* with an emphasis on the atomism and reductionism of the former, that is, the tendency to break the world into parts and focus on those parts in isolation (Nisbett et al., 2001). Analytic thinking is also used synonymously with reflective thinking in the dual-process literature. The two senses of the term analytic—reflective and atomistic—are often confounded. For instance, in their definition of analytic thinking, Nisbett et al. (2001, p. 293) also include "a tendency to focus on attributes of the object to assign it to categories, ... a preference for using rules about the categories to explain and predict the object's behavior, ... [and] the use of formal logic" which parallel the characterization of Type 2 processes as rule-based, abstract, and logical by dual-process theorists (Epstein et al., 1996; Evans & Stanovich, 2013b).[27]

If the purported alignment between reflective and piecemeal processing on the one hand, and intuitive and holistic processing on the other hand, is accurate, then a clear downside of reflective processes might be the inability to support seeing the forest and the connections between the analyzed elements. Even though no direct empirical test of these purported alignments has been conducted to date, Talhelm et al. (2015, Study 2) reported a non-negligible positive correlation between cognitive reflection test scores and analytic (vs. holistic) thinking as measured by the triad categorization task.[28] It seems safe to argue that reflective processes may indeed be better at making finer distinctions in whatever is attended to, compared to intuitive processes. On the other hand, there is no necessity for holistic thinking to be correlated with a tendency to think intuitively at the individual level or to be carried out primarily by Type 1 processes as a matter of cognitive architecture.[29] Research that specifies the components of holistic thinking does not make such an assumption and also highlights that there is more to holistic thinking than a focus on the whole and on the interrelationships among entities (Choi et al., 2007). In fact, the other components—also referred to as *naïve dialecticism* (e.g., acceptance of the ever-changing nature of the universe and a positive attitude toward contradictions; Peng et al., 2006)—could easily be viewed as requiring more complex, hence more effortful and reflective, thought even if they support a different way of approaching life compared to Western, formal logic. Moreover, if holistic thinking was an integral part of Type 1 processes, and as people are cognitively miserly in general and intuitive processes govern much of daily life, one would expect holistic thinking to be very common across cultures, as well. However, the literature portrays holistic thinking as relatively more dominant in Eastern cultures (Nisbett, 2004). Thus, lumping holistic thinking into the category of Type 1 processes appears to not be based on evidence and may reflect a mostly Western prejudice toward both holism and intuition. In line with these arguments, Buchtel and Norenzayan's (2009) review concluded that both holistic and analytic thinking can be reflective or intuitive. For example, holistic thinking might be an intuitively endorsed and practiced cultural orientation for an Easterner, while analytic cultural orientation could be an intuitively endorsed and practiced cultural orientation for a Westerner. In this context, the positive relationship between analytic cultural orientation and the cognitive reflection test should be reconsidered (Talhelm et al., 2015; Study 2), as most findings in the literature predominantly involve participants from the WEIRD cultures or the most WEIRD ones of non-WEIRD cultures (e.g., university students, English-speaking online participants) (see Endnote 2 in Yilmaz & Saribay, 2017b). In any case, reflective thought can sometimes benefit from assuming a holistic mode in terms of avoiding the pitfalls of atomism and exercising a greater capacity to conceptualize the interconnectedness of elements in a problem space.

Systems Thinking

Systems thinking is similar to holistic thinking in that it heavily emphasizes interconnectedness and dynamicism and stands in opposition to linear and reductionist thought (Meadows & Wright, 2008). Unlike holism, it stems more from Western science (e.g., biology, cybernetics), has influenced respectable modern efforts in various areas (e.g., engineering, complexity science), and thus mostly escapes the prejudice that holism has faced. Interestingly, research shows that a tendency to adopt systems thinking at the individual level is positively associated with *both* reflectiveness (e.g., need for cognition) and holistic thinking (Thibodeau et al., 2016). Such a tendency also appears to heighten sensitivity toward complex macro-level (e.g., environmental) problems (Ballew et al., 2019). Unfortunately, even a strong background in science does not guarantee the ability to think systemically (Sterman & Sweeney, 2007). Because systems thinking can be cognitively demanding, individuals rely on heuristics, such as that the output of a system should roughly match its inputs (Sweeney & Sterman, 2000), which are unlikely to do the job well enough. Similar to expertise, both strong reflection—to identify the many elements and to explicate the precise ways in which they are related—and delegation to intuitive processes via automatization and chunking—to enable efficient thought without becoming overwhelmed—are likely needed for systems thinking. These issues are crucial if we are to successfully tackle issues involving such complex systems as the climate.

Insight and Unconscious Integration of Complex Information

Our definition of intuition focuses on initial, rapid responses that are not subject to careful reflective scrutiny. Still, the discussion of holistic and systems thinking, as well as pattern recognition, highlights a different mental process that is sometimes discussed under the term intuition. In some cases, individuals, after being exposed to a good deal of novel information, might go through an *incubation* phase that they are not necessarily aware of and that leads to new ideas or to the integration of the new information into an *insight* (e.g., a sudden, creative solution to a complex problem; an "Aha" experience). The processes of incubation and insight do not fit neatly into either Type 1 or 2 processes. On the one hand, Gestalt psychologists who were the first to study insight systematically (e.g., Köhler, 1925), placed it in opposition to *analysis* (i.e., reflection) and this view also characterizes many modern approaches to insight (see Weisberg, 2015). On the other hand, there is evidence that insight problem-solving has strong affinity with reflective thought—e.g., that it relies on working memory and fluid intelligence (Chuderski & Jastrzębski, 2018). In any case, the general idea that complex information can be *intelligently* integrated by the operation of Type 1 processes over relatively long periods of time (e.g., hours, days, months) is an assumption that needs to be empirically tested. This idea goes beyond the learning of simple associations and regularities in the environment via experience, as discussed earlier.

Unconscious thought theory (Dijksterhuis & Nordgren, 2006) was proposed to highlight such a mental capacity. Unlike our focus in this book on intuition as relatively fast, initial responses (e.g., occurring within seconds of encountering a stimulus), this theory focused on unconscious information processing over relatively longer periods of time—a few minutes at the least—which only then may result in a task-relevant intuition. For instance, as both authors have experienced, looking for an apartment in a crowded and poorly planned city like Istanbul—which faces the ongoing threat of a major earthquake—is likely to cause headaches due to the cognitively demanding task of finding the optimum choice among alternatives. One needs to properly weigh many features such as size, rent, deposit, amenities, neighborhood, landlord, building residents, commute, noise levels, earthquake resistance, and so on, and combine them into an overall judgment. The initial test of unconscious-thought theory (Dijksterhuis, 2004, Experiment 1) presented 12 such features for 4 hypothetical apartments in Amsterdam to Dutch participants, arranged such that one apartment had the most positive features combined, another the most negative, and the remaining two falling in between. Participants were then asked to rate the desirability of each apartment either immediately, after 3 minutes of conscious deliberation, or after 3 minutes of being distracted by a cognitively demanding task. The latter condition was assumed to leave unconscious thought as the only possible mechanism with which the apartment features could be cognitively processed. Participants' ratings distinguished between the best and worst apartments only in this unconscious thought condition. Consistent with the popular advice to "sleep on it," this implies that unconscious thought facilitates better decisions than conscious thought, especially with increasing decisional complexity.

Like the literature on fast and frugal heuristics, unconscious thought promises better judgments and decisions when serial and resource-limited Type 2 processes are not up to the task. Such a feat would tremendously aid citizens of our complex modern world. There is not much doubt that unconscious processes exist. At the same time, the positive capacities attributed to unconscious thought and related notions such as incubation and insight may have been exaggerated (Newell & Shanks, 2014). Notwithstanding the greater difficulty of empirically investigating these notions compared to reflective thought (e.g., because of lack of introspective access to the former), there are important statistical, methodological, and theoretical challenges in the literature that preclude confident conclusions. The kind of effect reported by Dijksterhuis (2004) did not survive some tests of replication (e.g., Newell & Rakow, 2011), re-analysis (González-Vallejo & Phillips, 2010), and meta-analysis (Nieuwenstein et al., 2015; Vadillo et al., 2015). In addition, unconscious thought experiments have been criticized as providing impoverished conditions for deliberation in their conscious thought conditions. When participants are allowed to carry out self-paced conscious thought, instead of being given a fixed period of time as in the apartment experiment above, they actually perform equally well or better than participants in the unconscious thought condition (Payne et al., 2008). Finally, the effects of the distraction or incubation period need not be attributed to unconscious thought. In their scathing review of this area in which they call the idea of unconscious work an "imaginary meme," Smith and Beda (2023) list several mechanisms tested as viable alternatives to incubation-based explanations. In sum, as fascinating as the possibility is, the idea of unconscious information integration needs, at the least, further research to emerge as an empirically supported mechanism.

Coda

Our review indicates that reflection has several important downsides. Especially when it remains superficial and works in a pre-determined direction, it can lead to bias and error instead of boosting accuracy and rationality. Reflection may fail to find proper direction by itself, for which it needs the help of intuitive (e.g., motivational, emotional, bodily) processes. Reflection might also entail a bias to consider information in a piecemeal fashion rather than holistically. On the other hand, intuition can support accuracy and operate much more efficiently (time- and energy-wise). It can enable expertise by learning and recognizing patterns and protect one's chances of survival by detecting threats rapidly. Beyond what was reviewed above, intuitiveness may confer other advantages over reflectiveness, such as when decisions made intuitively foster stronger impressions of authenticity (Oktar & Lombrozo, 2022) and greater commitment (Maglio & Reich, 2020). It may be counterproductive to introspectively examine subjective experiences that are less inviting of symbolic thought and verbalization (Schooler et al., 1993; Schooler & Engstler-Schooler, 1990) or the reasons for one's attitudes and decisions (Wilson & Schooler, 1991).

Despite the early cautions of dual-process theorists against idealizing Type 2 processes, laboratory tasks created a somewhat artificial coupling between the use of those processes and correct, normative solutions; and between the use of Type 1 processes and bias. This appears to have led to a skewed view of both reflection and intuition both in scientific and (some) popular circles. It is not a coincidence that researchers in more applied fields, dealing more heavily with the messy data of real life compared to data from the highly controlled but sterile psychology laboratory, have tended to value intuition more than their counterparts pursuing basic research.[30] Part of the problem seems to be that the term intuition is too broad. Those in the basic research camp focus on rapid, initial responses in unfamiliar (to participants) laboratory environments. Those in applied settings focus on intuition that results from participants' prolonged experience in the same domain. Naturally, the latter type of intuition has much greater value than the former. In any case, among these two clusters of researchers, those going to extremes have ended up with versions of reflectionism and intuitionism that are both indefensible in our view.

Many impressive feats—expertise, elite-level performance in various domains, creativity, complex systems thinking—seem to require the extensive collaboration of reflective and intuitive processes. The critical task is to distinguish between intuition that stems from experience and expertise instead of invalid heuristics, irrelevant impulses, incidental feelings, and mere guesswork; and between truly effortful and open-minded reflection from low-effort and misguided forms of reflection. After spending more than nearly a quarter of a century researching dual processes, Evans (2019, p. 28) came to hold the view that

> we need to recognise the importance of intuitive processing in reasoning and decision making, neither dismissing it as a mere cause of cognitive biases, nor allowing ourselves to be deceived by philosophical tradition into thinking that slow reflective reasoning is the main basis for rational thought.

Our own review of the literature also leads us to believe that both science and society would do well to heed his advice. We believe that studies focusing specifically on the evolutionary-cultural context in which these cognitive styles evolved, the influence of metacognitive processes and other thinking styles (e.g., holistic and systemic thinking), as well as the importance of the virtues and motivations (e.g., open-mindedness and humility) accompanying those cognitive styles, can facilitate the discovery of aspects of reflection that we may not have previously realized.

Notes

1 Frankish and Evans (2009) remind us that this basic idea was present in philosophical writings from earlier centuries (e.g., Leibniz's "petites perceptions"; Helmholtz's "unconscious inferences").

2 An alternative view is that intuition continues to enjoy wide appeal, not despite, but *because of* its shortcomings, such as non-traceability. The human brain is vastly complex. Our internal (e.g., thoughts, feelings) and external (i.e., overt behaviors) responses are driven by a multitude of mechanisms, many of which are intuitive. Individuals thus have very limited introspective access to the actual mechanisms that drive their responses (Wilson & Dunn, 2004). Attributing one's responses to intuition provides a relatively easy way out when the individual is required to justify those responses but cannot. Combined with an obedient followership with strong faith in intuition, this provides a dangerously effective recipe for a leader to do as they please and not be held accountable. Freely attributing responses (e.g., business decisions) to intuition creates practical problems that obscure the real value of intuition (e.g., Blume & Covin, 2011).

3 We use this as a technical term, as is common in our field (e.g., Pennycook, Cheyne, et al., 2015), to refer to assertions that disregard the truth (Frankfurt, 2005).

4 Reflection—especially in the sense of conscious attention to the body and one's motor behavior—also has a critical role in continued improvements and recovery of old, superior habits (e.g., after injury) of elite performers (Toner et al., 2015).

5 Some readers may be confused because especially in the domain of sports and physical skills, these reflective processes may not primarily look and feel like the

sustained cognitive effort individuals show when they are, say, making tough life decisions. We have emphasized the latter kind of reflection, which involves symbolic propositions and abstract concepts, more in this book. However, we have also made reference to capacities that support reflection, as well, such as emotion regulation, impulse inhibition, and the control of attention. These may not involve mentally processing propositions or concepts. As Bermúdez (2017, p. 900) also stated, the reflective processes that go into skillful performance

> require exerting some cognitive effort, since executive functions are costly mental operations, and (...) need not imply the manipulation of propositions, since there can be non-propositional cognitive complexity (as in mentally rotating a three-dimensional object or sustaining attention despite distracting forces).

6 To add to emphasis, competitive sports have elements of a *hostile environment* where "other agents discern the simple cues that are being used to trigger miserly defaults and arrange them for their own advantage" (Stanovich, 2018, p. 426). Consider all the fakes and feints in football (e.g., the Cruyff turn, the lunge, the elastico); these work by setting off a habitual or reflexive response in the opponent that puts them at a disadvantage. Stanovich argues that "[o]ur responses might be suboptimal when we default to miserly processing in a hostile environment."

7 Conspiracy theories are similar: The ease with which they provoke fear and are adopted and spread by intuitive thinkers suggests that they may serve as an alarm signal (see Chapter 5).

8 This is true more broadly for the development of valid intuitions, as well. Simply put, "[i]f an environment provides valid cues and good feedback, skill and expert intuition will eventually develop in individuals of sufficient talent" (Kahneman & Klein, 2009, p. 524). Thus, the utility of intuitive responses and heuristics needs to be judged in context. Moreover, valid intuitions and heuristics are more likely to be domain-specific than to work across many different domains. This is self-evident if one compares tasks across different fields where heuristics or intuitive responses may be employed, such as diagnosing disease from X-ray or magnetic resonance images or a set of patient complaints versus forecasting the value of stocks based on their history and the current economic context. These tasks share little and so are unlikely to benefit from generalized heuristics applied rigidly.

9 This can be taken as another sense of reflection's fragility: Reflection needs more push (e.g., incentive, social guidance) from the environment to be activated.

10 We do not pretend we are immune from this risk. We have delayed the discussion of serial associative cognition up to this point in the book and some of the phenomena we discussed as stemming from intuitive processes could be instances of serial associative cognition with a focal bias. Empirical evidence of cognitive mechanisms is needed to distinguish the two. For example, Stanovich (2009a) explains how Evans was able to decide that low-effort reflective processes (i.e., serial associative cognition with a focal bias) were responsible for some typical errors in well-known research paradigms (e.g., the Wason selection task). In any case, it is critical but generally quite difficult both conceptually and empirically "to make firm distinctions between autonomous processes and processes that closely resemble them" (Thompson & Newman, 2017, p. 132).

11 To be sure, both reflective and intuitive processes are involved in creativity, which requires many distinct types of mental activity and consists of multiple, distinct stages (Allen & Thomas, 2011; Barr, 2018).

12 Some studies (e.g., Critcher & Gilovich, 2008) found anchoring effects using anchors completely incidental to the task and not even remembered afterwards by participants (e.g., making estimates about an athlete whose jersey number is high vs. low in the experimental conditions). Other studies demonstrated the influence of anchors presented outside of conscious awareness (e.g., Reitsma-van Rooijen & Daamen, 2006). Recent research failed to replicate these effects and suggested that anchoring effects occur only when the anchor is consciously attended to (Röseler et al., 2021; Shanks et al., 2020).

13 The rationalizing function of Type 2 processes is explicitly acknowledged in contemporary dual-process models, as well (e.g., Pennycook, Fugelsang, et al., 2015). A critical addition of the new wave of theorizing is that this type of process (i.e., rationalization) sometimes involves verifying and explicating correct intuitions (Bago & De Neys, 2019; see also Chapter 10). This compensates for a major limitation of intuitive responses, making them traceable and convincing to others (Mercier & Sperber, 2017). Interestingly, this was also acknowledged in the ending paragraph of the earliest dual-process article: "(…) mathematicians (e.g., Poincaré) sometimes report that the solutions to their problems occur 'intuitively' and that the conscious construction of the proof is worked out after the insight" (Wason & Evans, 1974, p. 152). Rationalization may also have the positive function of "extracting valuable information from [intuitive responses] and then allowing it to influence the network of beliefs and desires that support reasoning" (Cushman, 2020, p. 2).

14 However, a correlate of intuitive thought is also a big part of the problem: Intuitive responses are typically accompanied by high confidence, which appears to serve as an internal signal that serious scrutiny by reflective processes is not necessary (e.g., Thompson, Evans, et al., 2013). See Chapter 10.

15 The construct of *intellectual humility*—e.g., the tendency to recognize one's intellectual limitations and to avoid both intellectual arrogance and self-deprecation (Whitcomb et al., 2017; for a more comprehensive list of definitions, see Porter, Baldwin, et al., 2022)—overlaps with actively open-minded thinking and has been receiving increasing research attention in the past several years in psychology. Even if the two constructs were to be clearly distinguished conceptually and operationally, which is not always the case in research, they are both considered intellectual virtues and would be expected to build off of each other. For instance, recognizing one's intellectual limitations should make one more open to receiving alternative views and new information from others (see Krumrei-Mancuso & Worthington, Jr., 2023). Not surprisingly, intellectual humility and open-mindedness are found to be positively correlated in many studies (see Porter, Elnakouri, et al., 2022). Thus, the points in our discussion of actively open-minded thinking should generally apply to intellectual humility, as well.

16 One of the earlier operationalizations of actively open-minded thinking by Stanovich and West (1997) also explicitly included reflectiveness (and related factors such as "willingness to postpone closure"). After decades of research on this topic, Stanovich and Toplak (2023b) recently recommended keeping

reflectiveness as part of actively open-minded thinking. They also argue that cognitive decoupling, which we have discussed throughout the book as a key element of true reflectiveness and which we have discussed in this chapter as being absent from superficial forms of reflection (e.g., serial associative cognition with focal bias), is the key cognitive capacity assessed by actively open-minded thinking measures.

17 At the same time, there is a surprising level of empirical disconnect between myside bias and actively open-minded thinking: Many studies fail to find a correlation between measures of these constructs (for a review, see Stanovich & Toplak, 2023b). The reason has not been clarified empirically but Stanovich and Toplak (2023b) offer some possibilities. Myside bias concerns pre-existing beliefs. When studied in domains such as religion and politics, these are not just any set of beliefs but rather *convictions* (i.e., emotionally charged beliefs with a high degree of ego involvement). Convictions might entail the limits of the human ability to reason properly. In any case, the literature is currently stuck with the paradox that actively open-minded thinking appears to be irrelevant in domains most relevant to its conceptual definition and where it is most direly needed. There is a chilling possibility here—that the balance of evolutionary benefits and costs is simply more advantageous for holding convictions than for engaging in actively open-minded thinking (Stanovich, 2021).

18 We examine rumination in detail because there is an extensive literature on it but there are other forms of repetitive thought, some of which (e.g., worry) fit into our analysis of rumination better than others (Watkins, 2008).

19 Bernstein et al. (2015) treat self-distancing as related to the broader construct of *decentering*, which involves a set of metacognitive reflective processes. Research on some of the other decentering-related constructs, such as mindfulness, has also shown negative associations with rumination (Parmentier et al., 2019).

20 A separate line of work finds that rumination is more beneficial when it is focused on concrete/experiential (vs. abstract/analytic) thoughts (see Watkins & Roberts, 2020). Concrete thinking asks questions of "what" (e.g., specific sensations, feelings) with regard to the target of rumination (e.g., self, events, symptoms) whereas abstract thinking asks "why" (e.g., the reasons behind their feelings) questions. Like self-distancing, this may switch the nature of rumination from hot to cool: When individuals are led to think repetitive thoughts more concretely (vs. abstractly) via experimental manipulation, they show lowered emotional reactivity (Kornacka et al., 2019; Watkins et al., 2008). This is sensible because depressive rumination is known to be relatively abstract and thinking abstractly when depressed may facilitate overgeneralizing from single events (e.g., "I am worthless"), feeding back into depression. There is a seeming contradiction between the two literatures here because self-distancing is aligned with abstract, not concrete, thought; both are high-level construals (Trope & Liberman, 2010). How is it possible then for both self-distancing and concrete thought to turn rumination into something more beneficial? Kross and Ayduk (2008, p. 935) point to similarities between their self-distancing manipulation and the concrete thinking manipulation of Watkins and colleagues. Moran and Eyal (2022) offer another partial resolution by showing that high-level (i.e., self-distancing, abstract) thought may attenuate low-level (i.e., basic, primary) emotions (e.g., sadness) because of the mismatch in construal. They may not have the same effect

on high-level emotions (e.g., depression, anxiety). For instance, thinking abstractly would support overgeneralization of negative incidents to the self-concept. It is also likely that the immediate needs of individuals already suffering from depression are different than non-depressed individuals (e.g., to downregulate negative affect vs. to make symbolic meaning out of negative emotions, respectively). Thus, the former may benefit more from concrete thinking and the latter from abstract thinking. In any case, further high-quality research is needed (see also Murdoch et al., 2023) to attain better insight into how these thinking styles work in this context.

21 Reflective/distanced (vs. ruminative/immersed) processing may also dampen positive emotions (Gruber et al., 2009). Though this may be protective in the case of bipolar disorder, it would be undesirable for the rest of us. Cognitive flexibility—another reflectively supported capacity—may aid individuals in adopting different thinking styles flexibly as it suits them in terms of their overarching goals (e.g., general well-being). Very few studies have explored this possibility so far (e.g., Altan-Atalay et al., 2022).

22 The next chapter discusses a phenomenological state called the *feeling of rightness* as an internal cue that (when low) signals the need for further reflection (Thompson, 2009). This intuitively generated cue is stronger for initial, intuitive responses and this may facilitate naïve realism (see Chapter 2). On average, reflective responses take more effort and time to generate and suffer from lower levels of an accompanying feeling of rightness. Given that serious cognitive effort is also aversive (Kurzban et al., 2013), this may be considered another downside of reflection—that it does not engender as much psychological comfort (pleasance and confidence) as relying on intuition. Consistent with this reasoning, the tendency to maximize—to deliberate on options exhaustively as opposed to satisficing—is associated with lower well-being (e.g., happiness, optimism) and negative emotions (e.g., depression and regret; Schwartz et al., 2002). Likewise, intuitive cognitive style (e.g., as measured by the faith in intuition scale) is positively associated with meaning in life and more reflective thinkers (i.e., participants who perform better on the cognitive reflection test) report lower meaning in life (Heintzelman & King, 2016).

23 This is one disadvantage of Type 1 processes—that they learn slowly and are also difficult to modify once learning has taken place. In comparison, Type 2 processes can immediately represent new information, propositions, associations, and models that run counter to what is stored in memory. Because they respond at different speeds to new information, representations created by these two sets of processes can become disconnected over time. With contradictory new information, such as learning that one's beloved partner intentionally committed a horrible crime, representations undergirded by Type 2 processes will rapidly change where as those undergirded by Type 1 processes will remain relatively stable. In line with this idea, much research in social psychology creates or measures the dissociations between implicit and explicit evaluations/attitudes or the spontaneous/automatic and effortful/controlled behaviors that stem from them (e.g., McConnell & Rydell, 2014).

24 Learning patterns, associations, and rules or regularities that characterize the constellation of stimuli and information in the environment does not require conscious intention to do so or awareness that the stimuli are patterned—i.e.,

implicit learning—and the resulting knowledge structures are not always available for introspective reflection—i.e., *tacit knowledge* (Reber, 1989). This capacity of Type 1 processes plays a fundamental role across various crucial human abilities such as language acquisition. Some recent efforts suggest to us that more systematic tests of such intuitive capacities are underway. For instance, Kalra et al. (2019) found that, as predicted by dual-process models, performance on a variety of implicit learning tasks was unrelated to the algorithmic mind (cognitive ability and working memory), but also that, contrary to dual-process models (which predict few differences in the autonomous mind), there were sizeable individual differences in such performance. Weinberger and Green (2022) attempted to track how implicit learning gives rise to intuitions which in turn give rise to explicit knowledge about the learned pattern. While the quality of implicit learning did not translate into more accurate intuitions, the latter was related to more accurate explicit knowledge. Continued research along these lines could shed light on the nature of Type 1 processes, as well as the interplay between intuitive and reflective processes. However, research on unconscious processes is plagued by measurement error (Vadillo et al., 2022), which casts doubt on many findings, making it difficult to reach conclusions for the time being.

25 For a similar argument regarding how to conduct and report empirical research, see Kump (2022).

26 Of course, as the mismatch grows, the novelty of the situation increases and one's past experience and implicit learning become less applicable. A full understanding of the situation begins to require greater information search and mental simulation, which necessarily bring in reflective processes. The point here is that intuitive processes can detect the mismatch and trigger a course of action that at least serves to ensure safety or to buy more time.

27 Similarly, Allinson and Hayes (1996, p. 122) characterize intuition as "immediate judgement based on feeling and the adoption of a global perspective" and analytic thought as "judgement based on mental reasoning and a focus on detail." Epstein's model (Epstein et al., 1996) explicitly includes "holistic" as a feature of the experiential (Type 1) system. More recent findings appear to support these pairings but there is reason to be skeptical about such findings (e.g., Klauer & Singmann, 2015).

28 The association between cultural thought style (i.e., analytic vs. holistic) and reflective (vs. intuitive) cognitive style may depend on culture. For individuals socialized in East Asian cultures where holistic thinking is widespread (see Nisbett, 2004), thinking holistically may become intuitive via practice, whereas for individuals socialized in cultures where analytic thinking is dominant (e.g., North America and Western Europe), holistic thinking may require Type 2 processes (see also Chapter 10).

29 Consistent with this speculation, one study reported that individuals with a stronger tendency to think holistically were, contrary to the authors' prediction, less susceptible to anchoring (Cheek & Norem, 2017), a bias that we would expect to be dampened by reflective thought (see the section on anchoring-and-adjustment, above).

30 We have encountered similar situations in other areas of research. For example, in political science, Lodge and Taber (2013) note how the very act of asking questions about political issues or using sterile and artificial materials in surveys may itself lead respondents to give "intellectualized" answers. In contrast, politics is filled with controversial figures and topics and emotionally charged exchanges. This might lead to an affect-centered theory of political behavior to appear much less valid when tested on survey versus field data.

10
REVISITING THE DUAL-PROCESS MODEL OF THE MIND

In the previous chapters, we have attempted to demonstrate that a domain-general, prototypical version of the dual-process model of the mind can shed insight into a variety of seemingly unrelated phenomena from human prosociality, to violent extremism, to skilled sports performance, to sociopolitical, and moral convictions. At an abstract level, the model may appear to explain everything by flexibly accommodating any empirical observation—i.e., to be unfalsifiable. Proponents of dual-process theory have warned that this generic "received" version creates confusion as it may contain various myths—features defended by none of the individual dual-process theory proponents (or defended only by a minority of them) but attacked by the critics (Evans, 2012; Evans & Stanovich, 2013a). We have corrected for some such myths along the way. For instance, the previous chapter, by discussing the downsides of reflection and upsides of intuition, should have made it clear that the most widespread of these myths—equating Type 2 processes with rationality and Type 1 processes with bias (i.e., *the normative fallacy*)—is unwarranted.

In our reading, unfalsifiability is not a problem for dual-process theory (see Evans & Stanovich, 2013b).[1] As one of our favorite sayings goes, "all models are wrong" (Box, 1979, p. 202). Dual-process theory is also necessarily wrong because at the least, strictly speaking, nature probably never works according to our abstract linguistic categories (e.g., reflection vs. intuition; reflective vs. algorithmic vs. autonomous mind).[2] Writing about the Gestalt

DOI: 10.4324/9781003300366-13

approach to the psychology of problem-solving, one of our colleagues made a thought-provoking remark that:

> Gestalt theory does not confine itself to a narrow either-or dichotomy ... the biggest problem with American-centric psychology is that it almost always deals with the phenomena it examines in a dichotomizing, polarizing way. ... Just as the nature-nurture debate has become a thing of the past especially with epigenetics (i.e., because it has been understood that genes and environment are an inseparable whole), similarly, "conflicts" such as subjectivity versus objectivity, body versus mind, emotion versus cognition will also become meaningless. As we better understand the concepts that are currently settled in opposite poles, we will realize that they are actually an inseparable whole.
>
> *(Mungan, 2023a, p. 135)*[3]

This holds for reflection versus intuition as well. Indeed, such concepts are scientific "fictions" (see Kahneman, 2011, p. 28) or "heuristics" (see De Neys, 2023b, p. 71) and come with risks if we take them too seriously and pretend they are essences—like homunculi inside the minds of individuals— or that they have perfect correspondence to neurobiological structures (Brick et al., 2022). Box argued that "all models are wrong" but he also added the important qualification that "some are useful." Looking into some of the limitations of and debates surrounding the dual-process model of the mind is a good way to be reminded that it is just a model, though we also hope you are by now convinced that it is an extremely useful one.

In fact, wrongness and usefulness can go hand in hand. From a researcher's point of view, one way that a scientific model is useful is by being wrong in specific ways. That is, we think the best test of the scientific utility of a model is that by generating a lot of questions and drawing criticisms, it is eventually proven wrong, at least on some specific issues, and leads to revised, improved models. Tinghög et al. (2023, pp. 63–64) said it the best when they remarked that the key function of the general dual-process model is as a "benchmark theory" (or a metatheory; Evans & Stanovich, 2013b), that

> can serve as a starting point for more refined research questions and domain-specific models. Thus, dual-process theories have much in common with the fictional character Barbapapa, a blob-shaped creature with the notable ability to shapeshift and thereby smoothly overcome any obstacle. Just like Barbapapa, dual-process theory is liked by many and can easily be reshaped to fit in many contexts. ... The world needs Barbapapa and social science needs dual-process theory.

This highlights two points: First, we have not emphasized the nuances of domain-specific dual-process models even though we relied on them throughout the book. However, it is important to capture the domain-specific nuances in serious empirical and applied work. Second, the general dual-process model can be criticized on many fronts indeed. Fortunately, there is a lot of healthy debate amongst dual-process theorists and there are many interesting empirical findings and theoretical proposals that promise to advance our knowledge of the mind while also keeping this topic exciting (see especially De Neys, 2017b). In this chapter, we aim to give a glimpse of some such debates.

Conflict Sensitivity and Logical Intuition

As Chapter 9 revealed, the autonomous mind may be more capable than sometimes assumed. Research has relied heavily on tasks that have been designed to evoke misleading intuitions and to be solvable by the application of reflective processes and the use of appropriate mindware (e.g., knowledge of logic and probability). In other words, there is an overreliance on tasks that trigger conflict between intuition and reflection and data from these tasks naturally favor the default-interventionism (i.e., a misleading intuition is activated, and only if there is sufficient reflection is it suppressed in favor of a more principled (e.g., logical) approach).[4] Moreover, the majority of participants sampled in this area are university students or otherwise well-educated in the Western sense. The observation that even these samples display a high proportion of errors in these tasks has served to bolster the argument that people are cognitively miserly and typically unable or unwilling to show the cognitive effort to inhibit intuitive responses and apply their learned mindware towards attaining the normative solution.

De Neys (2012) reviewed several different kinds of evidence challenging this picture and supporting the idea that individuals show *conflict sensitivity*—that is, they detect the conflict between biased intuitions triggered by classical reasoning tasks and the normative solution that can be reached by reflection, *even when they fail to report the correct answer* (i.e., they appear to be unaware of the normative, logical solution). To give an example, in a seminal study, De Neys and Glumicic (2008) used base-rate neglect problems. Take a look at a classic version that we have used also in our own research:

In a study 1000 people were tested. Among the participants there were 4 kindergarten teachers and 996 executive managers. Lilly is a randomly chosen participant of this study. Lilly is 37 years old. She is married and has 3 kids. Her husband is a veterinarian. She is committed to her family and always watches the daily cartoon shows with her kids.

What is most likely?

a) Lilly is an executive manager
b) Lilly is a kindergarten teacher

This question is designed so that the cultural stereotype of a kindergarten teacher is activated—a Type 1 process—and is in conflict with the base-rate respecting solution that can be reached by suppressing the intuitively appealing stereotype-driven response and paying attention to the base rate—a Type 2 process. Versions of this question that do not trigger the conflict can be created, for instance, by stating that "there were 4 executive managers and 996 kindergarten teachers" instead (see De Neys, 2012, Box 1). In that case, both intuitive (i.e., the stereotype activated by Lilly's description) and reflective (i.e., base-rate information) should lead participants to choose the correct option (b). De Neys and Glumicic (2008, Experiment 1) administered such conflict and no-conflict versions of the base-rate neglect problem while asking participants to report their thought processes. This revealed no evidence that participants were *consciously aware* of the conflict between the responses generated by Type 1 and Type 2 processes in the conflict version—e.g., only 18% mentioned base rates. However, participants successfully recalled the base-rate information in a subsequent surprise test, showing that they had registered it. In the no-conflict version, participants had a much poorer recall of base-rate information. If people simply ignored base rates altogether, there would be no reason for recall performance to differ between the conflict and no-conflict versions. Instead, even if they produced an incorrect response and did not explicitly report paying attention to base rates, participants somehow detected the importance of the base-rate information—they seemed to realize that there was a potential conflict.[5] The second experiment applied a similar logic to response times in the same task. Monitoring and detecting conflict while attempting a problem should theoretically slow individuals down. Therefore, people should take longer to respond to base-rate conflict problems when they produce an incorrect answer compared to correctly solving the no-conflict version. The findings supported this prediction as well.

Similar findings with other tasks and paradigms began to accumulate in the following years (see De Neys, 2017a). This line of work has implications for how we conceptualize the interaction of Type 1 and Type 2 processes. Initially, De Neys interpreted these results in terms of *shallow analytic monitoring*—a Type 2 process—operating in parallel with Type 1 processes. This weaker Type 2 process "only recruits and keeps activated some general analytic principles" and "allows the reasoner to determine whether or not the heuristically cued response can be sanctioned but does not suffice to make a decision in case of a conflict" (De Neys & Glumicic, 2008, p. 1278).

This was a happy middle ground between a fully parallel architecture (which admits that precious cognitive resources are wasted by always engaging Type 2 processes for monitoring) and default-interventionism (which cannot explain how conflict is detected without Type 2 involvement).

Subsequently, De Neys (2012, p. 29) re-interpreted such findings as showing that Type 1 processes were capable of "an intuitive grasping of the standard logical and probability theory principles (e.g., conjunction rule, proportionality principle, logical validity) that are evoked in the classic reasoning problems," which he termed as *logical intuition*.[6] That is, individuals have not only biased and incorrect intuitions (e.g., based on the heuristics or affect that the task is designed to trigger) but also intuitions about the correct (logical, normative) response; and they sense the conflict between the two thanks to an intuitive monitoring process, even when they fail to resolve the conflict and simply produce the incorrect response. This converges with some other observations we discussed in Chapter 9 to suggest a view of the intuitive mind as more capable than was initially assumed by dual-process theorists. For instance, it is sensible that through years of Western education emphasizing logic, probability, and mathematics, judgments using such mindware become somewhat automatized.[7] If this is the mechanism underlying logical intuition effects, then people with higher cognitive ability would show stronger intuitive logic as they are better able to absorb such education. In fact, some findings show that cognitive ability is positively correlated with the ability to generate logical intuitions in reasoning tasks (Raoelison et al., 2020; Thompson et al., 2018). At the same time, the smartness of intuition should not be exaggerated because more recent work supports the idea that intuitive processes are not truly smart or logical but are simply sensitive to superficial cues of tasks that happen to coincide with the logically correct solution (Ghasemi et al., 2022, 2023). Thus, the exact nature of logical intuitions is still open to debate.

Exclusivity, Switch, and a New Working Model

Building on such findings, De Neys (2023a) recently put forth a more systematic criticism of dual-process theory in which he identified two related problems. First, the assumption of *exclusivity* in dual-process models holds that Type 1 and Type 2 processes cannot take over each other's capabilities. That is, mental calculations based on probability and logic,[8] for instance, are assumed to be handled exclusively by Type 2 processes and it is impossible for Type 1 processes to take this responsibility over. De Neys pointed out that while earlier studies provided evidence in support of the exclusivity assumption, more recent studies have muddied the picture by either failing to find support (e.g., Gürçay & Baron, 2017) or revealing the small size of the effects involved (e.g., Lawson et al., 2020).[9] More critically, newer paradigms provided evidence that is very difficult to explain with exclusivity. We already mentioned the work on conflict detection. Consider also the *two-response paradigm* (e.g., Thompson et al., 2011) in which participants attempt a classic reasoning problem twice; once fast and intuitively (sometimes under cognitive load so that reflection is even less of a possibility) and again without time pressure, reflecting on it as long as they wish. If exclusivity holds, most individuals' first attempts should be incorrect, even for individuals whose second attempts are correct, because being forced to give a fast and intuitive answer cannot lead to the correct, normative solution which is possible exclusively with the engagement of Type 2 processes. On the contrary, several studies observed that individuals' fast initial responses were often correct (e.g., Bago & De Neys, 2017).

The second problem—*switch*—is a by-product of the first. If the two processes are exclusive, then there needs to be a mechanism that switches between them. But what cognitive mechanism decides whether to keep running Type 1 processes or to instantiate Type 2 processes (and also to switch the latter off when their job is done)? In some situations, this is not a problem, such as when intuition is silent because the problem is too novel or when external demands guide our thinking (e.g., there is a clear indication that our intuitive response is misleading so one knows in advance to rely only on reflection). But attempting a classic reasoning task is not one of those situations; the switch must operate internally. De Neys (2023a) reviewed the solutions offered by dual-process theorists to this problem and argued that they are not convincing or even paradoxical. For instance, if it is assumed that Type 2 processes are constantly monitoring the output of Type 1 processes for potential conflict, then this creates the paradox that Type 2 processes activate themselves.[10]

The solution offered by De Neys (2023a) required assuming that the switch operation can be performed by Type 1 processes and abandoning the exclusivity assumption—that is, accepting that Type 1 processes can generate the kinds of outputs traditionally considered to be exclusive to Type 2 processes (e.g., logical, or in the moral domain, utilitarian, responses).[11] Thus, Type 1 processes produce different intuitions, some of which respect logic and probability (or are otherwise aligned with Type 2 thinking) and others being misleading (e.g., based on heuristics, salient environmental cues, momentary affect). When these various intuitions potentiate diverging responses, the resulting conflict triggers Type 2 engagement. To offer a more precise idea about the switch process, De Neys drew attention to the strength (i.e., activation level) of intuitions. Some of our intuitions, such as responses that we have practiced to a high degree of automaticity, are particularly strong, whereas others might be quite weak, such as when a novel stimulus weakly resembles an existing mental representation and generates a faint response tendency associated with that mental representation. Depending on our ongoing cognitive activity and our interactions with the environment, these intuitions can grow stronger or weaker over time (e.g., over the course of several hundred milliseconds or a few seconds), as well. To this, De Neys added an *uncertainty monitoring process*—itself a Type 1 process—which continuously checks the strength of different intuitions against one another, along with the assumption that small differences between the strength of different intuitions trigger Type 2 engagement. This is sensible: If one intuition greatly overpowers others, there is no uncertainty; but if two or more intuitions are at a similar activation level (e.g., two highly and equally attractive potential mates),[12] the individual needs help from Type 2 processes to figure out which of them should be prioritized and translated into action. Once triggered, Type 2 processes do their typical work, such as inhibiting one or more of the intuitions, boosting the strength of a favored intuition and justifying it (see Chapter 9), or generating novel ideas and responses not cued by intuition. Finally, the results of these Type 2 operations are fed back into Type 1 processes. For instance, inhibiting an intuition will decrease its strength, which in turn will decrease the level of uncertainty, which will release Type 2 processes from work if the uncertainty falls below a threshold. Thus, De Neys' model specifies not only when Type 2 is engaged but also when it is disengaged. It also highlights the value of thinking about the time course of competing intuitions and the interplay between Type 1 and Type 2 processes, instead of a more static approach focused, for instance, on individual differences in terms of the average level of reflective capacity and tendency. Another model sharing some of these features was recently offered by Pennycook, Fugelsang, et al. (2015) and is briefly described later in this chapter.[13]

(Some) Responses to De Neys

De Neys' proposal received 34 commentaries and reviewing some of those further helps to discover areas of debate and future directions for dual-process models. Responses ranged from enthusiastic endorsement (e.g., Frankish, 2023) to rejection of model assumptions (e.g., Handley et al., 2023). Some researchers (Newman & Thompson, 2023; Stanovich & Toplak, 2023a) stated that the exclusivity assumption has long been dropped from prominent dual-process models, citing the automatization of processes (i.e., what is initially an output generated by Type 2 process being taken over by Type 1 processes via practice) that we mentioned in Chapter 9. Other researchers confidently asserted that findings in their specific research areas firmly support exclusivity (e.g., mindreading, Low et al., 2023; threat perception and social cognition, March et al., 2023). Now that so much wisdom relevant to dual-process models has accumulated in specific domains, we expect that the future will see increased comparison of conclusions reached across various domains in which dual-process models have been tested. This could be immensely beneficial because, by this point in the book, it should be clear to the reader that overreliance on specific tasks and paradigms—which is characteristic of most communities of researchers working on the same topic—gives rise to a narrow and potentially skewed view of the studied phenomena. The previous chapter suggested how findings stemming from the classic reasoning tasks facilitated a default-interventionist version of the dual-process theory and how researching real-life phenomena, where implicit learning and pattern recognition are possible, paints a more positive picture of intuition.

Single-Process Models

As some of the responses to De Neys (e.g., Melnikoff & Bargh, 2023) show, another point of debate with a longer history has been whether instead of assuming two qualitatively different processes, it is more realistic to assume a single process that differs quantitatively (e.g., increasing in the strength of reflection going from one end of a continuum to the other) or to somehow just get rid of the reflection–intuition distinction altogether (e.g., Keren & Schul, 2009; Kruglanski & Gigerenzer, 2011; Osman, 2004). The single-versus dual-process debate involves several different issues (see De Neys, 2021). To take an example, opponents of dual-process models argue that features attributed to Type 1 and Type 2 processes (e.g., fast, automatic, parallel, associative vs. slow, controlled, serial, and rule-based) do not align perfectly. Melnikoff and Bargh (2018b) review several types of *misalignments between features*.[14] For instance, they note that in the bat-and-ball problem from the cognitive reflection test (see Chapter 2) producing the wrong answer ("10 cents") is uncontrollable (a Type 1 feature), but is intentional (a Type 2 feature) in the sense of requiring the test taker to not just be exposed to the problem but to intend to solve it. Moreover, these authors point out that there are *misalignments within features*—i.e., that "lower-order dimensions" of features like consciousness, efficiency, intentionality, and controllability do not necessarily cohere together. For instance, even though we have talked about working memory—central to dual-process models—as a unitary construct in this book, it might be better conceptualized as having dedicated types, such as for verbal versus visuospatial information, that are governed by a "central executive" (Baddeley & Hitch, 1994). Melnikoff and Bargh (2018b) mention evidence that taxing these separate working memory stores has opposite effects and depending on which type of store is taxed, different conclusions about the *efficiency* of behavior (a Type 1 feature) might emerge (e.g., Amit & Greene, 2012). They conclude that, therefore, dual-process models are "oversimplified" because of their reliance on a "unitary efficiency feature."

In response, dual-process theorists (e.g., Pennycook et al., 2018) point out that they do not hold (at least not currently) the unrealistic and extreme expectation that these various features will always be perfectly aligned. On the contrary, they explicitly discuss these features as "typical correlates" and distinguish them from a much narrower set of "defining characteristics." For instance, according to Evans and Stanovich (2013a, Table 1), only working memory involvement, cognitive decoupling/mental simulation, and autonomy distinguish the two processes (i.e., defining features). Further, dual-process proponents argue that a "single dichotomy," not alignment of multiple features, is logically sufficient to put forth a dual-process model (Pennycook et al., 2018). For some (e.g., Pennycook, 2017), autonomy—i.e., the distinction between responses that are mandatory upon the presence of their triggering stimuli and those that are not—alone does the job. This does not mean that dual-process models can steer clear of criticism[15] but in our view, the claims of opponents that dual-process models are "systematically thwarting scientific progress" (Melnikoff & Bargh, 2018b, p. 280), are "highly speculative" (p. 290) or that they have "been propelled not by scientific evidence but by the human tendency to be seduced by simplifying but baseless stereotypes" (p. 284) are overkill.[16] Even though we see many reasons to favor dual-process models, they may need better theoretical specification and empirical support on specific issues if their proponents wish to demonstrate unequivocally that they are more viable than single-process models. Opponents are right to argue that the alignment of features mentioned above (i.e., the assumption that a response that has one Type 1 feature, such as rapidity, should also exhibit other Type 1 features, such as unintentionality, parallel processing, etc.) has not been tested rigorously and empirical evidence on this issue could change the way we think about the dual-process models, though we do not believe such developments have strong potential to invalidate the conclusions about reflection and intuition we reached in this book. De Neys' (2021, p. 1413) opinion is that "there is currently no empirical data or theoretical principle that allows one to decide the debate" and that the debate is empirically irresolvable and unlikely to advance science in any case. For this reason, De Neys (2023a) designed his working model, summarized above, to be usable regardless of the position one wishes to take on this issue.

Metareasoning

Several authors (e.g., Ackerman & Morsanyi, 2023; Baron, 2023a; Newman & Thompson, 2023) brought up metacognitive issues and some of them specifically argued that De Neys failed to properly acknowledge earlier work on *metareasoning*. Throughout the book, we have occasionally referred to the importance of metacognition, which we view as a component, or at least a facilitator of proper reflectiveness, broadly defined. The term metareasoning is intended to draw attention to the operation of metacognitive processes in the context of reasoning and problem-solving tasks. Thompson (2009) was one of the first to note that relative to other cognitive functions (e.g., memory[17]), the role of metacognitive processes had been neglected in reasoning. A simple example (based on a similar one from Thompson, 2009) can convince one that metareasoning is highly relevant for dual-process models. Consider this modified version of the bat-and-ball problem (see Chapter 2):

A bat and a ball cost $3.28 in total. The bat costs $1.24 more than the ball. How much does the ball cost?

Compared to the original, not only does this version no longer cue a misleading intuition, but it also leads to a metacognitive judgment, unless you are a math wizard, that a solution can only be reached if you take the time to make the necessary calculations—i.e., if you use Type 2 processes. The absence of any intuitive response in a situation is expected to trigger Type 2 processes. But even when a problem or stimulus cues a Type 1 process or output, these are accompanied by other, metacognitive processes and outputs[18] of import. Thompson (2009) asserted that any Type 1 response toward a problem is accompanied by some degree of *feeling of rightness*—that this response is correct—as a metacognitive experience that is itself also generated by Type 1 processes. This feeling in turn plays a key role in whether Type 2 processes are recruited to help solve the problem. Roughly speaking, a strong feeling of rightness gives the person license to go along with the intuitive response that is associated with it, whereas a weak feeling of rightness triggers Type 2 processes

Subsequent work provided direct evidence in support of this early proposal (e.g., Thompson et al., 2011) and eventually advanced it into a full-fledged metareasoning framework (Ackerman & Thompson, 2017). Similar to De Neys' (2023a) model, Thompson and colleagues found that conflicting responses (e.g., as in base-rate conflict problems; see above) affect monitoring processes—specifically, they lower the feeling of rightness (see Experiment 3 in Thompson et al., 2011)—and trigger additional reflection. Newman and Thompson (2023) noted that uncertainty in De Neys' model plays a role similar to feelings of rightness in the metareasoning framework because these two concepts seem to be the inverse of each other and both are posited to drive Type 2 engagement. Thus, what is known about determinants of feelings of rightness and other similar metacognitive experiences and judgments could be integrated into De Neys' model, thereby making the latter more precise in terms of the factors that govern the "deliberation threshold" (i.e., the level of uncertainty above which Type 2 processes are triggered). In any case, it is important that these research teams, with minor differences in specifics,[19] converge in the view that Type 1 processes feature prominently in monitoring and controlling cognitive activity.

The advantage of the metareasoning framework is that it is based on a broader literature (i.e., metacognition) and paints a richer picture of the metacognitive processes at work during reasoning and problem-solving (see Figure 1 in Ackerman & Thompson, 2017). The feeling of rightness is not the only relevant monitoring signal. When a problem is first encountered, *initial judgments of solvability* (i.e., "Does this problem have a solution, regardless of whether I can arrive at it or not?") influence whether to take up or give up the problem. If the problem is taken up, an initial solution arises mentally, accompanied by a feeling of rightness that influences whether to suffice with this initial solution or not. For more complex problems and/or under continued effort (see Ackerman, 2014), as the solution is updated so too is the person's *intermediate confidence* level until a final solution is decided upon, accompanied by *final confidence*.[20] An interesting observation is that the more time people take on a problem, the more they tend to relax the final confidence level that they require for settling on a final solution (Ackerman, 2014). That is, people require higher levels of confidence to declare a solution in earlier stages of problem-solving but grow more accepting of lower confidence solutions in later stages, with the passage of more time. One can speculate that this is an additional downside of extensive reflection: even if a solution is declared, it may no longer be possible to trust it. If an individual is constantly faced with such complex problems in daily life (e.g., due to their occupation), they may even develop persistent feelings of uncertainty, doubt, and low self-efficacy. Thus, metacognition may even have implications for well-being.

We have occasionally emphasized the flexible use of cognitive resources in earlier chapters. The metacognitive monitoring and control processes make concrete what such flexibility entails. Metacognitive experiences and judgments such as feelings of rightness, error, and judgments of solvability influence whether an individual attempts a problem at all and their duration of persistence in search of a solution. For the outcome of this process to be worth the Type 2 resources they use up, these metacognitive experiences and judgments need to be accurate (e.g., a low feeling of rightness actually indicating a suboptimal or erroneous solution). However, often they are not, because they are based on cues that are independent of or weakly associated with the actual validity of responses or solutions. Moreover, they are also largely impenetrable by introspective reflection,[21] giving individuals very little chance to test whether they are useful and accurate or not (Ackerman & Thompson, 2017; Thompson, 2009).

The suspect nature of metacognitive experiences such as feelings of rightness is revealed by research on *processing fluency*, the foremost cue on which those experiences are based (Thompson, Turner, et al., 2013). Fluency, which we also mentioned in Chapter 3, is the sense of ease regarding cognitive activity and probably accompanies all such activities (Alter & Oppenheimer, 2009). For instance, if you are in a well-lit environment, holding this book at a comfortable distance from your eyes, you would be experiencing greater fluency than if you were in a darker environment or there were other impediments (e.g., a shaky subway car).[22] Now that we have repeated the word fluency three times, you will be processing it more fluently than before you started this paragraph.[23] To study the effects of fluency, researchers artificially heighten it (vs. leave it be or lower it) by repeatedly exposing participants to the same stimulus (usually surreptitiously, so that the effect is not driven by experimental demand). Among the most well-known of such demonstrations is *the truth effect* whereby statements processed more fluently are attributed greater truth value (Dechêne et al., 2010). While fluency may partially track truth value under certain conditions (Reber & Unkelbach, 2010) and may have been a valid cue for safety in our ancestral environment,[24] it is clear that in hostile environments fluency can become dissociated from the truth. The established advertising practice of repeatedly exposing consumers to simple, easy-to-process language and images is just one example in which judgments about the content of the advertisement would be driven largely by fluency and familiarity instead of relevant facts and information about a brand or product. Fluency stems from intuitive processes, arising spontaneously and efficiently; often drives various judgments that importantly guide behavior (e.g., truth, liking, trustworthiness, safety); generates positive affect (Winkielman & Cacioppo, 2001)[25] which in turn facilitates continued reliance on intuitive processes and heuristics (Schwarz & Bless, 1991);[26] and signals that there is no need for reflection (Ackerman & Thompson, 2017; Thompson, Turner, et al., 2013). Thus, research on fluency suggests that contextual factors and interventions that facilitate proper calibration of metacognitive experiences and judgments (e.g., so that they track response accuracy or the validity of the chosen problem-solving method more closely) should help to maximize the benefits of reflective thought.

A Three-Stage Dual-Process Model

Pennycook, Fugelsang, et al. (2015) integrated De Neys' focus on conflict and Thompson's emphasis on metacognition into a three-stage model. In this model, Stage 1 signifies Type 1 processes, characterized by automatic activations. Stage 2 involves the detection of conflict between competing intuitive responses, thereby involving metacognition. Stage 3 encompasses reflection, which can vary from trivial, such as Stanovich's serial associative cognition with a focal bias, to more extended reflection processes. If no conflict is detected in Stage 2, the prevailing intuition becomes the decision. However, if conflict is identified, reflection serves two primary functions: firstly, to reinforce and rationalize the initial intuition (motivated reasoning), and secondly, to facilitate cognitive decoupling that necessitates mental simulation and belief change.

This model strives to illustrate the decision-making sequence by integrating components from diverse dual-process theories. It addresses a vital deficiency in dual-process models by acknowledging the presence of conflicting intuitions. Additionally, the model includes metacognitive processes and conflict detection mechanisms. Moreover, it distinguishes between the *consequences* and *functions* of reflection, thereby establishing this framework as a viable and promising approach for future research (Pennycook, 2023). In essence, beyond the discovery that reflection diminishes epistemically suspect beliefs or alters political attitudes (i.e., the consequences of reflection), recognizing whether such changes stem from the motivated reasoning or cognitive decoupling functions of reflection necessitates considering individuals' pre-existing attitudes. This model distinguishes itself from other existing models by emphasizing not only the outcomes of reflection but also its various functions.

Coda

We attempted to outline some of the current debates concerning the dual-process model of the mind. The debates show that this area of inquiry is vibrant and fertile. New proposals that attempt to handle the criticisms signal that the newer generation of dual-process theorizing will be more focused on dynamic questions, such as the interaction of intuitive and reflective processes over time, compared to the relatively greater focus of earlier work on individual differences and cognitive structures (e.g., Stanovich, 2011), though the latter certainly remains important (e.g., De Neys, 2017a, p. 59). The new wave of research also shifts the earlier focus from the idealized situation, whereby reflection competes with a single (misleading) intuition to situations that involve multiple competing intuitions. These developments go along with the use of novel paradigms (e.g., two-response) and a change in the focal dependent variable from single-shot response accuracy—whether a participant produces the normative answer to a reasoning problem— to online behavior—whether a participant's bodily movements during a reasoning task are consistent with theoretical assumptions about the temporal interplay of intuition and reflection (e.g., Travers et al., 2016). Many key insights into the human mind will probably emerge from these debates and the research innovations they inspire, even though the debates sometimes appear irresolvable and point to fundamental and definitional disagreements between opponents. The content of these debates raises the possibility that some opponents are criticizing idealized and extreme versions of dual-process assumptions. Those versions are bound to fail, and it is not clear that anyone ever subscribed to them. In any case, dual-process theorists are not under the impression that the debates are unimportant or will be easily won. As De Neys (2017c, p. 4), one of the most prominent contributors to dual-process theory, remarked, "the field is still in full development and the last word on key debates has not been said. More work is definitely needed." The status of psychology and cognitive science may hinge heavily on the success of dual-process models—i.e., their ability to continue to serve as both highly useful fictions and logically coherent organizers of empirical findings that also generate novel predictions (or their alternatives) in the near future. As implied at the outset of this chapter, we would consider it a success of these models if they were to inspire new research and theorizing that eventually leads to them being replaced by new models. If dual-process theory continues to be fruitful in this broad sense, many novel real-world applications are likely to emerge and benefit humanity.

Notes

1   Pennycook (2017, p. 7) argues that "dual process theory is irrefutable, but falsifiable" and we completely agree. The distinction at the heart of the theory (reflection vs. intuition) can safely be taken as a given fact.
2   Similarly, all measures are imperfect. Human responses are overdetermined and "the pursuit of process-pure tests is largely a hopeless enterprise" (Jacoby et al., 1992, p. 806). That is, no measure is likely to tap Type 1 or Type 2 processes exclusively because constructing and administering such clean measures is nearly impossible, and because Type 1 and Type 2 processes are likely to "regularly interact" (Betsch & Glöckner, 2010) Similarly, we noted in Chapter 2 that scores on measures of the reflective and algorithmic mind are often correlated. For instance, scores on the cognitive reflection test are confounded with intelligence test scores (e.g., Frederick, 2005). Despite this fact, cognitive reflection test scores are frequently treated as if they only index reflectiveness, not intelligence. We are thus forced to admit that some unknown but non-negligible (judging by the magnitude of correlations just mentioned) portion of the effects we have attributed to reflectiveness throughout the book is due *also* (or sometimes even *solely*) to intelligence. With the same logic, intelligence test scores partly overlap with the test taker's level of reflectiveness, as well as being correlated with other factors, such as educational attainment and socioeconomic status (e.g., Strenze, 2007). The picture would be clearer if more studies measured both constructs and statistically controlled for their effects, leaving aside the perils of statistical control (Christenfeld et al., 2004; Westfall & Yarkoni, 2016). When we were able to do this in our research, we observed associations unique to each construct (e.g., Saribay & Yilmaz, 2017). Last but not least, measures of the same overarching construct do not consistently show the same associations as each other, something we have observed also in our research on reflectiveness (Yilmaz & Saribay, 2017d).
3   The quote is from a book in Turkish (the translation is ours). For an English version of some of the ideas in Mungan's book, see Mungan (2023b).
4   To reiterate, this point is admitted by dual-process theorists: "No doubt older work in the dual-process tradition overemphasized the importance and frequency of the override function" (Stanovich & Toplak, 2023a, p. 61). Overreliance on these tasks is also probably responsible for the "Type 1 = bad" and "Type 2 = good" association, which the dual-process theorists are careful to dismiss as a fallacy (e.g., Evans & Stanovich, 2013a).

5 Like many other findings, this one is based on a comparison of group means. De Neys and colleagues also explored individual differences in conflict detection ability and observed that only a small minority of participants appear to lack it (Frey et al., 2018).

6 That De Neys changed his conceptualizations of the monitoring process from being Type 2 to Type 1 exemplifies the difficulty of separating some reflective forms of thought from intuition. As discussed in the previous chapter via the concept of serial associative cognition with a focal bias, some of the blame for cognitive biases and thinking errors are probably wrongly attributed to intuitive processes because of such difficulty. Thus, it is important for future research to become more precise in the categorization of thought processes.

7 Evidence supports this developmental/educational mechanism (Raoelison et al., 2021) but also shows that even much shorter periods of specific training may be sufficient to instill correct intuitions (see Boissin et al., 2021).

8 De Neys (2023a) based his review on three research areas: the classic reasoning problems, morality, and prosociality. He showed that the same exclusivity assumption applies to all. For instance, in the morality literature, generating utilitarian (vs. deontological) responses is assumed to be the exclusive responsibility of Type 2 processes (see also Chapter 7).

9 As we warned in the preface to this book, when effects are detected in psychology research, they tend to be small because of reasons such as measurement error and the overdetermined nature of human responses. The presence of mixed findings (i.e., null effects or effects that are the opposite of a model's predictions or a commonly reported finding) is also the norm in our experience. Therefore, these kinds of criticisms probably apply to the majority of hypotheses and models in psychology, not just to dual-process models. Moreover, these patterns—mixed findings and small effects—also hold for the very studies challenging a dominant model. For instance, several articles have challenged the previously-mentioned intuitive conflict detection phenomenon, either with inconsistent findings (Ferreira et al., 2016; Singmann et al., 2014; Travers et al., 2016) or by discovering moderators of the effect (Pennycook, Fugelsang, et al., 2012).

10 The other solutions, none of which were considered viable by De Neys, are (1) assuming the monitoring to be a shallow version of Type 2 processes, as we covered earlier in the case of logical intuition; (2) assuming a third type of process (*Type 3*) whose task is to automatically monitor the outputs of both Type 1 and Type 2 processes; (3) assuming continuous parallel activation of Type 1 and Type 2 processes; and (4) a no-switch account whereby only the complete lack of a Type 1 response brings about Type 2 engagement.

11 De Neys' (2023a, p. 12) non-exclusivity assumption concerns responses (outputs), not processes. That is, he assumes that Type 1 and Type 2 processes can generate the same responses, *not* that the processes underlying these responses (or other characteristics of the responses) would be the same. For instance, as we have noted in Chapter 9 and as De Neys also stated, one clear advantage of generating a response via Type 2 processes is the traceability ("transparency" in De Neys' words) of the sequence of mental operations employed to arrive at it (Bago & De Neys, 2019). This is critical when we are trying to reach a non-deceptive and non-coercive consensus (i.e., persuading others without manipulating or forcing them) in the social sphere or to personally hold defensible opinions. Findings mentioned

earlier (e.g., Ghasemi et al., 2022) showing that logical intuition may not be truly logical after all, also necessitate this kind of approach.

12 The importance of these types of conflicts in human and animal behavior has long been recognized in psychology (e.g., Lewin, 1935).

13 See also Evans (2019). It is noteworthy that the offerings by both Evans and Pennycook, Fugelsang, et al. (2015) explicitly include a rationalization function for reflection (see Chapter 9).

14 In Chapter 9, we discussed unconscious information integration, incubation, and insight. These could be seen as examples of misalignment, e.g., as being slow but automatic.

15 For instance, De Neys (2021) points out that dual-process theorists have not specified what amount of working memory engagement should serve as the threshold for distinguishing reflection from intuition; how researchers should decide whether an individual is actually engaging in mental simulation or not; and that they have failed to acknowledge that the autonomy of a process depends on context and current goals. And for Melnikoff and Bargh (2018b), even assuming that the features are correlated, let alone perfectly aligned, is a mistake until this is tested empirically. It does seem that the debate partly stems from the tendency of dual-process theorists to argue that feature alignment is not a requirement and that even a single dichotomy can suffice while also frequently making statements that present multiple features as meaningfully going together without sufficient empirical support (see Melnikoff & Bargh, 2018a).

16 As we stated at the outset of this chapter, of course, these models are fiction and heuristics. Science proceeds by simplifying complex phenomena. Any act of scientific measurement or modeling is necessarily a simplification, though the preferred and realized degree of simplification will vary across applications. And so, there is indeed an overlap with stereotypes, which also simplify the complex social reality. However, scientific models are periodically revised and replaced with better alternatives that are progressively better aligned with reality. To equate attempts at building scientific models to the stereotypes of lay persons is what is overkill in our view, not the act of pointing out the lack of empirical support for an assumption. The latter is perfectly fine and just points to a neglected issue and the need for further research. We find the following statement by Trippas and Handley (2017, pp. 42–43) more fair:

> … as a meta-theory, dual process theory is matched by no other account of reasoning and judgment in two respects. First, dual process theory is a great way to generate novel and testable predictions, facilitating the framing of scientific debates … Second, the willingness of dual process researchers … to update their theories in light of new experimental evidence is particularly admirable. Indeed, if the trajectory traversed by [them] … is even just partially indicative of the things yet to come, we think it is fair to say that dual process theory will be alive and kicking for at least a few more decades.

17 In the domain of memory, the specific term for metacognition would be *metamemory* which can include many different types of cognitions regarding memory. For instance, a scholar writing an academic article might suspect that her memory for older literature has faded to a degree that she should not cite an older piece without verifying that it contains the information she is citing it for. In this example, a metacognitive judgment stops the scholar from trusting

her initial thought and compels her to spend time verifying it. Thompson (2009) recognized that metacognition should have similar functions in reasoning and drew inspiration from and formed parallels to metacognitive work in other domains to propose a "metacognitive framework for reasoning."

18 Later work referred to these two classes as *object-level* and *meta-level*, respectively (Ackerman & Thompson, 2017). Meta-level processes monitor (i.e., assess whether a process is up to standards, whatever they may be) and control (i.e., change the course of the process by terminating it and/or recruiting other types of processes) object-level processes.

19 For instance, De Neys (2023b) does not view the uncertainty signal in his model as affective, while the meta-reasoning framework (Thompson, 2009) explicitly asserts that the feeling of rightness is affective.

20 At least two other metacognitive monitoring signals have been identified for the final stage of problem-solving (see Ackerman & Thompson, 2017, for references to specific work). The *feeling of error* indexes the subjective sense of having made a mistake. The *final judgment of solvability* is particularly important in determining if one should give up or seek help from others to produce a solution (or change the parameters of the problem space so that a solution becomes possible).

21 For instance, according to Thompson (2009, p. 181) the feeling of rightness "is assumed to be an affective response that carries little cognitive content and that is generated by implicit processes whose origins are not likely available to conscious processes."

22 This would be a subcategory called *perceptual fluency*. Fluency can arise in other ways, as well, but the effects of fluency (e.g., on truth, liking, and confidence judgments) seem to be common regardless of the source of fluency (see Alter & Oppenheimer, 2009).

23 Note that, compared to Type 2 processes, Type 1 processes generally take place more rapidly and efficiently and are thus accompanied by greater processing fluency. In Chapter 2, we mentioned that intuitions, due to how rapidly they are mentally generated, are often mistaken for objective reality. Fluency is a key aspect of this phenomenon.

24 By simple logic, any stimulus that one had the chance of being repeatedly exposed to was more likely to be safe than not because such exposure did not lead to death, and repeated exposure would increase processing fluency. This is also a sensible distal explanation for the *mere exposure effect*—i.e., the tendency to like and prefer stimuli that have been encountered before, even in the absence of reward (Zajonc, 2001).

25 Recent work shows that fluency also amplifies a judgmental orientation, such as making a stimulus appear more negative if it is already negatively evaluated (Landwehr & Eckmann, 2020).

26 While much work is consistent with the proposition that positive and negative affect are associated with heuristic and systematic thinking, respectively, a more nuanced position might be that positive affect is a signal that the *current* processing style is fine (Isbell et al., 2013). If people are cognitive misers overall, then this would mean that under positive affect, they simply continue to not show cognitive effort. Thus, the two views (i.e., that positive affect facilitates heuristic thinking and that positive affect facilitates reliance on the current style of thinking) may practically overlap more than is apparent at first glance.

CONCLUSION

Final Thoughts

This book is our sincere effort to answer the question "What can we gain from thinking harder?" Although we tried to keep our focus on the core sense of reflectiveness as cognitively effortful thinking, we implicitly adopted a wider meaning of reflectiveness as a cognitive capacity and trait that is supported by many other capacities. The latter are represented by self-control and self-regulation, emotion regulation, metacognition, cognitive control, executive functions, and many other concepts in the literature that we did not always have the chance to cover in detail. In the process of writing the book, we realized better how large the corpus on even the narrow sense of reflectiveness already is. It was not possible to include (or to discuss in detail) so much more work that we see as relevant to reflectiveness. The book (and the number of gray hairs on our heads, if hair remained) would have to quadruple in size. That is for another life. Omissions due to ignorance probably exist, too. These should give the reader good reasons to keep reading about this topic from other sources.

If we were to summarize some key insights we derived from our effort, we could start by noting that inhibition of intuitive responses—or in any case, inhibition of the first thing that pops up in one's mind regardless of whether we call that an intuition or something else—is a central part of reflectiveness. It is difficult to deny that this component of reflectiveness is associated with many desirable characteristics for citizens in the modern world. For instance, weak reflectiveness is implicated in susceptibility to epistemically suspect beliefs, such as conspiracy beliefs, which have an erosive effect on democracy. Even in science, widespread use of questionable research practices implies the need for stronger reflectiveness and criticisms mention how intuitive,

DOI: 10.4324/9781003300366-14

"knee-jerk responses" (see van Zomeren, 2024, p. 26) impede progress. But the full story turned out to be much more nuanced.

Is Reflection Sufficient to Address Today's Most Pressing Problems?

Although recent arguments suggest that logical intuitions can exist and conflict monitoring is possible even between contradictory intuitive responses (De Neys, 2014), it is also possible that using reflection to resolve such conflicts may be one of the primary factors distinguishing accurate thinkers from less accurate ones (De Neys, 2023a). In modern media environments, especially where social media creates echo chambers and reinforces exposure to a single perspective, reflection becomes crucial. The lack of exposure to alternative views hampers cognitive decoupling, making intuition- and heuristics-based judgments highly dangerous in terms of spreading epistemically suspect beliefs and even narratives that fuel violent extremism. Hence, even in the extremely complicated real-world case of violent extremism, we were able to trace a preventive role of reflectiveness.

However, social media algorithms, by customizing content according to user preferences, strengthen existing beliefs and boost the likelihood of using reflection for motivated reasoning. Readers may recall that, as proposed in the three-stage model (Pennycook, Fugelsang, et al., 2015), reflection can only be employed when individuals detect conflict between competing intuitions. In these instances, they can engage in motivated reasoning to justify their initial intuitions. Similar to how a lawyer selectively searches for arguments to defend a client within legal boundaries, people can use reflection for motivated reasoning, particularly in cases where they hold strong intuitions, such as extreme political views. This use of reflection for motivated reasoning limits exposure to and serious consideration of varied perspectives, thereby preventing individuals from breaking free from low-effortful thought patterns and considering alternative viewpoints. As a result, moral intuitions are intensified through reflection, leading to parochialism and tribalism. Such a narrowing in the moral circle presents considerable challenges to the public sphere, especially during times of heightened exchange between people from different cultures and subcultures.

Relatedly, substantial evidence indicates that human nature is inherently tribalistic (Clark et al., 2019). That means, when left to our own devices and given scarce resources, we tend to prioritize our personal or group interests, and no political or ideological group seems to be immune to this strong bias. As reflection evolved in a social context to reinforce our own beliefs and to convince others of our arguments, and intuitive biases also arise functionally to increase the plausibility of our own arguments (Mercier & Sperber, 2017), neither logical intuitions nor reflection can be solutions to parochialism and tribalism. The basic premise here is that reflection does not operate in everyday life as it does when a scientist uses the scientific method to seek the truth. Instead, like a lawyer defending a client under all circumstances, reflection helps us avoid cognitive contradictions by justifying ourselves. In other words, as Mercier and Spencer (2017) argue, the main purpose of the evolution of reflection is to construct arguments and persuade others in a social context. Our intuitive biases are actually used to make our arguments more compelling and unshakable. This suggests that neither intuition nor reflection alone can solve the complex problems we face today, and their impact will be limited. That is why, in addition to reflection, one should seek help from virtues and motivations such as actively open-minded thinking and intellectual humility that may allow for cognitive decoupling when engaging with alternative viewpoints and seeking solutions to those issues.

At the same time, using reflection for motivated reasoning implies a narrower view and an inability to shift focus from one's own strong intuitions to alternative perspectives. Therefore, especially in moral disagreements, it is crucial for people to be cognitively flexible and adopt a holistic view, recognizing that cultures are not monolithic; that others may have differing moral convictions than their own; and that moral principles can be evaluated subjectively (i.e., the belief that moral claims are subjectively true). For example, variables such as closed-mindedness and prejudice are positively related to objective moral belief, which corresponds to the meta-ethical belief that one's own moral principles are absolutely and objectively true (Goodwin & Darley, 2012; Wright & Pölzler, 2022). Similarly, people tend to be more subjectivist when arguing with someone from a different culture, whereas they are more objectivist with someone from their own culture (Sarkissian et al., 2014). In addition, there is a positive relationship between interpersonal tolerance and subjectivism, with an increase in subjectivism when people enhance tolerance by engaging in tasks that form group pairs stereotypically perceived as difficult to coexist (Yilmaz, Bahçekapili, et al., 2020). These findings suggest that in moral disagreements, people may set different criteria depending on the context and the person, avoiding intuitive judgments, and thus their capacity to use reflection may vary accordingly.

Moreover, certain contexts can exploit the capacity for reflection and intuition. In some cases, political elites may manipulate intuitive and reflective mechanisms to increase societal polarization to gain benefits. Hence, the manipulation of human proclivities by populist leaders, who leverage conformity and epistemically suspect beliefs, further intensifies a critical issue of our time: polarization based on motivated reasoning. In a similar vein, public debates now often showcase reflection as a tool for motivated reasoning. The proliferation of different moral convictions, especially on social media, where everyone tries to convince others of their arguments, along with the increasing use of reflection for motivated reasoning, and the decreased exposure to alternative ideas due to social media algorithms, indicates that we are in a challenging century regarding this critical issue.

As a solution to this pressing problem, it has been previously argued that having more moral convictions may pose a problem for political disagreement (e.g., Burgess, 2007; Garner, 2007; Marks, 2014) and that reducing polarization might be achieved by agreeing on fewer convictions, especially when seeking common ground between different political groups on social issues (Sauer, 2015). One problem with this is that moral convictions in domains such as religion and politics are not just any set of beliefs but rather *convictions*—emotionally charged beliefs with a high degree of ego involvement, and it is very difficult to revise the initial position in these domains. Convictions may therefore illustrate the limits of human capacity for proper reasoning. Especially in cultures characterized by harsh environments and social norms centered on selfishness and parochialism, it is challenging to resolve political disagreements by advocating for fewer convictions through reflection. This in turn is because, as discussed throughout the book, people use reflection for motivated reasoning when strong moral convictions and supporting social norms are present. This underscores the need for dual-process theorists to more thoroughly explore the consequences and functions of intuition and reflection, as well as their practical application in varied real-life contexts with differing accepted social norms and environmental pressures.

While we may not yet have a complete understanding of the conditions under which our intuitive and reflective cognitive processes lead us to cooperate versus act selfishly, especially when facing anonymous others or out-groups, it is evident that a significant portion of our capacity for large-scale cooperation, especially within our in-groups, is rooted in the intuitive cognitive mechanisms that we covered in Chapter 1. As we have traced through the evolutionary history of cooperation, these mechanisms correspond to those ingrained in the human mind by evolution and shaped by cultural influences (Henrich, 2020). All of this underscores the pressing need to elucidate which specific intuitive aspects of our mind foster cooperation and which ones hinder it, and the conditions that favor cooperative outcomes of intuitive versus reflective thought processes. Such clarity is indispensable to maintain cooperation among humans in the face of impending challenges. Additionally, it serves as a foundation upon which democratic institutions can be safeguarded and rational discourse can be preserved in today's escalating polarized political environment.

However, it is crucial to understand that increased cooperation with anonymous others fostered by reflective thinking does not necessarily translate into reduced polarization. People often exhibit empathy-based cooperation primarily within their in-groups, potentially widening the gap with out-groups (Bloom, 2016). The perceptions of anonymous participants in economic games, especially by individuals with varying social or epistemic norms, have not been thoroughly examined. For instance, religious or conservative participants might perceive anonymous players in these games as more aligned with their in-group, influenced by their social norms. Conversely, groups with more universalistic values, like atheists or liberals, may perceive these anonymous participants as out-group members. To understand these dynamics, we need to move beyond the commonly used anonymous scenarios in behavioral economics. It is crucial to discern when reflection prompts motivated reasoning, leading to parochial in-group cooperation, and when it facilitates cognitive decoupling, helping overcome intuitive us-versus-them distinctions. Without this understanding, the role of reflection in potentially reducing polarization remains unclear. In other words, as argued by Stanovich (2021) in his recent book, even among the most sophisticated individuals, there exists a fundamental tendency to rationalize our own beliefs. This innate inclination runs so deep that the responses generated by our intuitive minds are often subsequently confirmed by our reflective thought processes. Consequently, our reflective thought processes often serve as the basis upon which we construct arguments that align with our existing intuitions (Pennycook, 2023). Hence, while reflective thinking can, in some cases, lead to a shift in attitudes toward rational or optimal decisions (e.g., cognitive decoupling), it can, in certain situations, give rise to motivated reasoning that reinforces pre-existing worldviews, often referred to as the expressive rationality account (Kahan & Stanovich, 2016). This leads to the prediction that merely inducing reflection may not suffice to mitigate polarization in the social sphere. For example, if an individual has been conditioned toward a particular mindset or behavior, reflection might merely serve to rationalize existing beliefs or self-interested actions, rather than fostering positive change (Pennycook, 2023). This suggests that the impact of reflection is not always beneficial. Recognizing the possibility that current beliefs or positions may be wrong, or being open to re-evaluating them in light of new evidence, could play a moderating role in these relationships (Baron et al., 2023). Future research should identify these influencing factors.

As thoroughly explored in Chapter 2, our reflective mind also comprises an algorithmic aspect that corresponds to our capacity and ability for rational thought, while our willingness and motivation to engage in such thinking seem to establish the boundary conditions for the utility of our reflective thought processes. Consequently, future research in this field should not only examine the direct increase or decrease in polarization or the endorsement of universalistic attitudes by activating reflection, but should unveil the empirical nature of these relationships by addressing their boundary conditions. Subsequently, theoretical frameworks can be developed based on robust phenomena identified in empirical relationships (Borsboom et al., 2021; Haig, 2005). Without knowledge of the empirical relationships between the variables and their boundary conditions, it is very likely that the resulting theoretical constructs will possess limited explanatory power.

Hence, an integrative perspective should explore the conditions under which reflective thinking can be activated among individuals with strong beliefs, such as those holding anti-vaccine views. It should also delve into the underlying motivations, such as actively open-minded versus closed-minded thinking, the desire for rational thought, motivation for consistency, and intellectual humility as well as holistic and systemic thinking. Furthermore, it should examine the contexts—whether in-group or out-group interactions, harsh or peaceful environments, tight or loose norm enforcement—in which reflective thinking leads to the adoption of specific types of moral convictions. To date, empirical studies have not fully achieved this integration. As a pioneering example, Gervais et al. (2018) proposed the counter-normative rationality model to explain the impact of reflection on religious belief. As the primary function of reflection is to challenge accepted social norms, this relationship is likely to manifest differently in cultures with high versus low levels of religiosity. However, the findings so far do not provide definitive evidence for this hypothesis, largely because the cultural data were not gathered using a probabilistic sampling method, making comparisons difficult (Baimel et al., 2021b). Therefore, while proposing such hypotheses is crucial, the quality of the cross-cultural studies conducted to uncover robust phenomena and their boundary conditions is equally vital. Instead of relying on random advertisements and individuals collecting data from their own cultures, it is clear that substantial funding should be allocated for such research, and data should be collected using probabilistic sampling from each culture to effectively test such cognition-by-culture interaction hypotheses. Researchers working on the dual-process model also bear responsibility in this regard. Incorporating measurement methods, such as the standardized Cognitive Reflection Test, into large-scale data collection frameworks like the World Values Survey could be a practical step toward identifying robust phenomena and their boundary conditions in this domain.

In addition to such practical actions, the need to broaden our definition of reflection is evident. Despite extensive research, there remains no definitive conceptual framework of what reflection entails or the different types that exist. Considering the motivated reasoning function of reflection, especially in morally charged and pressing issues, expanding our understanding of reflection could help address many contemporary problems, including polarization and climate change. Expansion is fundamentally about not getting bogged down in the details, as typically dictated by an analytic (vs. holistic) cultural orientation, but being able to evaluate issues and approach moral debates in a more holistic manner.

Although humans have evolved over millions of years genetically and culturally, we typically only envisage our lives over the next 100 years. This limitation stems from our relatively short lifespans in comparison to our species' history and our tendency to think in concrete terms, which makes it difficult to grasp issues that seem psychologically distant. While reflection alone enables us to recognize the critical aspects of these challenges, taking collaborative action requires more than just reflection. This is where holistic and systemic thinking come into play, assisting individuals in developing more comprehensive strategies for the future and envisioning what the world will look like for future generations.

Hence, while certain forms of reflection can protect us from dogmatically evaluating an issue through inhibition or reevaluation, holistic and systemic thinking are essential for understanding complex issues like climate change. This might explain why the capacity for reflection or experience alone does not predict success in fields such as chess, the stock market, management, or medical diagnosis, which also require a holistic perspective and systemic thinking. The character Dr. House from the TV show "House" is highly successful in his job largely because he operates within an imaginary department that embraces a holistic perspective. Although the human body functions as an integrated system, medical fields often analyze issues in isolation. It is rare for physicians from multiple specialties to collaborate and diagnose a patient from an integrative perspective, as portrayed by Dr. House. Therefore, it is crucial that we adopt holistic thinking alongside reflection, not only for issues that impact our future like climate change but also for everyday concerns such as health.

It is also important to acknowledge that holistic thinking alone is unlikely to give us optimum outcomes. An important component of holistic thinking is the recognition of a wide network of causal factors. Without reflection, this would take the form of simply believing that any random factor under consideration is, by definition, related to almost everything else imaginable. Such a loose application of holistic thinking is conducive to conspiracist ideation. This might be the reason that some dual-process models characterize holism as an intuitive style of thought. Reflection enables the holistic thinker to specify and scrutinize the precise nature of interrelations, as some forms of systemic thinking excellently demonstrate. In this sense, reflectiveness is necessary but not sufficient and the same applies to holistic thinking. It is the combination of both that we should pursue. While this message does not seem to be widely touted in the literature, we think that others besides us have reached a similar conclusion. For instance, coming from a very different (neo-Piagetian) perspective and using qualitative data, Rosenberg (2002) identified three thinking styles. One of these—*systematic thinking*—involves "isolating key elements of the situation and interpretatively reconstructing their apparent nature or meaning by redefining them as exemplars of a particular principle or abstract rule" (p. 139). This is a reflective process because it requires abstract thought and hence, cognitive decoupling

(Rosenberg also explicitly states that proper systematic thinking is effortful). Systematic thinking also involves "considering elements of a situation and then locating them in the context of a large systemic whole of which they are part" (p. 139), which is clearly a holistic way of thinking. Importantly, Rosenberg views systematic thinking as the "most sophisticated" of the thinking styles he identified. Thus, it appears that Rosenberg independently arrived at a similar appreciation of the combination of reflective and holistic styles of thinking. His effort, like ours, also highlights that it is the *structure* of one's thinking that matters; not simply how hard or slowly one is thinking.

The reason why reflection alone is not sufficient to address contemporary issues lies not only in its occasionally leading to motivated reasoning and narrower perspectives but also in its reliance on specific epistemic norms, or standards of belief and knowledge. For instance, while some individuals may regard empirical findings observed through scientific methods as valid evidence upon reflection, others, guided by different sources of belief such as faith or religious texts, might respond differently to hypothetical reflection training, potentially showing no effect (Acem, 2023). Consequently, enhancing reflection alone may not necessarily foster rationality or optimal decision-making but might instead serve as a means for individuals to rationalize their pre-existing norms based on their epistemic standards. In hypothetical experiments applying reflection to individuals with varied epistemic norms, it might be beneficial to complement reflection with motivations like actively open-minded thinking or a drive for rational thought for those who value scientific evidence. Conversely, pairing reflection with intellectual humility and holism may be more effective for individuals whose epistemic norms are rooted in religious texts, faith, and authority. Therefore, future research should consider this vital aspect, recognizing that the outcomes and functions of reflection may vary among people with diverse epistemic norms (Baron, 2020; Metz et al., 2018).

In sum, thinking per se can be unreliable and even dangerous. Other complementary capacities are needed and we have discussed our candidates. The Gestalt psychologist Max Wertheimer expressed a similar insight with remarkable flair in the opening paragraph of his 1934 essay, "On Truth":

> Science is rooted in the will to truth. With the will to truth it stands or falls. Lower the standard even slightly and science becomes diseased at the core. Not only science, but man. The will to truth, pure and unadulterated, is among the essential conditions of his existence; if the standard is compromised he easily becomes a kind of tragic caricature of himself.
>
> *(Wertheimer, 1934, p. 135)*

These words echoed in our minds throughout the process of writing the book as we became more acutely aware of the extent of human-caused limitations of both science and society that we diagnose in terms of weak reflectiveness but also a weak will to truth. The latter turns reflection into a caricature of itself, as concepts such as serial associative cognition with a focal bias and motivated reasoning exemplify. In our minds, this is related to the value of holistic thinking, as well, because such thinking should facilitate keeping one's broader, overarching goals in sight as opposed to getting trapped in the narrow world of details. Motivation and virtue need to be an integral part of reflectiveness research. Both as laypersons and as scientists, we need this more holistic approach. Reflection begins to shine when one remembers that the long-term goals of participating in politics or pursuing a career in science are not winning debates and prizes, but seeking the truth.

Other Key Insights of the Book

It is important to note that "good thinking" cannot be reduced to a single rule such as "always ignore your intuitions and replace them as soon as you can with reflection." It is clear that pairing intuition with "biased," and reflection with "rational," works well only in specific contexts. In most of daily life, intuitive processes serve us well and we would become paralyzed if they were removed from our lives. Via repetition and practice, intuition can take over complicated action sequences normally requiring reflection, and this critically underlies high-level, skilled performance, as well as many mundane daily tasks. Even the absence of a strong intuition (e.g., moral conviction) or the presence of multiple conflicting intuitions is beneficial because these conditions trigger reflection.

Knowing when to rely on intuition helps us reserve our limited cognitive resources for the areas in which reflectiveness is much more critical. Thus, in the broader scheme, it can be wise to rely on intuition when we can do so safely. With the same logic, one should feel free to "stop thinking just because thinking is not making progress or because the answer is not worth more time and effort" (Baron, 2023a, p. 23). Flexibility regarding when to think harder is a useful skill. Intuitive processes also play an important role in metacognitive processes that enable such flexibility.

Likewise, reflection has some serious downsides such as being sluggish and fragile. It can get stuck on minor details and miss the big picture. This is a threat even in science where criticisms bring up the failure to contextualize our efforts, appreciate the implicit assumptions behind research practices, and connect the dots in terms of integrating theories and research areas (e.g., Henriques, 2013). The challenge of dealing with the overwhelming and exponentially increasing amount of information produced by our civilization highlights a major weakness of human reflective capacity. Perhaps, this challenge will be tackled by tools like artificial intelligence but until we can rely on such tools with enough confidence, individuals may have to resort to receiving aid from intuitive processes if they wish to carry out the kinds of complementary thinking styles—more integrative, holistic, and systemic—mentioned throughout the book.

In some situations, useful heuristics may be developed (with the aid of reflection at first) to facilitate judgment. Likewise, individuals may benefit from explicitly focusing (reflectively, if needed) on the gist of information at the expense of precise details to derive memorable insights that they can transfer to other situations. After all, "[i]n the era of big data and overwhelming access to detailed information, appreciating the essence of information is more important than ever to improve human reasoning, judgment, and decision-making" (Reyna et al., 2017, p. 95). These processes do not preclude reflection or decrease its value. On the contrary, many theorists are fully aware that successful problem-solving is a matter of the collaboration of our reflective and intuitive capacities (this itself is a holistic view of cognition). It is telling that older adults typically have lower reflective capacity than perhaps even adolescents but they are typically wiser, thereby suggesting that something other than reflection, likely life experience condensed into intuitions, is involved in wisdom (see Romer et al., 2017, p. 27). Hence, mainstream dual-process models should seriously consider challenging viewpoints such as the work of Gigerenzer on heuristics and Fuzzy-Trace Theory, and work on how to theoretically and practically incorporate their offerings.

Viewed more broadly, while our effort was designed to focus specifically on reflectiveness, we could not help but notice at its concluding phase that these emerging themes point to *wisdom* as a potentially more important overarching construct. Interestingly, recent cross-cultural evidence uncovered two common components underlying people's perceptions of wisdom (Rudnev et al., 2023). Unsurprisingly, one of them is reflectiveness. The other component is "socio-emotional awareness," which involves some degree of intuitive capacity (e.g., "paying attention to emotions" and "caring for others' feelings"). This suggests that it is natural for people to see reflection and intuition as together contributing to a highly prized human capacity—unlike the tendency of dual-process theorists to view them in opposition (at least until recently). More interestingly, a close look at the literature reveals that the constructs of holistic thinking and wisdom overlap: At least one well-known framework synthesizing cognitive aspects of wise reasoning across the literature includes four components (see Figure 1 in Grossmann, 2017). Two of these—recognizing change in life and valuing compromise between opposing views—are more or less identical to two (out of the four) components of holistic thinking put forth by the most widely used framework on the latter (Choi et al., 2007). A third component was defined as "appreciation of perspectives broader than the issue at hand" (Grossmann, 2017, p. 235) and is thus also related to the core meaning of holism.[1] These emerging insights in the wisdom literature point to the utility of considering reflectiveness and holistic thinking together. This may be humdrum to those working on wisdom, holism, and systemic thinking; but independently arriving at this realization in a journey that started from the heart of the dual-process model of the mind has been meaningful for us and points to the need for more cross-talk across these pockets of theorizing and research.

We have also seen through the debates in the field that the scientific models of human cognitive architecture harbor some empirically untested assumptions, may have incoherent aspects, and are therefore open to criticism and revision on various fronts. The field will surely go beyond these models, though it is not easy to tell exactly in what way, how, or when. For now, at the least, the generic dual-process model of the mind continues to serve as a great entry point into the literature we covered and to the general topic of human cognition. Recent developments such as Pennycook, Fugelsang, et al.'s (2015) three-stage model offer promising advancements in the field of dual process theories. This model aims to synthesize debates among dual-process theorists by including the existence of competing intuitions, metacognition as a conflict detection mechanism, and distinguishing between reflection's motivated reasoning and cognitive decoupling functions. Similarly, De Neys' (2023a) threshold approach could guide future research by emphasizing the dynamic nature of cognition. Traditional methods, which often measure cognitive processes at a single point in time, overlook the dynamic aspects of decision-making (Thelen & Smith, 1994). De Neys' model underscores the importance of considering cognition as a continuous and evolving process. However, for dual-process theories to advance further, it becomes essential to refine the definitions of reflection and intuition and better understand the empirical relationships of their correlated features. This includes distinguishing various types of reflection and intuition, particularly cognitive versus affective intuitions or verbal versus arithmetic reflection, and clarifying related concepts such as open-mindedness, impulsivity, self-control, and metacognition.

Surprisingly, most studies in this area have relied on correlational methods, focusing on individual differences. The literature to date also has extensively explored the effects of reflection and intuition through experimental manipulations. However, it is noteworthy that these methods had not been thoroughly examined in high-powered experiments until recently. This gap has been addressed by a series of studies conducted by our research group (Isler et al., 2020; Isler & Yilmaz, 2023), which provide new insights into the empirical effects of these cognitive processes. A notable finding from this series of preregistered experiments (total N = 5,415) is that the conventional 10- and 20-second time delay methods, commonly employed against time pressure in the literature, did not enhance reflective scores compared to the control group, regardless of whether they were used in the two-response paradigm or as a standard between-subjects design. Intriguingly, participants in the time pressure condition exhibited lower reflective scores than those in both the control and delay conditions. This outcome aligns with the perspective we present in this book. It suggests that when we directly provide individuals with time for reflection, without the requisite motivation and guidance (e.g., the necessary mindware), they often do not engage in reflection independently, at least not in the manner envisioned by researchers. These findings highlight a need within dual-process research to develop and standardize tools that can more effectively manipulate and measure the underlying theoretical concepts.

However, it is important to note that the challenges identified here are not unique to dual-process theories but are indicative of broader issues within behavioral sciences. The social contexts in which human cognitive activity takes place may be critical. Our review highlighted how social factors such as group identities and the social network one is embedded in and its narratives may be decisive in terms of driving reflection into motivated reasoning versus a truly open-minded form. The lack of integration across silos of research taking place in very different contexts (e.g., the psychology laboratory vs. a business organization or the voting booth) leads to confusion in the sense of equally strong but opposing views regarding the nature of reflection and intuition in those different silos. Going forward, the field would do well to acknowledge that "even if one seems to be engaged in a solitary set of mental reflections in one's head, decision making is really a matter of embodied, emotion-rich, environmentally modulated processes" and that "[e]ven if we are trained as hard-nosed rationalist philosophers, or no-nonsense business executives, or data-driven scientists, ... our decisions are influenced by various institutional practices" (Gallagher, 2013, p. 11)—that is, to take a holistic approach and take into account the social context, not just cognitive processes. In this vein, Raeff (2020) applies a systems perspective to conceptualize thinking as an action that is founded on several subsystems (e.g., individual, social, cultural, bodily, and environmental processes). This unique perspective stands in sharp contrast to the "pure cognitive function" view—i.e., cognition as a set of relatively static capacities that can be captured by standardized laboratory tasks—espoused by most dual-process theorists. Closer integration of these approaches could move the field toward resolving some of the conflictual conceptualizations and contradictory findings in isolated research areas that we identified in our effort.

The major challenge confronting behavioral sciences today in taking such a holistic approach is the absence of a comprehensive overarching theory (Muthukrishna & Henrich, 2019). This deficiency is tied to the lack of a reference model to guide the interpretation of new discoveries. Similar to the broader field of psychology, dual-process approaches have predominantly relied on the hypothetico-deductive method, formulating theories without first thoroughly establishing the relationships between variables and their well-defined boundary conditions. However, recent critiques have highlighted the inadequacy of this method for psychological sciences (Borsboom et al., 2021; Haig, 2005, 2018; Muthukrishna & Henrich, 2019). In the spirit of Darwin, who formulated the theory of natural selection as the best explanation of existing evidence, we should focus on data collection followed by *abduction*—the process of seeking the most plausible explanations (Haig, 2005). As outlined by Borsboom et al. (2021), theory construction involves first pinpointing robust phenomena and their established boundary conditions, then developing verbal prototheories, which are subsequently mathematically modeled and tested against competing theories. These steps emphasize the creation of valid tools and the establishment of robust phenomena with their well-defined boundary conditions before theorizing. Such steps are crucial for advancing toward a comprehensive theory in behavioral sciences. Identifying robust phenomena necessitates understanding how a phenomenon manifests across different cultures and its context-specific moderators. Considering our limited knowledge about non-WEIRD cultures, it may be prudent to pause theory development based on yet-to-be-consolidated concepts without valid tools and instead prioritize the validity of research tools and the representation of the full diversity of *Homo sapiens* in our studies. Any work on the theoretical front should employ greater reflectiveness toward theory selection and construction (e.g., Kruglanski, 2001) and a more holistic approach toward theory integration (e.g., van Zomeren, 2024).

Coda

Our exploration of the literature we presented in the book pointed in different ways to the importance of the need to be reflective *while also* approaching issues holistically. Interestingly, this characterizes an ancient system of thought very well. The Stoics understood the value of reflection for generating thoughts and interpretations of reality that are congenial to one's goals but also understood that those goals need to be virtuous—the alternatives are disastrous for both the individual and society. They understood that human nature is not a collection of parts such as reason and emotion but is a unified whole that is also a part of the entire cosmos. They viewed human life in its broad context and living in harmony with nature as a fundamental principle. They aimed to create a philosophical system that integrated logic, virtue, and physics. While working on the final touches to our book, we serendipitously discovered that we are both very fond of Stoicism. Coincidentally, many ancient Stoic philosophers roamed around the region where we now live. Perhaps the most famous among them, the Greek philosopher Epictetus, was born in present-day Türkiye. These are the lands where the East meets the West figuratively and literally: Both of us cross the Bosphorus strait to travel from the Asian to the European halves of Istanbul every time we go to work. Hence, we would like to believe that our effort was able to offer a unique and fresh viewpoint from the heart of this cultural fusion. Concluding our effort with a pleasant surprise that connected our thoughts to great thinkers from more than 2000 years ago, we also find ourselves excited to imagine that revisiting their ideas with the tools of modern psychology could be, at least for us, a worthwhile path for the future of research on reflectiveness.

Note

1   The fourth component in Grossman's wisdom framework is "intellectual humility," which is a virtue we have frequently referred to throughout the book as an important complement to reflectiveness. Thus, if Grossman's framework captures wisdom successfully, one could say that we ended up writing a book about the importance of wisdom without intending to. Some other research traditions take a similar approach by highlighting how reflectiveness needs to be joined by various other cognitive skills and styles discussed in this book. For instance, similar to our effort and Grossman's framework, the literature on "critical thinking" gives special import to intellectual humility, as well (Halpern, 2013).

REFERENCES

Abelson, R. P. (1995). Attitude extremity. In R. E. Petty & Krosnick, Jon A. (Eds.), *Attitude strength: Antecedents and consequences* (pp. 25–41). Lawrence Erlbaum Associates.

Abramson, L. Y., Seligman, M. E., & Teasdale, J. D. (1978). Learned helplessness in humans: Critique and reformulation. *Journal of Abnormal Psychology, 87*(1), 49–74. https://doi.org/10.1037/0021-843X.87.1.49

Abulof, U. (2015). The malpractice of "rationality" in international relations. *Rationality and Society, 27*(3), 358–384. https://doi.org/10.1177/104346311 5593144

Acem, E. (2023). *Does cognitive reflection predict cooperation behavior after a seven-month period?* Kadir Has University.

Açıkgöz, E., & Alp, H. (Eds.). (2014). *"Biz de insanız yavrum ya!": Nefret suçları: Vakalar, tanıklıklar* (1. baskı). İletişim.

Ackerman, J. M., Hill, S. E., & Murray, D. R. (2018). The behavioral immune system: Current concerns and future directions. *Social and Personality Psychology Compass, 12*(2), e12371. https://doi.org/10.1111/spc3.12371

Ackerman, R. (2014). The diminishing criterion model for metacognitive regulation of time investment. *Journal of Experimental Psychology: General, 143*(3), 1349–1368. https://doi.org/10.1037/a0035098

Ackerman, R., & Morsanyi, K. (2023). We know what stops you from thinking forever: A metacognitive perspective. *Behavioral and Brain Sciences, 46*, e112. https://doi.org/10.1017/S0140525X22003065

Ackerman, R., & Thompson, V. A. (2017). Meta-reasoning: Monitoring and control of thinking and reasoning. *Trends in Cognitive Sciences, 21*(8), 607–617. https://doi.org/10.1016/j.tics.2017.05.004

Adam-Troian, J., & Bélanger, J. J. (2024). "Consumed by creed": Obsessive–compulsive symptoms underpin ideological obsession and support for political violence. *Aggressive Behavior, 50*(1), e22124. https://doi.org/10.1002/ab.22124

Adam-Troian, J., Tecmen, A., & Kaya, A. (2021). Youth extremism as a response to global threats?: A threat-regulation perspective on violent extremism among the youth. *European Psychologist*, 26(1), 15–28. https://doi.org/10.1027/1016-9040/a000415

Adorno, T. W., Frenkel-Brunswik, E., Levinson, D. J., & Sanford, R. N. (1950). *The authoritarian personality*. Norton.

Ahearn, E.-R., Bhui, K., & Jones, E. (2021). What factors are truly associated with risk for radicalisation? A secondary data analysis within a UK sample. *Transcultural Psychiatry*, 58(5), 645–653. https://doi.org/10.1177/1363461520933755

Akay, A., Bargain, O., & Elsayed, A. (2020). Global terror, well-being and political attitudes. *European Economic Review*, 123, 103394. https://doi.org/10.1016/j.euroecorev.2020.103394

Albert, K. E. (2022). What is rebel governance? Introducing a new dataset on rebel institutions, 1945–2012. *Journal of Peace Research*, 59(4), 622–630. https://doi.org/10.1177/00223433211051848

Alford, J. R., Funk, C. L., & Hibbing, J. R. (2005). Are political orientations genetically transmitted? *American Political Science Review*, 99(2), 153–167. https://doi.org/10.1017/S0003055405051579

Allen, A. P., & Thomas, K. E. (2011). A dual process account of creative thinking. *Creativity Research Journal*, 23(2), 109–118. https://doi.org/10.1080/10400419.2011.571183

Allinson, C. W., & Hayes, J. (1996). The cognitive style index: A measure of intuition-analysis for organizational research. *Journal of Management Studies*, 33(1), 119–135. https://doi.org/10.1111/j.1467-6486.1996.tb00801.x

Allport, G. W. (1937). *Personality: A psychological interpretation*. Holt & Co.

Almond, G. A., Appleby, R. S., & Sivan, E. (2003). *Strong religion: The rise of fundamentalisms around the world*. University of Chicago Press.

Alper, S. (2023). There are higher levels of conspiracy beliefs in more corrupt countries. *European Journal of Social Psychology*, 53(3), 503–517. https://doi.org/10.1002/ejsp.2919

Alper, S., Bayrak, F., Us, E. Ö., & Yilmaz, O. (2020). Do changes in threat salience predict the moral content of sermons? The case of Friday Khutbas in Turkey. *European Journal of Social Psychology*, 50(3), 662–672. https://doi.org/10.1002/ejsp.2632

Alper, S., Yelbuz, B. E., Akkurt, S. B., & Yilmaz, O. (2024). The positive association of education with the trust in science and scientists is weaker in highly corrupt countries. *Public Understanding of Science*, 33(1), 2–19. https://doi.org/10.1177/09636625231176935

Alper, S., & Yilmaz, O. (2023). What is wrong with conspiracy beliefs? *Routledge Open Research*, 2, 28. https://doi.org/10.12688/routledgeopenres.17926.1

Alper, S., Yilmaz, O., & Saribay, S. A. (2021). How do cognitive styles influence political attitudes? A joint consideration of dual-process model and construal level theory. In J. D. Sinnott & J. S. Rabin (Eds.), *The psychology of political behavior in a time of change* (pp. 177–193). Springer International Publishing. https://doi.org/10.1007/978-3-030-38270-4_6

Altan-Atalay, A., Kaya-Kızılöz, B., İlkmen, Y. S., & Kozol, E. (2022). Impact of abstract vs. concrete processing on state rumination: An exploration of the role of cognitive flexibility. *Journal of Behavior Therapy and Experimental Psychiatry*, 74, 101691. https://doi.org/10.1016/j.jbtep.2021.101691

Alter, A. L., & Oppenheimer, D. M. (2009). Uniting the tribes of fluency to form a metacognitive nation. *Personality and Social Psychology Review*, *13*(3), 219–235. https://doi.org/10.1177/1088868309341564

Alter, A. L., Oppenheimer, D. M., Epley, N., & Eyre, R. N. (2007). Overcoming intuition: Metacognitive difficulty activates analytic reasoning. *Journal of Experimental Psychology: General*, *136*(4), 569–576. https://doi.org/10.1037/0096-3445.136.4.569

Altier, M. B., Thoroughgood, C. N., & Horgan, J. G. (2014). Turning away from terrorism: Lessons from psychology, sociology, and criminology. *Journal of Peace Research*, *51*(5), 647–661. https://doi.org/10.1177/002234331 4535946

Amit, E., & Greene, J. D. (2012). You see, the ends don't justify the means: Visual imagery and moral judgment. *Psychological Science*, *23*(8), 861–868. https://doi. org/10.1177/0956797611434965

Andersen, S. M., & Saribay, S. A. (2012). Brainwashing and totalitarian influence. In *Encyclopedia of human behavior* (pp. 406–412). Elsevier. https://doi.org/10.1016/B978-0-12-375000-6.00075-6

Anticevic, A., Barch, D. M., & Repovs, G. (2010). Resisting emotional interference: Brain regions facilitating working memory performance during negative distraction. *Cognitive, Affective, & Behavioral Neuroscience*, *10*(2), 159–173. https://doi.org/10.3758/CABN.10.2.159

Artavia-Mora, L., Bedi, A. S., & Rieger, M. (2018). Help, prejudice and headscarves. *SSRN Electronic Journal*. https://doi.org/10.2139/ssrn.3170249

Asch, S. E. (1956). Studies of independence and conformity: I. A minority of one against a unanimous majority. *Psychological Monographs: General and Applied*, *70*(9), 1–70. https://doi.org/10.1037/h0093718

Aßmann, L., Betsch, T., Lang, A., & Lindow, S. (2022). When even the smartest fail to prioritise: Overuse of information can decrease decision accuracy. *Journal of Cognitive Psychology*, *34*(5), 675–690. https://doi.org/10.1080/20445 911.2022.2055560

Atari, M., Davani, A. M., Kogon, D., Kennedy, B., Ani Saxena, N., Anderson, I., & Dehghani, M. (2022). Morally homogeneous networks and radicalism. *Social Psychological and Personality Science*, *13*(6), 999–1009. https://doi.org/10.1177/19485506211059329

Atari, M., Haidt, J., Graham, J., Koleva, S., Stevens, S. T., & Dehghani, M. (2023). Morality beyond the WEIRD: How the nomological network of morality varies across cultures. *Journal of Personality and Social Psychology*, *125*(5), 1157–1188. https://doi.org/10.1037/pspp0000470

Atran, S. (2001) The trouble with memes: Inference versus imitation in cultural creation. *Human Nature*, *12*(4), 351–381. https://doi.org/10.1007/s12110-001-1003-0

Atran, S. (2002). The neuropsychology of religion. In R. Joseph (Ed.), *NeuroTheology: Brain, science, spirituality, religious experience* (pp. 147–166). University Press California. https://hal.science/ijn_00000110

Axelrod, R., & Hamilton, W. D. (1981). The evolution of cooperation. *Science*, *211*(4489), 1390–1396. https://doi.org/10.1126/science.7466396

Baddeley, A. D., & Hitch, G. J. (1994). Developments in the concept of working memory. *Neuropsychology*, *8*(4), 485–493. https://doi.org/10.1037/0894-4105.8.4.485

Baele, S. J. (2017). Lone-actor terrorists' emotions and cognition: an evaluation beyond stereotypes: Lone-actor terrorists' emotions and cognition. *Political Psychology*, 38(3), 449–468. https://doi.org/10.1111/pops.12365

Baele, S. J. (2019). Conspiratorial narratives in violent political actors' language. *Journal of Language and Social Psychology*, 38(5–6), 706–734. https://doi.org/10.1177/0261927X19868494

Bago, B., & De Neys, W. (2017). Fast logic?: Examining the time course assumption of dual process theory. *Cognition*, 158, 90–109. https://doi.org/10.1016/j.cognit ion.2016.10.014

Bago, B., & De Neys, W. (2019). The smart system 1: Evidence for the intuitive nature of correct responding on the bat-and-ball problem. *Thinking & Reasoning*, 25(3), 257–299. https://doi.org/10.1080/13546783.2018.1507949

Bago, B., Rand, D. G., & Pennycook, G. (2022). Does deliberation decrease belief in conspiracies? *Journal of Experimental Social Psychology*, 103, 104395. https://doi.org/10.1016/j.jesp.2022.104395

Bahçekapili, H. G., & Yilmaz, O. (2017). The relation between different types of religiosity and analytic cognitive style. *Personality and Individual Differences*, 117, 267–272. https://doi.org/10.1016/j.paid.2017.06.013

Bahçekapili, H. G., Yilmaz, O., & Sevi, B. (2019). Evolutionary perspectives on religion. In T. K. Shackelford, & V. A. Weekes-Shackelford (Eds.), *Encyclopedia of evolutionary psychological science* (pp. 1–4). Springer International Publishing. https://doi.org/10.1007/978-3-319-16999-6_3802-1

Baimel, A., White, C. J. M., Sarkissian, H., & Norenzayan, A. (2021). How is analytical thinking related to religious belief? A test of three theoretical models. *Religion, Brain & Behavior*, 11(3), 239–260. https://doi.org/10.1080/21535 99X.2021.1878259

Bakhti, R. (2018). Religious versus reflective priming and susceptibility to the conjunction fallacy. *Applied Cognitive Psychology*, 32(2), 186–191. https://doi.org/10.1002/acp.3394

Ballew, M. T., Goldberg, M. H., Rosenthal, S. A., Gustafson, A., & Leiserowitz, A. (2019). Systems thinking as a pathway to global warming beliefs and attitudes through an ecological worldview. *Proceedings of the National Academy of Sciences*, 116(17), 8214–8219. https://doi.org/10.1073/pnas.1819310116

Bandura, A. (1990). Mechanisms of moral disengagement. In W. Reich (Ed.), *Origins of terrorism: Psychologies, ideologies, theologies, states of mind* (pp. 161–191). Cambridge University Press.

Banerjee, A. V., & Duflo, E. (2012). *Poor economics: A radical rethinking of the way to fight global poverty* (Paperback ed.). PublicAffairs.

Bargh, J. A. (1994). The four horsemen of automaticity: Awareness, intention, efficiency, and control as separate issues. In R. S. Wyer & T. K. Srull (Eds.), *Handbook of social cognition* (2nd ed., Vol. 1, pp. 1–40). Lawrence Erlbaum Associates.

Bargh, J. A., Chaiken, S., Raymond, P., & Hymes, C. (1996). The automatic evaluation effect: Unconditional automatic attitude activation with a pronunciation task. *Journal of Experimental Social Psychology*, 32(1), 104–128. https://doi.org/10.1006/jesp.1996.0005

Bargh, J. A., Gollwitzer, P. M., Lee-Chai, A., Barndollar, K., & Trötschel, R. (2001). The automated will: Nonconscious activation and pursuit of behavioral goals. *Journal of Personality and Social Psychology*, 81(6), 1014–1027. https://doi.org/10.1037/0022-3514.81.6.1014

Baron, J. (2017). Comment on Kahan and Corbin: Can polarization increase with actively open-minded thinking? *Research & Politics*, 4(1), 205316801668812. https://doi.org/10.1177/2053168016688122

Baron, J. (2019). Actively open-minded thinking in politics. *Cognition*, 188, 8–18. https://doi.org/10.1016/j.cognition.2018.10.004

Baron, J. (2020). Religion, cognitive style, and rational thinking. *Current Opinion in Behavioral Sciences*, 34, 64–68. https://doi.org/10.1016/j.cobeha.2019.12.015

Baron, J. (2023a). Individual differences and multi-step thinking. *Behavioral and Brain Sciences*, 46, e114. https://doi.org/10.1017/S0140525X2200320X

Baron, J. (2023b). *Thinking and deciding* (5th ed.). Cambridge University Press.

Baron, J., Isler, O., & Yilmaz, O. (2023). Actively open-minded thinking and the political effects of its absence. In V. Ottati & C. Stern (Eds.), *Divided: Open-mindedness and dogmatism in a polarized world*. Oxford University Press.

Baron, J., & Jost, J. T. (2019). False equivalence: Are liberals and conservatives in the United States equally biased? *Perspectives on Psychological Science*, 14(2), 292–303. https://doi.org/10.1177/1745691618788876

Baron, J., Scott, S., Fincher, K., & Emlen Metz, S. (2015). Why does the cognitive reflection test (sometimes) predict utilitarian moral judgment (and other things)? *Journal of Applied Research in Memory and Cognition*, 4(3), 265–284. https://doi.org/10.1016/j.jarmac.2014.09.003

Baron, R. S. (2000). Arousal, capacity, and intense indoctrination. *Personality and Social Psychology Review*, 4(3), 238–254. https://doi.org/10.1207/S15327957PSPR0403_3

Baron-Cohen, S. (1991). Precursors to a theory of mind: Understanding attention in others. In A. Whiten (Ed.), *Natural theories of mind: Evolution, development and simulation of everyday mindreading* (pp. 233–251). Basil Blackwell.

Barr, N. (2018). Intuition, reason, and creativity: An integrative dual-process perspective. In G. Pennycook (Ed.), *The new reflectionism in cognitive psychology* (0 ed., pp. 99–124). Routledge. https://doi.org/10.4324/9781315460178-11

Barr, N., Pennycook, G., Stolz, J. A., & Fugelsang, J. A. (2015). Reasoned connections: A dual-process perspective on creative thought. *Thinking & Reasoning*, 21(1), 61–75. https://doi.org/10.1080/13546783.2014.895915

Barrett, J. L. (2004). Bringing data to mind: Empirical claims of Lawson and McCauley's theory of religious ritual. In T. Light, & B. C. Wilson (Eds.), *Religion as a human capacity* (pp. 265–288). BRILL. https://doi.org/10.1163/9789047401698_016

Bas, J., & Sebastian-Galles, N. (2021). Infants' representation of social hierarchies in absence of physical dominance. *PLoS ONE*, 16(2), e0245450. https://doi.org/10.1371/journal.pone.0245450

Bassili, J. N. (1996). Meta-judgmental versus operative indexes of psychological attributes: The case of measures of attitude strength. *Journal of Personality and Social Psychology*, 71(4), 637–653. https://doi.org/10.1037/0022-3514.71.4.637

Batson, C. D., & Schoenrade, P. A. (1991). Measuring religion as quest: 1) Validity concerns. *Journal for the Scientific Study of Religion*, 30(4), 416. https://doi.org/10.2307/1387277

Baumeister, R. F. (1984). Choking under pressure: Self-consciousness and paradoxical effects of incentives on skillful performance. *Journal of Personality and Social Psychology*, 46(3), 610–620. https://doi.org/10.1037/0022-3514.46.3.610

Baumeister, R. F., DeWall, C. N., Ciarocco, N. J., & Twenge, J. M. (2005). Social exclusion impairs self-regulation. *Journal of Personality and Social Psychology*, *88*(4), 589–604. https://doi.org/10.1037/0022-3514.88.4.589

Baumeister, R. F., Twenge, J. M., & Nuss, C. K. (2002). Effects of social exclusion on cognitive processes: Anticipated aloneness reduces intelligent thought. *Journal of Personality and Social Psychology*, *83*(4), 817–827. https://doi.org/10.1037/0022-3514.83.4.817

Baumgartner, H. A., Alessandroni, N., Byers-Heinlein, K., Frank, M. C., Hamlin, J. K., Soderstrom, M., Voelkel, J. G., Willer, R., Yuen, F., & Coles, N. A. (2023). How to build up big team science: A practical guide for large-scale collaborations. *Royal Society Open Science*, *10*(6), 230235. https://doi.org/10.1098/rsos.230235

Bausell, R. B. (2021). *The problem with science: The reproducibility crisis and what to do about it*. Oxford University Press.

Bear, A., & Rand, D. G. (2016). Intuition, deliberation, and the evolution of cooperation. *Proceedings of the National Academy of Sciences*, *113*(4), 936–941. https://doi.org/10.1073/pnas.1517780113

Beilock, S. L., Bertenthal, B. I., Mccoy, A. M., & Carr, T. H. (2004). Haste does not always make waste: Expertise, direction of attention, and speed versus accuracy in performing sensorimotor skills. *Psychonomic Bulletin & Review*, *11*(2), 373–379. https://doi.org/10.3758/BF03196585

Beilock, S. L., Wierenga, S. A., & Carr, T. H. (2002). Expertise, attention, and memory in sensorimotor skill execution: Impact of novel task constraints on dual-task performance and episodic memory. *The Quarterly Journal of Experimental Psychology Section A*, *55*(4), 1211–1240. https://doi.org/10.1080/02724980244000170

Bélanger, J. J. (2021). The sociocognitive processes of ideological obsession: Review and policy implications. *Philosophical Transactions of the Royal Society B: Biological Sciences*, *376*(1822), 20200144. https://doi.org/10.1098/rstb.2020.0144

Bélanger, J. J., Schumpe, B. M., Nisa, C. F., & Moyano, M. (2021). When countermessaging backfires: The role of obsessive passion in psychological reactance. *Motivation Science*, *7*(1), 83–95. https://doi.org/10.1037/mot0000206

Bélanger, J. J., Snook, D. W., Dzitac, D., & Cheppih, A. (2023). Challenging extremism: A randomized control trial examining the impact of counternarratives in the Middle East and North Africa. *Current Research in Ecological and Social Psychology*, *4*, 100097. https://doi.org/10.1016/j.cresp.2023.100097

Bell, D. (1962). *The end of ideology: On the exhaustion of political ideas in the fifties*. Harvard University Press.

Bellah, R. N. (2011). *Religion in human evolution: From the paleolithic to the axial age*. Harvard University Press. https://doi.org/10.4159/harvard.9780674063099

Bergson, H. (1999). *An introduction to metaphysics (T. E. Hulme, Trans.)*. Hackett Publishing. (Original work published 1903)

Bering, J. M. (2006). The folk psychology of souls. *Behavioral and Brain Sciences*, *29*(5), 453–462. https://doi.org/10.1017/S0140525X06009101

Berman, E., & Laitin, D. D. (2008). Religion, terrorism and public goods: Testing the club model. *Journal of Public Economics*, *92*(10–11), 1942–1967. https://doi.org/10.1016/j.jpubeco.2008.03.007

Bermúdez, J. P. (2017). Do we reflect while performing skillful actions? Automaticity, control, and the perils of distraction. *Philosophical Psychology*, *30*(7), 896–924. https://doi.org/10.1080/09515089.2017.1325457

Bernstein, A., Hadash, Y., Lichtash, Y., Tanay, G., Shepherd, K., & Fresco, D. M. (2015). Decentering and related constructs: a critical review and metacognitive processes model. *Perspectives on Psychological Science*, 10(5), 599–617. https://doi.org/10.1177/1745691615594577

Berrebi, C. (2007). Evidence about the link between education, poverty and terrorism among Palestinians. *Peace Economics, Peace Science and Public Policy*, 13(1). https://doi.org/10.2202/1554-8597.1101

Betsch, T., & Glöckner, A. (2010). Intuition in judgment and decision making: Extensive thinking without effort. *Psychological Inquiry*, 21(4), 279–294. https://doi.org/10.1080/1047840X.2010.517737

Bialek, M., & Pennycook, G. (2018). The cognitive reflection test is robust to multiple exposures. *Behavior Research Methods*, 50(5), 1953–1959. https://doi.org/10.3758/s13428-017-0963-x

Binnendyk, J., & Pennycook, G. (2022). Intuition, reason, and conspiracy beliefs. *Current Opinion in Psychology*, 47, 101387. https://doi.org/10.1016/j.copsyc.2022.101387

Black, M. (1964). The gap between "is" and "should." *The Philosophical Review*, 73(2), 165. https://doi.org/10.2307/2183334

Blackmore, S. (2010). Why I no longer believe religion is a virus of the mind. www.theguardian.com/commentisfree/belief/2010/sep/16/why-no-longer-believe-religion-virus-mind

Blalock, S. J., & Reyna, V. F. (2016). Using fuzzy-trace theory to understand and improve health judgments, decisions, and behaviors: A literature review. *Health Psychology*, 35(8), 781–792. https://doi.org/10.1037/hea0000384

Block, J., & Block, J. H. (2006). Nursery school personality and political orientation two decades later. *Journal of Research in Personality*, 40(5), 734–749. https://doi.org/10.1016/j.jrp.2005.09.005

Bloom, P. (2016). *Against empathy: The case for rational compassion* (1st ed.). Ecco, an imprint of HarperCollins Publishers.

Blume, B. D., & Covin, J. G. (2011). Attributions to intuition in the venture founding process: Do entrepreneurs actually use intuition or just say that they do? *Journal of Business Venturing*, 26(1), 137–151. https://doi.org/10.1016/j.jbusvent.2009.04.002

Boaz, D., & Kirby, D. (2006). The libertarian vote. *SSRN Electronic Journal*. https://doi.org/10.2139/ssrn.975672

Boehmer, C., & Daube, M. (2013). The curvilinear effects of economic development on domestic terrorism. *Peace Economics, Peace Science and Public Policy*, 19(3). https://doi.org/10.1515/peps-2013-0043

Boissin, E., Caparos, S., & De Neys, W. (2023). Examining the role of deliberation in de-bias training. *Thinking & Reasoning*, 1–29. https://doi.org/10.1080/13546783.2023.2259542

Boissin, E., Caparos, S., Raoelison, M., & De Neys, W. (2021). From bias to sound intuiting: Boosting correct intuitive reasoning. *Cognition*, 211, 104645. https://doi.org/10.1016/j.cognition.2021.104645

Bonanno, G. A., & Jost, J. T. (2006). Conservative shift among high-exposure survivors of the September 11th terrorist attacks. *Basic and Applied Social Psychology*, 28(4), 311–323. https://doi.org/10.1207/s15324834basp2804_4

Booth, A. (1984). Responses to scarcity. *The Sociological Quarterly*, 25(1), 113–124. https://doi.org/10.1111/j.1533-8525.1984.tb02242.x

Borsboom, D., Maas, H. L. J. van der, Dalege, J., Kievit, R. A., & Haig, B. D. (2021). Theory construction methodology: A practical framework for building theories in psychology. *Perspectives on Psychological Science, 16*(4), 756–766. https://doi.org/10.1177/1745691620969647

Borum, R. (2011). Radicalization into violent extremism I: A review of social science theories. *Journal of Strategic Security, 4*(4), 7–36. https://doi.org/10.5038/1944-0472.4.4.1

Bostyn, D. H., Sevenhant, S., & Roets, A. (2019). Beyond physical harm: How preference for consequentialism and primary psychopathy relate to decisions on a monetary trolley dilemma. *Thinking & Reasoning, 25*(2), 192–206. https://doi.org/10.1080/13546783.2018.1497536

Bouchard, T. J., & McGue, M. (2003). Genetic and environmental influences on human psychological differences. *Journal of Neurobiology, 54*(1), 4–45. https://doi.org/10.1002/neu.10160

Bouchard, T. J., Segal, N. L., Tellegen, A., McGue, M., Keyes, M., & Krueger, R. (2003). Evidence for the construct validity and heritability of the Wilson–Patterson conservatism scale: A reared-apart twins study of social attitudes. *Personality and Individual Differences, 34*(6), 959–969. https://doi.org/10.1016/S0191-8869(02)00080-6

Boudry, M., & Hofhuis, S. (2018). Parasites of the mind. Why cultural theorists need the meme's eye view. *Cognitive Systems Research, 52*, 155–167. https://doi.org/10.1016/j.cogsys.2018.06.010

Bouwmeester, S., Verkoeijen, P. P. J. L., Aczel, B., Barbosa, F., Bègue, L., Brañas-Garza, P., Chmura, T. G. H., Cornelissen, G., Døssing, F. S., Espín, A. M., Evans, A. M., Ferreira-Santos, F., Fiedler, S., Flegr, J., Ghaffari, M., Glöckner, A., Goeschl, T., Guo, L., Hauser, O. P., … Wollbrant, C. E. (2017). Registered replication report: Rand, Greene, and Nowak (2012). *Perspectives on Psychological Science, 12*(3), 527–542. https://doi.org/10.1177/1745691617693624

Bowlby, J. (1969). *Attachment and loss. Vol 1: Attachment.* Basic Books.

Bowles, S., & Gintis, H. (2011). *A cooperative species: human reciprocity and its evolution.* Princeton University Press. https://doi.org/10.1515/9781400838837

Box, G. E. P. (1979). Robustness in the strategy of scientific model building. In *Robustness in statistics* (pp. 201–236). Elsevier. https://doi.org/10.1016/B978-0-12-438150-6.50018-2

Boyd, R., & Richerson, P. J. (1989). The evolution of indirect reciprocity. *Social Networks, 11*(3), 213–236. https://doi.org/10.1016/0378-8733(89)90003-8

Boyer, P. (2001). *Religion explained: The evolutionary origins of religious thought.* Basic Books.

Brainerd, C. J., & Reyna, V. F. (1990). Gist is the grist: Fuzzy-trace theory and the new intuitionism. *Developmental Review, 10*(1), 3–47. https://doi.org/10.1016/0273-2297(90)90003-M

Brainerd, C. J., & Reyna, V. F. (2002). Fuzzy-trace theory: Dual processes in memory, reasoning, and cognitive neuroscience. In *Advances in child development and behavior* (Vol. 28, pp. 41–100). Elsevier. https://doi.org/10.1016/S0065-2407(02)80062-3

Brainerd, C. J., Reyna, V. F., & Forrest, T. J. (2002). Are young children susceptible to the false–memory illusion? *Child Development, 73*(5), 1363–1377. https://doi.org/10.1111/1467-8624.00477

Brandt, M. J., Evans, A. M., & Crawford, J. T. (2015). The unthinking or confident extremist? Political extremists are more likely than moderates to reject experimenter-generated anchors. *Psychological Science*, 26(2), 189–202. https://doi.org/10.1177/0956797614559730

Brandt, M. J., Turner-Zwinkels, F. M., Karapirinler, B., Van Leeuwen, F., Bender, M., Van Osch, Y., & Adams, B. (2021). The association between threat and politics depends on the type of threat, the political domain, and the country. *Personality and Social Psychology Bulletin*, 47(2), 324–343. https://doi.org/10.1177/01461 67220946187

Brandt, M. J., Wetherell, G., & Reyna, C. (2014). Liberals and conservatives can show similarities in negativity bias. *Behavioral and Brain Sciences*, 37(3), 307–308. https://doi.org/10.1017/S0140525X13002513

Brewer, M. B. (1988). A dual process model of impression formation. In R. S. Wyer, Jr. & T. K. Srull (Eds.), *Advances in social cognition* (Vol. I, pp. 13–48). Psychology Press. https://doi.org/10.4324/9781315801940-6

Brick, C., Hood, B., Ekroll, V., & de-Wit, L. (2022). Illusory essences: a bias holding back theorizing in psychological science. *Perspectives on Psychological Science*, 17(2), 491–506. https://doi.org/10.1177/1745691621991838

Brouard, S., Vasilopoulos, P., & Foucault, M. (2018). How terrorism affects political attitudes: France in the aftermath of the 2015–2016 attacks. *West European Politics*, 41(5), 1073–1099. https://doi.org/10.1080/01402382.2018.1429752

Bruine De Bruin, W., Parker, A. M., & Fischhoff, B. (2007). Individual differences in adult decision-making competence. *Journal of Personality and Social Psychology*, 92(5), 938–956. https://doi.org/10.1037/0022-3514.92.5.938

Bruns, S., Dalheimer, B., & Musshoff, O. (2022). The effect of cognitive function on the poor's economic performance: Evidence from Cambodian smallholder farmers. *Agricultural Economics*, 53(3), 468–480. https://doi.org/10.1111/agec.12685

Brush, J. E., Sherbino, J., & Norman, G. R. (2017). How expert clinicians intuitively recognize a medical diagnosis. *The American Journal of Medicine*, 130(6), 629–634. https://doi.org/10.1016/j.amjmed.2017.01.045

Buchtel, E. E., & Norenzayan, A. (2009). Thinking across cultures: Implications for dual processes. In J. Evans & K. Frankish (Eds.), *In two minds: Dual processes and beyond* (1st ed., pp. 217–238). Oxford University Press. https://doi.org/10.1093/acprof:oso/9780199230167.003.0010

Burgess, J. P. (2007). Against ethics. *Ethical Theory and Moral Practice*, 10(5), 427–439. https://doi.org/10.1007/s10677-007-9063-9

Burgoyne, A. P., Mashburn, C. A., Tsukahara, J. S., Hambrick, D. Z., & Engle, R. W. (2023) Understanding the relationship between rationality and intelligence: A latent-variable approach. *Thinking & Reasoning*, 29(1), 1–42. https://doi.org/10.1080/13546783.2021.2008003

Burke, B. L., Kosloff, S., & Landau, M. J. (2013). Death goes to the polls: A meta-analysis of mortality salience effects on political attitudes. *Political Psychology*, 34(2), 183–200. https://doi.org/10.1111/pops.12005

Byrd, N. (2021). Reflective reasoning & philosophy. *Philosophy Compass*, 16(11), e12786. https://doi.org/10.1111/phc3.12786

Cacioppo, J. T., & Berntson, G. G. (2007). Affective distinctiveness: Illusory or real? *Cognition & Emotion*, 21(6), 1347–1359. https://doi.org/10.1080/0269993070 1502262

Cacioppo, J. T., & Hawkley, L. C. (2009). Perceived social isolation and cognition. *Trends in Cognitive Sciences*, *13*(10), 447–454. https://doi.org/10.1016/j.tics.2009.06.005

Cacioppo, J. T., & Petty, R. E. (1982). The need for cognition. *Journal of Personality and Social Psychology*, *42*(1), 116–131. https://doi.org/10.1037/0022-3514.42.1.116

Cacioppo, J. T., Petty, R. E., Feinstein, J. A., & Jarvis, W. B. G. (1996). Dispositional differences in cognitive motivation: The life and times of individuals varying in need for cognition. *Psychological Bulletin*, *119*(2), 197–253. https://doi.org/10.1037/0033-2909.119.2.197

Cacioppo, J. T., Petty, R. E., & Feng Kao, C. (1984). The efficient assessment of need for cognition. *Journal of Personality Assessment*, *48*(3), 306–307. https://doi.org/10.1207/s15327752jpa4803_13

Caldwell-Harris, C. L., Hocaoğlu, S., & Morgan, J. (2020). Do social constraints inhibit analytical atheism? Cognitive style and religiosity in Turkey. *Journal of Cognition and Culture*, *20*(1–2), 1–21. https://doi.org/10.1163/15685373-12340071

Cameron, C. D., Hutcherson, C. A., Ferguson, A. M., Scheffer, J. A., Hadjiandreou, E., & Inzlicht, M. (2019). Empathy is hard work: People choose to avoid empathy because of its cognitive costs. *Journal of Experimental Psychology: General*, *148*(6), 962–976. https://doi.org/10.1037/xge0000595

Caplan, B. (2006). Terrorism: The relevance of the rational choice model. *Public Choice*, *128*(1–2), 91–107. https://doi.org/10.1007/s11127-006-9046-8

Capraro, V. (2024). The dual-process approach to human sociality: Meta-analytic evidence for a theory of internalized heuristics for self-preservation. *Journal of Personality and Social Psychology*, *126*(5), 719–757. https://doi.org/10.1037/pspa0000375

Capraro, V., & Cococcioni, G. (2016). Rethinking spontaneous giving: Extreme time pressure and ego-depletion favor self-regarding reactions. *Scientific Reports*, *6*(1), 27219. https://doi.org/10.1038/srep27219

Carman, M. (2022). Unpacking a charge of emotional irrationality: An exploration of the value of anger in thought. *Philosophical Papers*, *51*(1), 45–68. https://doi.org/10.1080/05568641.2021.1984981

Caroti, D., Adam-Troian, J., Theraud, M., & Bagneux, V. (2023). *Critical thinking education to decrease conspiracy and paranormal beliefs among secondary school students: A phase I trial*. PsyArXiv. https://doi.org/10.31234/osf.io/p5qzg

Carraro, L., Castelli, L., & Macchiella, C. (2011). The automatic conservative: Ideology-based attentional asymmetries in the processing of valenced information. *PLoS ONE*, *6*(11), e26456. https://doi.org/10.1371/journal.pone.0026456

Carthy, S. L., Doody, C. B., Cox, K., O'Hora, D., & Sarma, K. M. (2020). Counter-narratives for the prevention of violent radicalisation: A systematic review of targeted interventions. *Campbell Systematic Reviews*, *16*(3), e1106. https://doi.org/10.1002/cl2.1106

Cassam, Q. (2022). *Extremism: A philosophical analysis*. Routledge, Taylor & Francis Group.

Castanho Silva, B. (2018). The (non)impact of the 2015 Paris trrorist attacks on political attitudes. *Personality and Social Psychology Bulletin*, *44*(6), 838–850. https://doi.org/10.1177/0146167217752118

Čehajić-Clancy, S., Janković, A., Opačin, N., & Bilewicz, M. (2023). The process of becoming 'we' in an intergroup conflict context: How enhancing intergroup moral similarities leads to common-ingroup identity. *British Journal of Social Psychology*, 62(3), 1251–1270. https://doi.org/10.1111/bjso.12632

Chaiken, S. (1980). Heuristic versus systematic information processing and the use of source versus message cues in persuasion. *Journal of Personality and Social Psychology*, 39(5), 752–766. https://doi.org/10.1037/0022-3514.39.5.752

Chaiken, S., & Ledgerwood, A. (2012). A theory of heuristic and systematic information processing. In P. Van Lange, A. Kruglanski, & E. Higgins (Eds.), *Handbook of theories of social psychology: Volume 1* (pp. 246–266). SAGE Publications Ltd. https://doi.org/10.4135/9781446249215.n13

Chaiken, S., & Trope, Y. (Eds.). (1999). *Dual-process theories in social psychology*. Guilford Press.

Chamberlain, S. R., Blackwell, A. D., Fineberg, N. A., Robbins, T. W., & Sahakian, B. J. (2005). The neuropsychology of obsessive compulsive disorder: The importance of failures in cognitive and behavioural inhibition as candidate endophenotypic markers. *Neuroscience & Biobehavioral Reviews*, 29(3), 399–419. https://doi.org/10.1016/j.neubiorev.2004.11.006

Chambers, C. (2019). *The seven deadly sins of psychology: A manifesto for reforming the culture of scientific practice*. Princeton University Press. https://doi.org/10.1515/9780691192031

Chandrasekharan, S. (2014). Becoming knowledge: Cognitive and neural mechanisms that support scientific intuition. In L. M. Osbeck, & B. S. Held (Eds.), *Rational intuition* (1st ed., pp. 307–337). Cambridge University Press. https://doi.org/10.1017/CBO9781139136419.017

Chang, Y., & Durante, K. M. (2022). Why consumers have everything but happiness: An evolutionary mismatch perspective. *Current Opinion in Psychology*, 46, 101347. https://doi.org/10.1016/j.copsyc.2022.101347

Chase, W. G., & Simon, H. A. (1973). The mind's eye in chess. In *Visual information processing* (pp. 215–281). Elsevier. https://doi.org/10.1016/B978-0-12-170 150-5.50011-1

Chatard, A., Hirschberger, G., & Pyszczynski, T. (2020). *A word of caution about many labs 4: If you fail to follow your preregistered plan, you may fail to find a real effect*. https://doi.org/10.31234/osf.io/ejubn

Cheek, N. N., Coe-Odess, S., & Schwartz, B. (2015). What have I just done? Anchoring, self-knowledge, and judgments of recent behavior. *Judgment and Decision Making*, 10(1), 76–85. https://doi.org/10.1017/S1930297500003193

Cheek, N. N., & Norem, J. K. (2017). Holistic thinkers anchor less: Exploring the roles of self-construal and thinking styles in anchoring susceptibility. *Personality and Individual Differences*, 115, 174–176. https://doi.org/10.1016/j.paid.2016.01.034

Chester, D. S., & Lasko, E. N. (2021). Construct validation of experimental manipulations in social psychology: Current practices and recommendations for the future. *Perspectives on Psychological Science*, 16(2), 377–395. https://doi.org/10.1177/1745691620950684

Cheung, E. O., Slotter, E. B., & Gardner, W. L. (2015). Are you feeling what I'm feeling? The role of facial mimicry in facilitating reconnection following social exclusion. *Motivation and Emotion*, 39(4), 613–630. https://doi.org/10.1007/s11 031-015-9479-9

Choi, I., Koo, M., & Jong An Choi. (2007). Individual differences in analytic versus holistic thinking. *Personality and Social Psychology Bulletin, 33*(5), 691–705. https://doi.org/10.1177/0146167206298568

Christenfeld, N. J. S., Sloan, R. P., Carroll, D., & Greenland, S. (2004). Risk factors, confounding, and the illusion of statistical control. *Psychosomatic Medicine, 66*(6), 868–875. https://doi.org/10.1097/01.psy.0000140 008.70959.41

Christensen, W., Sutton, J., & McIlwain, D. (2015). Putting pressure on theories of choking: Towards an expanded perspective on breakdown in skilled performance. *Phenomenology and the Cognitive Sciences, 14*(2), 253–293. https://doi.org/10.1007/s11097-014-9395-6

Chuderski, A., & Jastrzębski, J. (2018). The relationship of insight problem solving to analytical thinking. In F. Vallée-Tourangeau (Ed.), *Insight* (1st ed., pp. 120–142). Routledge. https://doi.org/10.4324/9781315268118-7

Cichocka, A., Marchlewska, M., & De Zavala, A. G. (2016). Does self-love or self-hate predict conspiracy beliefs? Narcissism, self-esteem, and the endorsement of conspiracy theories. *Social Psychological and Personality Science, 7*(2), 157–166. https://doi.org/10.1177/1948550615616170

Clark, C. J., Liu, B. S., Winegard, B. M., & Ditto, P. H. (2019). Tribalism is human nature. *Current Directions in Psychological Science, 28*(6), 587–592. https://doi.org/10.1177/0963721419862289

Clark, L., Li, R., Wright, C. M., Rome, F., Fairchild, G., Dunn, B. D., & Aitken, M. R. F. (2012). Risk-avoidant decision making increased by threat of electric shock. *Psychophysiology, 49*(10), 1436–1443. https://doi.org/10.1111/j.1469-8986.2012.01454.x

Clarke, S. (2014). *The justification of religious violence.* Wiley Blackwell.

Clifford, S., Iyengar, V., Cabeza, R., & Sinnott-Armstrong, W. (2015). Moral foundations vignettes: A standardized stimulus database of scenarios based on moral foundations theory. *Behavior Research Methods, 47*(4), 1178–1198. https://doi.org/10.3758/s13428-014-0551-2

Cohen, F., Ogilvie, D. M., Solomon, S., Greenberg, J., & Pyszczynski, T. (2005). American Roulette: The effect of reminders of death on support for George W. Bush in the 2004 presidential election. *Analyses of Social Issues and Public Policy, 5*(1), 177–187. https://doi.org/10.1111/j.1530-2415.2005.00063.x

Coles, N. A., Hamlin, J. K., Sullivan, L. L., Parker, T. H., & Altschul, D. (2022). Build up big-team science. *Nature, 601*(7894), 505–507. https://doi.org/10.1038/d41586-022-00150-2

Conway, A. R. A., Cowan, N., & Bunting, M. F. (2001). The cocktail party phenomenon revisited: The importance of working memory capacity. *Psychonomic Bulletin & Review, 8*(2), 331–335. https://doi.org/10.3758/BF03196169

Conway, L. G., Gornick, L. J., Houck, S., Towgood, K. H., & Conway, K. R. (2011). The hidden implications of radical group rhetoric: Integrative complexity and terrorism. *Dynamics of Asymmetric Conflict, 4*(2), 155–165. https://doi.org/10.1080/17467586.2011.627938

Conway, L. G., Thoemmes, F., Allison, A. M., Towgood, K. H., Wagner, M. J., Davey, K., Salcido, A., Stovall, A. N., Dodds, D. P., Bongard, K., & Conway, K. R. (2008). Two ways to be complex and why they matter: Implications for attitude strength and lying. *Journal of Personality and Social Psychology, 95*(5), 1029–1044. https://doi.org/10.1037/a0013336

Corner, E., Taylor, H., Van Der Vegt, I., Salman, N., Rottweiler, B., Hetzel, F., Clemmow, C., Schulten, N., & Gill, P. (2021). Reviewing the links between violent extremism and personality, personality disorders, and psychopathy. *The Journal of Forensic Psychiatry & Psychology*, 32(3), 378–407. https://doi.org/10.1080/14789949.2021.1884736

Correll, J., Park, B., Judd, C. M., & Wittenbrink, B. (2002). The police officer's dilemma: Using ethnicity to disambiguate potentially threatening individuals. *Journal of Personality and Social Psychology*, 83(6), 1314–1329. https://doi.org/10.1037/0022-3514.33.6.1314

Costello, T. H., & Bowes, S. M. (2023). Absolute certainty and political ideology: A systematic test of curvilinearity. *Social Psychological and Personality Science*, 14(1), 93–102. https://doi.org/10.1177/19485506211070410

Cottee, S., & Hayward, K. (2011). Terrorist (e)motives: The existential attractions of terrorism. *Studies in Conflict & Terrorism*, 34(12), 963–986. https://doi.org/10.1080/1057610X.2011.621116

Coutinho, S., Wiemer-Hastings, K., Skowronski, J. J., & Britt, M. A. (2005). Metacognition, need for cognition and use of explanations during ongoing learning and problem solving. *Learning and Individual Differences*, 15(4), 321–337. https://doi.org/10.1016/j.lindif.2005.06.001

Craig, M. A., & Richeson, J. A. (2014). On the precipice of a "Majority-Minority" America: Perceived status threat from the racial demographic shift affects White Americans' political ideology. *Psychological Science*, 25(6), 1189–1197. https://doi.org/10.1177/0956797614527113

Crawford, J. T. (2017). Are conservatives more sensitive to threat than liberals? It depends on how we define threat and conservatism. *Social Cognition*, 35(4), 354–373. https://doi.org/10.1521/soco.2017.35.4.354

Crawford, J. T., Brandt, M. J., Inbar, Y., Chambers, J. R., & Motyl, M. (2017). Social and economic ideologies differentially predict prejudice across the political spectrum, but social issues are most divisive. *Journal of Personality and Social Psychology*, 112(3), 383–412. https://doi.org/10.1037/pspa0000074

Critcher, C. R., & Gilovich, T. (2008). Incidental environmental anchors. *Journal of Behavioral Decision Making*, 21(3), 241–251. https://doi.org/10.1002/bdm.586

Curry, O. S. (2016). Morality as cooperation: A problem-centred approach. In T. K. Shackelford, & R. D. Hansen (Eds.), *The evolution of morality* (pp. 27–51). Springer International Publishing. https://doi.org/10.1007/978-3-319-19671-8_2

Curşeu, P. L. (2011). Need for cognition and active information search in small student groups. *Learning and Individual Differences*, 21(4), 415–418. https://doi.org/10.1016/j.lindif.2011.02.005

Cushman, F. (2020). Rationalization is rational. *Behavioral and Brain Sciences*, 43, e28. https://doi.org/10.1017/S0140525X19001730

Da Silva, C., Trottier, D., Amadio, N., Domingo, B., Sarg, R., & Benbouriche, M. (2023). Significance quest: A meta-analysis on the association between the variables of the 3N model and violent extremism. *Trauma, Violence, & Abuse*, 25(2), 1184–1200. https://doi.org/10.1177/15248380231176056

Dalgaard-Nielsen, A. (2013). Promoting exit from violent extremism: Themes and approaches. *Studies in Conflict & Terrorism*, 36(2), 99–115. https://doi.org/10.1080/1057610X.2013.747073

Damasio, A. R. (1994). *Descartes' error: Emotion, reason and the human brain.* Penguin Books.

Damasio, A. R. (1996). The somatic marker hypothesis and the possible functions of the prefrontal cortex. *Philosophical Transactions of the Royal Society of London. Series B: Biological Sciences, 351*(1346), 1413–1420. https://doi.org/10.1098/rstb.1996.0125

David, L., Vassena, E., & Bijleveld, E. (2022). *The aversiveness of mental effort: A meta-analysis* [Preprint]. *PsyArXiv.* https://doi.org/10.31234/osf.io/m8zf6

Davies, C. L., Sibley, C. G., & Liu, J. H. (2014). Confirmatory factor analysis of the moral foundations questionnaire: Independent scale validation in a New Zealand sample. *Social Psychology, 45*(6), 431–436. https://doi.org/10.1027/1864-9335/a000201

Davies, L. (2009). Educating against extremism: Towards a critical politicisation of young people. *International Review of Education, 55*(2–3), 183–203. https://doi.org/10.1007/s11159-008-9126-8

Davis, W. (2009). *The wayfinders: Why ancient wisdom matters in the modern world.* House of Anansi Press.

Dawkins, R. (1976). *The selfish gene.* Oxford University Press.

De Neys, W. (2012). Bias and conflict: A case for logical intuitions. *Perspectives on Psychological Science, 7*(1), 28–38. https://doi.org/10.1177/1745691611429354

De Neys, W. (2014). Conflict detection, dual processes, and logical intuitions: Some clarifications. *Thinking & Reasoning, 20*(2), 169–187. https://doi.org/10.1080/13546783.2013.854725

De Neys, W. (2017a). Bias, conflict, and fast logic: Towards a hybrid dual process future? In W. De Neys (Ed.), *Dual process theory 2.0* (1st ed., pp. 47–65). Routledge. https://doi.org/10.4324/9781315204550-4

De Neys, W. (Ed.). (2017b). *Dual process theory 2.0* (1st ed.). Routledge.

De Neys, W. (2017c). Dual process theory 2.0: An introduction. In W. De Neys (Ed.), *Dual process theory 2.0* (1st ed., pp. 1–4). Routledge. https://doi.org/10.4324/9781315204550-1

De Neys, W. (2021). On dual- and single-process models of thinking. *Perspectives on Psychological Science, 16*(6), 1412–1427. https://doi.org/10.1177/1745691620964172

De Neys, W. (2023a). Advancing theorizing about fast-and-slow thinking. *Behavioral and Brain Sciences, 46*, e111. https://doi.org/10.1017/S0140525X2200142X

De Neys, W. (2023b). Further advancing fast-and-slow theorizing. *Behavioral and Brain Sciences, 46*, e146. https://doi.org/10.1017/S0140525X23000559

De Neys, W., & Glumicic, T. (2008). Conflict monitoring in dual process theories of thinking. *Cognition, 106*(3), 1248–1299. https://doi.org/10.1016/j.cognition.2007.06.002

De Neys, W., & Vanderputte, K. (2011). When less is not always more: Stereotype knowledge and reasoning development. *Developmental Psychology, 47*(2), 432–441. https://doi.org/10.1037/a0021313

Deary, I. J., Spinath, F. M., & Bates, T. C. (2006). Genetics of intelligence. *European Journal of Human Genetics, 14*(6), 690–700. https://doi.org/10.1038/sj.ejhg.5201588

DeCaro, M. S., Thomas, R. D., Albert, N. B., & Beilock, S. L. (2011). Choking under pressure: Multiple routes to skill failure. *Journal of Experimental Psychology: General, 140*(3), 390–406. https://doi.org/10.1037/a0023466

Decety, J., Pape, R., & Workman, C. I. (2018). A multilevel social neuroscience perspective on radicalization and terrorism. *Social Neuroscience*, *13*(5), 511–529. https://doi.org/10.1080/17470919.2017.1400462

Dechêne, A., Stahl, C., Hansen, J., & Wänke, M. (2010). The truth about the truth: A meta-analytic review of the truth effect. *Personality and Social Psychology Review*, *14*(2), 238–257. https://doi.org/10.1177/1088868309352251

Deppe, K. D., Gonzalez, F. J., Neiman, J. L., Jacobs, C., Pahlke, J., Smith, K. B., & Hibbing, J R. (2015). Reflective liberals and intuitive conservatives: A look at the cognitive reflection test and ideology. *Judgment and Decision Making*, *10*(4), 314–331. https://doi.org/10.1017/S1930297500005131

Descartes, R. (2013). *Meditations on first philosophy: With selections from the objections and replies; a Latin-English edition* (J. Cottingham, Ed.). Cambridge University Press. (Original work published 1641).

Desmarais, S. L., Simens-Rudolph, J., Brugh, C. S., Schilling, E., & Hoggan, C. (2017). The state of scientific knowledge regarding factors associated with terrorism. *Journal of Threat Assessment and Management*, *4*(4), 180–209. https://doi.org/10.1037/tam0000090

Dewey, J. (1933). *How we think: A restatement of the relation of reflective thinking to the educative process*. D.C. Heath.

Di Santo, D., Gelfand, M. J., Baldner, C., & Pierro, A. (2022). The moral foundations of desired cultural tightness moral foundations of desired cultural tightness. *Frontiers in Psychology*, *13*, 739579. https://doi.org/10.3389/fpsyg.2022.739579

Diamond, S. (1980). Wundt before Leipzig. In R. W. Rieber (Ed.), *Wilhelm Wundt and the making of a scientific psychology* (pp. 3–70). Springer US. https://doi.org/10.1007/978-1-4684-8340-6_1

Diesendruck. G., & Shatz, M. (2001). Two-year-olds' recognition of hierarchies. *Cognitive Development*, *16*(1), 577–594. https://doi.org/10.1016/S0885-2014(01)00047-8

Dijksterhuis, A. (2004). Think different: The merits of unconscious thought in preference development and decision making. *Journal of Personality and Social Psychology*, *87*(5), 586–598. https://doi.org/10.1037/0022-3514.87.5.586

Dijksterhuis, A., & Nordgren, L. F. (2006). A theory of unconscious thought. *Perspectives on Psychological Science*, *1*(2), 95–109. https://doi.org/10.1111/j.1745-6916.2006.00007.x

Ditto, P. H., Clark, C. J., Liu, B. S., Wojcik, S. P., Chen, E. E., Grady, R. H., Celniker, J. B., & Zinger, J. F. (2019). Partisan bias and its discontents. *Perspectives on Psychological Science*, *14*(2), Article 2. https://doi.org/10.1177/1745691618817753

Ditto, P. H., Liu, B. S., Clark, C. J., Wojcik, S. P., Chen, E. E., Grady, R. H., Celniker, J. B., & Zinger, J. F. (2019). At least bias is bipartisan: A meta-analytic comparison of partisan bias in liberals and conservatives. *Perspectives on Psychological Science*, *14*(2), 273–291. https://doi.org/10.1177/1745691617746796

Dodd, M. D., Balzer, A., Jacobs, C. M., Gruszczynski, M. W., Smith, K. B., & Hibbing, J. R. (2012). The political left rolls with the good and the political right confronts the bad: Connecting physiology and cognition to preferences. *Philosophical Transactions of the Royal Society B: Biological Sciences*, *367*(1589), 640–649. https://doi.org/10.1098/rstb.2011.0268

Douglas, K. M., & Sutton, R. M. (2023). What are conspiracy theories? A definitional approach to their correlates, consequences, and communication. *Annual Review of Psychology*, 74(1), 271–298. https://doi.org/10.1146/annurev-psych-032420-031329

Douglas, K. M., Sutton, R. M., & Cichocka, A. (2017). The psychology of conspiracy theories. *Current Directions in Psychological Science*, 26(6), 538–542. https://doi.org/10.1177/0963721417718261

Douglas, K. M., Sutton, R. M., & Cichocka, A. (2019). Belief in conspiracy theories. In J. P. Forgas, & R. F. Baumeister (Eds.), *The social psychology of gullibility* (1st ed., pp. 61–76). Routledge. https://doi.org/10.4324/9780429203787-4

Downey, G., & Feldman, S. I. (1996). Implications of rejection sensitivity for intimate relationships. *Journal of Personality and Social Psychology*, 70(6), 1327–1343. https://doi.org/10.1037/0022-3514.70.6.1327

Dreu, C. K. W. D., Dussel, D. B., & Velden, F. S. T. (2015). In intergroup conflict, self-sacrifice is stronger among pro-social individuals, and parochial altruism emerges especially among cognitively taxed individuals. *Frontiers in Psychology*, 6. https://doi.org/10.3389/fpsyg.2015.00572

Duarte, J. L., Crawford, J. T., Stern, C., Haidt, J., Jussim, L., & Tetlock, P. E. (2015). Political diversity will improve social psychological science. *Behavioral and Brain Sciences*, 38, e130. https://doi.org/10.1017/S0140525X14000430

Dubray, C. (1912). Teleology. In *The Catholic encyclopedia*. Robert Appleton Company. www.newadvent.org/cathen/14474a.htm

Duckitt, J., & Sibley, C. G. (2010). Personality, ideology, prejudice, and politics: A dual-process motivational model: dual-process motivational model. *Journal of Personality*, 78(6), 1861–1894. https://doi.org/10.1111/j.1467-6494.2010.00672.x

Duncan, S., & Barrett, L. F. (2007). Affect is a form of cognition: A neurobiological analysis. *Cognition & Emotion*, 21(6), 1184–1211. https://doi.org/10.1080/02699930701437931

Durkheim, É. (2008). *The elementary forms of religious life* (Trans. K. E. Fields). Oxford University Press. (Original work published 1912).

Duru, H., Onat, I., Akyuz, K., & Akbas, H. (2021). Microcycles of terrorist violence in Turkey: A spatio-temporal analysis of the PKK attacks. *Asian Journal of Criminology*, 16(3), 235–256. https://doi.org/10.1007/s11417-020-09326-z

Eadeh, F. R., & Chang, K. K. (2020). Can threat increase support for liberalism? New insights into the relationship between threat and political attitudes. *Social Psychological and Personality Science*, 11(1), 88–96. https://doi.org/10.1177/1948550618815919

Echebarria-Echabe, A., & Fernández-Guede, E. (2006). Effects of terrorism on attitudes and ideological orientation. *European Journal of Social Psychology*, 36(2), 259–265. https://doi.org/10.1002/ejsp.294

Eidelman, S., Crandall, C. S., Goodman, J. A., & Blanchar, J. C. (2012). Low-effort thought promotes political conservatism. *Personality and Social Psychology Bulletin*, 38(6), 808–820. https://doi.org/10.1177/0146167212439213

Ellemers, N. (2013). Connecting the dots: Mobilizing theory to reveal the big picture in social psychology (and why we should do this). *European Journal of Social Psychology*, 43(1), 1–8. https://doi.org/10.1002/ejsp.1932

Englich, B., Mussweiler, T., & Strack, F. (2006). Playing dice with criminal sentences: the influence of irrelevant anchors on experts' judicial decision making. *Personality and Social Psychology Bulletin*, 32(2), 188–200. https://doi.org/10.1177/0146167205282152

Epley, N., & Gilovich, T. (2005). When effortful thinking influences judgmental anchoring: Differential effects of forewarning and incentives on self-generated and externally provided anchors. *Journal of Behavioral Decision Making, 18*(3), 199–212. https://doi.org/10.1002/bdm.495

Epley, N., & Gilovich, T. (2006). The anchoring-and-adjustment heuristic: why the adjustments are insufficient. *Psychological Science, 17*(4), 311–318. https://doi.org/10.1111/j.1467-9280.2006.01704.x

Epley, N., Keysar, B., Van Boven, L., & Gilovich, T. (2004). Perspective taking as egocentric anchoring and adjustment. *Journal of Personality and Social Psychology, 87*(3), 327–339. https://doi.org/10.1037/0022-3514.87.3.327

Epley, N., Waytz, A., & Cacioppo, J. T. (2007). On seeing human: A three-factor theory of anthropomorphism. *Psychological Review, 114*(4), 864–886. https://doi.org/10.1037/0033-295X.114.4.864

Epstein, S. (1994). Integration of the cognitive and the psychodynamic unconscious. *American Psychologist, 49*(8), 709–724. https://doi.org/10.1037/0003-066X.49.8.709

Epstein, S., Pacini, R., Denes-Raj, V., & Heier, H. (1996). Individual differences in intuitive–experiential and analytical–rational thinking styles. *Journal of Personality and Social Psychology, 71*(2), 390–405. https://doi.org/10.1037/0022-3514.71.2.390

Ericsson, K. A., Krampe, R. T., & Tesch-Römer, C. (1993). The role of deliberate practice in the acquisition of expert performance. *Psychological Review, 100*(3), 363–406. https://doi.org/10.1037/0033-295X.100.3.363

Erişen, C. (2013). Emotions as a determinant in Turkish political behavior. *Turkish Studies, 14*(1), 115–135. https://doi.org/10.1080/14683849.2013.766987

Eronen, M. I., & Bringmann, L. F. (2021). The theory crisis in psychology: How to move forward. *Perspectives on Psychological Science, 16*(4), 779–788. https://doi.org/10.1177/1745691620970586

Essien, I., Stelter, M., Kalbe, F., Koehler, A., Mangels, J., & Meliß, S. (2017). The shooter bias: Replicating the classic effect and introducing a novel paradigm. *Journal of Experimental Social Psychology, 70*, 41–47. https://doi.org/10.1016/j.jesp.2016.12.009

Eva, K. W., Hatala, R. M., LeBlanc, V. R., & Brooks, L. R. (2007). Teaching from the clinical reasoning literature: Combined reasoning strategies help novice diagnosticians overcome misleading information: clinical expertise. *Medical Education, 41*(12), 1152–1153. https://doi.org/10.1111/j.1365-2923.2007.02923.x

Evans, J. St. B. T. (1984). Heuristic and analytic processes in reasoning. *British Journal of Psychology, 75*(4), 451–468. https://doi.org/10.1111/j.2044-8295.1984.tb01915.x

Evans, J. St. B. T. (2007). *Hypothetical thinking: Dual processes in reasoning and judgement.* Psychology Press.

Evans, J. St. B. T. (2008). Dual-processing accounts of reasoning, judgment, and social cognition. *Annual Review of Psychology, 59*(1), 255–278. https://doi.org/10.1146/annurev.psych.59.103006.093629

Evans, J. St. B. T. (2012). Dual-process theories of deductive reasoning: Facts and fallacies. In K. J. Holyoak, & R. G. Morrison (Eds.), *The Oxford handbook of thinking and reasoning* (1st ed., pp. 115–133). Oxford University Press. https://doi.org/10.1093/oxfordhb/9780199734689.013.0008

Evans, J. St. B. T. (2019). Reflections on reflection: The nature and function of type 2 processes in dual-process theories of reasoning. *Thinking & Reasoning, 25*(4), 383–415. https://doi.org/10.1080/13546783.2019.1623071

Evans, J. St. B. T. (2020). Bounded rationality, reasoning and dual processing. In R. Viale (Ed.), *Routledge handbook of bounded rationality* (1st ed., pp. 185–195). Routledge. https://doi.org/10.4324/9781315658353-11

Evans, J. St. B. T., Handley, S. J., Neilens, H., & Over, D. (2010). The influence of cognitive ability and instructional set on causal conditional inference. *Quarterly Journal of Experimental Psychology, 63*(5), 892–909. https://doi.org/10.1080/17470210903111821

Evans, J. St. B. T., & Stanovich, K. E. (2013a). Dual-process theories of higher cognition: Advancing the debate. *Perspectives on Psychological Science, 8*(3), 223–241. https://doi.org/10.1177/1745691612460685

Evans, J. St. B. T., & Stanovich, K. E. (2013b). Theory and metatheory in the study of dual processing: Reply to comments. *Perspectives on Psychological Science, 8*(3), 263–271. https://doi.org/10.1177/1745691613483774

Evans, J. St. B. T., & Wason, P. C. (1976). Rationalization in a reasoning task. *British Journal of Psychology, 67*(4), 479–486. https://doi.org/10.1111/j.2044-8295.1976.tb01536.x

Everett, J. A. C. (2013). The 12 item social and economic conservatism scale (SECS). *PLoS ONE, 8*(12), e82131. https://doi.org/10.1371/journal.pone.0082131

Everett, J. A. C., Ingbretsen, Z., Cushman, F., & Cikara, M. (2017). Deliberation erodes cooperative behavior—even towards competitive out-groups, even when using a control condition, and even when eliminating selection bias. *Journal of Experimental Social Psychology, 73*, 76–81. https://doi.org/10.1016/j.jesp.2017.06.014

Everton, S. F. (2018). *Networks and religion: Ties that bind, loose, build up, and tear down.* Cambridge University Press.

Eysenck, H. J. (1954). *The psychology of politics* (0 ed.). Routledge. https://doi.org/10.4324/9781351303088

Ezekiel, R. S. (2002). An ethnographer looks at Neo-Nazi and Klan Groups: The racist mind revisited. *American Behavioral Scientist, 46*(1), 51–71. https://doi.org/10.1177/0002764202046001005

Fair, C. C., Goldstein, J. S., & Hamza, A. (2017). Can knowledge of Islam explain lack of support for terrorism? Evidence from Pakistan. *Studies in Conflict & Terrorism, 40*(4), 339–355. https://doi.org/10.1080/1057610X.2016.1197692

Fair, C. C., Malhotra, N., & Shapiro, J. N. (2014). Democratic values and support for militant politics: Evidence from a national survey of Pakistan. *Journal of Conflict Resolution, 58*(5), 743–770. https://doi.org/10.1177/0022002713478564

Fanelli, D. (2010). "Positive" results increase down the hierarchy of the sciences. *PLoS ONE, 5*(4), e10068. https://doi.org/10.1371/journal.pone.0010068

Farias, M., Van Mulukom, V., Kahane, G., Kreplin, U., Joyce, A., Soares, P., Oviedo, L., Hernu, M., Rokita, K., Savulescu, J., & Möttönen, R. (2017). Supernatural belief is not modulated by intuitive thinking style or cognitive inhibition. *Scientific Reports, 7*(1), 15100. https://doi.org/10.1038/s41598-017-14090-9

Faulkner, J., Schaller, M., Park, J. H., & Duncan, L. A. (2004). Evolved disease-avoidance mechanisms and contemporary xenophobic attitudes. *Group Processes*

& *Intergroup Relations*, 7(4), 333–353. https://doi.org/10.1177/13684302C
4046142

Federico, C. M., Weber, C. R., Ergun, D., & Hunt, C. (2013). Mapping the connections
between politics and morality: the multiple sociopolitical orientations involved in
moral intuition. *Political Psychology*, 34(4), 589–610. https://doi.org/10.1111/
pops.12006

Fehr, E., Fischbacher, U., & Gächter, S. (2002). Strong reciprocity, human cooperation,
and the enforcement of social norms. *Human Nature*, 13(1), 1–25. https://doi.org/
10.1007/s12110-002-1012-7

Fehse, K., Silveira, S., Elvers, K., & Blautzik, J. (2015). Compassion, guilt and
innocence: An fMRI study of responses to victims who are responsible for
their fate. *Social Neuroscience*, 10(3), 243–252. https://doi.org/10.1080/17470
919.2014.980587

Fekete, L. (2012). The Muslim conspiracy theory and the Oslo massacre. *Race &
Class*, 53(3), 30–47. https://doi.org/10.1177/0306396811425984

Feldman, S. (2003). Values, ideology, and the structure of political attitudes. In D. O.
Sears, L. Huddy, & R. Jervis (Eds.), *Oxford handbook of political psychology* (pp.
477–508). Oxford University Press.

Feldman, S., & Johnston, C. (2014). Understanding the determinants of political
ideology: Implications of structural complexity. *Political Psychology*, 35(3), 337–
358. https://doi.org/10.1111/pops.12055

Ferreira, M. B., Mata, A., Donkin, C., Sherman, S. J., & Ihmels, M. (2016). Analytic
and heuristic processes in the detection and resolution of conflict. *Memory &
Cognition*, 44(7), 1050–1063. https://doi.org/10.3758/s13421-016-0618-7

Festinger, L. (1962). Cognitive dissonance. *Scientific American*, 207(4), 93–106.
https://doi.org/10.1038/scientificamerican1062-93

Festinger, L., & Carlsmith, J. M. (1959). Cognitive consequences of forced compliance.
The Journal of Abnormal and Social Psychology, 58(2), 203–210. https://doi org/
10.1037/h0041593

Fincher, C. L., & Thornhill, R. (2012). Parasite-stress promotes in-group
assortative sociality: The cases of strong family ties and heightened religiosity.
Behavioral and Brain Sciences, 35(2), 61–79. https://doi.org/10.1017/S01405
25X11000021

Findley, M. G., & Young, J. K. (2012). More combatant groups, more terror?: empirical
tests of an outbidding logic. *Terrorism and Political Violence*, 24(5), 706–721.
https://doi.org/10.1080/09546553.2011.639415

Finseraas, H., & Listhaug, O. (2013). It can happen here: The impact of the Mumbai
terror attacks on public opinion in Western Europe. *Public Choice*, 156(1–2),
213–228. https://doi.org/10.1007/s11127-011-9895-7

Fischbacher, U., Gächter, S., & Fehr, E. (2001). Are people conditionally cooperative?
Evidence from a public goods experiment. *Economics Letters*, 71(3), 397–404.
https://doi.org/10.1016/S0165-1765(01)00394-9

Fischer, C., Dailler, F., & Morlet, D. (2008). Novelty P3 elicited by the subject's
own name in comatose patients. *Clinical Neurophysiology*, 119(10), 2224–2230.
https://doi.org/10.1016/j.clinph.2008.03.035

Fiske, S. T., & Neuberg, S. L. (1990). A continuum of impression formation,
from category-based to individuating processes: influences of information and
motivation on attention and interpretation. In M. P. Zanna (Ed.), *Advances in*

experimental social psychology (Vol. 23, pp. 1–74). Academic Press. https://doi.org/10.1016/S0065-2601(08)60317-2

Fitch, W. T. (2005). The evolution of language: A comparative review. *Biology & Philosophy*, 20(2–3), 193–203. https://doi.org/10.1007/s10539-005-5597-1

Fitts, P. M. (1964). Perceptual-motor skill learning. In A. W. Melton (Ed.), *Categories of human learning* (pp. 243–285). Elsevier. https://doi.org/10.1016/B978-1-4832-3145-7.50016-9

Flake, J. K., Davidson, I. J., Wong, O., & Pek, J. (2022). Construct validity and the validity of replication studies: A systematic review. *American Psychologist*, 77(4), 576–588. https://doi.org/10.1037/amp0001006

Flanigan, J. (2013). Charisma and moral reasoning. *Religions*, 4(2), 216–229. https://doi.org/10.3390/rel4020216

Fleeson, W. (2004). Moving personality beyond the person-situation debate: The challenge and the opportunity of within-person variability. *Current Directions in Psychological Science*, 13(2), 83–87. https://doi.org/10.1111/j.0963-7214.2004.00280.x

Fleeson, W., Miller, C., Furr, R. M., Knobel, A., & Jayawickreme, E. (2022). Moral, extreme, and positive: What are the key issues for the study of the morally exceptional? In A. W. Kruglanski, C. E. Kopetz, & E. Szumowska (Eds.), *The psychology of extremism: A motivational perspective* (pp. 230–258). Routledge.

Fleischhauer, M., Enge, S., Brocke, B., Ullrich, J., Strobel, A., & Strobel, A. (2010). Same or different? Clarifying the relationship of need for cognition to personality and intelligence. *Personality and Social Psychology Bulletin*, 36(1), 82–96. https://doi.org/10.1177/0146167209351886

Fletcher, J. M., Marks, A. D. G., Hine, D. W., & Coventry, W. L. (2014). Heritability of preferred thinking styles and a genetic link to working memory capacity. *Twin Research and Human Genetics*, 17(6), 526–534. https://doi.org/10.1017/thg.2014.62

Foley, R. (1995). The adaptive legacy of human evolution: A search for the environment of evolutionary adaptedness. *Evolutionary Anthropology: Issues, News, and Reviews*, 4(6), 194–203. https://doi.org/10.1002/evan.1360040603

Forscher, P. S., Wagenmakers, E.-J., Coles, N. A., Silan, M. A., Dutra, N., Basnight-Brown, D., & IJzerman, H. (2023). The benefits, barriers, and risks of big-team science. *Perspectives on Psychological Science*, 18(3), 607–623. https://doi.org/10.1177/17456916221082970

Forstmann, M., & Burgmer, P. (2017). Antecedents, manifestations, and consequences of belief in mind–body dualism. In C. M. Zedelius, B. C. N. Müller, & J. W. Schooler (Eds.), *The science of lay theories* (pp. 181–205). Springer International Publishing. https://doi.org/10.1007/978-3-319-57306-9_8

Fox, E., Lester, V., Russo, R., Bowles, R. J., Pichler, A., & Dutton, K. (2000). Facial expressions of emotion: Are angry faces detected more efficiently? *Cognition & Emotion*, 14(1), 61–92. https://doi.org/10.1080/026999300378996

Franco, A., Malhotra, N., & Simonovits, G. (2014). Publication bias in the social sciences: Unlocking the file drawer. *Science*, 345(6203), 1502–1505. https://doi.org/10.1126/science.1255484

Frankfurt, H. G. (2005). *On bullshit*. Princeton University Press.

Frankish, K. (2023). Toward dual-process theory 3.0. *Behavioral and Brain Sciences*, 46, e122. https://doi.org/10.1017/S0140525X22003144

Frankish, K., & Evans, J. St. B. T. (2009). The duality of mind: An historical perspective. In J. Evans, & K. Frankish (Eds.), *In two minds: Dual processes and beyond* (1st ed., pp. 1–30). Oxford University Press. https://doi.org/10.1093/acprof:oso/9780199230167.003.0001

Frederick, S. (2005). Cognitive reflection and decision making. *Journal of Economic Perspectives*, 19(4), 25–42. https://doi.org/10.1257/089533005775196732

Freud, S. (1946). Why war. *Free World*, 11(4), 18–24.

Freud, S. (1953). The interpretation of dreams. In J. Strachey (Ed. & Trans.), *The standard edition of the complete psychological works of Sigmund Freud* (Vols. 4-5). London, England: Hogarth. (Original work published 1900).

Freud, S. (2017). *Three essays on the theory of sexuality: The 1905 edition (U. Kistner, Trans.)*. Verso. (Original work published 1905).

Frey, D., Johnson, E. D., & De Neys, W. (2018). Individual differences in conflict detection during reasoning. *Quarterly Journal of Experimental Psychology*, 71(5), 1188–1208. https://doi.org/10.1080/17470218.2017.1313283

Fu, F., Nowak, M. A., Christakis, N. A., & Fowler, J. H. (2012). The evolution of homophily. *Scientific Reports*, 2(1), 845. https://doi.org/10.1038/srep00845

Fukuyama, F. (1992). *The end of history and the last man* (1st Free Press trade pbk. ed.). Free Press.

Fukuyama, F. (2011). *The origins of political order: From prehuman times to the French Revolution*. Farrar, Straus and Giroux.

Furnham, A., & Boo, H. C. (2011). A literature review of the anchoring effect. *The Journal of Socio-Economics*, 40(1), 35–42. https://doi.org/10.1016/j.socec.2010.10.008

Gächter, S., Kölle, F., & Quercia, S. (2022). Preferences and perceptions in provision and maintenance public goods. *Games and Economic Behavior*, 135, 338–355. https://doi.org/10.1016/j.geb.2022.06.009

Galanter, M., & Forest, J. J. F. (2006). Cults, charismatic groups, and social systems: Understanding the transformation of terrorist recruits. In J. J. F. Forest (Ed.), *The making of a terrorist: Recruitment, training, and root causes* (pp. 51–70). Praeger.

Galinsky, A. D., Magee, J. C., Rus, D., Rothman, N. B., & Todd, A. R. (2014). Acceleration with steering: the synergistic benefits of combining power and perspective-taking. *Social Psychological and Personality Science*, 5(6), 627–635. https://doi.org/10.1177/1948550613519685

Galinsky, A. D., & Mussweiler, T. (2001). First offers as anchors: The role of perspective-taking and negotiator focus. *Journal of Personality and Social Psychology*, 81(4), 657–669. https://doi.org/10.1037/0022-3514.81.4.657

Galla, B. M., & Duckworth, A. L. (2015). More than resisting temptation: Beneficial habits mediate the relationship between self-control and positive life outcomes. *Journal of Personality and Social Psychology*, 109(3), 508–525. https://doi.org/10.1037/pspp0000026

Gallagher, S. (2013). The socially extended mind. *Cognitive Systems Research*, 25–26, 4–12. https://doi.org/10.1016/j.cogsys.2013.03.008

Garner, R. (2007). Abolishing morality. *Ethical Theory and Moral Practice*, 10(5), 499–513. https://doi.org/10.1007/s10677-007-9085-3

Garrison, K. E., & Schmeichel, B. J. (2022). Getting over it: Working memory capacity and affective responses to stressful events in daily life. *Emotion*, 22(3), 418–429. https://doi.org/10.1037/emo0000755

Gaub, F. (2016). The cult of ISIS. *Survival*, 58(1), 113–130. https://doi.org/10.1080/00396338.2016.1142142

Gawronski, B., & Bodenhausen, G. V. (2006). Associative and propositional processes in evaluation: An integrative review of implicit and explicit attitude change. *Psychological Bulletin*, 132(5), 692–731. https://doi.org/10.1037/0033-2909.132.5.692

Gelfand, M. J. (2018). *Rule makers, rule breakers: How culture wires our minds.* Scribner.

Gelfand, M. J., Harrington, J. R., & Jackson, J. C. (2017). The strength of social norms across human groups. *Perspectives on Psychological Science*, 12(5), 800–809. https://doi.org/10.1177/1745691617708631

Gentile, E. (2006). *Politics as religion.* Princeton University Press.

Gerber, A. S., Huber, G. A., Doherty, D., Dowling, C. M., & Ha, S. E. (2010). Personality and political attitudes: relationships across issue domains and political contexts. *American Political Science Review*, 104(1), 111–133. https://doi.org/10.1017/S0003055410000031

Gervais, W. M., Najle, M. B., & Caluori, N. (2021). The origins of religious disbelief: A dual inheritance approach. *Social Psychological and Personality Science*, 12(7), 1369–1379. https://doi.org/10.1177/1948550621994001

Gervais, W. M., & Norenzayan, A. (2012). Analytic thinking promotes religious disbelief. *Science*, 336(6080), 493–496. https://doi.org/10.1126/science.1215647

Gervais, W. M., & Norenzayan, A. (2018). Analytic atheism revisited. *Nature Human Behaviour*, 2(9), 609–609. https://doi.org/10.1038/s41562-018-0426-0

Gervais, W. M., van Elk, M., Xygalatas, D., McKay, R. T., Aveyard, M., Buchtel, E. E., Dar-Nimrod, I., Klocová, E. K., Ramsay, J. E., Riekki, T., Svedholm-Häkkinen, A. M., & Bulbulia, J. (2018). Analytic atheism: A cross-culturally weak and fickle phenomenon? *Judgment and Decision Making*, 13(3), 268–274.

Ghasemi, O., Handley, S., & Howarth, S. (2023). Illusory intuitive inferences: Matching heuristics explain logical intuitions. *Cognition*, 235, 105417. https://doi.org/10.1016/j.cognition.2023.105417

Ghasemi, O., Handley, S., Howarth, S., Newman, I. R., & Thompson, V. A. (2022). Logical intuition is not really about logic. *Journal of Experimental Psychology: General*, 151(9), 2009–2028. https://doi.org/10.1037/xge0001179

Gigerenzer, G. (2004). Mindless statistics. *The Journal of Socio-Economics*, 33(5), 587–606. https://doi.org/10.1016/j.socec.2004.09.033

Gigerenzer, G. (2008a). *Gut feelings: The intelligence of the unconscious.* Penguin Books.

Gigerenzer, G. (2008b). Why heuristics work. *Perspectives on Psychological Science*, 3(1), 20–29. https://doi.org/10.1111/j.1745-6916.2008.00058.x

Gigerenzer, G. (2010). Personal reflections on theory and psychology. *Theory & Psychology*, 20(6), 733–743. https://doi.org/10.1177/0959354310378184

Gigerenzer, G., & Gaissmaier, W. (2011). Heuristic decision making. *Annual Review of Psychology*, 62(1), 451–482. https://doi.org/10.1146/annurev-psych-120709-145346

Gigerenzer, G., Hertwig, R., & Pachur, T. (2011). *Heuristics: The foundations of adaptive behavior.* Oxford University Press.

Gigerenzer, G., & Todd, P. M. (1999). *Simple heuristics that make us smart.* Oxford University Press.

Gilbert, D. T. (1991). How mental systems believe. *American Psychologist*, 46(2), 107–119. https://doi.org/10.1037/0003-066X.46.2.107

Gill, P., Clemmow, C., Hetzel, F., Rottweiler, B., Salman, N., Van Der Vegt, I., Marchment, Z., Schumann, S., Zolghadriha, S., Schulten, N., Taylor, H., & Corner, E. (2021). Systematic review of mental health problems and violent extremism. *The Journal of Forensic Psychiatry & Psychology*, 32(1), 51–78. https://doi.org/10.1080/14789949.2020.1820067

Gilovich, T., & Savitsky, K. (1999). The spotlight effect and the illusion of transparency: egocentric assessments of how we are seen by others. *Current Directions in Psychological Science*, 8(6), 165–168. https://doi.org/10.1111/1467-8721.00039

Ginges, J., Hansen, I., & Norenzayan, A. (2009). Religion and support for suicide attacks. *Psychological Science*, 20(2), 224–230. https://doi.org/10.1111/j.1467-9280.2009.02270.x

Gintis, H. (2003). The Hitchhiker's guide to altruism: Gene-culture coevolution, and the internalization of norms. *Journal of Theoretical Biology*, 220(4), 407–418 https://doi.org/10.1006/jtbi.2003.3104

Goldenberg, J. L., & Arndt, J. (2008). The implications of death for health: A terror management health model for behavioral health promotion. *Psychological Review*, 115(4), 1032–1053. https://doi.org/10.1037/a0013326

Goldstein, D. G., & Gigerenzer, G. (2002). Models of ecological rationality: The recognition heuristic. *Psychological Review*, 109(1), 75–90. https://doi.org/10.1037/0033-295X.109.1.75

Goldstein, D. G., & Gigerenzer, G. (2009). Fast and frugal forecasting. *International Journal of Forecasting*, 25(4), 760–772. https://doi.org/10.1016/j.ijforec ast.2009.05.010

Golec De Zavala, A., Cichocka, A., & Iskra-Golec, I. (2013). Collective narcissism moderates the effect of in-group image threat on intergroup hostility. *Journal of Personality and Social Psychology*, 104(6), 1019–1039. https://doi.org/10.1037/a0032215

Gómez, D.M., Jiménez, A., Bobadilla, R., Reyes, C., & Dartnell, P. (2015). The effect of inhibitory control on general mathematics achievement and fraction comparison in middle school children. *ZDM Mathematics Education*, 47, 801–811. https://doi.org/10.1007/s11858-015-0685-4

Gong, T., Young, A. G., & Shtulman, A. (2021). The development of cognitive reflection in China. *Cognitive Science*, 45(4), e12966. https://doi.org/10.1111/cogs.12966

González-Vallejo, C., & Phillips, N. (2010). Predicting soccer matches: A reassessment of the benefit of unconscious thinking. *Judgment and Decision Making*, 5(3), 200–206. https://doi.org/10.1017/S193029750000108X

Goodwin, G. P., & Darley, J. M. (2012). Why are some moral beliefs perceived to be more objective than others? *Journal of Experimental Social Psychology*, 48(1), 250–256. https://doi.org/10.1016/j.jesp.2011.08.006

Götz, F. M., Gosling, S. D., & Rentfrow, P. J. (2022). Small effects: The indispensable foundation for a cumulative psychological science. *Perspectives on Psychological Science*, 17(1), 205–215. https://doi.org/10.1177/1745691620984483

Gouldner, A. W. (1960). The norm of reciprocity: A preliminary statement. *American Sociological Review*, 25(2), 161. https://doi.org/10.2307/2092623

Graham, J. (2010). Left gut, right gut: Ideology and automatic moral reactions [PhD Thesis]. University of Virginia.

Graham, J., & Haidt, J. (2010). Beyond beliefs: Religions bind individuals into moral communities. *Personality and Social Psychology Review*, *14*(1), 140–150. https://doi.org/10.1177/1088868309353415

Graham, J., Haidt, J., & Nosek, B. A. (2009). Liberals and conservatives rely on different sets of moral foundations. *Journal of Personality and Social Psychology*, *96*(5), 1029–1046. https://doi.org/10.1037/a0015141

Graham, J., Nosek, B. A., Haidt, J., Iyer, R., Koleva, S., & Ditto, P. H. (2011). Mapping the moral domain. *Journal of Personality and Social Psychology*, *101*(2), 366–385. https://doi.org/10.1037/a0021847

Graham, L. K., Yoon, T., & Kim, J. J. (2010). Stress impairs optimal behavior in a water foraging choice task in rats. *Learning & Memory*, *17*(1), 1–4. https://doi.org/10.1101/lm.1605510

Greenberg, J., Pyszczynski, T., & Solomon, S. (1986). The causes and consequences of a need for self-esteem: A terror management theory. In R. F. Baumeister (Ed.), *Public self and private self* (pp. 189–212). Springer New York. https://doi.org/10.1007/978-1-4613-9564-5_10

Greenberg, J., Pyszczynski, T., Solomon, S., Rosenblatt, A., Veeder, M., Kirkland, S., & Lyon, D. (1990). Evidence for terror management theory II: The effects of mortality salience on reactions to those who threaten or bolster the cultural worldview. *Journal of Personality and Social Psychology*, *58*(2), 308–318. https://doi.org/10.1037/0022-3514.58.2.308

Greenberg, J., Pyszczynski, T., Solomon, S., Simon, L., & Breus, M. (1994). Role of consciousness and accessibility of death-related thoughts in mortality salience effects. *Journal of Personality and Social Psychology*, *67*(4), 627–637. https://doi.org/10.1037/0022-3514.67.4.627

Greenberg, J., Schimel, J., Martens, A., Solomon, S., & Pyszcznyski, T. (2001). Sympathy for the devil: Evidence that reminding whites of their mortality promotes more favorable reactions to white racists. *Motivation and Emotion*, *25*(2), 113–133. https://doi.org/10.1023/A:1010613909207

Greenberg, J., Simon, L., Pyszczynski, T., Solomon, S., & Chatel, D. (1992). Terror management and tolerance: Does mortality salience always intensify negative reactions to others who threaten one's worldview? *Journal of Personality and Social Psychology*, *63*(2), 212–220. https://doi.org/10.1037/0022-3514.63.2.212

Greenland, A., Proulx, D., & Savage, D. A. (2020). Dying for the cause: The rationality of martyrs, suicide bombers and self-immolators. *Rationality and Society*, *32*(1), 93–115. https://doi.org/10.1177/1043463119900327

Grisham, J. R., & Williams, A. D. (2009). Cognitive control of obsessional thoughts. *Behaviour Research and Therapy*, *47*(5), 395–402. https://doi.org/10.1016/j.brat.2009.01.014

Griskevicius, V., Ackerman, J. M., Cantú, S. M., Delton, A. W., Robertson, T. E., Simpson, J. A., Thompson, M. E., & Tybur, J. M. (2013). When the economy falters, do people spend or save? Responses to resource scarcity depend on childhood environments. *Psychological Science*, *24*(2), 197–205. https://doi.org/10.1177/0956797612451471

Grossman, H. I., & Mendoza, J. (2003). Scarcity and appropriative competition. *European Journal of Political Economy*, *19*(4), 747–758. https://doi.org/10.1016/S0176-2680(03)00033-8

Grossmann, I. (2017). Wisdom in context. *Perspectives on Psychological Science*, 12(2), 233–257. https://doi.org/10.1177/1745691616672066

Gruber, J., Harvey, A. G., & Johnson, S. L. (2009). Reflective and ruminative processing of positive emotional memories in bipolar disorder and healthy controls. *Behaviour Research and Therapy*, 47(8), 697–704. https://doi.org/10.1016/j.brat.2009.05.005

Guest, O., & Martin, A. E. (2021). How computational modeling can force theory building in psychological science. *Perspectives on Psychological Science*, 16(4), 789–802. https://doi.org/10.1177/1745691620970585

Guo, L., Trueblood, J. S., & Diederich, A. (2017). Thinking fast increases framing effects in risky decision making. *Psychological Science*, 28(4), 530–543. https://doi.org/10.1177/0956797616689092

Gürçay, B., & Baron, J. (2017). Challenges for the sequential two-system model of moral judgement. *Thinking & Reasoning*, 23(1), 49–80. https://doi.org/10.1080/13546783.2016.1216011

Haidt, J. (2007). The new synthesis in moral psychology. *Science*, 316(5827), 998–1002. https://doi.org/10.1126/science.1137651

Haidt, J. (2012). *The righteous mind: Why good people are divided by politics and religion* (1st ed.). Pantheon Books.

Haidt, J., Graham, J., & Joseph, C. (2009). Above and below left–right: ideological narratives and moral foundations. *Psychological Inquiry*, 20(2–3), 110–119. https://doi.org/10.1080/10478400903028573

Haidt, J., & Kesebir, S. (2010). Morality. In S. T. Fiske, D. T. Gilbert, & G. Lindzey (Eds.), *Handbook of social psychology* (1st ed.). Wiley. https://doi.org/10.1002/9780470561119.socpsy002022

Haig, B. D. (2005). An abductive theory of scientific method. *Psychological Methods*, 10(4), 371–388. https://doi.org/10.1037/1082-989X.10.4.371

Haig, B. D. (2018). The philosophy of quantitative methods. In *Method matters in psychology: Essays in applied philosophy of science* (pp. 159–186). Springer International Publishing. https://doi.org/10.1007/978-3-030-01051-5_8

Haig, B. D. (2019). The importance of scientific method for psychological science. *Psychology, Crime & Law*, 25(6), 527–541. https://doi.org/10.1080/1068316X.2018.1557181

Haller, H., & Krauss, S. (2002). Misinterpretations of significance: A problem students share with their teachers? *Methods of Psychological Research Online*, 7, 1–20.

Halpern, D. F. (2013). *Thought and knowledge: An introduction to critical thinking* (5th ed.). Psychology Press. https://doi.org/10.4324/9781315885278

Hamilton, W. D. (1964). The genetical evolution of social behaviour. II. *Journal of Theoretical Biology*, 7(1), 17–52. https://doi.org/10.1016/0022-5193(64)90039-6

Hamlin, J. K., Wynn, K., & Bloom, P. (2007). Social evaluation by preverbal infants. *Nature*, 450(7169), 557–559. https://doi.org/10.1038/nature06288

Handley, S. J., Ghasemi, O., & Bialek, M. (2023). Illusory intuitions: Challenging the claim of non-exclusivity. *Behavioral and Brain Sciences*, 46, e125. https://doi.org/10.1017/S0140525X22003168

Hanscombe, K. B., Trzaskowski, M., Haworth, C. M. A., Davis, O. S. P., Dale, P. S., & Plomin, R. (2012). Socioeconomic status (SES) and children's intelligence (IQ): In a UK-representative sample SES moderates the environmental, not genetic, effect on IQ. *PLoS ONE*, 7(2), e30320. https://doi.org/10.1371/journal.pone.0030320

Hansen, S. J., & Lid, S. (2020). Why do we need a handbook on disengagement and deradicalisation? In S. J. Hansen & S. Lid (Eds.), *Routledge handbook of deradicalisation and disengagement* (1st ed., pp. 1–8). Routledge. https://doi.org/10.4324/9781315387420-1

Hardin, G. (1968). The tragedy of the commons: The population problem has no technical solution; it requires a fundamental extension in morality. *Science, 162*(3859), 1243–1248. https://doi.org/10.1126/science.162.3859.1243

Harris, C. R., Coburn, N., Rohrer, D., & Pashler, H. (2013). Two failures to replicate high-performance-goal priming effects. *PLoS ONE, 8*(8), e72467. https://doi.org/10.1371/journal.pone.0072467

Harris, L. T., & Fiske, S. T. (2011). Dehumanized perception: A psychological means to facilitate atrocities, torture, and genocide? *Zeitschrift Für Psychologie, 219*(3), 175–181. https://doi.org/10.1027/2151-2604/a000065

Haslam, S. A., & Reicher, S. D. (2012). When prisoners take over the prison: A social psychology of resistance. *Personality and Social Psychology Review, 16*(2), 154–179. https://doi.org/10.1177/1088868311419864

Hastie, R., & Dawes, R. M. (2010). *Rational choice in an uncertain world: The psychology of judgment and decision making* (2nd ed.). SAGE.

Hatemi, P. K., Crabtree, C., & Smith, K. B. (2019). Ideology justifies morality: Political beliefs predict moral foundations. *American Journal of Political Science, 63*(4), 788–806. https://doi.org/10.1111/ajps.12448

Hatemi, P. K., Hibbing, J. R., Medland, S. E., Keller, M. C., Alford, J. R., Smith, K. B., Martin, N. G., & Eaves, L. J. (2010). Not by twins alone: Using the extended family design to investigate genetic influence on political beliefs. *American Journal of Political Science, 54*(3), 798–814. https://doi.org/10.1111/j.1540-5907.2010.00461.x

Hatemi, P. K., Medland, S. E., Klemmensen, R., Oskarsson, S., Littvay, L., Dawes, C. T., Verhulst, B., McDermott, R., Nørgaard, A. S., Klofstad, C. A., Christensen, K., Johannesson, M., Magnusson, P. K. E., Eaves, L. J., & Martin, N. G. (2014). Genetic influences on political ideologies: Twin analyses of 19 measures of political ideologies from five democracies and genome-wide findings from three populations. *Behavior Genetics, 44*(3), 282–294. https://doi.org/10.1007/s10519-014-9648-8

Hayes, J., Schimel, J., Arndt, J., & Faucher, E. H. (2010). A theoretical and empirical review of the death-thought accessibility concept in terror management research. *Psychological Bulletin, 136*(5), 699–739. https://doi.org/10.1037/a0020524

Heintzelman, S. J., & King, L. A. (2016). Meaning in life and intuition. *Journal of Personality and Social Psychology, 110*(3), 477–492. https://doi.org/10.1037/pspp0000062

Helzer, E. G., & Pizarro, D. A. (2011). Dirty liberals!: Reminders of physical cleanliness influence moral and political attitudes. *Psychological Science, 22*(4), 517–522. https://doi.org/10.1177/0956797611402514

Henrich, J. (2020). *The WEIRDest people in the world: How the west became psychologically peculiar and particularly prosperous* (1st ed.). Farrar, Straus and Giroux.

Henrich, J., Heine, S. J., & Norenzayan, A. (2010). The weirdest people in the world? *Behavioral and Brain Sciences, 33*(2–3), 61–83. https://doi.org/10.1017/S0140525X0999152X

Henriques, G. (2013). Evolving from methodological to conceptual unification. *Review of General Psychology*, *17*(2), 168–173. https://doi.org/10.1037/a0032929

Heppner, W. L., Kernis, M. H., Lakey, C. E., Campbell, W. K., Goldman, B. M., Davis, P. J., & Cascio, E. V. (2008). Mindfulness as a means of reducing aggressive behavior: Dispositional and situational evidence. *Aggressive Behavior*, *34*(5), 486–496. https://doi.org/10.1002/ab.20258

Hermes, H., Hett, F., Mechtel, M., Schmidt, F., Schunk, D., & Wagner, V. (2020). Do children cooperate conditionally? Adapting the strategy method for first-graders. *Journal of Economic Behavior & Organization*, *179*, 638–652. https://doi.org/10.1016/j.jebo.2018.12.032

Hertwig, R., & Ortmann, A. (2001). Experimental practices in economics: A methodological challenge for psychologists? *Behavioral and Brain Sciences*, *24*(3), 383–403. https://doi.org/10.1017/S0140525X01004149

Hibbing, J. R., Smith, K. B., & Alford, J. R. (2014). Differences in negativity bias underlie variations in political ideology. *Behavioral and Brain Sciences*, *37*(3), 297–307. https://doi.org/10.1017/S0140525X13001192

Higgins, E. T. (1996). Knowledge activation: Accessibility, applicability, and salience. In E. T. Higgins & A. W. Kruglanski (Eds.), *Social psychology: Handbook of basic principles* (pp. 133–168). Guilford Press.

Higgins, E. T., & Pittman, T. S. (2008). Motives of the human animal: Comprehending, managing, and sharing inner states. *Annual Review of Psychology*, *59*(1), 361–385. https://doi.org/10.1146/annurev.psych.59.103006.093726

Higgins, E. T., Rossignac-Milon, M., & Echterhoff, G. (2021). Shared reality: From sharing-is-believing to merging minds. *Current Directions in Psychological Science*, *30*(2), 103–110. https://doi.org/10.1177/0963721421992027

Hogg, M. A. (2021). Uncertain self in a changing world: A foundation for radicalisation, populism, and autocratic leadership. *European Review of Social Psychology*, *32*(2), 235–268. https://doi.org/10.1080/10463283.2020.1827628

Holbrook, D., & Horgan, J. (2019). Terrorism and ideology: Cracking the nut. *Perspectives on Terrorism*, *13*(6), 2–15.

Holmes, A. J., Hollinshead, M. O., Roffman, J. L., Smoller, J. W., & Buckner, R. L. (2016). Individual differences in cognitive control circuit anatomy link sensation seeking, impulsivity, and substance use. *The Journal of Neuroscience*, *36*(14), 4038–4049. https://doi.org/10.1523/JNEUROSCI.3206-15.2016

Holzer, J. C., Dew, A. J., Recupero, P. R., & Gill, P. (2022). Introduction: Scope of the problem, definitions, and concepts. In J. C. Holzer, A. J. Dew, P. R. Recupero, & P. Gill, *Lone-actor terrorism* (pp. 1–12). Oxford University Press. https://doi.org/10.1093/med/9780190929794.003.0001

Hood, R. W., Hill, P. C., & Williamson, W. P. (2005). *The psychology of religious fundamentalism*. Guilford Press.

Horgan, J. G. (2014). *The psychology of terrorism* (0 ed.). Routledge. https://doi.org/10.4324/9781315882246

Horgan, J. G. (2017). Psychology of terrorism: Introduction to the special issue *American Psychologist*, *72*(3), 199–204. https://doi.org/10.1037/amp0000148

Horita, Y., & Takezawa, M. (2018). Cultural differences in strength of conformity explained through pathogen stress: A statistical test using hierarchical Bayesian estimation. *Frontiers in Psychology*, *9*, 1921. https://doi.org/10.3389/fpsyg.2018.01921

Hudgins, B. B., & Edelman, S. (1988). Children's self-directed critical thinking. *The Journal of Educational Research*, *81*(5), 262–273. https://doi.org/10.1080/00220 671.1988.10885834

Hudgins, B. B., Riesenmy, M., Ebel, D., & Edelman, S. (1989). Children's critical thinking: A model for its analysis and two examples. *The Journal of Educational Research*, *82*(6), 327–339. https://doi.org/10.1080/00220671.1989.10885915

Iannaccone, L. R., & Berman, E. (2006). Religious extremism: The good, the bad, and the deadly. *Public Choice*, *128*(1–2), 109–129. https://doi.org/10.1007/s11 127-006-9047-7

Ichheiser, G. (1970). *Appearances and realities* (1st ed.). Jossey-Bass.

Igou, E. R., & Bless, H. (2007). On undesirable consequences of thinking: Framing effects as a function of substantive processing. *Journal of Behavioral Decision Making*, *20*(2), 125–142. https://doi.org/10.1002/bdm.543

IJzerman, H., Lewis Jr, N. A., Przybylski, A. K., Weinstein, N., DeBruine, L., Ritchie, S. J., Vazire, S., Forscher, P. S., Morey, R. D., Ivory, J. D., & Anvari, F. (2020). Use caution when applying behavioural science to policy. *Nature Human Behaviour*, *4*(11), 1092–1094. https://doi.org/10.1038/s41562-020-00990-w

Imhoff, R., Dieterle, L., & Lamberty, P. (2021). Resolving the puzzle of conspiracy worldview and political activism: Belief in secret plots decreases normative but increases nonnormative political engagement. *Social Psychological and Personality Science*, *12*(1), 71–79. https://doi.org/10.1177/1948550619896491

Inbar, Y., Pizarro, D. A., & Bloom, P. (2009). Conservatives are more easily disgusted than liberals. *Cognition & Emotion*, *23*(4), 714–725. https://doi.org/10.1080/ 02699930802110007

Ioannidis, J. P. A. (2005). Why most published research findings are false. *PLoS Medicine*, *2*(8), e124. https://doi.org/10.1371/journal.pmed.0020124

Irwin, H. J., & Watt, C. (2007). *An introduction to parapsychology* (5th ed.). McFarland & Co.

Isbell, L. M., Lair, E. C., & Rovenpor, D. R. (2013). Affect-as-information about processing styles: A cognitive malleability approach: Cognitive malleability. *Social and Personality Psychology Compass*, *7*(2), 93–114. https://doi.org/10.1111/ spc3.12010

Isler, O., Gächter, S., Maule, A. J., & Starmer, C. (2021). Contextualised strong reciprocity explains selfless cooperation despite selfish intuitions and weak social heuristics. *Scientific Reports*, *11*(1), 13868. https://doi.org/10.1038/s41 598-021-93412-4

Isler, O., Maule, J., & Starmer, C. (2018). Is intuition really cooperative? Improved tests support the social heuristics hypothesis. *PLoS ONE*, *13*(1), e0190560. https:// doi.org/10.1371/journal.pone.0190560

Isler, O., & Yilmaz, O. (2019). Intuition and deliberation in morality and cooperation: An overview of the literature. In J. Liebowitz (Ed.), *Developing informed intuition for decision-making (pp. 101-113)*. Taylor & Francis.

Isler, O., & Yilmaz, O. (2023). How to activate intuitive and reflective thinking in behavior research? A comprehensive examination of experimental techniques. *Behavior Research Methods*, *55*(7), 3679–3698. https://doi.org/10.3758/s13 428-022-01984-4

Isler, O., Yilmaz, O., & Dogruyol, B. (2020). Activating reflective thinking with decision justification and debiasing training. *Judgment and Decision Making*, *15*(6), 926–938. https://doi.org/10.1017/S1930297500008147

Isler, O., Yilmaz, O., & Doğruyol, B. (2021). Are we at all liberal at heart? High-powered tests find no effect of intuitive thinking on moral foundations. *Journal of Experimental Social Psychology*, 92, 104050. https://doi.org/10.1016/j.jesp.2020.104050

Isler, O., Yilmaz, O., & Maule, A. J. (2021). Religion, parochialism and intuitive cooperation. *Nature Human Behaviour*, 5(4), 512–521. https://doi.org/10.1038/s41562-020-01014-3

Iyer, R., Koleva, S., Graham, J., Ditto, P., & Haidt, J. (2012). Understanding libertarian morality: The psychological dispositions of self-identified libertarians. *PLoS ONE*, 7(8), e42366. https://doi.org/10.1371/journal.pone.0042366

Jacoby, L. L., Lindsay, D. S., & Toth, J. P. (1992). Unconscious influences revealed: Attention, awareness, and control. *American Psychologist*, 47(6), 802–809. https://doi.org/10.1037/0003-066X.47.6.802

Jakobsson, N., & Blom, S. (2014). Did the 2011 terror attacks in norway change citizens' attitudes toward immigrants? *International Journal of Public Opinion Research*, 26(4), 475–486. https://doi.org/10.1093/ijpor/edt036

Janis, I. L. (1982). *Groupthink: Psychological studies of policy decisions and fiascoes* (2nd ed.). Houghton Mifflin.

Janoff-Bulman, R., & Carnes, N. C. (2013). Surveying the moral landscape: Moral motives and group-based moralities. *Personality and Social Psychology Review*, 17(3), 219–236. https://doi.org/10.1177/1088868313480274

Janoff-Bulman, R., & Carnes, N. C. (2016). Social justice and social order: Binding moralities across the political spectrum. *PLoS ONE*, 11(3), e0152479. https://doi.org/10.1371/journal.pone.0152479

Janoff-Bulman, R., & Usoof-Thowfeek, R. (2009). Shifting moralities: Post-9/11 responses to shattered national assumptions. In M. J. Morgan (Ed.), *The impact of 9/11 on psychology and education* (pp. 81–96). Palgrave Macmillan US. https://doi.org/10.1057/9780230101593_7

John, L. K., Loewenstein, G., & Prelec, D. (2012). Measuring the prevalence of questionable research practices with incentives for truth telling. *Psychological Science*, 23(5), 524–532. https://doi.org/10.1177/0956797611430953

Johnson, D. (2016). *God is watching you: How the fear of God makes us human.* Oxford University Press.

Johnson, M. K., Nolen-Hoeksema, S., Mitchell, K. J., & Levin, Y. (2009). Medial cortex activity, self-reflection and depression. *Social Cognitive and Affective Neuroscience*, 4(4), 313–327. https://doi.org/10.1093/scan/nsp022

Johnston, C. D., & Madson, G. J. (2022). Negativity bias, personality and political ideology. *Nature Human Behaviour*, 6(5), 666–676. https://doi.org/10.1038/s41562-022-01327-5

Jones, A., & Fitness, J. (2008). Moral hypervigilance: The influence of disgust sensitivity in the moral domain. *Emotion*, 8(5), 613–627. https://doi.org/10.1037/a0013435

Jost, J. T. (2006). The end of the end of ideology. *American Psychologist*, 61(7), 651–670. https://doi.org/10.1037/0003-066X.61.7.651

Jost, J. T. (2012). Left and right, right and wrong. *Science*, 337(6094), 525–526. https://doi.org/10.1126/science.1222565

Jost, J. T. (2017). Ideological asymmetries and the essence of political psychology. *Political Psychology*, 38(2), 167–208. https://doi.org/10.1111/pops.12407

Jost, J. T., & Amodio, D. M. (2012). Political ideology as motivated social cognition: Behavioral and neuroscientific evidence. *Motivation and Emotion*, 36(1), 55–64. https://doi.org/10.1007/s11031-011-9260-7

Jost, J. T., Federico, C. M., & Napier, J. L. (2009). Political ideology: its structure, functions, and elective affinities. *Annual Review of Psychology*, 60(1), 307–337. https://doi.org/10.1146/annurev.psych.60.110707.163600

Jost, J. T., Glaser, J., Kruglanski, A. W., & Sulloway, F. J. (2003). Political conservatism as motivated social cognition. *Psychological Bulletin*, 129(3), 339–375. https://doi.org/10.1037/0033-2909.129.3.339

Jost, J. T., Ledgerwood, A., & Hardin, C. D. (2008). Shared reality, system justification, and the relational basis of ideological beliefs. *Social and Personality Psychology Compass*, 2(1), 171–186. https://doi.org/10.1111/j.1751-9004.2007.00056.x

Jost, J. T., Napier, J. L., Thorisdottir, H., Gosling, S. D., Palfai, T. P., & Ostafin, B. (2007). Are needs to manage uncertainty and threat associated with political conservatism or ideological extremity? *Personality and Social Psychology Bulletin*, 33(7), 989–1007. https://doi.org/10.1177/0146167207301028

Jost, J. T., Sterling, J., & Stern, C. (2017). Getting closure on conservatism, or the politics of epistemic and existential motivation. In J. P. Forgas, K. Fiedler, & W. D. Crano (Eds.), *Motivated social perception: The Ontario symposium* (Vol. 14, pp. 56–87). Psychology Press.

Jost, J. T., Stern, C., Rule, N. O., & Sterling, J. (2017). The politics of fear: Is there an ideological asymmetry in existential motivation? *Social Cognition*, 35(4), 324–353. https://doi.org/10.1521/soco.2017.35.4.324

Kagan, J., Pearson, L., & Welch, L. (1966). Conceptual impulsivity and inductive reasoning. *Child Development*, 37(3), 583. https://doi.org/10.2307/1126680

Kagan, J., Rosman, B. L., Day, D., Albert, J., & Phillips, W. (1964). Information processing in the child: Significance of analytic and reflective attitudes. *Psychological Monographs: General and Applied*, 78(1), 1–37. https://doi.org/10.1037/h0093830

Kagitcibasi, C., Sunar, D., & Bekman, S. (2001). Long-term effects of early intervention: Turkish low-income mothers and children. *Journal of Applied Developmental Psychology*, 22(4), 333–361. https://doi.org/10.1016/S0193-3973(01)00071-5

Kagitcibasi, C., Sunar, D., Bekman, S., Baydar, N., & Cemalcilar, Z. (2009). Continuing effects of early enrichment in adult life: The Turkish Early Enrichment Project 22 years later. *Journal of Applied Developmental Psychology*, 30(6), 764–779. https://doi.org/10.1016/j.appdev.2009.05.003

Kahan, D. M. (2013). Ideology, motivated reasoning, and cognitive reflection. *Judgment and Decision Making*, 8(4), 407–424. https://doi.org/10.1017/S1930297500005271

Kahan, D. M., & Stanovich, K. (2016). *Rationality and belief in human evolution* (SSRN Scholarly Paper 2838668). https://papers.ssrn.com/abstract=2838668

Kahneman, D. (2003). Maps of bounded rationality: Psychology for behavioral economics. *American Economic Review*, 93(5), 1449–1475. https://doi.org/10.1257/000282803322655392

Kahneman, D. (2011). *Thinking, fast and slow*. Farrar, Straus and Giroux.

Kahneman, D., & Klein, G. (2009). Conditions for intuitive expertise: A failure to disagree. *American Psychologist*, 64(6), 515–526. https://doi.org/10.1037/a0016755

Kahneman, D., & Tversky, A. (1973). On the psychology of prediction. *Psychological Review*, 80(4), 237–251. https://doi.org/10.1037/h0034747

Kahneman, D., & Tversky, A. (1979). Prospect theory: An analysis of decision under risk. *Econometrica*, *47*(2), 263–291. https://doi.org/10.2307/1914185

Kallis, A. (2013). Far-right "Contagion" or a failing "mainstream"? How dangerous ideas cross borders and blur boundaries. *Democracy and Security*, *9*(3), 221–246. https://doi org/10.1080/17419166.2013.792251

Kalra, P. B., Gabrieli, J. D., & Finn, A. S. (2019). Evidence of stable individual differences in implicit learning. *Cognition*, *190*, 199–211. https://doi.org/10.1016/j.cognition.2019.05.007

Kanai, R., Feilden, T., Firth, C., & Rees, G. (2011). Political orientations are correlated with brain structure in young adults. *Current Biology*, *21*(8), 677–680. https://doi.org/10.1016/j.cub.2011.03.017

Kane, M. J., Bleckley, M. K., Conway, A. R. A., & Engle, R. W. (2001). A controlled-attention view of working-memory capacity. *Journal of Experimental Psychology: General*, *130*(2), 169–183. https://doi.org/10.1037/0096-3445. 130.2.169

Kane, M. J., & Engle, R. W. (2003). Working-memory capacity and the control of attention: The contributions of goal neglect, response competition, and task set to Stroop interference. *Journal of Experimental Psychology: General*, *132*(1), 47–70. https://doi.org/10.1037/0096-3445.132.1.47

Kang, Y., Gruber, J., & Gray, J. R. (2013). Mindfulness and de-automatization. *Emotion Review*, *5*(2), 192–201. https://doi.org/10.1177/1754073912451629

Karwowski, M., Kowal, M., Groyecka, A., Białek, M., Lebuda, I., Sorokowska. A., & Sorokowski, P. (2020). When in danger, turn right: does Covid-19 threat promote social conservatism and right-wing presidential candidates? *Human Ethology*, *35*(1), 37–48. https://doi.org/10.22330/he/35/037-048

Kassam, K. S., Koslov, K., & Mendes, W. B. (2009). Decisions under distress: stress profiles influence anchoring and adjustment. *Psychological Science*, *20*(11), 1394–1399. https://doi.org/10.1111/j.1467-9280.2009.02455.x

Kelemen, D. (2004). Are children "intuitive theists"?: Reasoning about purpose and design in nature. *Psychological Science*, *15*(5), 295–301. https://doi.org/10.1111/j.0956-7976.2004.00672.x

Kempthorne, J. C., & Terrizzi, J. A. (2021). The behavioral immune system and conservatism as predictors of disease-avoidant attitudes during the COVID-19 pandemic. *Personality and Individual Differences*, *178*, 110857. https://doi.org/10.1016/j.paid.2021.110857

Keren, G., & Schul, Y. (2009). Two is not always better than one: A critical evaluation of two-system theories. *Perspectives on Psychological Science*, *4*(6), 533–550. https://doi.org/10.1111/j.1745-6924.2009.01164.x

Kernis, M. H., Grannemann, B. D., & Barclay, L. C. (1989). Stability and level of self-esteem as predictors of anger arousal and hostility. *Journal of Personality and Social Psychology*, *56*(6), 1013–1022. https://doi.org/10.1037/0022-3514.56.6.1013

Kerr, N. L. (1998). HARKing: Hypothesizing after the results are known. *Personality and Social Psychology Review*, *2*(3), 196–217. https://doi.org/10.1207/s15327957pspr0203_4

Kierkegaard, S. (1846/2009). *Concluding unscientific postscript to the philosophical crumbs (A. Hannay, Trans.).* Cambridge University Press. (Original work published 1846).

King, P. M., & Kitchener, K. S. (2004). Reflective judgment: Theory and research on the development of epistemic assumptions through adulthood. *Educational Psychologist*, *39*(1), 5–18. https://doi.org/10.1207/s15326985ep3901_2

Kinsman, L., & Frimer, J. A. (2021). A psychological profile of extreme Trump supporters. In J.-W. Van Prooijen (Ed.), *The psychology of political polarization* (1st ed., pp. 53–76). Routledge. https://doi.org/10.4324/9781003042433-6

Klauer, K. C., & Singmann, H. (2015). Does global and local vision have an impact on creative and analytic thought? Two failed replications. *PLoS ONE, 10*(10), e0132885. https://doi.org/10.1371/journal.pone.0132885

Klein, G., Calderwood, R., & Clinton-Cirocco, A. (2010). Rapid decision making on the fire ground: The original study plus a postscript. *Journal of Cognitive Engineering and Decision Making, 4*(3), 186–209. https://doi.org/10.1518/15553 4310X12844000801203

Klein, G. A. (1998). *Sources of power: How people make decisions.* MIT Press.

Klein, R. A., Cook, C. L., Ebersole, C. R., Vitiello, C., Nosek, B. A., Hilgard, J., Ahn, P. H., Brady, A. J., Chartier, C. R., Christopherson, C. D., Clay, S., Collisson, B., Crawford, J. T., Cromar, R., Gardiner, G., Gosnell, C. L., Grahe, J., Hall, C., Howard, I., … Ratliff, K. A. (2022). Many labs 4: Failure to replicate mortality salience effect with and without original author involvement. *Collabra: Psychology, 8*(1), 35271. https://doi.org/10.1525/collabra.35271

Kliegr, T., Bahník, Š., & Fürnkranz, J. (2020). Advances in machine learning for the behavioral sciences. *American Behavioral Scientist, 64*(2), 145–175. https://doi. org/10.1177/0002764219859639

Knauff, M., & Spohn, W. (Eds.). (2021). *The handbook of rationality.* The MIT Press. https://doi.org/10.7551/mitpress/11252.001.0001

Knežević, G., Lazarevic, L. B., Međedović, J., Petrović, B., & Stankov, L. (2022). The relationship between closed-mindedness and militant extremism in a post-conflict society. *Aggressive Behavior, 48*(2), 253–263. https://doi.org/10.1002/ab.22017

Knight, K. (1999). Liberalism and conservatism. In J. P. Robinson, P. R. Shaver, & L. S. Wrightsman (Eds.), *Measures of political attitudes* (pp. 59–158). Academic Press.

Koehler, D. (2017). *Understanding deradicalization: Methods, tools and programs for countering violent extremism.* Routledge, Taylor & Francis Group.

Koehler, D. (2020). Terminology and definitions. In S. J. Hansen, & S. Lid (Eds.), *Routledge handbook of deradicalisation and disengagement* (1st ed., pp. 10–25). Routledge. https://doi.org/10.4324/9781315387420-3

Kohlberg, L. (1969). Stage and sequence: The cognitive developmental approach to socialization. In D. Goslin (Ed.), *Handbook of socialization theory and research* (pp. 347–480). Rand McNally.

Kohlberg, L. (1971). From is to ought: How to commit the naturalistic fallacy and get away with it in the study of moral development. In T. Mischel (Ed.), *Cognitive development and epistemology* (pp. 151–235). Academic Press. https://doi.org/ 10.1016/B978-0-12-498640-4.50011-1

Kohlberg, L. (1981). *The philosophy of moral development* (Vol. 1). Harper & Row.

Köhler, W. (1925). *The mentality of apes* (E. Winter, Trans.). Vintage Books.

Kornacka, M., Krejtz, I., & Douilliez, C. (2019). Concrete vs. abstract processing in repetitive negative thinking: Distinct functional effects on emotional reactivity and attentional control. *Frontiers in Psychology, 10*, 1372. https://doi.org/10.3389/ fpsyg.2019.01372

Koster, E. H. W., De Lissnyder, E., Derakshan, N., & De Raedt, R. (2011). Understanding depressive rumination from a cognitive science perspective: The impaired disengagement hypothesis. *Clinical Psychology Review, 31*(1), 138–145. https://doi.org/10.1016/j.cpr.2010.08.005

Krapohl, E., Rimfeld, K., Shakeshaft, N. G., Trzaskowski, M., McMillan, A., Pingault, J.-B., Asbury, K., Harlaar, N., Kovas, Y., Dale, P. S., & Plomin, R. (2014). The high heritability of educational achievement reflects many genetically influenced traits, not just intelligence. *Proceedings of the National Academy of Sciences*, 111(42), 15273–15278. https://doi.org/10.1073/pnas.1408777111

Kross, E., & Ayduk, O. (2008). Facilitating adaptive emotional analysis: distinguishing distanced-analysis of depressive experiences from immersed-analysis and distraction. *Personality and Social Psychology Bulletin*, 34(7), 924–938. https://doi.org/10.1177/0146167208315938

Kross, E., Ayduk, O., & Mischel, W. (2005). When asking "why" does not hurt distinguishing rumination from reflective processing of negative emotions. *Psychological Science*, 16(9), 709–715. https://doi.org/10.1111/j.1467-9280.2005.01600.x

Krueger, A. B (2008). *What makes a terrorist: Economics and the roots of terrorism: Lionel Robbins lectures* (4. print., and 1. paperback print. with a new afterw. by the author). Princeton University Press.

Kruglanski, A. W. (2001). That "vision thing": The state of theory in social and personality psychology at the edge of the new millennium. *Journal of Personality and Social Psychology*, 80(6), 871–875. https://doi.org/10.1037/0022-3514.80.6.871

Kruglanski, A. W., & Gigerenzer, G. (2011). Intuitive and deliberate judgments are based on common principles. *Psychological Review*, 118(1), 97–109. https://doi.org/10.1037/a0020762

Kruglanski, A. W., Kopetz, C. E., & Szumowska, E. (Eds.). (2022). *The psychology of extremism: A motivational perspective*. Routledge.

Kruglanski, A. W., Molinario, E., Ellenberg, M., & Di Cicco, G. (2022). Terrorism and conspiracy theories: A view from the 3N model of radicalization. *Current Opinion in Psychology*, 47, 101396. https://doi.org/10.1016/j.copsyc.2022.101396

Kruglanski, A. W., Molinario, E., Jasko, K., Webber, D., Leander, N. P., & Pierro, A. (2022). Significance-quest theory. *Perspectives on Psychological Science*, 17(4), 1050–1071. https://doi.org/10.1177/17456916211034825

Kruglanski, A. W., & Orehek, E. (2011). The need for certainty as a psychological nexus for individuals and society. In M. A. Hogg & D. L. Blaylock (Eds.), *Extremism and the psychology of uncertainty* (1st ed., pp. 1–18). Wiley. https://doi.org/10.1002/9781444344073.ch1

Kruglanski, A. W., Webber, D., & Koehler, D. (2019). *The Radical's journey: How German Neo-Nazis voyaged to the edge and back* (1st ed.). Oxford University Press. https://doi.org/10.1093/oso/9780190851095.001.0001

Kruglanski, A. W., Webster, D. M., & Klem, A. (1993). Motivated resistance and openness to persuasion in the presence or absence of prior information. *Journal of Personality and Social Psychology*, 65(5), 861–876. https://doi.org/10.1037/0022-3514.65.5.861

Krumrei-Mancuso, E J., & Worthington, Jr., E. L. (2023). Links between intellectual humility and open-mindedness: Does strength of belief matter? In V. Ottati & C. Stern (Eds.), *Divided* (1st ed., pp. 81-C5P95). Oxford University Press. https://doi.org/10.1093/oso/9780197655467.003.0005

Krupenye, C., & Call, J. (2019). Theory of mind in animals: Current and future directions. *WIREs Cognitive Science*, 10(6), e1503. https://doi.org/10.1002/wcs.1503

Kugler, M., Jost, J. T., & Noorbaloochi, S. (2014). Another look at moral foundations theory: Do authoritarianism and social dominance orientation explain liberal-conservative differences in "Moral" intuitions? *Social Justice Research*, 27(4), 413–431. https://doi.org/10.1007/s11211-014-0223-5

Kukla, A., & Walmsley, J. (2006). *Mind: A historical and philosophical introduction to the major theories*. Hackett Publishing Co.

Kump, B. (2022). No need to hide: Acknowledging the researcher's intuition in empirical organizational research. *Human Relations*, 75(4), 635–654. https://doi.org/10.1177/0018726720984837

Kunda, Z. (1990). The case for motivated reasoning. *Psychological Bulletin*, 108(3), 480–498. https://doi.org/10.1037/0033-2909.108.3.480

Kunst-Wilson, W. R., & Zajonc, R. B. (1980). Affective discrimination of stimuli that cannot be recognized. *Science*, 207(4430), 557–558. https://doi.org/10.1126/science.7352271

Kurzban, R., Duckworth, A., Kable, J. W., & Myers, J. (2013). An opportunity cost model of subjective effort and task performance. *Behavioral and Brain Sciences*, 36(6), 661–679. https://doi.org/10.1017/S0140525X12003196

Kushner Gadarian, S., & Brader, T. (2023). Emotion and political psychology. In L. Huddy, D. O. Sears, J. S. Levy, & J. Jerit (Eds.), *The Oxford handbook of political psychology* (3rd ed., pp. 191–247). Oxford University Press. https://doi.org/10.1093/oxfordhb/9780197541302.013.5

Kvarven, A., Strømland, E., Wollbrant, C., Andersson, D., Johannesson, M., Tinghög, G., Västfjäll, D., & Myrseth, K. O. R. (2020). The intuitive cooperation hypothesis revisited: A meta-analytic examination of effect size and between-study heterogeneity. *Journal of the Economic Science Association*, 6(1), 26–42. https://doi.org/10.1007/s40881-020-00084-3

Kwak, Y., Payne, J. W., Cohen, A. L., & Huettel, S. A. (2015). The rational adolescent: Strategic information processing during decision making revealed by eye tracking. *Cognitive Development*, 36, 20–30. https://doi.org/10.1016/j.cogdev.2015.08.001

Kydd, A. H., & Walter, B. F. (2006). The strategies of terrorism. *International Security*, 31(1), 49–80. https://doi.org/10.1162/isec.2006.31.1.49

LaBerge, D., & Samuels, S. J. (1974). Toward a theory of automatic information processing in reading. *Cognitive Psychology*, 6(2), 293–323. https://doi.org/10.1016/0010-0285(74)90015-2

Lalande, D., Vallerand, R. J., Lafrenière, M.-A. K., Verner-Filion, J., Laurent, F.-A., Forest, J., & Paquet, Y. (2017). Obsessive passion: A compensatory response to unsatisfied needs: passion and need satisfaction. *Journal of Personality*, 85(2), 163–178. https://doi.org/10.1111/jopy.12229

Lambert, A. J., Scherer, L. D., Schott, J. P., Olson, K. R., Andrews, R. K., O'Brien, T. C., & Zisser, A. R. (2010). Rally effects, threat, and attitude change: An integrative approach to understanding the role of emotion. *Journal of Personality and Social Psychology*, 98(6), 886–903. https://doi.org/10.1037/a0019086

Landau, M. J., Solomon, S., Greenberg, J., Cohen, F., Pyszczynski, T., Arndt, J., Miller, C. H., Ogilvie, D. M., & Cook, A. (2004). Deliver us from evil: The effects of mortality salience and reminders of 9/11 on support for President George W. Bush. *Personality and Social Psychology Bulletin*, 30(9), 1136–1150. https://doi.org/10.1177/0146167204267988

Landwehr, J. R., & Eckmann, L. (2020). The nature of processing fluency: Amplification versus hedonic marking. *Journal of Experimental Social Psychology*, *90*, 103997. https://doi.org/10.1016/j.jesp.2020.103997

Landy, J. F. (2016). Representations of moral violations: Category members and associated features. *Judgment and Decision Making*, *11*(5), 496–508. https://doi.org/10.1017/S1930297500004587

Landy, J. F., & Royzman, E. B. (2018). The moral myopia model: Why and how reasoning matters in moral judgment. In G. Pennycook (Ed.), *The new reflectionism in cognitive psychology* (0 ed., pp. 76–98). Routledge. https://doi.org/10.4324/9781315460178-10

Lantian, A., Muller, D., Nurra, C., & Douglas, K. M. (2017). "I Know Things They Don't Know!": The role of need for uniqueness in belief in conspiracy theories. *Social Psychology*, *48*(3), 160–173. https://doi.org/10.1027/1864-9335/a0C0306

Lau, R. R., & Redlawsk, D. P. (2001). Advantages and disadvantages of cognitive heuristics in political decision making. *American Journal of Political Science*, *45*(4), 951. https://doi.org/10.2307/2669334

Lawson, M. A., Larrick, R. P., & Soll, J. B. (2020). Comparing fast thinking and slow thinking: The relative benefits of interventions, individual differences, and inferential rules. *Judgment and Decision Making*, *15*(5), 660–684. https://doi.org/10.1017/S1930297500007865

Lazarus, R. S., & Smith, C. A. (1988). Knowledge and appraisal in the cognition—Emotion relationship. *Cognition & Emotion*, *2*(4), 281–300. https://doi.org/10.1080/02699938808412701

LeDoux, J. E. (1996). *The emotional brain: The mysterious underpinnings of emotional life.* Simon & Schuster.

Lefevere, J., Tresch, A., & Walgrave, S. (2015). Introduction: Issue ownership. *West European Politics*, *38*(4), 755–760. https://doi.org/10.1080/01402382.2015.1039375

Lenharo, M., & Wolf, L. (2023). US COVID-origins hearing renews debate over lab-leak hypothesis. *Nature*, *615*(7952), 380–381. https://doi.org/10.1038/d41586-023-00701-1

Levine, J. M., & Kruglanski, A. W. (2021). The extreme group. In A. W. Kruglanski, C. Kopetz, & E. Szumowska (Eds.), *The psychology of extremism* (1st ed., pp. 96–139). Routledge. https://doi.org/10.4324/9781003030898-6

Levitan, L., & Wronski, J. (2014). Social context and information seeking: examining the effects of network attitudinal composition on engagement with political information. *Political Behavior*, *36*(4), 793–816. https://doi.org/10.1007/s11109-013-9247-z

Levitan, L. C., & Verhulst, B. (2016). Conformity in groups: The effects of others' views on expressed attitudes and attitude change. *Political Behavior*, *38*(2), 277–315. https://doi.org/10.1007/s11109-015-9312-x

Levitan, L. C., & Visser, P. S. (2008). The impact of the social context on resistance to persuasion: Effortful versus effortless responses to counter-attitudinal information. *Journal of Experimental Social Psychology*, *44*(3), 640–649. https://doi.org/10.1016/j.jesp.2007.03.004

Lewin, K. (1935). *A dynamic theory of personality.* McGraw-Hill.

Li, N. P., Van Vugt, M., & Colarelli, S. M. (2018). The evolutionary mismatch hypothesis: Implications for psychological science. *Current Directions in Psychological Science*, *27*(1), 38–44. https://doi.org/10.1177/0963721417731378

Li, Q., & Schaub, D. (2004). Economic globalization and transnational terrorism: A pooled time-series analysis. *Journal of Conflict Resolution*, 48(2), 230–258. https://doi.org/10.1177/0022002703262869

Lieberman, M. D. (2011). Why symbolic processing of affect can disrupt negative affect: Social cognitive and affective neuroscience investigations. In A. Todorov, S. T. Fiske, & D. A. Prentice (Eds.), *Social neuroscience: Toward understanding the underpinnings of the social mind* (pp. 188–209). Oxford University Press.

Lieberman, M. D., Gaunt, R., Gilbert, D. T., & Trope, Y. (2002). Reflexion and reflection: A social cognitive neuroscience approach to attributional inference. In *Advances in experimental social psychology* (Vol. 34, pp. 199–249). Elsevier. https://doi.org/10.1016/S0065-2601(02)80006-5

Liebowitz, J. (Ed.). (2021). *Developing informed intuition for decision-making.* CRC Press.

Lieder, F., Griffiths, T. L., M. Huys, Q. J., & Goodman, N. D. (2018). Empirical evidence for resource-rational anchoring and adjustment. *Psychonomic Bulletin & Review*, 25(2), 775–784. https://doi.org/10.3758/s13423-017-1288-6

Liekefett, L., Christ, O., & Becker, J. C. (2023). Can conspiracy beliefs be beneficial? Longitudinal linkages between conspiracy beliefs, anxiety, uncertainty aversion, and existential threat. *Personality and Social Psychology Bulletin*, 49(2), 167–179. https://doi.org/10.1177/01461672211060965

Lifton, R. J. (1961). *Thought reform and the psychology of totalism: A study of "Brainwashing" in China.* W. W. Norton.

Liht, J., & Savage, S. (2013). Preventing violent extremism through value complexity: Being Muslim being British. *Journal of Strategic Security*, 6(4), 44–66. https://doi.org/10.5038/1944-0472.6.4.3

Lilienfeld, S. O., Basterfield, C., Bowes, S. M., & Costello, T. H. (2020). Nobelists gone wild: Case studies in the domain specificity of critical thinking. In R. J. Sternberg, & D. F. Halpern (Eds.), *Critical thinking in psychology* (2nd ed., pp. 10–38). Cambridge University Press. https://doi.org/10.1017/9781108684354.003

Lin, S., Keysar, B., & Epley, N. (2010). Reflexively mindblind: Using theory of mind to interpret behavior requires effortful attention. *Journal of Experimental Social Psychology*, 46(3), 551–556. https://doi.org/10.1016/j.jesp.2009.12.019

Lindeman, M. (2011). Biases in intuitive reasoning and belief in complementary and alternative medicine. *Psychology & Health*, 26(3), 371–382. https://doi.org/10.1080/08870440903440707

Lindeman, M., & Svedholm, A. M. (2012). What's in a term? Paranormal, superstitious, magical and supernatural beliefs by any other name would mean the same. *Review of General Psychology*, 16(3), 241–255. https://doi.org/10.1037/a0027158

Lipset, S. M. (1960). *Political man: The social bases of politics.* Hopkins.

Liu, R. T., Kleiman, E. M., Nestor, B. A., & Cheek, S. M. (2015). The hopelessness theory of depression: A quarter-century in review. *Clinical Psychology: Science and Practice*, 22(4), 345–365. https://doi.org/10.1111/cpsp.12125

Lobato, E., Mendoza, J., Sims, V., & Chin, M. (2014). Examining the relationship between conspiracy theories, paranormal beliefs, and pseudoscience acceptance among a university population. *Applied Cognitive Psychology*, 28(5), 617–625. https://doi.org/10.1002/acp.3042

Lodge, M., & Taber, C. S. (2013). *The rationalizing voter.* Cambridge University Press.

LoGiudice, A. B., Sherbino, J., Norman, G., Monteiro, S., & Sibbald, M. (2021). Intuitive and deliberative approaches for diagnosing 'well' versus 'unwell': Evidence from eye tracking, and potential implications for training. *Advances in Health Sciences Education, 26*(3), 811–825. https://doi.org/10.1007/s10459-020-10023-w

Low, J., Butterfill, S. A., & Michael, J. (2023). A view from mindreading on fast-and-slow thinking. *Behavioral and Brain Sciences, 46*, e130. https://doi.org/10.1017/S0140525X22002858

Ma, Y., Liu, Y., Rand, D. G., Heatherton, T. F., & Han, S. (2015). Opposing oxytocin effects on intergroup cooperative behavior in intuitive and reflective minds. *Neuropsychopharmacology, 40*(10), 2379–2387. https://doi.org/10.1038/npp.2015.87

Mac Aonghusa, P., & Michie, S. (2020). Artificial intelligence and behavioral science through the looking glass: Challenges for real-world application. *Annals of Behavioral Medicine, 54*(12), 942–947. https://doi.org/10.1093/abm/kaaa095

Macrae, C. N., Milne, A. B., & Bodenhausen, G. V. (1994). Stereotypes as energy-saving devices: A peek inside the cognitive toolbox. *Journal of Personality and Social Psychology, 66*(1), 37–47. https://doi.org/10.1037/0022-3514.66.1.37

Maglio, S. J., & Reich, T. (2020). Choice protection for feeling-focused decisions. *Journal of Experimental Psychology: General, 149*(9), 1704–1718. https://doi.org/10.1037/xge0000735

Maij, David. L. R., Van Harreveld, F., Gervais, W., Schrag, Y., Mohr, C., & Van Elk, M. (2017). Mentalizing skills do not differentiate believers from non-believers, but credibility enhancing displays do. *PLoS ONE, 12*(8), e0182764. https://doi.org/10.1371/journal.pone.0182764

Ma-Kellams, C., & Lerner, J. (2016). Trust your gut or think carefully? Examining whether an intuitive, versus a systematic, mode of thought produces greater empathic accuracy. *Journal of Personality and Social Psychology, 111*(5), 674–685. https://doi.org/10.1037/pspi0000063

Malka, A., Soto, C. J., Inzlicht, M., & Lelkes, Y. (2014). Do needs for security and certainty predict cultural and economic conservatism? A cross-national analysis. *Journal of Personality and Social Psychology, 106*(6), 1031–1051. https://doi.org/10.1037/a0036170

Malson, L. (1972). *Wolf children and the problem of human nature*. Monthly Review Press.

Mamayek, C., Loughran, T., & Paternoster, R. (2015). Reason taking the reins from impulsivity: The promise of dual-systems thinking for criminology. *Journal of Contemporary Criminal Justice, 31*(4), 426–448. https://doi.org/10.1177/1043986215608532

Mani, A., Mullainathan, S., Shafir, E., & Zhao, J. (2013). Poverty impedes cognitive function. *Science, 341*(6149), 976–980. https://doi.org/10.1126/science.1238041

Mankiw, N. G. (2014). *Principles of economics* (7th ed.). Cengage Learning.

Mar, K., Townes, P., Pechlivanoglou, P., Arnold, P., & Schachar, R. (2022). Obsessive compulsive disorder and response inhibition: Meta-analysis of the stop-signal task. *Journal of Psychopathology and Clinical Science, 131*(2), 152–161. https://doi.org/10.1037/abn0000732

March, D. S., Gaertner, L., & Olson, M. A. (2017). In Harm's way: On preferential response to threatening stimuli. *Personality and Social Psychology Bulletin, 43*(11), 1519–1529. https://doi.org/10.1177/0146167217722558

March, D. S., Gaertner, L., & Olson, M. A. (2018). On the prioritized processing of threat in a dual implicit process model of evaluation. *Psychological Inquiry*, 29(1), 1–13. https://doi.org/10.1080/1047840X.2018.1435680

March, D. S., Gaertner, L., & Olson, M. A. (2022). On the automatic nature of threat: Physiological and evaluative reactions to survival-threats outside conscious perception. *Affective Science*, 3(1), 135–144. https://doi.org/10.1007/s42 761-021-00090-6

March, D. S., Olson, M. A., & Gaertner, L. (2023). Automatic threat processing shows evidence of exclusivity. *Behavioral and Brain Sciences*, 46, e131. https://doi. org/10.1017/S0140525X22002928

Marewski, J. N., & Gigerenzer, G. (2012). Heuristic decision making in medicine. *Dialogues in Clinical Neuroscience*, 14(1), 77–89. https://doi.org/10.31887/ DCNS.2012.14.1/jmarewski

Marks, J. (1991). *The search for the "Manchurian Candidate."* Norton.

Marks, J. (2014). *Ethics without morals: In defence of amorality* (First issued in paperback 2014). Routledge.

Martin, L. L., & Tesser, A. (1996). Some ruminative thoughts. In R. S. Wyer, *Advances in social cognition* (Vol. 9, pp. 1–47). Lawrence Erlbaum Associates.

Martin, L. L., & Van Den Bos, K. (2014). Beyond terror: Towards a paradigm shift in the study of threat and culture. *European Review of Social Psychology*, 25(1), 32–70. https://doi.org/10.1080/10463283.2014.923144

Martinsson, P., Myrseth, K. O. R., & Wollbrant, C. (2014). Social dilemmas: When self-control benefits cooperation. *Journal of Economic Psychology*, 45, 213–236. https://doi.org/10.1016/j.joep.2014.09.004

Marx, K., & Engels, F. (1970). *The German ideology* (K. Marx, Ed.). International Publishers.

Mattsson, C., & Johansson, T. (2022). *Radicalization and disengagement in neo-nazi movements: Social psychology perspective*. Routledge.

McBeath, M. K., Shaffer, D. M., & Kaiser, M. K. (1995). How baseball outfielders determine where to run to catch fly balls. *Science*, 268(5210), 569–573. https:// doi.org/10.1126/science.7725104

McConnell, A. R., & Rydell, R. J. (2014). The systems of evaluation model: A dual-systems approach to attitudes. In J. W. Sherman, B. Gawronski, & Y. Trope (Eds.), *Dual process theories of the social mind* (pp. 204–217). Guilford Press.

McDermott, R. (2022). Genetic contributions to political phenomena. In D. Osborne, & C. G. Sibley (Eds.), *The Cambridge handbook of political psychology* (1st ed., pp. 37–49). Cambridge University Press. https://doi.org/10.1017/9781108779 104.004

McPherson, M., Smith-Lovin, L., & Cook, J. M. (2001). Birds of a feather: Homophily in social networks. *Annual Review of Sociology*, 27(1), 415–444. https://doi.org/ 10.1146/annurev.soc.27.1.415

Meadows, D. H., & Wright, D. (2008). *Thinking in systems: A primer*. Chelsea Green Publishing.

Meehl, P. E. (1967). Theory-testing in psychology and physics: A methodological paradox. *Philosophy of Science*, 34(2), 103–115.

Melnikoff, D. E., & Bargh, J. A. (2018a). The insidious number two. *Trends in Cognitive Sciences*, 22(8), 668–669. https://doi.org/10.1016/j.tics.2018.05.005

Melnikoff, D. E., & Bargh, J. A. (2018b). The mythical number two. *Trends in Cognitive Sciences*, 22(4), 280–293. https://doi.org/10.1016/j.tics.2018.02.001

Melnikoff, D. E., & Bargh, J. A. (2023). Hoist by its own petard: The ironic and fatal flaws of dual-process theory. *Behavioral and Brain Sciences*, 46, e132. https://doi.org/10.1017/S0140525X22003077

Mercier, H., & Sperber, D. (2017). *The enigma of reason.* Harvard University Press.

Mernyk, J. S., Pink, S. L., Druckman, J. N., & Willer, R. (2022). Correcting inaccurate metaperceptions reduces Americans' support for partisan violence. *Proceedings of the National Academy of Sciences*, 119(16), e2116851119. https://doi.org/10.1073/pnas.2116851119

Merton, R. K. (1973). The normative structure of science. In R. K. Merton & N. W. Storer (Eds.), *The sociology of science: Theoretical and empirical investigations* (pp. 267–278). The University of Chicago Press.

Metcalfe, J., & Mischel, W. (1999). A hot/cool-system analysis of delay of gratification: Dynamics of willpower. *Psychological Review*, 106(1), 3–19. https://doi.org/10.1037/0033-295X.106.1.3

Metz, S. E., Weisberg, D. S., & Weisberg, M. (2018). Non-scientific criteria for belief sustain counter-scientific beliefs. *Cognitive Science*, 42(5), 1477–1503. https://doi.org/10.1111/cogs.12584

Meyer, A., Frederick, S., Burnham, T. C., Guevara Pinto, J. D., Boyer, T. W., Ball, L. J., Pennycook, G., Ackerman, R., Thompson, V. A., & Schuldt, J. P. (2015). Disfluent fonts don't help people solve math problems. *Journal of Experimental Psychology: General*, 144(2), e16–e30. https://doi.org/10.1037/xge0000049

Mieth, L., Buchner, A., & Bell, R. (2021). Cognitive load decreases cooperation and moral punishment in a Prisoner's Dilemma game with punishment option. *Scientific Reports*, 11(1), 24500. https://doi.org/10.1038/s41598-021-04217-4

Miller, H. L., Odegard, T. N., & Allen, G. (2014). Evaluating information processing in Autism Spectrum Disorder: The case for Fuzzy Trace Theory. *Developmental Review*, 34(1), 44–76. https://doi.org/10.1016/j.dr.2013.12.002

Miller, P. M., & Fagley, N. S. (1991). The effects of framing, problem variations, and providing rationale on choice. *Personality and Social Psychology Bulletin*, 17(5), 517–522. https://doi.org/10.1177/0146167291175006

Miller, T. (2019). Explanation in artificial intelligence: Insights from the social sciences. *Artificial Intelligence*, 267, 1–38. https://doi.org/10.1016/j.artint.2018.07.007

Milojev, P., Osborne, D., Greaves, L. M., Bulbulia, J., Wilson, M. S., Davies, C. L., Liu, J. H., & Sibley, C. G. (2014). Right-wing authoritarianism and social dominance orientation predict different moral signatures. *Social Justice Research*, 27(2), 149–174. https://doi.org/10.1007/s11211-014-0213-7

Mittone, L., & Savadori, L. (2009). The scarcity bias. *Applied Psychology*, 58(3), 453–468. https://doi.org/10.1111/j.1464-0597.2009.00401.x

Mitze, T., Kosfeld, R., Rode, J., & Wälde, K. (2020). Face masks considerably reduce COVID-19 cases in Germany. *Proceedings of the National Academy of Sciences*, 117(51), 32293–32301. https://doi.org/10.1073/pnas.2015954117

Moghaddam, F. M. (2005). The staircase to terrorism: A psychological exploration. *American Psychologist*, 60(2), 161–169. https://doi.org/10.1037/0003-066X.60.2.161

Molinario, E., Jasko, K., Webber, D., & Kruglanski, A. W. (2021). The social psychology of violent extremism. In A. W. Kruglanski, C. Kopetz, & E. Szumowska, *The psychology of extremism* (1st ed., pp. 259–279). Routledge. https://doi.org/10.4324/9781003030898-13

Monsay, E. H. (1997). Intuition in the development of scientific theory and practice. In R. Davis-Floyd & P. S. Arvidson (Eds.), *Intuition: The inside story* (pp. 103–120). Routledge.

Moon, J. W. (2021). Why are world religions so concerned with sexual behavior? *Current Opinion in Psychology, 40,* 15–19. https://doi.org/10.1016/j.copsyc.2020.07.030

Moore, G. E. (2004). *Principia ethica.* Dover Publications. (Original work published 1903).

Moran, T., & Eyal, T. (2022). Emotion regulation by psychological distance and level of abstraction: Two meta-analyses. *Personality and Social Psychology Review, 26*(2), 112–159. https://doi.org/10.1177/10888683211069025

Moran, T. P. (2016). Anxiety and working memory capacity: A meta-analysis and narrative review. *Psychological Bulletin, 142*(8), 831–864. https://doi.org/10.1037/bul0000051

Morgan, J., Wood, C., & Caldwell-Harris, C. (2018). Reflective thought, religious belief, and the social foundations hypothesis. In G. Pennycook (Ed.), *The new reflectionism in cognitive psychology* (0 ed., pp. 16–38). Routledge. https://doi.org/10.4324/9781315460178-7

Morson, G. S., & Schapiro, M. (2021). Minds Wide Shut: How the New Fundamentalisms Divide Us. Princeton University Press. https://doi.org/10.1515/9780691214931

Mullainathan, S., & Shafir, E. (2013). Decision making and policy in contexts of poverty. In E. Shafir (Ed.), *The behavioral foundations of public policy* (pp. 281–298). Princeton University Press. https://doi.org/10.1515/9781400845347-020

Mungan, E. (2023a). *Geştalt Kuramı.* Metis Yayınları. www.metiskitap.com/catalog/book/37157

Mungan, E. (2023b). Gestalt theory: A revolution put on pause? Prospects for a paradigm shift in the psychological sciences. *New Ideas in Psychology, 71,* 101036. https://doi.org/10.1016/j.newideapsych.2023.101036

Murdoch, E. M., Chapman, M. T., Crane, M., & Gucciardi, D. F. (2023). The effectiveness of self-distanced versus self-immersed reflections among adults: Systematic review and meta-analysis of experimental studies. *Stress and Health, 39*(2), 255–271. https://doi.org/10.1002/smi.3199

Murray, D. R., & Schaller, M. (2012). Threat(s) and conformity deconstructed: Perceived threat of infectious disease and its implications for conformist attitudes and behavior. *European Journal of Social Psychology, 42*(2), 180–188. https://doi.org/10.1002/ejsp.863

Murray, D. R., Schaller, M., & Suedfeld, P. (2013). Pathogens and politics: Further evidence that parasite prevalence predicts authoritarianism. *PLoS ONE, 8*(5), e62275. https://doi.org/10.1371/journal.pone.0062275

Muthukrishna, M., Bell, A. V., Henrich, J., Curtin, C. M., Gedranovich, A., McInerney, J., & Thue, B. (2020). Beyond Western, Educated, Industrial, Rich, and Democratic (WEIRD) psychology: Measuring and mapping scales of cultural and psychological distance. *Psychological Science, 31*(6), 678–701. https://doi.org/10.1177/0956797620916782

Muthukrishna, M., & Henrich, J. (2019). A problem in theory. *Nature Human Behaviour, 3*(3), 221–229. https://doi.org/10.1038/s41562-018-0522-1

Mutz, D. C., & Mondak, J. J. (2006). The workplace as a context for cross-cutting political discourse. *The Journal of Politics*, 68(1), 140–155. https://doi.org/10.1111/j.1468-2508.2006.00376.x

Myrseth, K. O. R., & Wollbrant, C. E. (2017). Cognitive foundations of cooperation revisited: Commentary on Rand et al. (2012, 2014). *Journal of Behavioral and Experimental Economics*, 69, 133–138. https://doi.org/10.1016/j.socec.2017.01.005

Nail, P. R., & McGregor, I. (2009). Conservative shift among liberals and conservatives following 9/11/01. *Social Justice Research*, 22(2–3), 231–240. https://doi.org/10.1007/s11211-009-0098-z

Nail, P. R., McGregor, I., Drinkwater, A. E., Steele, G. M., & Thompson, A. W. (2009). Threat causes liberals to think like conservatives. *Journal of Experimental Social Psychology*, 45(4), 901–907. https://doi.org/10.1016/j.jesp.2009.04.013

Narmashiri, A., Akbari, F., Sohrabi, A., & Hatami, J. (2023). Conspiracy beliefs are associated with a reduction in frontal beta power and biases in categorizing ambiguous stimuli. *Heliyon*, 9(10), e20249. https://doi.org/10.1016/j.heli yon.2023.e20249

Navarrete, C. D., & Fessler, D. M. T. (2005). Normative bias and adaptive challenges: A relational approach to coalitional psychology and a critique of terror management theory. *Evolutionary Psychology*, 3(1), 147470490500300. https://doi.org/10.1177/147470490500300121

Navarrete, C. D., & Fessler, D. M. T. (2006). Disease avoidance and ethnocentrism: The effects of disease vulnerability and disgust sensitivity on intergroup attitudes. *Evolution and Human Behavior*, 27(4), 270–282. https://doi.org/10.1016/j.evolh umbehav.2005.12.001

Nemr, C., & Savage, S. (2019). *Integrative complexity interventions to prevent and counter violent extremism*. Global Center on Cooperative Security. www.globa lcenter.org/resource/integrative-complexity-interventions-to-prevent-and-counter-violent-extremism/

Newell, B. R., & Rakow, T. (2011). Revising beliefs about the merit of unconscious thought: Evidence in favor of the null hypothesis. *Social Cognition*, 29(6), 711–726. https://doi.org/10.1521/soco.2011.29.6.711

Newell, B. R., & Shanks, D. R. (2014). Unconscious influences on decision making: A critical review. *Behavioral and Brain Sciences*, 37(1), 1–19. https://doi.org/10.1017/S0140525X12003214

Newman, I. R., & Thompson, V. A. (2023). Not feeling right about uncertainty monitoring. *Behavioral and Brain Sciences*, 46, e133. https://doi.org/10.1017/S0140525X22003089

Nickerson, R. S. (1998). Confirmation bias: A ubiquitous phenomenon in many guises. *Review of General Psychology*, 2(2), 175–220. https://doi.org/10.1037/1089-2680.2.2.175

Nieuwenstein, M. R., Wierenga, T., Morey, R. D., Wicherts, J. M., Blom, T. N., Wagenmakers, E.-J., & Van Rijn, H. (2015). On making the right choice: A meta-analysis and large-scale replication attempt of the unconscious thought advantage. *Judgment and Decision Making*, 10(1), 1–17. https://doi.org/10.1017/S19302 9750003144

Nilson, C., Fetherston, C., McMurray, A., & Fetherston, T. (2013). Creative arts: An essential element in the teacher's toolkit when developing critical thinking in children. *Australian Journal of Teacher Education, 38*(7). https://doi.org/10.14221/ajte.2013v38n7.4

Nir, Y., & Tononi, G. (2010). Dreaming and the brain: From phenomenology to neurophysiology. *Trends in Cognitive Sciences, 14*(2), 88–100. https://doi.org/10.1016/j.tics.2009.12.001

Nisbett, R. E. (2004). *The geography of thought: How Asians and Westerners think differently ... and why.* Free Press.

Nisbett, R. E., Peng, K., Choi, I., & Norenzayan, A. (2001). Culture and systems of thought: Holistic versus analytic cognition. *Psychological Review, 108*(2), 291–310. https://doi.org/10.1037/0033-295X.108.2.291

Nolen-Hoeksema, S., Wisco, B. E., & Lyubomirsky, S. (2008). Rethinking rumination. *Perspectives on Psychological Science, 3*(5), 400–424. https://doi.org/10.1111/j.1745-6924.2008.00088.x

Norenzayan, A. (2013). *Big Gods: How religion transformed cooperation and conflict.* Princeton University Press. https://doi.org/10.1515/9781400848324

Norenzayan, A., & Gervais, W. M. (2013). The origins of religious disbelief. *Trends in Cognitive Sciences, 17*(1), 20–25. https://doi.org/10.1016/j.tics.2012.11.006

Norenzayan, A., Gervais, W. M., & Trzesniewski, K. H. (2012). Mentalizing deficits constrain belief in a personal god. *PLoS ONE, 7*(5), e36880. https://doi.org/10.1371/journal.pone.0036880

Norman, G. R., Monteiro, S. D., Sherbino, J., Ilgen, J. S., Schmidt, H. G., & Mamede, S. (2017). The causes of errors in clinical reasoning: Cognitive biases, knowledge deficits, and dual process thinking. *Academic Medicine, 92*(1), 23–30. https://doi.org/10.1097/ACM.0000000000001421

Nosek, B. A., Hardwicke, T. E., Moshontz, H., Allard, A., Corker, K. S., Dreber, A., Fidler, F., Hilgard, J., Kline Struhl, M., Nuijten, M. B., Rohrer, J. M., Romero, F., Scheel, A. M., Scherer, L. D., Schönbrodt, F. D., & Vazire, S. (2022). Replicability, robustness, and reproducibility in psychological science. *Annual Review of Psychology, 73*(1), 719–748. https://doi.org/10.1146/annurev-psych-020821-114157

Obaidi, M., Bergh, R., Akrami, N., & Anjum, G. (2019). Group-based relative deprivation explains endorsement of extremism among Western-Born Muslims. *Psychological Science, 30*(4), 596–605. https://doi.org/10.1177/0956797619834879

Obaidi, M., Bergh, R., Sidanius, J., & Thomsen, L. (2018). The mistreatment of my people: Victimization by proxy and behavioral intentions to commit violence among Muslims in Denmark: Victimization by proxy. *Political Psychology, 39*(3), 577–593. https://doi.org/10.1111/pops.12435

Oktar, K., & Lombrozo, T. (2022). Deciding to be authentic: Intuition is favored over deliberation when authenticity matters. *Cognition, 223*, 105021. https://doi.org/10.1016/j.cognition.2022.105021

Onraet, E., Van Hiel, A., Dhont, K., & Pattyn, S. (2013). Internal and external threat in relationship with right-wing attitudes. *Journal of Personality, 81*(3), 233–248. https://doi.org/10.1111/jopy.12011

Open Science Collaboration. (2015). Estimating the reproducibility of psychological science. *Science, 349*(6251), aac4716. https://doi.org/10.1126/science.aac4716

Ortmann, A., Gigerenzer, G., Borges, B., & Goldstein, D. G. (2008). The recognition heuristic: A fast and frugal way to investment choice? In *Handbook of experimental economics results* (Vol. 1, pp. 993–1003). Elsevier. https://doi.org/10.1016/S1574-0722(07)00107-2

Osman, M. (2004). An evaluation of dual-process theories of reasoning. *Psychonomic Bulletin & Review, 11*(6), 988–1010. https://doi.org/10.3758/BF03196730

Osman, M. (2023). Using the study of reasoning to address the age of unreason. *Behavioral and Brain Sciences, 46*, e135. https://doi.org/10.1017/S0140525X2 2002953

Overmier, J. B., & Seligman, M. E. (1967). Effects of inescapable shock upon subsequent escape and avoidance responding. *Journal of Comparative and Physiological Psychology, 63*(1), 28–33. https://doi.org/10.1037/h0024166

Oxley, D. R., Smith, K. B., Alford, J. R., Hibbing, M. V., Miller, J. L., Scalora, M., Hatemi, P. K., & Hibbing, J. R. (2008). Political attitudes vary with physiological traits. *Science, 321*(5896), 1667–1670. https://doi.org/10.1126/science.1157627

Pacini, R., & Epstein, S. (1999). The relation of rational and experiential information processing styles to personality, basic beliefs, and the ratio-bias phenomenon. *Journal of Personality and Social Psychology, 76*(6), 972–987. https://doi.org/10.1037/0022-3514.76.6.972

Papageorgiou, C., & Wells, A. (2001). Metacognitive beliefs about rumination in recurrent major depression. *Cognitive and Behavioral Practice, 8*(2), 160–164. https://doi.org/10.1016/S1077-7229(01)80021-3

Papineau, D. (2015). Choking and the yips. *Phenomenology and the Cognitive Sciences, 14*(2), 295–308. https://doi.org/10.1007/s11097-014-9383-x

Parker, A. M., Bruine De Bruin, W., Fischhoff, B., & Weller, J. (2018). Robustness of decision-making competence: Evidence from two measures and an 11-year longitudinal study: Decision-making competence. *Journal of Behavioral Decision Making, 31*(3), 380–391. https://doi.org/10.1002/bdm.2059

Parmentier, F. B. R., García-Toro, M., García-Campayo, J., Yañez, A. M., Andrés, P., & Gili, M. (2019). Mindfulness and symptoms of depression and anxiety in the general population: the mediating roles of worry, rumination, reappraisal and suppression. *Frontiers in Psychology, 10*, 506. https://doi.org/10.3389/fpsyg.2019.00506

Payne, B. K. (2001). Prejudice and perception: The role of automatic and controlled processes in misperceiving a weapon. *Journal of Personality and Social Psychology, 81*(2), 181–192. https://doi.org/10.1037/0022-3514.81.2.181

Payne, J. W., Samper, A., Bettman, J. R., & Luce, M. F. (2008). Boundary conditions on unconscious thought in complex decision making. *Psychological Science, 19*(11), 1118–1123. https://doi.org/10.1111/j.1467-9280.2008.02212.x

Pedroni, A., Eisenegger, C., Hartmann, M. N., Fischbacher, U., & Knoch, D. (2014). Dopaminergic stimulation increases selfish behavior in the absence of punishment threat. *Psychopharmacology, 231*(1), 135–141. https://doi.org/10.1007/s00 213-013-3210-x

Pellegrini, V., De Cristofaro, V., Salvati, M., Giacomantonio, M., & Leone, L. (2021). Social exclusion and anti-immigration attitudes in Europe: The mediating role of interpersonal trust. *Social Indicators Research, 155*(2), 697–724. https://doi.org/10.1007/s11205-021-02618-6

Peng, K., Spencer-Rodgers, J., & Nian, Z. (2006). Naïve dialecticism and the tao of Chinese thought. In U. Kim, K.-S. Yang, & K.-K. Hwang (Eds.), *Indigenous and cultural psychology* (pp. 247–262). Springer US. https://doi.org/10.1007/0-387-28662-4_11

Pennycook, G. (2017). A perspective on the theoretical foundation of Dual Process Models. In W. De Neys (Ed.), *Dual process theory 2.0* (1st ed., pp. 5–27). Routledge. https://doi.org/10.4324/9781315204550-2

Pennycook, G. (2018). *The new reflectionism in cognitive psychology: Why reasons matter.* Routledge, Taylor & Francis Group.

Pennycook, G. (2023). A framework for understanding reasoning errors: From fake news to climate change and beyond. In *Advances in experimental social psychology* (Vol. 67, pp. 131–208). Elsevier. https://doi.org/10.1016/bs.aesp.2022.11.003

Pennycook, G., Cheyne, J. A., Barr, N., Koehler, D. J., & Fugelsang, J. A. (2014). The role of analytic thinking in moral judgements and values. *Thinking & Reasoning, 20*(2), 188–214. https://doi.org/10.1080/13546783.2013.865000

Pennycook, G., Cheyne, J. A., Barr, N., Koehler, D. J., & Fugelsang, J. A. (2015). On the reception and detection of pseudo-profound bullshit. *Judgment and Decision Making, 10*(6), 549–563. https://doi.org/10.1017/S1930297500006999

Pennycook, G., Cheyne, J. A., Koehler, D. J., & Fugelsang, J. A. (2020). On the belief that beliefs should change according to evidence: Implications for conspiratorial, moral, paranormal, political, religious, and science beliefs. *Judgment and Decision Making, 15*(4), 476–498. https://doi.org/10.1017/S1930297500007439

Pennycook, G., Cheyne, J. A., Seli, P., Koehler, D. J., & Fugelsang, J. A. (2012). Analytic cognitive style predicts religious and paranormal belief. *Cognition, 123*(3), 335–346. https://doi.org/10.1016/j.cognition.2012.03.003

Pennycook, G., Fugelsang, J. A., & Koehler, D. J. (2012). Are we good at detecting conflict during reasoning? *Cognition, 124*(1), 101–106. https://doi.org/10.1016/j.cognition.2012.04.004

Pennycook, G., Fugelsang, J. A., & Koehler, D. J. (2015). What makes us think? A three-stage dual-process model of analytic engagement. *Cognitive Psychology, 80*, 34–72. https://doi.org/10.1016/j.cogpsych.2015.05.001

Pennycook, G., Neys, W. D., Evans, J. St. B. T., Stanovich, K. E., & Thompson, V. A. (2018). The mythical dual-process typology. *Trends in Cognitive Sciences, 22*(8), 667–668. https://doi.org/10.1016/j.tics.2018.04.008

Pennycook, G., & Rand, D. G. (2019). Lazy, not biased: Susceptibility to partisan fake news is better explained by lack of reasoning than by motivated reasoning. *Cognition, 188*, 39–50. https://doi.org/10.1016/j.cognition.2018.06.011

Pennycook, G., Ross, R. M., Koehler, D. J., & Fugelsang, J. A. (2016). Atheists and agnostics are more reflective than religious believers: Four empirical studies and a meta-analysis. *PLoS ONE, 11*(4), e0153039. https://doi.org/10.1371/journal.pone.0153039

Perone, S., & Simmering, V. R. (2017). Applications of dynamic systems theory to cognition and development. In *Advances in child development and behavior* (Vol. 52, pp. 43–80). *Elsevier.* https://doi.org/10.1016/bs.acdb.2016.10.002

Petrocik, J. R. (1996). Issue ownership in presidential elections, with a 1980 case study. *American Journal of Political Science, 40*(3), 825. https://doi.org/10.2307/2111797

Petty, R. E., & Cacioppo, J. T. (1986). The elaboration likelihood model of persuasion. In *Advances in experimental social psychology* (Vol. 19, pp. 123–205). *Elsevier.* https://doi.org/10.1016/S0065-2601(08)60214-2

Petty, R. E., & Krosnick, J. A. (Eds.). (1995). *Attitude strength: Antecedents and consequences.* Lawrence Erlbaum Associates.

Piaget, J. (1952). *The origins of intelligence in children.* (M. Cook, Trans.). W. W. Norton & Co. https://doi.org/10.1037/11494-000

Piaget, J. (1965). *The moral judgment of the child.* Harcourt, Brace.

Piaget, J. (1967). *The psychology of intelligence.* Random House.

Piazza, J. A. (2011). Poverty, minority economic discrimination, and domestic terrorism. *Journal of Peace Research,* 48(3), 339–353. https://doi.org/10 1177/0022343310397404

Piazza, J., & Sousa, P. (2014). Religiosity, political orientation, and consequentialist moral thinking. *Social Psychological and Personality Science,* 5(3), 334–342. https://doi.org/10.1177/1948550613492826

Pigliucci, M. (2007). The trouble with memetics. *Skeptical Inquirer,* 31(5), 23–24.

Pinker, S. (2003). Language as an adaptation to the cognitive niche. In M. H. Christiansen & S. Kirby (Eds.), *Language evolution* (pp. 16–37). Oxford University Press. https://doi.org/10.1093/acprof:oso/9780199244843.003.0002

Pinker, S. (2021). *Rationality: What it is, why it seems scarce, why it matters* (1st ed). Viking.

Plato. (2002). *Phaedrus* (R. Waterfield, Trans.). Oxford University Press.

Pobiner, B. L. (2020). The zooarchaeology and paleoecology of early hominin scavenging. *Evolutionary Anthropology: Issues, News, and Reviews,* 29(2), 68–82. https://doi.org/10.1002/evan.21824

Pohl, R. F. (Ed.). (2022). *Cognitive illusions: Intriguing phenomena in judgement, thinking and memory* (3rd ed.). Routledge.

Popper, K. R. (1971). *The open society and its enemies: The spell of Plato* (5 ed., (rev.), 1. Princeton paperback print). Princeton University Press.

Porcelli, A. J., & Delgado, M. R. (2009). Acute stress modulates risk taking in financial decision making. *Psychological Science,* 20(3), 278–283. https://doi.org/10.1111/j.1467-9280.2009.02288.x

Porter, T., Baldwin, C. R., Warren, M. T., Murray, E. D., Cotton Bronk, K., Forgeard, M. J. C., Snow, N. E., & Jayawickreme, E. (2022). Clarifying the content of intellectual humility: A systematic review and integrative framework. *Journal of Personality Assessment,* 104(5), 573–585. https://doi.org/10.1080/00223 891.2021.1975725

Porter, T., Elnakouri, A., Meyers, E. A., Shibayama, T., Jayawickreme, E., & Grossmann, I. (2022). Predictors and consequences of intellectual humility. *Nature Reviews Psychology,* 1(9), 524–536. https://doi.org/10.1038/s44 159-022-00081-9

Post, J. M. (2010). "When hatred is bred in the bone:" The social psychology of terrorism: The social psychology of terrorism. *Annals of the New York Academy of Sciences,* 1208(1), 15–23. https://doi.org/10.1111/j.1749-6632.2010.05694 x

Potts, S. R., McCuddy, W. T., Jayan, D., & Porcelli, A. J. (2019). To trust, or not to trust? Individual differences in physiological reactivity predict trust under acute stress. *Psychoneuroendocrinology,* 100, 75–84. https://doi.org/10.1016/j.psyne uen.2018.09.019

Prentice, D. A., & Miller, D. T. (1992). When small effects are impressive. *Psychological Bulletin,* 112(1), 160–164. https://doi.org/10.1037/0033-2909.112.1.160

Pretz, J. E., & Totz, K. S. (2007). Measuring individual differences in affective, heuristic, and holistic intuition. *Personality and Individual Differences,* 43(5), 1247–1257. https://doi.org/10.1016/j.paid.2007.03.015

Pryor, C., Perfors, A., & Howe, P. D. L. (2018). Even arbitrary norms influence moral decision-making. *Nature Human Behaviour*, *3*(1), 57–62. https://doi.org/10.1038/s41562-018-0489-y

Pyszczynski, T., Greenberg, J., & Solomon, S. (1999). A dual-process model of defense against conscious and unconscious death-related thoughts: An extension of terror management theory. *Psychological Review*, *106*(4), 835–845. https://doi.org/10.1037/0033-295X.106.4.835

Pyszczynski, T., Greenberg, J., Solomon, S., Arndt, J., & Schimel, J. (2004). Why do people need self-esteem? A theoretical and empirical review. *Psychological Bulletin*, *130*(3), 435–468. https://doi.org/10.1037/0033-2909.130.3.435

Pyszczynski, T., Solomon, S., & Greenberg, J. (2015). Thirty years of terror management theory. In *Advances in experimental social psychology* (Vol. 52, pp. 1–70). *Elsevier.* https://doi.org/10.1016/bs.aesp.2015.03.001

Raeff, C. (2020). *Exploring the complexities of human action.* Oxford University Press.

Raichle, M. E. (2015). The brain's default mode network. *Annual Review of Neuroscience*, *38*(1), 433–447. https://doi.org/10.1146/annurev-neuro-071013-014030

Ramakrishnan, S., Robbins, T. W., & Zmigrod, L. (2022). Cognitive rigidity, habitual tendencies, and obsessive-compulsive symptoms: individual differences and compensatory interactions. *Frontiers in Psychiatry*, *13*, 865896. https://doi.org/10.3389/fpsyt.2022.865896

Rand, D. G. (2016). Cooperation, fast and slow: Meta-analytic evidence for a theory of social heuristics and self-interested deliberation. *Psychological Science*, *27*(9), 1192–1206. https://doi.org/10.1177/0956797616654455

Rand, D. G., Greene, J. D., & Nowak, M. A. (2012). Spontaneous giving and calculated greed. *Nature*, *489*(7416), 427–430. https://doi.org/10.1038/nature11467

Rand, D. G., Newman, G. E., & Wurzbacher, O. M. (2015). Social context and the dynamics of cooperative choice. *Journal of Behavioral Decision Making*, *28*(2), 159–166. https://doi.org/10.1002/bdm.1837

Rand, D. G., & Nowak, M. A. (2013). Human cooperation. *Trends in Cognitive Sciences*, *17*(8), 413–425. https://doi.org/10.1016/j.tics.2013.06.003

Rand, D. G., Peysakhovich, A., Kraft-Todd, G. T., Newman, G. E., Wurzbacher, O., Nowak, M. A., & Greene, J. D. (2014). Social heuristics shape intuitive cooperation. *Nature Communications*, *5*(1), 3677. https://doi.org/10.1038/ncomms4677

Raoelison, M., Boissin, E., Borst, G., & De Neys, W. (2021). From slow to fast logic: The development of logical intuitions. *Thinking & Reasoning*, *27*(4), 599–622. https://doi.org/10.1080/13546783.2021.1885488

Raoelison, M., Thompson, V. A., & De Neys, W. (2020). The smart intuitor: Cognitive capacity predicts intuitive rather than deliberate thinking. *Cognition*, *204*, 104381. https://doi.org/10.1016/j.cognition.2020.104381

Reber, A. S. (1989). Implicit learning and tacit knowledge. *Journal of Experimental Psychology: General*, *118*(3), 219–235. https://doi.org/10.1037/0096-3445.118.3.219

Reber, R., & Unkelbach, C. (2010). The epistemic status of processing fluency as source for judgments of truth. *Review of Philosophy and Psychology*, *1*(4), 563–581. https://doi.org/10.1007/s13164-010-0039-7

Reidy, K. (2019). Benevolent radicalization: An antidote to terrorism. *Perspectives on Terrorism*, *13*(4), 1–13.

Reitsma-van Rooijen, M., & Daamen, D. D. L. (2006). Subliminal anchoring: The effects of subliminally presented numbers on probability estimates. *Journal of Experimental Social Psychology*, *42*(3), 380–387. https://doi.org/10.1016/j.jesp.2005.05.001

Reyna, V. F (2012). A new intuitionism: Meaning, memory, and development in fuzzy-trace theory. *Judgment and Decision Making*, *7*(3), 332–359. https://doi.org/10.1017/S1930297500002291

Reyna, V. F., & Brainerd, C. J. (1995). Fuzzy-trace theory: An interim synthesis. *Learning and Individual Differences*, *7*(1), 1–75. https://doi.org/10.1016/1041-6030(95)90031-4

Reyna, V. F., Chick, C. F., Corbin, J. C., & Hsia, A. N. (2014). Developmental reversals in risky decision making: Intelligence agents show larger decision biases than college students. *Psychological Science*, *25*(1), 76–84. https://doi.org/10.1177/0956797613497022

Reyna, V. F, & Ellis, S. C. (1994). Fuzzy-trace theory and framing effects in children's risky decision making. *Psychological Science*, *5*(5), 275–279. https://doi.org/10.1111/j.1467-9280.1994.tb00625.x

Reyna, V. F., & Farley, F. (2006). Risk and rationality in adolescent decision making: Implications for theory, practice, and public policy. *Psychological Science in the Public Interest*, *7*(1), 1–44. https://doi.org/10.1111/j.1529-1006.2006.00026.x

Reyna, V. F., & Kiernan, B. (1994). Development of gist versus verbatim memory in sentence recognition: Effects of lexical familiarity, semantic content, encoding instructions, and retention interval. *Developmental Psychology*, *30*(2), 178–191. https://doi.org/10.1037/0012-1649.30.2.178

Reyna, V. F., & Lloyd, F. J. (2006). Physician decision making and cardiac risk: Effects of knowledge, risk perception, risk tolerance, and fuzzy processing. *Journal of Experimental Psychology: Applied*, *12*(3), 179–195. https://doi.org/10.1037/1076-898X.12.3.179

Reyna, V. F., & Mills, B. A. (2007). Interference processes in fuzzy-trace theory: Aging, Alzheimer's disease, and development. In D. S. Gorfein, & C. M. MacLeod (Eds.), *Inhibition in cognition* (pp. 185–210). American Psychological Association. https://doi.org/10.1037/11587-010

Reyna, V. F., & Mills, B. A. (2014). Theoretically motivated interventions for reducing sexual risk taking in adolescence: A randomized controlled experiment applying fuzzy-trace theory. *Journal of Experimental Psychology: General*, *143*(4), 1627–1648. https://doi.org/10.1037/a0036717

Reyna, V F., Rahimi-Golkhandan, S., Garavito, D. M. N., & Helm, R. K. (2017). The fuzzy-trace dual process model. In W. De Neys (Ed.), *Dual process theory 2.0* (1st ed., pp. 82–99). Routledge. https://doi.org/10.4324/9781315204550-6

Richard, F. D., Bond, C. F., & Stokes-Zoota, J. J. (2003). One hundred years of social psychology quantitatively described. *Review of General Psychology*, *7*(4), 331–363. https://doi.org/10.1037/1089-2680.7.4.331

Robertson, D. (2020). *The philosophy of cognitive-behavioural therapy (CBT): Stoic philosophy as rational and cognitive psychotherapy* (2nd ed.). Routledge.

Robila, M., & Robila, S. A. (2020). Applications of artificial intelligence methodologies to behavioral and social sciences. *Journal of Child and Family Studies*, *29*(10), 2954–2966. https://doi.org/10.1007/s10826-019-01689-x

Robinson, P. (2022). The relationship between reflective disposition and persistence in education. *Journal of Educational, Cultural and Psychological Studies (ECPS Journal)*, *25*, 1. https://doi.org/10.7358/ecps-2022-025-robi

Romer, D., Reyna, V. F., & Satterthwaite, T. D. (2017). Beyond stereotypes of adolescent risk taking: Placing the adolescent brain in developmental context. *Developmental Cognitive Neuroscience*, *27*, 19–34. https://doi.org/10.1016/j.dcn.2017.07.007

Röseler, L., Schütz, A., Blank, P. A., Dück, M., Fels, S., Kupfer, J., Scheelje, L., & Seida, C. (2021). Evidence against subliminal anchoring: Two close, highly powered, preregistered, and failed replication attempts. *Journal of Experimental Social Psychology*, *92*, 104066. https://doi.org/10.1016/j.jesp.2020.104066

Rosenberg, S. (2017). Unfit for democracy? Irrational, rationalizing, and biologically predisposed citizens. *Critical Review*, *29*(3), 362–387. https://doi.org/10.1080/08913811.2017.1410982

Rosenberg, S. W. (2002). *The not so common sense: Differences in how people judge social and political life*. Yale University Press.

Rosenblatt, A., Greenberg, J., Solomon, S., Pyszczynski, T., & Lyon, D. (1989). Evidence for terror management theory: I. The effects of mortality salience on reactions to those who violate or uphold cultural values. *Journal of Personality and Social Psychology*, *57*(4), 681–690. https://doi.org/10.1037/0022-3514.57.4.681

Ross, L., & Ward, A. (1996). *Naive realism in everyday life: Implications for social conflict and misunderstanding* (By E. S. Reed, E. Turiel, & T. Brown; pp. 103–135). Lawrence Erlbaum Associates.

Ross, M., & Sicoly, F. (1979). Egocentric biases in availability and attribution. *Journal of Personality and Social Psychology*, *37*(3), 322–336. https://doi.org/10.1037/0022-3514.37.3.322

Rottweiler, B., & Gill, P. (2022a). Conspiracy beliefs and violent extremist intentions: The contingent effects of self-efficacy, self-control and law-related morality. *Terrorism and Political Violence*, *34*(7), 1485–1504. https://doi.org/10.1080/09546553.2020.1803288

Rottweiler, B., & Gill, P. (2022b). Individual differences in personality moderate the effects of perceived group deprivation on violent extremism: Evidence from a United Kingdom nationally representative survey. *Frontiers in Psychology*, *13*, 790770. https://doi.org/10.3389/fpsyg.2022.790770

Roux, C., Goldsmith, K., & Bonezzi, A. (2015). On the psychology of scarcity: when reminders of resource scarcity promote selfish (and generous) behavior. *Journal of Consumer Research*, *ucv048*. https://doi.org/10.1093/jcr/ucv048

Rozin, P., & Royzman, E. B. (2001). Negativity bias, negativity dominance, and contagion. *Personality and Social Psychology Review*, *5*(4), 296–320. https://doi.org/10.1207/S15327957PSPR0504_2

Rudnev, M., Buckwalter, W., Barr, K., Bencherifa, A., Clancy, R. F., Crone, D. L., Deguchi, Y., Fabiano, E., Fodeman, A. D., Guennoun, B., Halamova, J., Hashimoto, T., Homan, J., Kanovský, M., Karasawa, K., Kim, H., Kiper, J., Lee, M., Liu, X., … Grossmann, I. (2023). *Social perception of wisdom across cultures*. https://doi.org/10.31234/osf.io/p9cv4

Ruscio, A. M., Seitchik, A. E., Gentes, E. L., Jones, J. D., & Hallion, L. S. (2011). Perseverative thought: A robust predictor of response to emotional challenge in generalized anxiety disorder and major depressive disorder. *Behaviour Research and Therapy*, 49(12), 867–874. https://doi.org/10.1016/j.brat.2011.10.001

Ruscio, A. M., Stein, D. J., Chiu, W. T., & Kessler, R. C. (2010). The epidemiology of obsessive–compulsive disorder in the National Comorbidity Survey Replication. *Molecular Psychiatry*, 15(1), 53–63. https://doi.org/10.1038/mp.2008.94

Russell, J. A. (2003). Core affect and the psychological construction of emotion. *Psychological Review*, 110(1), 145–172. https://doi.org/10.1037/0033-295X.110.1.145

Sadler-Smith, E. (2007). *Inside intuition*. Routledge.

Sætrevik, B., & Sjåstad, H. (2022). Mortality salience effects fail to replicate in traditional and novel measures. *Meta-Psychology*, 6. https://doi.org/10.15626/MP.2020.2628

Sageman, M. (2004). *Understanding terror networks*. University of Pennsylvania Press.

Salahshour, M. (2020). Coevolution of cooperation and language. *Physical Review E*, 102(4), 042409. https://doi.org/10.1103/PhysRevE.102.042409

Salter, M. E., Duymaç, F. Y., Yilmaz, O., Bahçekapili, H. G., & Harma, M. (2023). Is negativity bias intuitive for liberals and conservatives? *Current Psychology*, 42(15), 12374–12386. https://doi.org/10.1007/s12144-021-02557-y

Sanchez, C., Sundermeier, B., Gray, K., & Calin-Jageman, R. J. (2017). Direct replication of Gervais & Norenzayan (2012): No evidence that analytic thinking decreases religious belief. *PLoS ONE*, 12(2), e0172636. https://doi.org/10.1371/journal.pone.0172636

Sardoč, M., Coady, C. A. J., Bufacchi, V., Moghaddam, F. M., Cassam, Q., Silva, D., Miščević, N., Andrejč, G., Kodelja, Z., Vezjak, B., Peters, M. A., & Tesar, M. (2022). Philosophy of education in a new key: On radicalization and violent extremism. *Educational Philosophy and Theory*, 54(8), 1162–1177. https://doi.org/10.1080/00131857.2020.1861937

Sarıbay, S. A., Okcaysoy Ökten, I., & Yılmaz, O. (2017). Kişisel ve Toplumsal Düzeylerde Eşitliğe Karşıtlık ve Değişime Direnmenin Muhafazakârlıkla İlişkisi. *Türk Psikoloji Yazıları*, 39, 24–41.

Saribay, S. A., & Yilmaz, O. (2017). Analytic cognitive style and cognitive ability differentially predict religiosity and social conservatism. *Personality and Individual Differences*, 114, 24–29. https://doi.org/10.1016/j.paid.2017.03.056

Saribay, S. A., & Yilmaz, O. (2018). Relationships between core ideological motives, social and economic conservatism, and religiosity: Evidence from a Turkish sample. *Asian Journal of Social Psychology*, 21(3), 205–211. https://doi.org/10.1111/ajsp.12213

Saribay, S. A., Yilmaz, O., & Körpe, G. G. (2020). Does intuitive mindset influence belief in God? A registered replication of. *Judgment and Decision Making*, 15(2), 193–202. https://doi.org/10.1017/S1930297500007348

Sarkissian, H., Park, J., Tien, D., Wright, J. C., & Knobe, J. (2014). Folk moral relativism. In J. Knobe, & S. Nichols (Eds.), *Experimental philosophy* (pp. 169–192). Oxford University Press. https://doi.org/10.1093/acprof:osobl/9780199927418.003.0008

Sarma, K. M., Carthy, S. L., & Cox, K. M. (2022). Mental disorder, psychological problems and terrorist behaviour: A systematic review and meta-analysis. *Campbell Systematic Reviews*, 18(3), e1268. https://doi.org/10.1002/cl2.1268

Saucier, G., Akers, L. G., Shen-Miller, S., Knežević, G., & Stankov, L. (2009). Patterns of thinking in militant extremism. *Perspectives on Psychological Science*, *4*(3), 256–271. https://doi.org/10.1111/j.1745-6924.2009.01123.x

Sauer, H. (2015). Can't we all disagree more constructively? moral foundations, moral reasoning, and political disagreement. *Neuroethics*, *8*(2), 153–169. https://doi.org/10.1007/s12152-015-9235-6

Schachter, S., & Singer, J. (1962). Cognitive, social, and physiological determinants of emotional state. *Psychological Review*, *69*(5), 379–399. https://doi.org/10.1037/h0046234

Schäfer, T., & Schwarz, M. A. (2019). The meaningfulness of effect sizes in psychological research: differences between sub-disciplines and the impact of potential biases. *Frontiers in Psychology*, *10*, 813. https://doi.org/10.3389/fpsyg.2019.00813

Scheffer, J. A., Cameron, C. D., & Inzlicht, M. (2022). Caring is costly: People avoid the cognitive work of compassion. *Journal of Experimental Psychology: General*, *151*(1), 172–196. https://doi.org/10.1037/xge0001073

Schimmack, U. (2021). The validation crisis in psychology. *Meta-Psychology*, *5*. https://doi.org/10.15626/MP.2019.1645

Schindler, S., Reinhardt, N., & Reinhard, M.-A. (2021). Defending one's worldview under mortality salience: Testing the validity of an established idea. *Journal of Experimental Social Psychology*, *93*, 104087. https://doi.org/10.1016/j.jesp.2020.104087

Schmid, A. (Ed.). (2011). The definition of terrorism. In *The Routledge handbook of terrorism research* (0 ed., pp. 39–157). Routledge. https://doi.org/10.4324/9780203828731-10

Schnall, S. (2017). Disgust as embodied loss aversion. *European Review of Social Psychology*, *28*(1), 50–94. https://doi.org/10.1080/10463283.2016.1259844

Schoenemann, P. T. (2009). Evolution of brain and language. *Language Learning*, *59*, 162–186. https://doi.org/10.1111/j.1467-9922.2009.00539.x

Schooler, J. W., & Engstler-Schooler, T. Y. (1990). Verbal overshadowing of visual memories: Some things are better left unsaid. *Cognitive Psychology*, *22*(1), 36–71. https://doi.org/10.1016/0010-0285(90)90003-M

Schooler, J. W., Ohlsson, S., & Brooks, K. (1993). Thoughts beyond words: When language overshadows insight. *Journal of Experimental Psychology: General*, *122*(2), 166–183. https://doi.org/10.1037/0096-3445.122.2.166

Schreiber, D., Fonzo, G., Simmons, A. N., Dawes, C. T., Flagan, T., Fowler, J. H., & Paulus, M. P. (2013). Red brain, blue brain: Evaluative processes differ in democrats and Republicans. *PLoS ONE*, *8*(2), e52970. https://doi.org/10.1371/journal.pone.0052970

Schumpe, B. M., Bélanger, J. J., Moyano, M., & Nisa, C. F. (2020). The role of sensation seeking in political violence: An extension of the Significance Quest Theory. *Journal of Personality and Social Psychology*, *118*(4), 743–761. https://doi.org/10.1037/pspp0000223

Schut, H. (1999). The dual process model of coping with bereavement: Rationale and description. *Death Studies*, *23*(3), 197–224.

Schuurman, B., Lindekilde, L., Malthaner, S., O'Connor, F., Gill, P., & Bouhana, N. (2019). End of the Lone Wolf: The typology that should not have been. *Studies in Conflict & Terrorism*, *42*(8), 771–778. https://doi.org/10.1080/1057610X.2017.1419554

Schwartz, B., Ward, A., Monterosso, J., Lyubomirsky, S., White, K., & Lehman, D. R. (2002). Maximizing versus satisficing: Happiness is a matter of choice. *Journal of Personality and Social Psychology*, 83(5), 1178–1197. https://doi.org/10.1037/0022-3514.83.5.1178

Schwarz, N (2012). Feelings-as-information theory. In P. Van Lange, A. Kruglanski, & E. Higgins (Eds.), *Handbook of theories of social psychology: Volume 1* (pp. 289–308). SAGE Publications Ltd. https://doi.org/10.4135/9781446249215.n15

Schwarz, N., & Bless, H. (1991). Happy and mindless, but sad and smart? The impact of affective states on analytic reasoning. In J. P. Forgas (Ed.), *Emotion and social judgments* (1st ed., pp. 55–71). Pergamon Press. https://doi.org/10.4324/9781003058731-4

Scott, W. A. (1960). International ideology and interpersonal ideology. *Public Opinion Quarterly*, 24(3), 419. https://doi.org/10.1086/266961

Sedikides, C., & Brewer, M. B. (Eds.). (2015). *Individual self, relational self, collective self* (0 ed.). Psychology Press. https://doi.org/10.4324/9781315783024

Seeberg, H. B. (2017). How stable is political parties' issue ownership? A cross-time, cross-national analysis. *Political Studies*, 65(2), 475–492. https://doi.org/10.1177/0032321716650224

Shah, A. K., Mullainathan, S., & Shafir, E. (2012). Some consequences of having too little. *Science*, 338(6107), 682–685. https://doi.org/10.1126/science.1222426

Shanks, D. R., Barbieri-Hermitte, P., & Vadillo, M. A. (2020). Do incidental environmental anchors bias consumers' price estimations? *Collabra: Psychology*, 6(1), 19. https://doi.org/10.1525/collabra.310

Sharma, E., & Alter, A. L. (2012). Financial deprivation prompts consumers to seek scarce goods. *Journal of Consumer Research*, 39(3), 545–560. https://doi.org/10.1086/664038

Sheeran, P., & Webb, T. L. (2016). The intention–behavior gap. *Social and Personality Psychology Compass*, 10(9), 503–518. https://doi.org/10.1111/spc3.12265

Sheldrake, R. (2012). *The science delusion: Freeing the spirit of enquiriy*. Coronet.

Shenhav, A., Musslick, S., Lieder, F., Kool, W., Griffiths, T. L., Cohen, J. D., & Botvinick, M. M. (2017). Toward a rational and mechanistic account of mental effort. *Annual Review of Neuroscience*, 40(1), 99–124. https://doi.org/10.1146/annurev-neuro-072116-031526

Shenhav, A., Rand, D. G., & Greene, J. D. (2012). Divine intuition: Cognitive style influences belief in God. *Journal of Experimental Psychology: General*, 141(3), 423–428. https://doi.org/10.1037/a0025391

Sherbino, J., Dore, K. L., Wood, T. J., Young, M. E., Gaissmaier, W., Kreuger, S., & Norman, G. R. (2012). The relationship between response time and diagnostic accuracy. *Academic Medicine*, 87(6), 785–791. https://doi.org/10.1097/ACM.0b013e318253acbd

Sherif, M. (Ed.). (1988). *The robbers cave experiment: Intergroup conflict and cooperation (Reprint)*. Wesleyan University Press.

Sherman, J. W., Gawronski, B., & Trope, Y. (Eds.). (2014). *Dual-process theories of the social mind*. The Guilford Press.

Shiffrin, R. M., & Schneider, W. (1977). Controlled and automatic human information processing: II. Perceptual learning, automatic attending and a general theory. *Psychological Review*, 84(2), 127–190. https://doi.org/10.1037/0033-295X.84.2.127

Shweder, R. A., Much, N. C., Mahapatra, M., & Park, L. (1997). The "big three" of morality (autonomy, community, divinity) and the "big three" explanations of suffering. In A. Brandt & P. Rozin (Eds.), *Morality and health* (pp. 119–169). Routledge.

Sibley, C. G., Osborne, D., & Duckitt, J. (2012). Personality and political orientation: Meta-analysis and test of a threat-constraint model. *Journal of Research in Personality*, 46(6), 664–677. https://doi.org/10.1016/j.jrp.2012.08.002

Siegle, G. J., Price, R. B., Jones, N. P., Ghinassi, F., Painter, T., & Thase, M. E. (2014). You gotta work at it: Pupillary indices of task focus are prognostic for response to a neurocognitive intervention for rumination in depression. *Clinical Psychological Science*, 2(4), 455–471. https://doi.org/10.1177/2167702614536160

Sih, A., & Del Giudice, M. (2012). Linking behavioural syndromes and cognition: A behavioural ecology perspective. *Philosophical Transactions of the Royal Society B: Biological Sciences*, 367(1603), 2762–2772. https://doi.org/10.1098/rstb.2012.0216

Silke, A. (2008). Holy warriors: Exploring the psychological processes of Jihadi radicalization. *European Journal of Criminology*, 5(1), 99–123. https://doi.org/10.1177/1477370807084226

Simmons, J. P., LeBoeuf, R. A., & Nelson, L. D. (2010). The effect of accuracy motivation on anchoring and adjustment: Do people adjust from provided anchors? *Journal of Personality and Social Psychology*, 99(6), 917–932. https://doi.org/10.1037/a0021540

Simmons, J. P., Nelson, L. D., & Simonsohn, U. (2011). False-positive psychology: Undisclosed flexibility in data collection and analysis allows presenting anything as significant. *Psychological Science*, 22(11), 1359–1366. https://doi.org/10.1177/0956797611417632

Simon, H. A. (1955). A behavioral model of rational choice. *The Quarterly Journal of Economics*, 99–118. https://doi.org/10.2307/1884852

Simon, H. A. (1956). Rational choice and the structure of the environment. *Psychological Review*, 63(2), 129–138. https://doi.org/10.1037/h0042769

Simon, H. A. (1997). *Administrative behavior: A study of decision-making processes in administrative organizations* (4th ed.). Free Press.

Simpson, D. P. (1968). *Cassell's Latin dictionary: Latin–English, English–Latin* (5th ed.). Wiley.

Sinayev, A., & Peters, E. (2015). Cognitive reflection vs. calculation in decision making. *Frontiers in Psychology*, 6. https://doi.org/10.3389/fpsyg.2015.00532

Singmann, H., Klauer, K. C., & Kellen, D. (2014). Intuitive logic revisited: New data and a Bayesian mixed model meta-analysis. *PLoS ONE*, 9(4), e94223. https://doi.org/10.1371/journal.pone.0094223

Sinn, J. S. (2019). Mapping ideology: Combining the Schwartz value circumplex with evolutionary theory to explain ideological differences. *Evolutionary Psychological Science*, 5(1), 44–57. https://doi.org/10.1007/s40806-018-0165-5

Sinn, J. S., & Hayes, M. W. (2017). Replacing the moral foundations: an evolutionary-coalitional theory of liberal-conservative differences. *Political Psychology*, 38(6), 1043–1064. https://doi.org/10.1111/pops.12361

Sirota, M., Dewberry, C., Juanchich, M., Valuš, L., & Marshall, A. C. (2021). Measuring cognitive reflection without maths: Development and validation of the verbal cognitive reflection test. *Journal of Behavioral Decision Making*, 34(3), 322–343. https://doi.org/10.1002/bdm.2213

Sirota, M., Theodoropoulou, A., & Juanchich, M. (2021). Disfluent fonts do not help people to solve math and non-math problems regardless of their numeracy. *Thinking & Reasoning*, 27(1), 142–159. https://doi.org/10.1080/13546783.2020. 1759689

Skitka, L. J , Mullen, E., Griffin, T., Hutchinson, S., & Chamberlin, B. (2002). Dispositions, scripts, or motivated correction? Understanding ideological differences in explanations for social problems. *Journal of Personality and Social Psychology*, 83(2), 470–487. https://doi.org/10.1037/0022-3514.83.2.470

Slone, D. J. (2004). *Theological incorrectness: Why religious people believe what they shouldn't*. Oxford University Press.

Slovic, P., Finucane, M., Peters, E., & MacGregor, D. G. (2002). The affect heuristic. In T. Gilovich, D. Griffin, & D. Kahneman (Eds.), *Heuristics and biases* (1st ed., pp. 397–420). Cambridge University Press. https://doi.org/10.1017/CBO978051 1808098.025

Smith, E. R., & DeCoster, J. (2000). Dual-process models in social and cognitive psychology: conceptual integration and links to underlying memory systems. *Personality and Social Psychology Review*, 4(2), 108–131. https://doi.org/10.1207/ S15327957PSPR0402_01

Smith, S. M., & Beda, Z. (2023). Unconscious work doesn't work. *Creativity Research Journal*, 35(3), 369–379. https://doi.org/10.1080/10400419.2023.2189358

Solheim, Ø. B. (2021). Are we all Charlie? How media priming and framing affect immigration policy preferences after terrorist attacks. *West European Politics*, 44(2), 204–228. https://doi.org/10.1080/01402382.2019.1683791

Song, H., & Schwarz, N. (2008). If it's hard to read, it's hard to do: Processing fluency affects effort prediction and motivation. *Psychological Science*, 19(10), 986–988. https://doi.org/10.1111/j.1467-9280.2008.02189.x

Speckhard, A., & Yayla, A. S. (2015). Eyewitness accounts from recent defectors from Islamic state: Why they joined, what they saw, why they quit. *Perspectives on Terrorism*, 9(6), 95–118.

Spellman, B. A. (2015). A short (personal) future history of Revolution 2.0. *Perspectives on Psychological Science*, 10(6), 886–899. https://doi.org/10.1177/ 1745691615609918

Spiller, S. A. (2011). Opportunity cost consideration. *Journal of Consumer Research*, 38(4), 595–610. https://doi.org/10.1086/660045

Stagnaro, M. N., Ross, R. M., Pennycook, G., & Rand, D. G. (2019). Cross-cultural support for a link between analytic thinking and disbelief in God: Evidence from India and the United Kingdom. *Judgment and Decision Making*, 14(2), 179–186. https://doi.org/10.1017/S1930297500003417

Stall, L. M., & Petrocelli, J. V. (2023). Countering conspiracy theory beliefs: Understanding the conjunction fallacy and considering disconfirming evidence. *Applied Cognitive Psychology*, 37(2), 266–276. https://doi.org/10.1002/ acp.3998

Stankov, L., Knežević, G., Saucier, G., Radović, B., & Milovanović, B. (2018). Militant extremist mindset and the assessment of radicalization in the general population. *Journal of Individual Differences*, 39(2), 88–98. https://doi.org/10.1027/1614- 0001/a000253

Stankov, L., Saucier, G., & Knežević, G. (2010). Militant extremist mind-set: Proviolence, vile world, and divine power. *Psychological Assessment*, 22(1), 70–86. https://doi.org/10.1037/a0016925

Stanovich, K. E. (1993). Dysrationalia: A new specific learning disability. *Journal of Learning Disabilities, 26*(8), 501–515. https://doi.org/10.1177/00222194930 2600803

Stanovich, K. E. (1999). *Who is rational? Studies of individual differences in reasoning.* Lawrence Erlbaum Associates.

Stanovich, K. E. (2004). *The Robot's rebellion: Finding meaning in the age of Darwin.* University of Chicago Press.

Stanovich, K. E. (2009a). Distinguishing the reflective, algorithmic, and autonomous minds: Is it time for a tri-process theory? In J. Evans, & K. Frankish (Eds.), *In two minds: Dual processes and beyond* (1st ed., pp. 55–88). Oxford University Press. https://doi.org/10.1093/acprof:oso/9780199230167.003.0003

Stanovich, K. E. (2009b). *What intelligence tests miss: The psychology of rational thought.* Yale University Press.

Stanovich, K. E. (2011). *Rationality and the reflective mind.* Oxford University Press.

Stanovich, K. E. (2018). Miserliness in human cognition: The interaction of detection, override and mindware. *Thinking & Reasoning, 24*(4), 423–444. https://doi.org/ 10.1080/13546783.2018.1459314

Stanovich, K. E. (2021). *The bias that divides us: The science and politics of myside thinking.* The MIT Press.

Stanovich, K. E., & Toplak, M. E. (2023a). A good architecture for fast and slow thinking, but exclusivity is exclusively in the past. *Behavioral and Brain Sciences, 46*, e142. https://doi.org/10.1017/S0140525X22002904

Stanovich, K. E., & Toplak, M. E. (2023b). Actively open-minded thinking and its measurement. *Journal of Intelligence, 11*(2), 27. https://doi.org/10.3390/jintellige nce11020027

Stanovich, K. E., & West, R. F. (1997). Reasoning independently of prior belief and individual differences in actively open-minded thinking. *Journal of Educational Psychology, 89*(2), 342–357. https://doi.org/10.1037/0022-0663.89.2.342

Stanovich, K. E., & West, R. F. (2008). On the relative independence of thinking biases and cognitive ability. *Journal of Personality and Social Psychology, 94*(4), 672–695. https://doi.org/10.1037/0022-3514.94.4.672

Stanovich, K. E., West, R. F., & Toplak, M. E. (2016). *The rationality quotient: toward a test of rational thinking.* MIT Press.

Stavrova, O., Ehlebracht, D., & Vohs, K. D. (2020). Victims, perpetrators, or both? The vicious cycle of disrespect and cynical beliefs about human nature. *Journal of Experimental Psychology: General, 149*(9), 1736–1754. https://doi.org/10.1037/ xge0000738

Steinberg, L. (2008). A social neuroscience perspective on adolescent risk-taking. *Developmental Review, 28*(1), 78–106. https://doi.org/10.1016/j.dr.2007.08.002

Stephens, W., Sieckelinck, S., & Boutellier, H. (2021). Preventing violent extremism: A review of the literature. *Studies in Conflict & Terrorism, 44*(4), 346–361. https:// doi.org/10.1080/1057610X.2018.1543144

Sterman, J. D., & Sweeney, L. B. (2007). Understanding public complacency about climate change: Adults' mental models of climate change violate conservation of matter. *Climatic Change, 80*(3–4), 213–238. https://doi.org/10.1007/s10 584-006-9107-5

Stewart, P. A., Adams, T. G., & Senior, C. (2020). The effect of trait and state disgust on fear of God and sin. *Frontiers in Psychology, 11*, 51. https://doi.org/10.3389/ fpsyg.2020.00051

Stiglitz, J. E. (2003). *Globalization and its discontents.* W. W. Norton.

Storbeck, J., & Clore, G. L. (2007). On the interdependence of cognition and emotion. *Cognition & Emotion, 21*(6), 1212–1237. https://doi.org/10.1080/02699930701438020

Strack, F., & Deutsch, R. (2004). Reflective and impulsive determinants of social behavior. *Personality and Social Psychology Review, 8*(3), 220–247. https://doi.org/10.1207/s15327957pspr0803_1

Strenze, T. (2007). Intelligence and socioeconomic success: A meta-analytic review of longitudinal research. *Intelligence, 35*(5), 401–426. https://doi.org/10.1016/j.intell.2006.09.004

Strupp-Levitsky, M., Noorbaloochi, S., Shipley, A., & Jost, J. T. (2020). Moral "foundations" as the product of motivated social cognition: Empathy and other psychological underpinnings of ideological divergence in "individualizing" and "binding" concerns. *PLoS ONE, 15*(11), e0241144. https://doi.org/10.1371/journal.pone.0241144

Suedfeld, P. (2009) Integrative complexity. In M. Leary & R. H. Hoyle (Eds.), *Handbook of individual differences in social behavior* (pp. 354–366). Guilford Press.

Suedfeld, P., Cross, R. W., & Logan, C. (2013). Can thematic content analysis separate the pyramid of ideas from the pyramid of action? A comparison among different degrees of commitment to violence. In H. Cabayan, V. Sitterle, & M. Yandura, *Looking back, looking forward: Perspectives on terrorism and responses to it* (pp. 61–68). Office of the Secretary of Defense.

Suhay, E., & Erisen, C. (2018). The role of anger in the biased assimilation of political information: Role of anger in biased assimilation. *Political Psychology, 39*(4), 793–810. https://doi.org/10.1111/pops.12463

Sümer, V. (2023). *Reflection decreases the endorsement of conspiracy beliefs when stronger manipulation is used.* Kadir Has University.

Swami, V., Voracek, M., Stieger, S., Tran, U. S., & Furnham, A. (2014). Analytic thinking reduces belief in conspiracy theories. *Cognition, 133*(3), 572–585. https://doi.org/10.1016/j.cognition.2014.08.006

Swann, W. B., Jetten, J., Gómez, Á., Whitehouse, H., & Bastian, B. (2012). When group membership gets personal: A theory of identity fusion. *Psychological Review, 119*(3), 441–456. https://doi.org/10.1037/a0028589

Swedlow, B., & Wyckoff, M. L. (2009). Value preferences and ideological structuring of attitudes in American public opinion. *American Politics Research, 37*(6), 1048–1087. https://doi.org/10.1177/1532673X09333959

Sweeney, L. B., & Sterman, J. D. (2000). Bathtub dynamics: Initial results of a systems thinking inventory. *System Dynamics Review, 16*(4), 249–286. https://doi.org/10.1002/sdr.198

Szaszi, B., Palfi, B., Szollosi, A., Kieslich, P. J., & Aczel, B. (2018). Thinking dynamics and individual differences: Mouse-tracking analysis of the denominator neglect task. *Judgment and Decision Making, 13*(1), 23–32. https://doi.org/10.1017/S1930297500008792

Talhelm, T. (2018). Hong Kong liberals are WEIRD: Analytic thought increases support for liberal policies. *Personality and Social Psychology Bulletin, 44*(5), 717–728. https://doi.org/10.1177/0146167217746151

Talhelm, T., Haidt, J., Oishi, S., Zhang, X., Miao, F. F., & Chen, S. (2015). Liberals think more analytically (more "WEIRD") than conservatives. *Personality and*

Social Psychology Bulletin, *41*(2), 250–267. https://doi.org/10.1177/014616721 4563672

Tardiff, N., Bascandziev, I., Carey, S., & Zaitchik, D. (2020). Specifying the domain-general resources that contribute to conceptual construction: Evidence from the child's acquisition of vitalist biology. *Cognition*, *195*, 104090. https://doi.org/ 10.1016/j.cognition.2019.104090

Taylor, S. E. (1981). The interface of cognitive and social psychology. In J. H. Harvey (Ed.), *Cognition, social behavior, and the environment* (pp. 189–211). Lawrence Erlbaum Associates.

Teichert, T., Ferrera, V. P., & Grinband, J. (2014). Humans optimize decision-making by delaying decision onset. *PLoS ONE*, *9*(3), e89638. https://doi.org/10.1371/jour nal.pone.0089638

Ten Velden, F. S., Daughters, K., & De Dreu, C. K. W. (2017). Oxytocin promotes intuitive rather than deliberated cooperation with the in-group. *Hormones and Behavior*, *92*, 164–171. https://doi.org/10.1016/j.yhbeh.2016.06.005

Terrizzi, J. A., Shook, N. J., & McDaniel, M. A. (2013). The behavioral immune system and social conservatism: A meta-analysis. *Evolution and Human Behavior*, *34*(2), 99–108. https://doi.org/10.1016/j.evolhumbehav.2012.10.003

Thelen, E., & Smith, L. B. (1994). *A dynamic systems approach to the development of cognition and action*. MIT Press.

Thibodeau, P. H., Frantz, C. M., & Stroink, M. L. (2016). Situating a measure of systems thinking in a landscape of psychological constructs. *Systems Research and Behavioral Science*, *33*(6), 753–769. https://doi.org/10.1002/sres.2388

Thompson, V. A. (2009). Dual-process theories: A metacognitive perspective. In J. Evans, & K. Frankish (Eds.), *In two minds: Dual processes and beyond* (1st ed., pp. 171–196). Oxford University Press. https://doi.org/10.1093/acprof:oso/ 9780199230167.003.0008

Thompson, V. A., Evans, J. St. B. T., & Campbell, J. I. D. (2013). Matching bias on the selection task: It's fast and feels good. *Thinking & Reasoning*, *19*(3–4), 431–452. https://doi.org/10.1080/13546783.2013.820220

Thompson, V. A., & Newman, I. R. (2017). Logical intuitions and other conundra for dual process theories. In W. De Neys (Ed.), *Dual process theory 2.0* (1st ed., pp. 121–136). Routledge. https://doi.org/10.4324/9781315204550-8

Thompson, V. A., Pennycook, G., Trippas, D., & Evans, J. St. B. T. (2018). Do smart people have better intuitions? *Journal of Experimental Psychology: General*, *147*(7), 945–961. https://doi.org/10.1037/xge0000457

Thompson, V. A., Prowse Turner, J. A., & Pennycook, G. (2011). Intuition, reason, and metacognition. *Cognitive Psychology*, *63*(3), 107–140. https://doi.org/ 10.1016/j.cogpsych.2011.06.001

Thompson, V. A., Turner, J. A. P., Pennycook, G., Ball, L. J., Brack, H., Ophir, Y., & Ackerman, R. (2013). The role of answer fluency and perceptual fluency as metacognitive cues for initiating analytic thinking. *Cognition*, *128*(2), 237–251. https://doi.org/10.1016/j.cognition.2012.09.012

Thomson, K. S., & Oppenheimer, D. M. (2016). Investigating an alternate form of the cognitive reflection test. *Judgment and Decision Making*, *11*(1), 99–113. https:// doi.org/10.1017/S1930297500007622

Thornhill, R., Fincher, C. L., & Aran, D. (2009). Parasites, democratization, and the liberalization of values across contemporary countries. *Biological Reviews*, *84*(1), 113–131. https://doi.org/10.1111/j.1469-185X.2008.00062.x

Tiedens, L. Z., & Linton, S. (2001). Judgment under emotional certainty and uncertainty: The effects of specific emotions on information processing. *Journal of Personality and Social Psychology*, 81(6), 973–988. https://doi.org/10.1037/0022-3514.81.6.973

Tinghög, G., Andersson, D., Bonn, C., Böttiger, H., Josephson, C., Lundgren, G., Västfjäll, D., Kirchler, M., & Johannesson, M. (2013). Intuition and cooperation reconsidered. *Nature*, 498(7452), E1–E2. https://doi.org/10.1038/nature12194

Tinghög, G., Koppel, L., & Västfjäll, D. (2023). Dual-process theory is Barbapapa. *Behavioral and Brain Sciences*, 46, e144. https://doi.org/10.1017/S0140525X22003211

Tokdemir, E., Sedashov, E., Ogutcu-Fu, S. H., Leon, C. E. M., Berkowitz, J., & Akcinaroglu, S. (2021). Rebel rivalry and the strategic nature of rebel group ideology and demands. *Journal of Conflict Resolution*, 65(4), 729–758. https://doi.org/10.1177/0022002720967411

Tomasello, M. (2001). *The cultural origins of human cognition* (4. print). Harvard University Press.

Tomasello, M. (2016). *A natural history of human morality*. Harvard University Press.

Toner, J., Montero, B. G., & Moran, A. (2015). Considering the role of cognitive control in expert performance. *Phenomenology and the Cognitive Sciences*, 14(4), 1127–1144. https://doi.org/10.1007/s11097-014-9407-6

Toplak, M. E. (2022). *Cognitive sophistication and the development of judgment and decision-making*. Elsevier.

Toplak, M. E., West, R. F., & Stanovich, K. E. (2011). The cognitive reflection test as a predictor of performance on heuristics-and-biases tasks. *Memory & Cognition*, 39(7), 1275–1289. https://doi.org/10.3758/s13421-011-0104-1

Toplak, M. E., West, R. F., & Stanovich, K. E. (2014). Assessing miserly information processing: An expansion of the cognitive reflection test. *Thinking & Reasoning*, 20(2), 147–168. https://doi.org/10.1080/13546783.2013.844729

Topolinski, S. (2017). Flotsam on the shore of ignorance: Towards a definition of intuition. In R. Deutsch, B. Gawronski, & W. Hofmann (Eds.), *Reflective and impulsive determinants of human behavior* (pp. 87–102). Routledge, Taylor & Francis Group.

Trapnell, P. D., & Campbell, J. D. (1999). Private self-consciousness and the five-factor model of personality: Distinguishing rumination from reflection. *Journal of Personality and Social Psychology*, 76(2), 284–304. https://doi.org/10.1037/0022-3514.76.2.284

Travers, E., Rolison, J. J., & Feeney, A. (2016). The time course of conflict on the cognitive reflection test. *Cognition*, 150, 109–118. https://doi.org/10.1016/j.cognition.2016.01.015

Trémolière, B., De Neys, W., & Bonnefon, J.-F. (2012). Mortality salience and morality: Thinking about death makes people less utilitarian. *Cognition*, 124(3), 379–384. https://doi.org/10.1016/j.cognition.2012.05.011

Trémolière, B., De Neys, W., & Bonnefon, J.-F. (2014). The grim reasoner: Analytical reasoning under mortality salience. *Thinking & Reasoning*, 20(3), 333–351. https://doi.org/10.1080/13546783.2013.823888

Trippas, D., & Handley, S. J. (2017). The parallel processing model of belief bias review and extensions. In W. De Neys (Ed.), *Dual process theory 2.0* (1st ed., pp. 28–46). Routledge. https://doi.org/10.4324/9781315204550-3

Trivers, R. L. (1971). The evolution of reciprocal altruism. *The Quarterly Review of Biology, 46*(1), 35–57. https://doi.org/10.1086/406755

Trope, Y., & Liberman, N. (2010). Construal-level theory of psychological distance. *Psychological Review, 117*(2), 440–463. https://doi.org/10.1037/a0018963

Tversky, A., & Kahneman, D. (1974). Judgment under uncertainty: Heuristics and biases: Biases in judgments reveal some heuristics of thinking under uncertainty. *Science, 185*(4157), 1124–1131. https://doi.org/10.1126/science.185.4157.1124

Tversky, A., & Kahneman, D. (1981). The framing of decisions and the psychology of choice. *Science, 211*(4481), 453–458. https://doi.org/10.1126/science.7455683

Tversky, A., & Kahneman, D. (1991). Loss aversion in riskless choice: A reference-dependent model. *The Quarterly Journal of Economics, 106*(4), 1039–1061. https://doi.org/10.2307/2937956

Ullrich, J., & Cohrs, J. C. (2007). Terrorism salience increases system justification: experimental evidence. *Social Justice Research, 20*(2), 117–139. https://doi.org/10.1007/s11211-007-0035-y

Unkelbach, C., & Greifeneder, R. (2013). *The experience of thinking: How the fluency of mental processes influences cognition and behaviour.* Psychology Press.

Vadillo, M. A., Kostopoulou, O., & Shanks, D. R. (2015). A critical review and meta-analysis of the unconscious thought effect in medical decision making. *Frontiers in Psychology, 6.* https://doi.org/10.3389/fpsyg.2015.00636

Vadillo, M. A., Malejka, S., Lee, D. Y. H., Dienes, Z., & Shanks, D. R. (2022). Raising awareness about measurement error in research on unconscious mental processes. *Psychonomic Bulletin & Review, 29*(1), 21–43. https://doi.org/10.3758/s13423-021-01923-y

Van Berkel, L., Crandall, C. S., Eidelman, S., & Blanchar, J. C. (2015). Hierarchy, dominance, and deliberation: Egalitarian values require mental effort. *Personality and Social Psychology Bulletin, 41*(9), 1207–1222. https://doi.org/10.1177/0146167215591961

Van Boven, L., & Loewenstein, G. (2003). Social projection of transient drive states. *Personality and Social Psychology Bulletin, 29*(9), 1159–1168. https://doi.org/10.1177/0146167203254597

Van De Vyver, J., Houston, D. M., Abrams, D., & Vasiljevic, M. (2016). Boosting belligerence: How the July 7, 2005, London bombings affected liberals' moral foundations and prejudice. *Psychological Science, 27*(2), 169–177. https://doi.org/10.1177/0956797615615584

Van Der Maas, H. L. J., Dolan, C. V., Grasman, R. P. P. P., Wicherts, J. M., Huizenga, H. M., & Raijmakers, M. E. J. (2006). A dynamical model of general intelligence: The positive manifold of intelligence by mutualism. *Psychological Review, 113*(4), 842–861. https://doi.org/10.1037/0033-295X.113.4.842

Van Der Toorn, J., Nail, P. R., Liviatan, I., & Jost, J. T. (2014). My country, right or wrong: Does activating system justification motivation eliminate the liberal-conservative gap in patriotism? *Journal of Experimental Social Psychology, 54,* 50–60. https://doi.org/10.1016/j.jesp.2014.04.003

Van Lange, P. A. M. (Ed.). (2006). *Bridging social psychology: Benefits of transdisciplinary approaches.* L. Erlbaum Associates.

Van Lange, P. A. M. (2013). What we should expect from theories in social psychology: Truth, abstraction, progress, and applicability as standards (TAPAS). *Personality and Social Psychology Review, 17*(1), 40–55. https://doi.org/10.1177/1088868312453088

Van Leeuwen, F., & Petersen, M. B. (2018). The behavioral immune system is designed to avoid infected individuals, not outgroups. *Evolution and Human Behavior*, 39(2), 226–234. https://doi.org/10.1016/j.evolhumbehav.2017.12.003

Van Mulukom, V., Pummerer, L. J., Alper, S., Bai, H., Čavojová, V., Farias, J., Kay, C. S., Lazarevic, L. B., Lobato, E. J. C., Marinthe, G., Pavela Banai, I., Šrol, J., & Žeželj, I. (2022). Antecedents and consequences of COVID-19 conspiracy beliefs: A systematic review. *Social Science & Medicine*, 301, 114912. https://doi.org/10.1016/j.socscimed.2022.114912

Van Prooijen, J.-W., & Acker, M. (2015). The influence of control on belief in conspiracy theories: Conceptual and applied extensions. *Applied Cognitive Psychology*, 29(5), 753–761. https://doi.org/10.1002/acp.3161

Van Prooijen, J.-W. (2021). The psychology of political polarization: An introduction. In J.-W. Van Prooijen (Ed.), *The psychology of political polarization* (1st ed., pp. 1–13). Routledge. https://doi.org/10.4324/9781003042433-2

Van Um, E. (2011). Discussing concepts of terrorist rationality: Implications for counterterrorism policy. *Defence and Peace Economics*, 22(2), 161–179. https://doi.org/10.1080/10242694.2011.542337

van Zomeren, M. (2024). The ACES Guide for researchers in psychology: Fostering researchers' informed decision-making about theory selection and theoretical integration. *Review of General Psychology*, 28(1), 17–29. https://doi.org/10.1177/10892680231182033

Västfjäll, D., Slovic, P., Burns, W. J., Erlandsson, A., Koppel, L., Asutay, E., & Tinghög, G. (2016). The arithmetic of emotion: Integration of incidental and integral affect in judgments and decisions. *Frontiers in Psychology*, 7. https://doi.org/10.3389/fpsyg.2016.00325

Vazire, S. (2018). Implications of the credibility revolution for productivity, creativity, and progress. *Perspectives on Psychological Science*, 13(4), 411–417. https://doi.org/10.1177/1745691617751884

Vazire, S., Schiavone, S. R., & Bottesini, J. G. (2022). Credibility beyond replicability: Improving the four validities in psychological science. *Current Directions in Psychological Science*, 31(2), 162–168. https://doi.org/10.1177/09637214211067779

Većkalov, B., Gligorić, V., & Petrović, M. B. (2024). No evidence that priming analytic thinking reduces belief in conspiracy theories: A registered report of high-powered direct replications of Study 2 and Study 4 from. *Journal of Experimental Social Psychology*, 110, 104549. https://doi.org/10.1016/j.jesp.2023.104549

Velioglu, I. (2023). The effects of collective threats on cooperation and moral foundations. [Unpublished Master's thesis]. Kadir Has University.

Verkoeijen, P. P. J. L., & Bouwmeester, S. (2014). Does intuition cause cooperation? *PLoS ONE*, 9(5), e96654. https://doi.org/10.1371/journal.pone.0096654

Verkuyten, M. (2018). Religious fundamentalism and radicalization among Muslim minority youth in Europe. *European Psychologist*, 23(1), 21–31. https://doi.org/10.1027/1016-9040/a000314

Vigil, J. M. (2010). Political leanings vary with facial expression processing and psychosocial functioning. *Group Processes & Intergroup Relations*, 13(5), 547–558. https://doi.org/10.1177/1368430209356930

Visser, P. S., & Mirabile, R. R. (2004). Attitudes in the social context: The impact of social network composition on individual-level attitude strength. *Journal of

Personality and Social Psychology, 87(6), 779–795. https://doi.org/10.1037/0022-3514.87.6.779

Vlaev, I. (2012). How different are real and hypothetical decisions? Overestimation, contrast and assimilation in social interaction. *Journal of Economic Psychology, 33*(5), 963–972. https://doi.org/10.1016/j.joep.2012.05.005

Voelkel, J. G., & Brandt, M. J. (2019). The effect of ideological identification on the endorsement of moral values depends on the target group. *Personality and Social Psychology Bulletin, 45*(6), 851–863. https://doi.org/10.1177/0146167218798822

Vosniadou, S., Pnevmatikos, D., & Makris, N. (2018). The role of executive function in the construction and employment of scientific and mathematical concepts that require conceptual change learning. *Neuroeducation, 5*(2), 62–72. https://doi.org/10.24046/neuroed.20180502.62

Vygotsky, L. S. (2012). *Thought and language* (Rev. and expanded ed.). MIT Press.

Wallis, S. E., & Valentinov, V. (2017). A limit to our thinking and some unanticipated moral consequences: A science of conceptual systems perspective with some potential solutions. *Systemic Practice and Action Research, 30*(2), 103–116. https://doi.org/10.1007/s11213-016-9394-3

Wason, P. C., & Evans, J. St. B. T. (1974). Dual processes in reasoning? *Cognition, 3*(2), 141–154. https://doi.org/10.1016/0010-0277(74)90017-1

Watkins, E., Moberly, N. J., & Moulds, M. L. (2008). Processing mode causally influences emotional reactivity: Distinct effects of abstract versus concrete construal on emotional response. *Emotion, 8*(3), 364–378. https://doi.org/10.1037/1528-3542.8.3.364

Watkins, E. R. (2008). Constructive and unconstructive repetitive thought. *Psychological Bulletin, 134*(2), 163–206. https://doi.org/10.1037/0033-2909.134.2.163

Watkins, E. R., & Nolen-Hoeksema, S. (2014). A habit-goal framework of depressive rumination. *Journal of Abnormal Psychology, 123*(1), 24–34. https://doi.org/10.1037/a0035540

Watkins, E. R., & Roberts, H. (2020). Reflecting on rumination: Consequences, causes, mechanisms and treatment of rumination. *Behaviour Research and Therapy, 127*, 103573. https://doi.org/10.1016/j.brat.2020.103573

Webber, D., Babush, M., Schori-Eyal, N., Vazeou-Nieuwenhuis, A., Hettiarachchi, M., Bélanger, J. J., Moyano, M., Trujillo, H. M., Gunaratna, R., Kruglanski, A. W., & Gelfand, M. J. (2018). The road to extremism: Field and experimental evidence that significance loss-induced need for closure fosters radicalization. *Journal of Personality and Social Psychology, 114*(2), 270–285. https://doi.org/10.1037/pspi0000111

Webber, D., Kruglanski, A., Molinario, E., & Jasko, K. (2020). Ideologies that justify political violence. *Current Opinion in Behavioral Sciences, 34*, 107–111. https://doi.org/10.1016/j.cobeha.2020.01.004

Weinberger, A. B., & Green, A. E. (2022). Dynamic development of intuitions and explicit knowledge during implicit learning. *Cognition, 222*, 105008. https://doi.org/10.1016/j.cognition.2021.105008

Weisberg, R. W. (2015). Toward an integrated theory of insight in problem solving. *Thinking & Reasoning, 21*(1), 5–39. https://doi.org/10.1080/13546783.2014.886625

Wertheimer, M. (1934). On truth. *Social Research, 1*(2), 135–146.

West, R. F., Toplak, M. E., & Stanovich, K. E. (2008). Heuristics and biases as measures of critical thinking: Associations with cognitive ability and thinking dispositions. *Journal of Educational Psychology*, *100*(4), 930–941. https://doi.org/10.1037/a0012842

Westfall, J., & Yarkoni, T. (2016). Statistically controlling for confounding constructs is harder than you think. *PLoS ONE*, *11*(3), e0152719. https://doi.org/10.1371/journal.pone.0152719

Whitcomb, D., Battaly, H., Baehr, J., & Howard-Snyder, D. (2017). Intellectual humility: Owning our limitations. *Philosophy and Phenomenological Research*, *94*(3), 509–539. https://doi.org/10.1111/phpr.12228

White, C. J., Baimel, A., & Norenzayan, A. (2021). How cultural learning and cognitive biases shape religious beliefs. *Current Opinion in Psychology*, *40*, 34–39. https://doi.org/10.1016/j.copsyc.2020.07.033

Wicherts, J. M., Veldkamp, C. L. S., Augusteijn, H. E. M., Bakker, M., Van Aert, R. C. M., & Van Assen, M. A. L. M. (2016). Degrees of freedom in planning, running, analyzing, and reporting psychological studies: A checklist to avoid p-Hacking. *Frontiers in Psychology*, *7*. https://doi.org/10.3389/fpsyg.2016.01832

Williams, K. D. (2009). Ostracism: A Temporal Need-Threat Model. In M. P. Zanna (Ed.), *Advances in experimental social psychology* (Vol. 41, pp. 275–314). Academic Press. https://doi.org/10.1016/S0065-2601(08)00406-1

Wilson, T. D. (2002). *Strangers to ourselves: Discovering the adaptive unconscious*. Belknap Press of Harvard University Press.

Wilson, T. D., & Dunn, E. W. (2004). Self-knowledge: Its limits, value, and potential for improvement. *Annual Review of Psychology*, *55*(1), 493–518. https://doi.org/10.1146/annurev.psych.55.090902.141954

Wilson, T. D., Houston, C. E., Etling, K. M., & Brekke, N. (1996). A new look at anchoring effects: Basic anchoring and its antecedents. *Journal of Experimental Psychology: General*, *125*(4), 387–402. https://doi.org/10.1037/0096-3445.125.4.387

Wilson, T. D., Lindsey, S., & Schooler, T. Y. (2000). A model of dual attitudes. *Psychological Review*, *107*(1), 101–126. https://doi.org/10.1037/0033-295X.107.1.101

Wilson, T. D., & Schooler, J. W. (1991). Thinking too much: Introspection can reduce the quality of preferences and decisions. *Journal of Personality and Social Psychology*, *60*(2), 181–192. https://doi.org/10.1037/0022-3514.60.2.131

Wimmer, H., & Perner, J. (1983). Beliefs about beliefs: Representation and constraining function of wrong beliefs in young children's understanding of deception. *Cognition*, *13*(1), 103–128. https://doi.org/10.1016/0010-0277(83)90004-5

Winkielman, P., & Cacioppo, J. T. (2001). Mind at ease puts a smile on the face: Psychophysiological evidence that processing facilitation elicits positive affect. *Journal of Personality and Social Psychology*, *81*(6), 989–1000. https://doi.org/10.1037/0022-3514.81.6.989

Wintrobe, R. (2006). *Rational extremism: The political economy of radicalism*. Cambridge University Press.

Wojcieszak, M. (2011). Deliberation and attitude polarization. *Journal of Communication*, *61*(4), 596–617. https://doi.org/10.1111/j.1460-2466.2011.01568.x

Wolfowicz, M., Litmanovitz, Y., Weisburd, D., & Hasisi, B. (2021). Cognitive and behavioral radicalization: A systematic review of the putative risk and protective factors. *Campbell Systematic Reviews*, *17*(3), e1174. https://doi.org/10.1002/cl2.1174

Wood, M. J., & Douglas, K. M. (2018). Conspiracy theory psychology: Individual differences, worldviews, and states of mind. In J. E. Uscinski (Ed.), *Conspiracy Theories and the People Who Believe Them* (pp. 245–256). Oxford University Press.

Wright, J. C., & Baril, G. (2011). The role of cognitive resources in determining our moral intuitions: Are we all liberals at heart? *Journal of Experimental Social Psychology*, *47*(5), 1007–1012. https://doi.org/10.1016/j.jesp.2011.03.014

Wright, J. C., & Pölzler, T. (2022). Should morality be abolished? An empirical challenge to the argument from intolerance. *Philosophical Psychology*, *35*(3), 350–385. https://doi.org/10.1080/09515089.2021.1983160

Wu, B.-P., & Chang, L. (2012). The social impact of pathogen threat: How disease salience influences conformity. *Personality and Individual Differences*, *53*(1), 50–54. https://doi.org/10.1016/j.paid.2012.02.023

Wyszynski, M., & Diederich, A. (2023). Individual differences moderate effects in an unusual disease paradigm: A psychophysical data collection lab approach and an online experiment. *Frontiers in Psychology*, *14*, 1086699. https://doi.org/10.3389/fpsyg.2023.1086699

Xu, M., Li, Z., Qi, S., Fan, L., Zhou, X., & Yang, D. (2020). Social exclusion modulates dual mechanisms of cognitive control: Evidence from ERPs. *Human Brain Mapping*, *41*(10), 2669–2685. https://doi.org/10.1002/hbm.24970

Yechiam, E., & Zeif, D. (2023a). Revisiting the effect of incentivization on cognitive reflection: A meta-analysis. *Journal of Behavioral Decision Making*, *36*(1), e2286. https://doi.org/10.1002/bdm.2286

Yechiam, E., & Zeif, D. (2023b). The effect of incentivization on the conjunction fallacy in judgments: A meta-analysis. *Psychological Research*, *87*(8), 2336–2344. https://doi.org/10.1007/s00426-023-01837-5

Yelbuz, B. E., Madan, E., & Alper, S. (2022). Reflective thinking predicts lower conspiracy beliefs: A meta-analysis. *Judgment and Decision Making*, *17*(4), 720–744. https://doi.org/10.1017/S1930297500008913

Yen, C.-L., & Cheng, C.-P. (2013). Researcher effects on mortality salience research: A meta-analytic moderator analysis. *Death Studies*, *37*(7), 636–652. https://doi.org/10.1080/07481187.2012.682290

Yilmaz, O. (2021a). Cognitive styles and religion. *Current Opinion in Psychology*, *40*, 150–154. https://doi.org/10.1016/j.copsyc.2020.09.014

Yilmaz, O. (2021b). The evolutionary perspective. In T. K. Shackelford, & V. A. Weekes-Shackelford (Eds.), *Encyclopedia of evolutionary psychological science* (pp. 2759–2760). Springer International Publishing. https://doi.org/10.1007/978-3-319-19650-3_2207

Yilmaz, O., & Alper, S. (2019). The link between intuitive thinking and social conservatism is stronger in WEIRD societies. *Judgment and Decision Making*, *14*(2), 156–169. https://doi.org/10.1017/S1930297500003399

Yilmaz, O., & Bahçekapili, H. G. (2018). Meta-ethics and the mortality: Mortality salience leads people to adopt a less subjectivist morality. *Cognition*, *179*, 171–177. https://doi.org/10.1016/j.cognition.2018.06.014

Yilmaz, O., Bahçekapili, H. G., Harma, M., & Sevi, B. (2020). Intergroup tolerance leads to subjective morality, which in turn is associated with (but does not lead to) reduced religiosity. *Archive for the Psychology of Religion*, 42(2), 232–243. https://doi.org/10.1177/0084672419883349

Yilmaz, O., Harma, M., Bahçekapili, H. G., & Cesur, S. (2016). Validation of the Moral Foundations Questionnaire in Turkey and its relation to cultural schemas of individualism and collectivism. *Personality and Individual Differences*, 99, 149–154. https://doi.org/10.1016/j.paid.2016.04.090

Yilmaz, O., & Isler, O. (2019). Reflection increases belief in God through self-questioning among non-believers. *Judgment and Decision Making*, 14(6), 649–657. https://doi.org/10.1017/S1930297500005374

Yilmaz, O., & Isler, O. (2024). *Intuitive and Reflective Foundations of Moral Judgment and Cooperation*. [Manuscript submitted for publication].

Yilmaz, O., Karadöler, D. Z., & Sofuoglu, G. (2016). Analytic thinking, religion, and prejudice: An experimental test of the dual-process model of mind. *The International Journal for the Psychology of Religion*, 26(4), 360–369. https://doi.org/10.1080/10508619.2016.1151117

Yilmaz, O., & Saribay, S. A. (2016). An attempt to clarify the link between cognitive style and political ideology: A non-western replication and extension. *Judgment and Decision Making*, 11(3), 287–300. https://doi.org/10.1017/S1930297500003119

Yilmaz, O , & Saribay, S. A. (2017a). Activating analytic thinking enhances the value given to individualizing moral foundations. *Cognition*, 165, 88–96. https://doi.org/10.1016/j.cognition.2017.05.009

Yilmaz, O., & Saribay, S. A. (2017b). Analytic thought training promotes liberalism on contextualized (but not stable) political opinions. *Social Psychological and Personality Science*, 8(7), 789–795. https://doi.org/10.1177/1948550616687092

Yilmaz, O., & Saribay, S. A. (2017c). *Replication of Eidelman et al. (2012)* [dataset].

Yilmaz, O., & Saribay, S. A. (2017d). The relationship between cognitive style and political orientation depends on the measures used. *Judgment and Decision Making*, 12(2), 140–147. https://doi.org/10.1017/S1930297500005684

Yilmaz, O., & Saribay, S. A. (2018a). Lower levels of resistance to change (but not opposition to equality) is related to analytic cognitive style. *Social Psychology*, 49(2), 65–75. https://doi.org/10.1027/1864-9335/a000328

Yilmaz, O., & Saribay, S. A. (2018b). Moral foundations explain unique variance in political ideology beyond resistance to change and opposition to equality. *Group Processes & Intergroup Relations*, 22(8), 1124–1138. https://doi.org/10.1177/1368430218781012

Yilmaz, O., Saribay, S. A., Bahçekapılı, H. G., & Harma, M. (2016). Political orientations, ideological self-categorizations, party preferences, and moral foundations of young Turkish voters. *Turkish Studies*, 17(4), 544–566. https://doi.org/10.1080/14683849.2016.1221312

Yilmaz, O., Saribay, S. A., & Iyer, R. (2020). Are neo-liberals more intuitive? Undetected libertarians confound the relation between analytic cognitive style and economic conservatism. *Current Psychology*, 39(1), 25–32. https://doi.org/10.1007/s12144-019-0130-x

Yonker, J. E., Edman, L. R. O., Cresswell, J., & Barrett, J. L. (2016). Primed analytic thought and religiosity: The importance of individual characteristics. *Psychology of Religion and Spirituality*, 8(4), 298–308. https://doi.org/10.1037/rel0000095

Young, A. G., & Shtulman, A. (2020). How children's cognitive reflection shapes their science understanding. *Frontiers in Psychology, 11,* 1247. https://doi.org/10.3389/fpsyg.2020.01247

Youyou, W., Yang, Y., & Uzzi, B. (2023). A discipline-wide investigation of the replicability of psychology papers over the past two decades. *Proceedings of the National Academy of Sciences, 120*(6), e2208863120. https://doi.org/10.1073/pnas.2208863120

Zainal, N. H., & Newman, M. G. (2022). Curiosity helps: Growth in need for cognition bidirectionally predicts future reduction in anxiety and depression symptoms across 10 years. *Journal of Affective Disorders, 296,* 642–652. https://doi.org/10.1016/j.jad.2021.10.001

Zajonc, R. B. (1980). Feeling and thinking: Preferences need no inferences. *American Psychologist, 35*(2), 151–175. https://doi.org/10.1037/0003-066X.35.2.151

Zajonc, R. B. (2001). Mere exposure: A gateway to the subliminal. *Current Directions in Psychological Science, 10*(6), 224–228. https://doi.org/10.1111/1467-8721.00154

Zedelius, C. M., Gross, M. E., & Schooler, J. W. (2022). Inquisitive but not discerning: Deprivation curiosity is associated with excessive openness to inaccurate information. *Journal of Research in Personality, 98,* 104227. https://doi.org/10.1016/j.jrp.2022.104227

Zitek, E. M., & Tiedens, L. Z. (2012). The fluency of social hierarchy: The ease with which hierarchical relationships are seen, remembered, learned, and liked. *Journal of Personality and Social Psychology, 102*(1), 98–115. https://doi.org/10.1037/a0025345

Zmigrod, L., Eisenberg, I. W., Bissett, P. G., Robbins, T. W., & Poldrack, R. A. (2021). The cognitive and perceptual correlates of ideological attitudes: A data-driven approach. *Philosophical Transactions of the Royal Society B: Biological Sciences, 376*(1822), 20200424. https://doi.org/10.1098/rstb.2020.0424

Zmigrod, L., Rentfrow, P. J., & Robbins, T. W. (2019). Cognitive inflexibility predicts extremist attitudes. *Frontiers in Psychology, 10,* 989. https://doi.org/10.3389/fpsyg.2019.00989

INDEX

Printed and bound by CPI Group (UK) Ltd, Croydon, CR0 4YY

18/11/2024

01790617-0019